Jacob.

May all of your
dreams come true...

Jim Black

Jacob.

May all of your
dreams come true...

LEARN THE SECRETS OF SUCCESS IN THE **NEW ECONOMY**
FROM TODAY'S LEADING ENTREPRENEURS & PROFESSIONALS

SUCCESSONOMICS

LEARN THE SECRETS OF SUCCESS IN THE NEW ECONOMY
FROM TODAY'S LEADING ENTREPRENEURS & PROFESSIONALS

SUCCESSONOMICS

CONTENTS

CHAPTER 73

EVERYONE IS A WINNER — THERE ARE NO LOSERS

CHAPTER 1

THE U.S. ECONOMY: HOW TO RAMP UP OUR RECOVERY AND STABILIZE OUR FUTURE

BY STEVE FORBES

In 2008 we were hit by the possibility of a complete meltdown of our financial system. Since then things have, of course, calmed down tremendously, but the U.S. economy is still a source of much speculation. Is its current growth enough? Will that growth continue? The answers, of course, are important to all of us, whether you're a CEO, an entrepreneur or someone concerned about keeping their job – or getting one.

As of this writing, the U.S. economy has grown more in 2013 than it grew in the past three years and should end the fiscal year with an overall annual growth rate of 3%, barring any kind of international crisis. That's a better rate than we experienced during the previous three years, which was roughly 1.5% to 2%.

However, that growth is still not what it should be. I liken it to a talented baseball player, who has been routinely striking out for the last month or so. Now he's hitting .250 – but, with his natural abilities, he should be hitting .350. In other words, he remains competitive, but he's certainly not going to lead his team to the World Series. Our current economic progress is far from championship caliber.

We should, of course, acknowledge the positive signs. Private credit is beginning to flow again; the housing marketing has shown some improvement; and retail sales aren't too bad. The automatic budget cuts that triggered the Sequester did cause the government to take fewer resources from the economy than it had been, but those cuts were made in the worst way possible.

As far as job creation goes, when you look at what's called the Household Survey – which, I believe, measures small-business creation better than the so-called Corporate Survey or Establishment Survey – there are some heartening signs as well.

But, again, we're the guy who's only hitting .250. Because we're not achieving at a higher level, we're still very vulnerable to outside threats – and we must learn how to connect with the ball on a more consistent and powerful level.

INTERNATIONAL THREATS

Of course, to continue the baseball analogy, if we want to get our average up, there has to be a ball for us to swing at. Unfortunately, there are still some ominous clouds on the horizon that could rain out this game and put us right back in the dugout.

For example, the Middle East almost exploded in the spring of 2012. Everyone is now focused on Syria, but, as we all know, Egypt remains an ongoing question, and Iran and Israel continue to butt heads.

Then there's the lunatic who runs North Korea. The scary thing about Kim Jong-un is that he was brought up in a bubble. We have no idea how he sees the world; we only know that it's not our world. No one knows what he will do next - especially if he doesn't succeed in shaking down the U.S., Japan, and South Korea for another round of money. In that case, he may do something that has unforeseen consequences for the world.

On the financial side, Cyprus, a little country with a population of 800,000, established a truly frightening precedent. With the connivance of the European Central Bank, the IMF and others, Cyprus' government seized private citizens' deposits from the banks. The consequences of this? Anytime there's the threat of a financial crisis in any of the southern

European countries, the first thing people will do is pull their money out of the bank for fear that the government might seize it before rightful owners can withdraw it – and that, of course, makes any financial crisis worse.

Yes, we live in an uncertain world. Even China is having financial hiccups at the moment. But, having looked outward, let's do some inward soul-searching and analyze the reasons for our own weak economic growth.

THE REASONS BEHIND OUR WEAK RECOVERY

Here's the question we really need to answer: Why is this the feeblest recovery from a sharp economic downturn in American history?

Many of you don't remember the 1970s, but, during that decade we had three recessions in a row, each more severe than its predecessor. Each was followed by a sharp upturn. This kind of up-and-down shockwave made many wonder if our economy was sustainable.

It wasn't until the early 1980s when, with the Reagan reforms of the Federal Reserve, we finally got a sustainable boom of historic proportions. Remember the Great Depression, the worst economic disaster in history – at least in American history – did not finally bottom out until the early 1930s. After the initial crash, there was actually a sharp uptick in the economy. It didn't last, but, as had always happened previously, when there was a sharp downturn, we always got a subsequent sharp upturn.

But this time, it didn't happen. Why?

Here's the big thing that stands in the economy's way – monetary policy. Now, this is not the most exciting subject in the world, so I hope you had some caffeine to get through this. Better yet, let me put this in terms you might find a little more interesting. Think of it as you would a magnificent automobile you own and love to drive. Now, if you don't have enough fuel for that vehicle, it stalls. Of course, if you pump the gas pedal and give it too much fuel, you also stall, because you flood the engine. The ideal situation is, of course, to have the right amount of gas so you can move forward smoothly without any complications.

Well, the same is true of our economy. It may be a magnificent one, or at least, a very sturdy and usable one, but if the Federal Reserve doesn't supply enough money to meet the economy's natural needs, well, the economy is going to stall out.

However, just as too much fuel stalls your car, too much money from the Fed stalls the economy. And that's just what's been happening since the early part of the last decade. The Fed has been creating so much money that it has undermined the integrity of the U.S. dollar. People start distrusting our currency, and we don't get a sustainable recovery. This is a historical fact that's been proven time and time again, but memories, at least at the federal level, are very short.

WHEN YOU MESS WITH MONEY

Now, money is simply a means to simplify the ways in which we carry out transactions with each other. Wealth-creation happens through people conducting these transactions in the marketplace. Before there was a currency, we could only deal with each other through a barter system. Three thousand years ago, if I were to sell an ad in FORBES, the advertiser might have paid me with a herd of goats.

But let's say that things worked that way still, and I want to buy iPads for each of our writers. I go to the Apple store with a very large herd of goats. Naturally, this would take a lot of very obliging cab drivers, but let's not get too bogged down in the details. Anyway, the Apple store manager sees my goats and says, "I've got enough goats. What I need is sheep."

Now, I have to figure out how to exchange my goats for sheep to get the products I want. After I get the sheep, I have to hire a shepherd to make sure the wolves of Wall Street don't eat the sheep. But the available shepherds want to be paid in wine. I only have red wine, they want white. As you can see, this could go on forever – and that's without even considering the logistics of depositing a cow into an ATM.

So, 2600 years ago in Athens, Greece, which was a great commercial center, money was created in the form of coins. It made it easier to buy, sell and invest. But, let's remember, that for money to work, *it has to have a stable value,* just as all of our other weights and measures in the marketplace do.

For example, when you go to a store and buy a pound of apples, you expect those apples to weigh 16 ounces, not 15 or 10 (18 would be nice, of course, but unfair to the seller). Solid measurements ensure both sides are treated equally well. When you want a 2,500 square foot house, you don't expect the builder to suddenly assume there are only 11 inches in a foot.

So why in the world would we allow money – arguably, the most important system of measurement used – to be tinkered with?

What if the Federal Reserve did to clocks what it does to the dollar? Let's say they "floated" time. One day, there were 60 minutes in an hour and the next day, only 42. Now, say you hired someone to work for you at $15 an hour, you'd have to figure out whether that was a New York hour, a Texas hour, a Thailand hour or a Congo hour? You wouldn't know. It would be hard to even bake a cake – the recipe says, "Bake the batter 45 minutes." Do you have to adjust those minutes for inflation?

The goats, in comparison, are starting to look simple, right?

Whenever you engineer an environment in which people can't trust the fixed nature of money, the first problem is that capital gets misdirected. Investors suddenly lock it into hard assets. Why? To preserve what they have, instead of investing in a very uncertain future. When you invest in something, it may be three or more years before you get a payout. An investment is risky enough without having to worry about the uncertainty of what the dollar is worth when you actually get your payout. Will you be collecting it in dollars that are worth 100 cents? 80 cents? 20 cents?

This is the kind of thing that fueled the housing bubble in the early 2000s. Everyone thought, because the Fed had undermined the dollar, that prices would keep going up forever. It became the norm for the value of homes to always rise. Of course, that's not reality, but everyone's mindset was corrupted, which caused the bubble to grow until it finally blew up in everyone's faces.

CHEAP CREDIT = LESS JOBS

Today, you routinely hear about 0% interest rates, which distorts the credit markets. It brings to mind an old joke about the Soviet Union: "Healthcare is free, but you can't get any." And 0% interest rates absolutely direct capital to certain parties at the expense of others.

Who benefits by what Ben Bernanke's done at the Federal Reserve? First of all, the government itself, by creating cheap deficits. Who else gets helped? Fannie Mae and Freddie Mac, which are government-sponsored enterprises. They're, in effect, coining money, because the Fed's buying all these mortgage securities. Big companies also have access to cheap credit. Their balance sheets are spectacular today, probably the strongest in American history because of this.

Now, who gets hurt in this era of cheap credit? Small companies do, because they simply don't have reliable access to it. It is instead being directed to big players and to hard assets, as already noted, which is why we've had a weak job-creation environment. As you know, most jobs are created in *small* businesses. In an uncertain credit environment, job-creation is hurt. That's why only now, four years into the recovery, are we starting to see some real signs of life in terms of employment numbers.

That's beginning to change thankfully, because it looks like the 0% interest rate policy is finally coming to an end. It's hurt the recovery, not helped it. The Federal Reserve underestimated – or, to recall a Bushism, "misunderestimated" – the consequences of its policies. They thought of it as a stimulus, but all it did was create our current $2 trillion overhang. By printing money that went to preferred borrowers, such as Fannie and Freddie and the Federal Government, our national balance sheet has gone from $800 billion to more than $3 trillion.

THE PRICE OF UNCERTAINTY

Where is this ultimately going to lead, here and around the world? Well, this may sound very strange, but I believe, in the next few years we're going to see something that hasn't been since since the 1970s: The dollar is going to be relinked to gold. In the U.S., that link was in place for 180 years of our existence.

Why gold? Yes, it fluctuates in terms of dollars, but the value of the gold itself doesn't change - it's the *perception* of the value of the dollar that does. Gold retains its intrinsic value better than anything else – better than silver, better than copper, platinum, or you name it. It's the best thing we have, and its worked for 4,000 years.

Frankly, we need a hard and fast ruler with which we measure our money's worth. In a vibrant economy gold doesn't restrict money creation; it makes sure the currency's value remains consistent. It's like when building a highway, you know when construction begins that there are 5,280 feet in a mile. It doesn't restrict the number of miles or highways that you can build. It just means the mile is a fixed measure - the same as gold.

If a proper gold standard were in place, what would it mean? Well, let's assign it a random value of, say, $1200 an ounce. That means that if the price of gold rose above that $1200 an ounce, the Federal Reserve would stop creating money. If it fell below $1200, the Fed would create *more* money. The amount of money would be practically and accurately measured.

You might ask, "Can it actually be that simple?" The answer is "Yes." This is the essence of how a gold standard works. Does it hurt money creation in a vibrant economy? Absolutely not.

Here's a statistic that will make you sound profound the next time you attend a cocktail party. Start by pointing out that from the time we declared America's independence in the 1770s, when the U.S. was a small agricultural and relatively poor nation of 3.8 million people, to about 1900, when we had grown to 76 million people and had become the mightiest industrial nation in the world, the amount of gold mined in that period had increased the world's gold supply by a little more than three times. And even though the dollar was fixed to gold in terms of measurement, the money in the U.S. actually increased by *160 times*. This makes it clear that a gold standard would not be an anchor around our economic neck; it would bring a much needed stability to the value of our money, while still providing the flexibility to meet the needs of our economy.

And isn't that better than putting all our trust in the bureaucrats and politicians in Washington?

CHAPTER 2

12 STEPS TO FINANCIAL FREEDOM

BY CHERIF MEDAWAR

If you possess the spirit of entrepreneurship and are willing to start with little to no money but commit to success and financial freedom, then here are 12 specific steps that can evolve you in 3 stages:

First: You work for the Money (1-5)

Then: You work the Money (6-7)

Finally: The Money works for You (8-12)

1) GET THE BEST EDUCATION

Academic, professional and financial:

- Good: Get a basic education and know people, and numbers. Improve your communication skills, verbal and written, as well as your public speaking ability.

- Better: Get a college degree and learn the basics of business and accounting.

- Best: Study Law, Finance and Technology.

2) GET THE BEST CORPORATE JOB

Apprenticeship with steady income and good benefits:

- Good: Get in with a big corporation for potential growth or a small company ready for an initial public offering (IPO).

- Better: Become a broker in real estate or insurance and work with a reputable company to build clientele and/or residual income to potentially branch out on your own in the future.

- <u>Best</u>: Become a licensed professional and work in a large office with other attorneys, or dentists, or other professionals to eventually branch out on your own.

3) ACQUIRE LEADERSHIP SKILLS

Manage yourself, other people and projects (use latest technology in marketing, operations and finance):

- <u>Good</u>: Be efficient (Learn to prioritize and focus.)
- <u>Better</u>: Be effective (Master public speaking and selling.)
- <u>Best</u>: Get results by coordinating time, effort and money.

4) START SAVING

401k and other similar programs – Self-Directed Individual Retirement Accounts (SD-IRA):

- <u>Good</u>: Invest using Dollar Cost Averaging in market indices as offered by your employer's retirement program.
- <u>Better</u>: Manage your own retirement money in self-directed accounts like self-directed IRAs.
- <u>Best</u>: Start your own Solo 401K and use Roth to get your returns tax-free.

5) BUILD CREDIT

a) <u>Personal credit</u>
   Build your credit score:

- <u>Good</u>: Apply, receive and use credit cards carefully.
- <u>Better</u>: Keep increasing the credit by using one card for a couple months then a second one, then a third one etc. The ones you stop using start offering you better deals and even increase your credit to entice you back.
- <u>Best</u>: Deposit money in a bank CD (certificate of deposit) and borrow against it in your name, then pay on time on that loan, and pay it off after 6 months. The bank will report to the credit bureau that you have good credit. Instead of doing that with one bank, you can simultaneously build credit with six banks by doing it over and over. As soon as you borrow against the first CD you

opened in the first bank, take the money and go to another bank and do it again (repeat the process in 6 banks and pay on time each month then pay them off).

You will have great credit on the seventh month.

b) <u>Business credit</u>
   Start a separate legal entity and Build business credit:

Legal entities like an S Corp., an LLC or a C Corp. can have a separate Tax ID number, apart from your Social Security (SS) number and you can build business credit under any of these entities if you set up an account with Dun and Bradstreet as well as Business Equifax.

- <u>Good</u>: Apply, receive and use business credit cards carefully (start with department store credit cards, gas stations etc.)

- <u>Better</u>: Keep increasing the business credit by using one card for a month then a second one, then a third one etc. just like you did for your personal credit.

- <u>Best</u>: Deposit money in a bank CD (certificate of deposit) and borrow against it in your business name and tax ID number; then pay on time and pay it off after 6 months – do the same process you did for your personal credit with six banks and you will build great business credit.

6) BUY AND SELL ("FLIP") ASSETS - (To build your cash reserves):

Learn to borrow against the credit you built and buy assets to resell them at a profit.

- <u>Good</u>: Buy and sell residential properties in cash using your personal and business credit lines (The process is simple: a) Focus on an area, b) Focus on a type, (such as 3bed 2ba), c) Understand the values – You can see prices and comparable sales on line for free at www.zillow.com - Also look at what's listed in that market at: www.realtor.com and check if the price trend is moving up or down. Then finally check the DOM in the neighborhood/zip code (DOM is **D**ays **O**n **M**arket, which is: How long the listed properties sit on the market to sell - you want this to be less than 60 days). You will identify deals below market prices and will be able to access your credit to purchase quickly to either resell right away as is at a profit, or get a contractor to improve condition or add square footage to resell at a much higher profit. (This is all based on market prices, the per square foot cost of purchasing, plus cost of improvement versus resale price over time).

- Better: Build rapport with lenders including private equity ones to be able to get loans on larger acquisitions or rehab funds to increase the value of the properties.

- Best: Create partnerships with investors, relationships with banks and brokers and work closely with contractors to speed up the game and magnify the results.

(You can do the buying and selling using other assets like discounted mortgage notes, stock and options trading and/or small businesses. This is the easiest and fastest way to build cash reserve and usually flipping residential property is the easiest asset to resell.)

7) REDUCE YOUR TAXES

Taxes are between 30 to 50% when you calculate the federal and state tax throughout the US:

- Good: If you net less than $150K it is good to place your business in a separate legal entity to shift income and get good deductions, then start your Solo 401K to transfer some more income and reduce your taxes while netting more, which makes you attractive for lenders.

- Better: If you net over $150K but less than $350K it is better to set up the right entity in the right location where Congress offers some lucrative tax incentives for businesses like netting tax-free the first $150K in income. A small business owner netting $162K before tax in states like NY or CA will net approximately $98K after paying Federal and State tax. Using the proper jurisdiction in the US and entity structure, that same business will net the first $150K tax-free (over 50% more in tax-free profit).

- Best: If you net over $350K to millions of dollars in your business there is an additional incentive offered by Congress with a written decree for 20 years to drop your tax rate to less than 10% on your net income Most companies and their tax advisors are unaware of these special rules offered in the USA.

8) ACQUIRE AND HOLD VALUABLE ASSETS - (For reliable, increasing cash flow and higher net worth over time):

Get into a bigger game like commercial real estate or business joint Ventures and/or Syndications:

- Good: Find a good commercial property in a good location being under utilized. These properties derive their value from the cash flow they produce. I have a simple formula called the FACTS system:

a) **F**ind an empty single Tenant property and find a national tenant that would be interested in leasing it for a long term (10 years +).

b) **A**nalyze what is the potential rental income and what is the trend in the area.

c) **C**ontrol the negotiation process and place the property under contract (Remember: Under contract does not mean you are obligated to buy it. You can change your mind during the contingency period of several weeks, but you get access to the property to inspect it and tour potential tenants etc., with no obligation to buy).

d) **T**ime the process of due diligence, the financing and closing. Start by calling on National Tenants and giving them all the info about the location and see if they are interested. All you need is one Tenant to say: "Yes, we want the space." Once you get an interested Tenant to send you a letter of intent to lease (LOI), you have a gold mine, because based on the lease and the income anticipated from that Tenant, the property value increases based on a multiplier in each area and it gets easier to finance the purchase or raise capital for it by getting partners or investors – based on the value added.

e) **S**trategize and either assign the contract to an investor based on the added value of having a Tenant ready to sign a long term lease or buy the property at the lower contract price that you wrote when it was vacant. The banks like properties that will have a long term NNN lease (NNN means the Tenant pays the lease net of property tax, net of property insurance and net of property maintenance - The Tenant pays for almost everything). A national tenant usually also gives a corporate guarantee, meaning the payments are guaranteed for the length of the lease by the entire company.

The property value increases the day you close and sign the long-term lease with the Tenant. This is a phenomenal way to become wealthy in instant equity increase in value while enjoying reliable and increasing streams of secured cash flow income for several years down the road.

- Better: Get partners and line up banks to do several deals and if no Tenant is interested in any location, just cancel your contract within the contingency period and walk away with no risk or obligation. If you placed earnest money deposit, you get it back in full through escrow.

- Best: Create a Syndication, which is: group investing. You write a business plan. You submit it to an SEC attorney who drafts a Private Placement Memorandum (PPM) and files it with the SEC. Anyone can do it. There is no need for a real estate license or any other requirement other than knowing what you are doing. If you follow certain rules and regulations, you do not even need to have a high net worth or a lot of experience to start making yourself and your investors a lot of money in commercial real estate assets that produce long term streams of income.

Once you have your PPM filed with the SEC you can learn how to present/pitch your investments to investors to raise capital and deploy the funds wisely, safely and profitably. Opportunities are endless in commercial real estate such as apartment buildings, shopping malls, storage facilities, manufactured home parks and hotels, etc. You get paid in many ways as a Syndicator. Here are a few:

3% asset acquisition fee, 20% of the net cash flow of the property, and 30% to 50% of the upside increase in property value when you resell it in 3 to 5 years later.

(You can also buy stocks in quality companies and hold on to them for dividend income and potential increase in value. You can buy or start companies and build them up to larger entities that can produce huge income through license agreements or through a public offering.)

9) GET ASSET PROTECTION

You must protect your assets from the prying eyes of lawsuit hungry attorneys so you can keep the net worth and income you created:

- Good: Behave prudently and get insurance against your assets whether real estate or business.

- <u>Better</u>: Get umbrella insurance and/or Errors and Omissions coverage for your business.

- <u>Best</u>: Set up a separate legal entity such as an LLC. Draft a specially worded Operating Agreement to use the entity for asset protection. Create a Promissory Note with economic substance between you (Borrower) and the LLC (Lender). Record a mortgage lien secured by your asset to the benefit of the LLC (Lender). The lien must have a clearly defined legal and financial set of terms to eliminate any equity reflected in the public records on any of your assets.

The separate LLC entity, to which you would owe a substantial amount of money will have a lien recorded and cross collateralized against all your assets (properties and/or businesses – even if some are out of state). You will make periodic payments to the LLC. (This is tax neutral since you are paying your own entity.)

Anyone trying to sue you will be discouraged by the fact that the public records show that you owe more than you own.

Anyone successful at suing you will collect nothing even if the courts issue a charging order to force you to sell your assets. This is simply because if and when you sell, you would have to pay all the lenders first and that includes your own LLC as per lending and entity laws.

Any time you want to borrow against your assets or sell them, you can show the certificate of ownership of the LLC and as the Owner: You can cancel or substitute collateral or subordinate your lien positions as needed. You remain in full control.

This is by far the ultimate set up for asset protection because it is also a lawsuit deterrent and an asset preservation structure all at once.

You do not need to transfer assets out of your name and potentially trigger a due on sale clause with your bank or a tax reassessment with the county (you only get a loan against them).

You do not need to set up many entities and maintain them all at a high cost. (All you need is one legally structured LLC and one lien with the proper wording and terms.)

And finally you do not need to worry about having many assets spread out across the nation because the lien could be cross-collateralized.

No court has been able to challenge this structure provided it has the proper economic substance and all the documents have been prepared by expert experienced attorneys to stand up in any court in the US.

Most plaintiffs or creditors trying to sue you, will most likely avoid the matter altogether, or settle with you and/or accept whatever your insurance offers as a final and full settlement for their claim because they will see that it will be near impossible to get anything by force.

10) SET UP A RETIREMENT PLAN USING LIFE INSURANCE PROGRAM

Now that you have set up your business in a way that you are getting cash flow and netting a lot more after taxes, and protected your assets, you must use the extra money in the most effective way for your estate plan and probate for yourself and your loved ones:

- Good: Use the net difference after the tax saving to pay off your debt and to buy term life insurance.

- Better: Use the net difference to invest in private funds or other good commercial real estate properties to increase your cash flow and get mortgage insurance or enough term life insurance to pay off your debt when you die – whichever is less expensive.

- Best: Buy a special kind of insurance that gives you the best of both worlds: You get a life insurance coverage and a large portion gets invested into a tax deferred (possibly tax-free) investment account that allows you to compound the returns. You can borrow against your investment portion (tax-free) and enjoy the money while you are still alive (based on some basic rules). Over time your life insurance coverage increases as well as your investment account.

11) CREATE A BIGGER GAME-(Become an expert in your field and show the way to others):

Never stop growing. Write, speak and coach others on what you are passionate about. If you have followed the rules and succeeded, you may want to keep the momentum by inspiring and empowering others to grow and prosper with you through your own syndications and financial services.

- Good: Become a recognized expert and help others achieve their potential by writing and publishing a book.

- Better: Teach others how to reach their potential, speak at events and film your presentations to share them with more people.

- Best: Coach and demonstrate to others how they could achieve their highest potential by following your systems and methods.

12) BUILD A LEGACY

Contribute to others in need in a valuable way so you can leave the world a better place than you found it.

Our lives are never complete until and unless we leave the world a better place than we've found it:

- Good: Donate regularly money, time and effort to a good cause.

- Better: Create your own charity and manage it to produce the highest results you want. Use the same skills you acquired in the past when you were building and growing your businesses.

- Best: Create a structure for your charity and the good causes you pursue so you can continue helping, expanding and producing beyond your time, effort or money. Eventually the positive results you create will take a life of their own in the world and your legacy will be created to live a long time after you are gone.

While success could be defined in many ways, the ultimate success anyone could achieve is to live an ethical existence and demonstrate to others how to handle life, business and investments in a way that builds meaningful relationships, transforms challenges into opportunities and provides peace of mind for all.

About Cherif

Cherif Medawar was a Management Trainee at the Century Plaza hotel in Los Angeles California in the early 80's, when an International Financier and Billionaire hotel guest in the name of Edmond Baysari noticed Cherif's work ethics, enthusiasm and energy and asked him to come and work for him.

Cherif worked for Baysari* for a few years and became an expert in real estate investing, trading securities and developing and growing businesses. He got exposed to the intense and exciting world of high finance and participated in transactions worth tens of millions of dollars at an early age. He then decided to create his own wealth by branching out and doing his own real estate investing and building great companies with profitable business models.

In 1999, after becoming a multimillionaire, Cherif decided to start a training and investment company www.CMREI.com to share his wealth secrets with others. Today he has over 1000 video success stories on Youtube from people who followed his system and achieved their financial goals.

His California Real Estate Syndication has been growing for years and paying investors secured high rates of returns: www.MIGSIF.com.

Many of his clients are high net worth, high-income individuals and companies seeking expert advice and specific direction to set up their companies properly for exponential growth, strategic tax avoidance and powerful asset protection.

Cherif is known to have the best structures and cutting edge methods in the financial world including the best retirement company www.eFreedomIRA.com. He is getting ready to launch his own Private International Bank www.MedawarBank.com as he continues to grow his educational and financial companies.

Cherif lives part of the year in California where he teaches entrepreneurs his real estate programs and travels between Puerto Rico, where he holds over $50 Million Dollars of historic commercial properties, and Cancun where he enjoys life with his wife and two children.

For contact information visit: www.CMREI.com/Forbes
Email: CherifMedawar@yahoo.com

*Edmond Baysari: http://www.forbes.com/sites/morganbrennan/2013/03/28/inside-frances-100-million-palace-pompadour-a-royal-chateau-restored-by-a-press-shy-philanthropist/

CHAPTER 3

COSMETIC SURGERY AND THE ROI OF GIVING BACK

BY HARVEY "CHIP" COLE, III, MD, FACS

Now that the economy is showing signs of recovery from the Great Recession, what is the state of philanthropy in America? Well here's the good news: There's more money on U.S. corporate balance sheets than at any other time in our history. The S&P 500 and Dow have hit several high-water marks this year alone. So what does that mean for corporate and individual giving? Thankfully, these are also more robust than ever. In fact, everyone from private equity firms to venture capital to foundations and trusts are looking for more opportunities to put their assets to work. And that means generating positive returns—not just in terms of cash, but social and cultural value—something useful for the human condition.

And that's where my Face Change Foundation comes in, bringing hope to those who stand most to benefit from our work. As founder and president of Oculus Plastic Surgery, I'm grateful that my practice has weathered the storms of boom-bust cycles for over two decades. While contributing to pioneering advances in everything from laser treatments to botox, I've had the great fortune of building a successful business, not only for my family and 25 employees, but for the larger community. But for those of us who care about something larger than ourselves, no amount of commercial success provides the satisfaction of developing new ways to give back. I have always positioned *pro-bono* work as a central component to my practice, but over the last decade or so began looking at ways to expand our giving platform.

For me, charity begins close to home. I've always made it my policy that no patient will ever be turned away for financial reasons. People may have preconceptions about plastic surgery as a frivolous business, but I know it changes lives; and I would hate for someone to be denied the opportunity to improve their life because of the inability to pay. I'm on call to do facial reconstruction for the kinds of orbital fractures and other horrific damage done in domestic-abuse cases. Giving our time and our talents provides a sort of nourishment for the soul that always pays us back tenfold. Early on, I witnessed that altruistic spirit in the caregivers in my own life, from my mother to my wife to my own daughter—all nurses and all committed to helping others in times of trouble.

We have tried to impart to our own children that no matter what you have, 10% should be invested for emergencies and 10% should go toward helping mankind without expecting a penny back. To us, generosity and empathy yield a more thoughtful and evolved way of living.[*]

It's out of this spirit that The Face Change Foundation was formed. The Foundation is primarily focused on (temporarily) troubled teens, who no doubt have the capacity to become tomorrow's leaders, with just a quarter turn. They come from a variety of adverse conditions, be it around drugs, behavior, bullying, broken homes, or all the above. This is not just addressing a question of the physical health of victims, but equally important, their emotional health. Our self-image informs everything we do, from the types of relationships we pursue to our level of career…to the decision to have a family and friends in our lives. That's why it's so fundamental for returning soldiers and victims of abuse to recover their sense of self, and Oculus is honored to provide an avenue back in for so many.

So that's the philanthropic piece. And I must admit that some colleagues approach me and say, "Chip, let me ask you something… how can you afford to just leave 10 percent of your revenue on the table with these *pro-bono* procedures?"

And my answer is always the same. You know, business revenues are

---

[*] Some material excerpted from Face Change by Harvey "Chip" Cole, III, MD, FACS. Copyright 2014.

not a zero-sum game (one big pie, out of which comes charitable giving, simply leaving a smaller pie). No, each slice of civic engagement actually gives rise to multiple other pies. Let's leave aside questions of social consequence, and ethical duty, and just plain feeling good, that extend from this sort of work: The bottom-line benefits of corporate giving are legion. By upping your charitable quotient—and I'm talking to the business leaders out there—you will surely:

- increase marketing capacity.
- develop thought leadership around Corporate Social Responsibility (CSR).
- Improve your employee recruitment and retention efforts.
- deepen shareholder trust and stakeholder value.
- drive new business development.
- burnish your reputation.

The other leg of my philanthropic vision is for those who pursue plastic surgery as an elective procedure—to disabuse them of the notion that a cosmetic procedure is a panacea. Instead I want to convey that it's a way to enhance and bring expression to what's already there.

You may not expect to hear this from a plastic surgeon, but I'm going to let you in on a little secret: **cosmetic surgery alone is not going to change your life.** It's not going to make you happier… it's not going to make you a better person… or a better spouse, lover, friend. What it *will* do is amplify what's already deep down inside you. And with the right approach—one that errs on the side of subtlety, we have the capacity now to not only live longer and stronger, but also to look better, well into our silver years.

I've learned one thing in my three-plus decades on the cutting edge of this industry (pun intended); it's this: True beauty and happiness is an inside job. Simple as that. No amount of laser treatments and endoscopic surgery can cure a broken heart. Or make somebody fall in love with you. If you're harboring grudges, are driven by jealousy and striving ambition, maybe you'll keep getting that next procedure, hoping it will give you the peace of mind—the perfection—you've been striving for.

But let me share something with you: as you climb that mountain and get to the summit, there's always another peak, off in the distance. The finish line keeps receding. What you thought you wanted wasn't what you wanted after all, and then it's on to the next shiny object—the next nip, the next tuck.

Mind you, this is coming from someone who's performed over eighteen *thousand* procedures over the years, and I'm grateful for every minute of it... To study early on with trailblazers and even help forge new pathways on my own. To be featured on FOX and CNN, ABC, CBS, NBC and *Good Day Atlanta*, to be a pioneer in laser treatments and endoscopic surgery, and be handed awards from the American College of Surgeons and the Southern Medical Association and the Consumer Research Council and the list goes on...

But when Harper's Bazaar came to me and told me I was chosen by my physician peers as one of the top 10 cosmetic eye surgeons in the country, I wanted to say, "hold on guys, just wait a minute. Don't you realize it's about so much more than surgery alone...?" It's about diet, exercise, lifestyle, it's about being present in every moment and sharing your life with the ones you love the most. And here's the most important piece: it's about *happiness*.

When I first began reading John Stuart Mill and other 19th-Century Utilitarian philosophers, saying that the ultimate goal in life is *happiness*, I said to myself, "well, that's sort of naïve, isn't it? That may be all well and good for 1861, but this is 2013! What we really want in 2013 is power, sex, money, beauty, travel, shopping sprees, great wine, a juicy ribeye from Ruth's Chris." (Or Oysters and Pearls at *The French Laundry*, ladies?)

But wait a second, maybe J. Stu was on to something there. Because all those other things—all those trappings of modern life—don't have any inherent value, do they? They only work when they're making us *happy!* And this is something I try to share with my patients (it comes up frequently in my book *Face Change*):

Get your mind together and good health will follow.

Get healthy and real happiness is just around the corner...

Get happy and guess what? All of a sudden you're more beautiful. Your skin is more radiant. You beam positive energy, and *that's* what makes you magnetic. Not the perfect nose or the perfect breasts or right number of chins (just joking).

We all know the Ice Queen who's gone in for a li-i-i-ttle too much work over the years, right? She's one half of a type-A power couple who's somehow magically always *on*. She chairs every committee, plans every luncheon, donates generously to every cause, and she looks *damn good* doing it. But you look behind those eyes and there's something... missing—a deep sadness, or a fear, or some nameless, bottomless desire. She might be missing the most important ingredient of all: true happiness.

And that's what my Face Change Foundation is all about: bringing happy back... and at the same time, it's *more than that*. **It's about self-image and unleashing the beauty within.**

Let's face it: when we go in for that job interview or show up on a blind date, for better or worse we're being judged for our appearance. And most definitely for our personality, which is a direct reflection of how we see ourselves. There's a feedback loop there, where the better you feel about yourself, the more confidence you project, the more beautiful you become in the eyes of your beholder. This leads to more and better promotions, more affluence, increased social status and so many of the things that make our lives rich and rewarding. It's called the "halo effect."

But again, let's not take that to far. In *Face Change* I look at celebrity surgery over the years, at what I call "The Good," "The Bad," and "The OH NO!" It's staggering, really, that someone like, say, Raquel Welch, or Sophia Loren (I'm dating myself) could be such great beauties now, when they were just hitting their stride in the *1960's!* All because of judicious, skillful treatments over the years... not surgical overreach.

Or let's look at the usual suspects like Demi Moore, or Sharon Stone, or Christie Brinkley. These lovely women have been pop-culture icons for decades, and are knockouts to this day. The reason? Well, there are lots of reasons, and granted I'm biased, but I like to think that having the right cosmetic surgeon in your court can make a big difference... and also that degree of giving back, of civic engagement. Fortunately these days movie actors and other pop stars have a greater platform to fight for what's right than ever before. Think of Bono and his work with EDUN, a group dedicated to stimulating trade with poverty stricken countries. Or

Angelina Jolie standing up for humanitarian issues and girls' education. Let's face it: these are beautiful people on a beautiful mission, and for those who would aspire to their level of social consequence, the enhanced self-image that can extend from cosmetic treatment can be a great boon, and unleash the altruist within.

Who does this describe: "She was unquestionably gorgeous. She was lavish. She was a dark, unyielding largesse. She was, in short, too bloody much." Any guesses? That was Richard Burton, speaking about the first time he met Elizabeth Taylor. That stuck with her, that striking beauty. And who did she have to thank, a great plastic surgeon? No doubt, but also her *joie de vivre* and embrace of social causes, which lent her long life and glamour.

So where does that leave us regular folk who may not be to the Hollywood manor born? Well, the myth, I think, is that cosmetic procedures all cost an arm and a leg, lay you up for months, and can be spotted from the Hubble Space Telescope. But I'll tell you, in my experience that couldn't be further from the truth. The average cost of a procedure at Oculus Plastic Surgery, for example, is just $2,500.

You break it down, what does that mean? It's less than $7 per day, or a Venti latte at Starbucks. A laser eye treatment, which corrects for wrinkles, dark spots, loss of elasticity, is a little over a thousand dollars. You're in and out and healed in less than a week. Same goes for a laser facial resurfacing, where the recovery time is about a week and it's sort of astonishing how well it treats sun-damaged skin, wrinkles, acne scars, dyspigmentation and fine lines.

And even the more comprehensive surgical procedures, like a facelift, are in the mid-four figures and correct much more effectively for things like loose skin, jowls and deep folds around the mouth. And the recovery time is still only a couple of weeks. Done correctly, this isn't about stretching the skin into a drum-tight look of permanent surprise. It's about subtlety and art, and enhancing the natural plump resilience of the skin. It's about restoring and refreshing your own natural anatomy.

You get into the non-surgical procedures, and the investment is even lower. Things like microdermabrasion, botox, chemical peels, you're talking a few hundred dollars for a treatment that will heal immediately and may last for several years.

So to come back to the theme of economic impact, let's look at the macro: I must say, the landscape is somewhat different than it was when I was coming up in the industry. Heck, it's not even the same world. The American Society of Plastic Surgeons, the ASPS, have really been the standard bearers in the industry, and you see in the statistics they release a dramatic rise in the numbers of procedures over the years. In the 1960's when plastic surgery was really coming into prominence, there were what… a few thousand procedures? Do you know how many there are today? **Just in the year 2012, between surgical and non-surgical, there were almost *15 million procedures* at a cost of over 11 billion dollars.** That's 422 procedures for every man, woman and child in Beverly Hills.

So to the question of ROI. Whether you're a business leader in this or any other field, looking at the return on your philanthropic investment is of crucial importance. From the Greatest Generation and Baby Boomers down to Generation X and Gen Y, consumers are more informed than ever, thanks to the Internet. They have huge volumes of information at their disposal, to help them decide which companies they wish to do business with. And more than ever, they are choosing to engage with businesses that take a stand to improve the human condition, not just keep their shareholders flush.

The value proposition for giving back is easy to make on the human end: it helps us feel good and makes the world a better place. But here's the ethos I'm trying to bring to our industry, that the business case is equally compelling: The best individuals, companies and foundations are finding new ways of doing well by doing good. If every business chose from here on in to dedicate 10% of their billable hours to *pro bono* work, or 10% of their pre-tax revenue to social causes, just think what our world will look like in 10 years, in 20 years, in a century. If a rising tide raises all boats, *it's high time we all join together to be that tide*.

About Dr. Chip

An innovator in the cosmetic surgery field, Harvey "Chip" Cole, III, MD, FACS, has performed more than 18,000 surgeries since opening Atlanta's Oculus Plastic Surgery in 1994. An early pioneer of many techniques that have since become part of the medical mainstream, Dr. Cole was a Botox innovator who in 1986 trained in its use with Botox trailblazers Drs. Jean and Alastair Carruthers. In 1992, he gained vital early information regarding the cosmetic applications of lasers while learning from laser pioneer Dr. Sterling Baker. A groundbreaker in his own right, Dr. Cole has advanced the use of less invasive endoscopic surgery with minimal incisions, combining laser resurfacing, in his patented brow-lifting ABC technique.

Quadruple board certified by the American Society of Ophthalmic Plastic and Reconstructive Surgery, the American Board of Ophthalmology, the American Board of Cosmetic Surgery, and the American Board of Laser Surgery, Dr. Cole has also taught at some of the country's most prestigious medical institutions, including Harvard Medical School, UCLA, Stanford University, Cleveland Clinic, Tulane University, Emory University, and Vanderbilt Medical School. He serves as an invited board examiner for the American Board of Cosmetic Surgery, the American Society of Ophthalmic Plastic and Reconstructive Surgery, and the World Board of Cosmetic Surgery. He completed his ophthalmic surgical residency at Tulane, which was followed by a prestigious two-year fellowship in Oculo Facial Plastic Surgery at Vanderbilt, where he received the specialty's highest honor, the Marvin H. Quickert Award. He now serves as a facial plastic surgery preceptor for both Vanderbilt and the Medical College of Georgia.

Among his many professional honors, Dr. Cole was named one of America's top facial plastic surgeons by the Consumers Research Council of America for the past 18 consecutive years. He received the Southern Medical Association's Most Outstanding Research Award; the C.S. O'Brien Professorship; and the American College of Surgeons' Golden Scalpel Achievement Award for surgical excellence. As a multiple board certified Ophthalmic Microsurgeon, Dr. Cole combines his expertise in highly refined millimeter-precise eye surgeries with his work as a facial plastic surgeon, offering an even greater degree of precision and knowledge to his surgical practice.

He has been an invited medical expert on Fox, CNN, ABC, NBC, *Good Day Atlanta,* and several regional and national radio shows. In Town & Country, he has been named by his physician peers as one of the country's top cosmetic surgeons and by *Harper's Bazaar* as one of the top 10 cosmetic eye surgeons in the nation.

Dr. Cole has coauthored over a dozen medical books, has been invited to give numerous keynote-presentation speeches, and has given over 100 lectures around the world as an educator and surgical pioneer in his medical field. He attended Tulane Medical School, graduating in the top 10 percent of his class; he then did his surgical internship at Ochsner Clinic in New Orleans, where he was chosen Intern of the year.

In addition to his clinical practice, Dr. Cole is also the founder of the nonprofit FaceChange, which helps troubled teens. Learn more at: www.FaceChange.info.

CHAPTER 4

MINIMUM PAYMENTS, MAXIMUM CONSEQUENCES

BY ANDY EILERS, MA, CMC

"There are but two ways of paying debt: Increase of industry in raising income, increase of thrift in laying out."
~ Thomas Carlyle

INTRODUCTION

Did you know that the average amount of credit card debt per household in the United States right now is $15,799? How does that compare with you? The total US revolving debt is over $793,000,000,000, which is billion with a "B." Most of that is revolving credit card debt. The total US consumer debt is $2,430,000,000,000, which is trillion with a "T." Another interesting fact is that 20% of the people in the US control 80% of the wealth. That means people are spending billions of dollars that they don't have! Does this sound like anyone you know? If you are in this situation, do you make minimum payments each month or even worse live on these cards from time to time? Do you think the credit card companies and banks that issue these credit cards want this to change? Think about it for a minute and then answer.

It is important to understand that there is good debt and bad debt. Good debt is debt that allows you to get closer to your financial goals and dreams. That might include buying a home, owning a business, and student loans for formal education you need to advance your career. <u>Bad debt is what keeps you from reaching your financial goals. This includes any debt that you continue to make minimum payments on and don't get any closer to paying off the principal balances, like credit cards and unsecured loans.</u>

If you are one of the millions of Americans who has credit card and unsecured loan debt, here are some of the terms you need to understand in order to really see where you are now and where you are headed in the future. These include: compound interest, simple interest, self-management, debt management, debt settlement, and bankruptcy programs. Let's take a look at each of these in more detail so you can walk away after reading this with a plan that will change your life forever!

COMPOUND INTEREST VERSUS SIMPLE INTEREST

Imagine if you are one of those people with $15,799 on credit cards with an average of 18% compound interest (which may be low if you look at the average American), and you have decided to repay the debt completely in 60 months. Here is the challenge that you will be facing on those purchases, especially when you consider what it will cost to pay that money back with compounding interest on credit cards versus simple interest like you might pay on a home or auto loan. Simple interest is interest paid or computed on the original principal only of a loan. Compound interest is interest that is computed on the sum of an original principal and accrued interest. The difference between these two can be staggering and means thousands of dollars more that you have to pay back in an example like this one.

Starting with simple interest, in order to pay back that $15,799 over 60 months, without charging another penny on any of these cards during that time, at an annual percentage rate of 18%, you would have to pay back $30,018.10 with $14,219.10 in interest over that period. That is almost double the original balance with simple interest of 18%! That should already seem like an incredible amount to pay back versus what you started with, right? That is a little more than 90% of the original balance that you are paying back in addition to the principal. Just wait until you see what happens with compound interest, which is the kind you have on those credit cards right now!!

With compound interest of 1.5% per month, which is going to cost you more than 18% annual percentage interest using simple interest, on that same $15,799 balance over 60 months, you would pay back a staggering $38,600.43!! That is $22,801.43 in compound interest without adding a single penny to the cards and keeping that same interest rate over the same period of time. That is a little more than 144% of the original balance that you are paying back in addition to the principal. That's over 50% more of the original balance that you pay back just because of the type of interest! Can you imagine ever agreeing to this if you were to open a credit card today?

The fact is that millions of people have open credit cards with these exact same terms in which the credit card companies charge compound interest on their monthly balances, which makes those minimum payments even more painful in the big picture. If you are one of these people and after seeing just this one example you want to get out of debt as quickly as possible, let's take a look at what your options really are and how you can get started in the right direction right now! The four options you really have without acquiring any new debt include the following: the self-management program, a debt management program, a debt settlement program, and bankruptcy.

SELF-MANAGEMENT

A self-management program requires you to manage all of your credit cards and unsecured loans on your own. This may be what you are doing now if you haven't taken a formal approach to reducing or eliminating your debt. That means you are faced with some or all of the following questions every single month. The questions include:

1. How much do I owe on all of the cards or loans combined? What is the total amount I have to send out in minimum payments on all of my cards combined this month?

2. What are the compound interest rates I am paying now on each card?

3. How much is my minimum payment on each card or loan?

4. Will I pay the minimum or how much can I pay on each card?

5. How much of my payment is actually going to principal versus interest this month?

6. When is each of the payments due?

7. When do I have to mail the payment to avoid a late charge?

8. Will I need to use the card after I make the payment before making another payment?

9. Am I getting any closer to paying off the principal balances?

10. How much longer will I have to make these payments before I will be out of credit card and unsecured loan debt?

11. Have I created a realistic budget that I can stick to every month?

12. Is handling this debt on my own really the best way to go?

13. How much additional stress am I creating by handling my debt the way I am handling it now?

14. Am I relying on what I already know or am I getting the financial education I need to get this problem resolved once and for all?

15. How can I save money on monthly expenses so I can eliminate my debt even faster?

With all of these questions facing you every single month by using the self-management program, maybe it is time to consider the other available options. Remember, the self-management option is the one in which the credit card companies and banks will make the most money and you will be in debt the longest! Now let's take a look at the debt-management option that includes credit counseling.

DEBT MANAGEMENT

In a debt management program, you have the opportunity to pay off your credit card and unsecured loan debt in three to five years through a program that allows you to have the following:

1. Single program payment for all of the credit cards and unsecured loans in the program

2. Typically lower interest rates on credit cards and unsecured loans in the program

3. Interest rates and payment amounts will not be increased as long as payments are made on time

4. Like simple interest throughout the program – stacking the money toward principal

5. Frequently you will get reduced interest rates in these programs

6. No negative effect on your credit

7. Closed credit cards and unsecured loans so no debt can be added

8. Fees are charged for these programs and are included in your program payment

9. Set term to repay the debt

10. You can pay extra in order to accelerate paying off the debt while keeping the lower rates and reduced term

I know you are probably asking yourself why the credit card companies would be willing to make all of this available for you without this program affecting your credit score. The fact is that you are repaying the full balances and still paying interest. Just in case you forgot, even if the interest was eliminated while you are in the program, the credit card companies are getting everything you owe them if you complete the program, along with any interest in the program, plus they get to keep all of the interest you have already paid.

Also, the cards and credit lines are closed, so you won't be able to keep using the credit and the creditors are fully aware of that fact too. What does this mean to you at the end of the program? It means that even though you originally agreed to the terms and conditions that were provided when you opened the card you have now been able to save thousands of dollars without any negative effect on your credit and have the opportunity to change your financial life forever.

The biggest challenge that people have on occasion in a program like this comes when they are used to living on credit cards or are barely able to make minimum payments currently. Keep in mind that you are paying the full balances in this type of program in a shorter period of time, which usually means that the single program payment will be the same or higher than what the minimum payments add up to each month. As you can see though, the benefits in a program like this clearly outweigh any challenges, and the best part about it is that if you are approved and complete the program, the debt that was holding you back is gone forever!

DEBT SETTLEMENT

In a debt settlement program, you have the opportunity to settle your debt with your creditors and eliminate your debt in an average of three to five years. Debt settlement has some similarities with debt management, but also has some critical differences that you need to be aware of prior to getting involved. Here are the debt settlement program features you should understand prior to getting started:

1. Single program payment for all of the credit cards and unsecured loans in the program
2. The monthly payment is reduced an average of 35-50% based on the expected settlement amounts that the company you are working with expects to achieve
3. There will be a negative effect on your credit due to not repaying the full balances
4. There are different models – direct settlement and attorney model
5. Credit cards and unsecured loans are closed
6. Set term to settle the debts
7. You can be sued by the creditors
8. You can receive a 1099 for the uncollected debt amount
9. You will receive collection calls from the creditors or collection agencies on their behalf
10. Fees are charged to settle the debt and are included in your program payment

If you are struggling to make minimum payments and the debt is overwhelming you at this point in your life, debt settlement may make sense for you. Some of the challenges that people have with entering a debt settlement program include the negative effect on credit, closed cards, collection calls, potential lawsuits, the potential for 1099s on forgiven balances, and the mental hurdle of not repaying debts that they agreed to repay. The real benefit in the debt settlement program is the reduced monthly payment and the fact that these companies have vast experience settling debt with creditors that most consumers don't have.

Keep in mind; the creditors will still end up getting a percentage of the debt in addition to all of the interest and principal they have already collected from you for as long as you have had the debt. They will also write off whatever they are unable to collect as a result of you being in a debt settlement program and not repaying the full balances. In my opinion, debt settlement is not the right program for you if you are able to afford the payment in the debt management program because the benefits for most people who can make that payment outweigh the benefits in the debt settlement program in exchange for the savings. However, I believe the debt settlement program is a great option for people who need payment relief and otherwise would be unable to handle the debt without having to file for bankruptcy.

BANKRUPTCY

Bankruptcy is the fourth and final option for people who want to eliminate debt. This is an option in which you should meet with an attorney who specializes in bankruptcy to make sure that this is the right decision for your situation. Typically you will be discussing one of two possible options when it comes to bankruptcy, which are Chapter 7 bankruptcy or Chapter 13 bankruptcy.

Chapter 7 bankruptcy, also known as "straight bankruptcy," liquidates your assets to pay off as much of your debt as possible. Any cash that is raised from the sale of your assets is then distributed to creditors. The next step is receiving a notice of discharge within about four months, which leads to the bankruptcy being reported on your credit report for ten years. The challenge is that if you own a business, home, or any other personal assets, Chapter 7 bankruptcy may not be the best bankruptcy option for you.

Chapter 13 bankruptcy, also known as "reorganization bankruptcy," allows you to pay off your debts over a set term of three to five years in length. If you have a consistent, predictable monthly and annual income, Chapter 13 offers a grace period. Once the grace period is over the remaining debts are discharged. In Chapter 13 bankruptcy, once it is approved by the court, creditors must stop calling or contacting you. Chapter 13 bankruptcy allows you to continue working and paying off your debts over the set period of time – while allowing you to keep your property and possessions.

SUMMARY

Have you come to the point in your life where you are tired of waking up every single day to the frustration of *minimum payments and maximum consequences*? It's time for you to explore the options besides self-management. Ask yourself this... "Knowing what I now know, shouldn't I find out what the best way to eliminate my debt is?" **Call or email us right now and we will help you get started!!**

About Andy

Andy Eilers works with individuals and organizations as a consultant through his own company, Andrew J. Eilers Consulting (ajeconsult.com). Andy's goal is to serve them and their companies in achieving their personal and professional goals through teaching, leadership, sales and motivational training, and personal and professional coaching. For over 25 years, Andy has served families and companies in the financial industry. He has also studied the material of many of the great trainers and teachers of our time including: Steve Forbes, Les Brown, Stephen Covey, Peter Drucker, Tom Hopkins, Brian Tracy, Zig Ziglar, Tony Robbins, and Napoleon Hill. In addition, Andy has consulted for many companies in the areas of motivation and sales training throughout Northern California.

Andy has a BA in Economics, with a minor in Communication Studies from CSU Sacramento. He earned an MA in Psychology with an emphasis in Organizational and Business Psychology. He is also a member of the Golden Key International Honour Society, which recognizes graduate students who graduate with a GPA of 3.5 or higher. Andy is a Doctoral candidate in a program with the University of the Rockies studying for his PhD in Philosophy with an emphasis on Innovation and Entrepreneurship and will complete that program in 2016.

Andy is also Co-author of the Best-Selling Book *In It To Win It* with the legendary Tom Hopkins, *The Secret to Winning Big* with the legendary Brian Tracy, and is a member of The National Academy of Best-Selling Authors®. He received an Editor's Choice Award for his work in *The Secret to Winning Big*. Andy has also written and recorded an audio program with Tom Hopkins focusing on his *"Ask Yourself This… How Can I Create a Better Life?"* material for sales and motivational instruction.

Andy is an accomplished martial artist, holding a 1st degree black belt in Tae Kwon Do. He is also an avid reader, golfer, tennis player, singer, poet, and wine enthusiast. For more information on Andy Eilers, email him at: andrewjeilersconsulting@gmail.com or call him at 916-221-2639 (cell).

CHAPTER 5

REWIRE YOUR BRAIN TO SPEAK YOUR MIND AND BE HEARD IN THE WIDE, WIRED WORLD

BY ANASTASIA PRYANIKOVA

Opportunity often comes disguised, or so they say. My business breakthrough came disguised as a junk email message - talk about not missing your chance. Who has the time to check the junk folder when you have hundreds of unread messages in your Inbox? Nonetheless, that morning, I was waiting for a confirmation email from somcone, and it wouldn't come. Since legitimate messages sometimes get filtered out as junk, I decided to check. The subject lines promised various pharmaceutical products, the best deals ever, and some exorbitant sum of money about to be wired to me by unknown rich relatives in foreign lands. No, those were not my business opportunities.

As I kept scrolling down, a message caught my attention. It was from Craig Valentine, a 1999 World Champion of Pubic Speaking for Toastmasters International. The message described a launch of a new World Class Speaking Coach certification program. I was curious. I had been speaking and training for years, and loved it. I applied the social brain research to the areas of persuasion, communication, and conflict management. The program offered me a chance to take a deeper dive into the dynamics of how we communicate under pressure.

Several months earlier, I found myself delivering possibly the most difficult speech of my life. It was at a Memorial service for my own husband who we had lost unexpectedly a few months shy of his 40th birthday and what would have been our 10-year anniversary. It was an impromptu, unrehearsed speech. I didn't know I could or would speak. But as I stood there in front of friends and colleagues at his workplace, my family and our then six-year-old daughter, stories started pouring out. In the end, sharing those stories made us all feel a little bit better, more hopeful and more resilient. This is the power of stories in life and business.

We all want to be in control of our lives: to plan, set goals, and get results. Yet, unexpected and sometimes tragic things happen. When our world turns upside down, our instincts kick in to make it upright again. We have a lot of resources inside to cope with life's challenges, but we don't trust ourselves enough until bad things happen and we have no choice. Craig Valentine always says that our best stories come from the places where we don't want to go. His message resonated with me that morning, and I signed up for his program right then and there. Over the course of the following three months, as I was fine-tuning my speaking and coaching skills, I was also developing my own narrative of resilience, success, and vision for my business and my life.

Whatever your reason is for finding your voice and speaking up, especially when the stakes are high - to take your audiences on a transformational journey, inspire change, navigate a conflict, sell your idea, product or service - a brain-captivating blend of stories and facts can power up your words and magnify your message.

We live in the fast-paced world of crowded markets and short attention spans. Those who can capture attention, imagination and emotions of others can drive change and become influencers. The following nine principles of ICE Speak empower leaders to speak for *Impact, Connection,* and *Earning.* They will help you turn each instance of communication into an opportunity to sync the brains and engage the hearts of your employees, business partners, and customers, so you can:

- Grow your business and expand your brand.
- Build strong and resilient relationships with your customers and fans to boost loyalty.

- Manage your reputation and effectively deal with negativity.
- Gain your community's insights to improve your offerings and your brand experience.

IMPACT

To combat short attention spans and the multitude of distractions that constantly bombard us, you need the help of a few mind tricks, sprinkled with the current brain science pixie dust, which can turn your messages into attention-pulling magnets.

1. Be a facilitator of insights.

Your message will have more relevance and impact if you co-create it with the audience. We all want to have choices and influence decisions. Personal autonomy is a reward to the brain. We are more likely to implement solutions that we contributed to than to follow someone else's advice. Ask questions; invite people to share their own stories and experiences, and encourage them to identify their own solutions.

Whenever you tell a story, make sure your participants can see themselves in your story and can relate to the characters and their journeys. Your story can provide hooks for the participants to hang their own assumptions, beliefs, fears, and hopes. We all suffer from the so-called "egocentric bias" – we think we know better. Asking the audience to take perspectives of different characters in your story may help them overcome this bias and be more receptive to other points of view.

2. Write and speak for the senses.

Words have power – some more than others. Narratives stimulate not just the language regions in the brain, like Broca's and Wernicke's areas, but many other parts as well. For example, words associated with smells, like "perfume" or "coffee," activate the primary olfactory cortex. Similarly, words describing motion light up the motor cortex. It appears that words can cause the brain to create a vivid and real experience of whatever is described to us. Whenever you recall a scene, think about the sights, sounds, smells and textures it can evoke. Provide enough detail for your audience members to help them visualize the scenes of your narrative and remember them.

Use comparisons and metaphors that can turn abstract concepts into something tangible: *cold like ice, sharp like needles, smooth like silk.*

3. Dare to care and show it.

Be yourself. Avoid sounding like a faceless corporate entity. Show vulnerability. Show your passion. Passion is infectious. People want to feel and see passion. Emotions spread across our social networks. When we smile at someone, that person is likely to smile back. Even yawning is contagious. If you are bored with your own topic, don't expect your audience to jump up from their seats in excitement. In contrast, if you are passionate, and your words, voice, and body language show it, your audience will respond with emotion. It is a magical ingredient to earn attention.

CONNECTION

People crave connection and a sense of purpose and contribution. To communicate means to connect in the shared space of understanding. Speaking is about connection that unpacks assumptions and packs new perspectives.

4. Master your signature story.

Stories captivate the brain as the oldest form of communication and as a way for all of us to bond in our unique yet archetypal experiences of struggle and success. Stories can be rebellious, raw, and emotional. They allow for vulnerability, conflict, and struggle. Stories are a vehicle for finding meaning in the events of our lives. Research shows that when a story resonates with the listener, the brains of the speaker and listener synchronize, suggesting a deeper human connection.

What is your signature story of resilience and success? Uncover it, live it, and share it. People want to know who you are. Strong personal brands translate into loyal communities of customers and fans.

Think about your business as an evolving story:

- Who are the main characters in your story?
- What are they trying to accomplish?
- What challenges and conflicts do they face?
- How do your characters overcome the obstacles?
- What message does your story convey?

5. Zoom in on the common things you share with others, zoom out of the differences.

Our brains are wired to filter out information that does not support our own views. The confirmation bias causes us to give more weight to the opinions that we agree with. Therefore, we naturally gravitate towards people like us. The advantage is that we feel safe. The downside is that we are limiting ourselves to what we already know – to our comfort zone. Before you can influence people, you have to show what you share and that you care. With each choice of words, you can either disengage or connect, show up guarded or vulnerable, belittle or uplift, assume or explore, doubt or lead. What choices are you making today?

6. Be slow to talk and in a hurry to listen.

Effective leaders master the art of listening. They understand that people want to be heard. Active and empathetic listening is a rarity in our fast-paced world. Next time you talk to someone, watch for the common barriers to active listening: relying on the predetermined attitude and assumptions; jumping to conclusions; completing other people's thoughts; selective listening only to what you want to hear; ignoring body language. Practice listening with a compassionate heart and an open mind.

EARNING

Each form of communication has a goal. In business, we often communicate to earn a sale, trust, respect, credibility, and loyalty. Rewards come in many shapes and forms. Social acceptance, autonomy, fairness, increased self-esteem, enjoyment, and monetary gains - all promote the release of the feel-good neurotransmitter dopamine, which is implicated in motivation and learning.

7. Use constraints to encourage action.

The brain likes to conserve energy and resources and prefers the *status quo* over change because change requires more mental effort. Both urgency and scarcity are examples of constraints that shift the brain into action. Setting deadlines or highlighting a limited availability of your offerings can prompt people to take action. So can routines. Much of our behavior is habitual, often in response to some cues in the environment that we may not even be aware of. Become an expert in pattern recognition, tweak the patterns, and set new routines to drive change. Routines and rituals program the brain for a specific, predictable set of actions.

8. Play to win.

Contests tantalize the brain with the possibility of a random reward. Many people join virtual communities of their favorite brands to get access to exclusive promotions, coupons, and other benefits. Use contests to bring some fun and game elements and to boost engagement. Contests can serve a variety of purposes:

- Celebrate a special occasion.

- Feature your community members.

- Offer promotions, coupons, discounts, VIP tickets, etc.

- Motivate your members to participate in a challenge.

- Invite members to submit stories about how they use your product or service.

- Reward members who spread the word about your community and invite their friends to join.

9. Earn a stellar reputation.

Your reputation is about perceptions, not intentions. People may never know what was intended behind your remarks and actions, but they will trust their own perceptions and will make decisions accordingly. Here are some strategies for managing your reputation in the wide, wired world:

Be a connector. Shine a spotlight on your social network and introduce people if you think they should meet. Express gratitude and reciprocate when somebody does something nice for you. Reciprocity is a motivating force. Give support and encouragement. Ask people for advice and favors. People like to help. Helping others gives them a sense of autonomy and enhances their social standing.

Control your hot buttons to have cool conversations. Avoid defensive and abrasive language. Don't say anything online that you wouldn't say to a person face-to-face. Remember that people can't see your body language or hear the tone of your voice. Encourage good tone and friendliness.

Monitor your name and any trademarks to know what people are saying about you. Promptly respond to any business inquiries or complaints. In any crisis communication, time is of the essence. The longer you wait to take action, admit responsibility, apologize, or make amends, the less trustworthy you appear. When you respond to a negative review or complaint, be positive in tone and factual in substance. Acknowledge the damage done and the pain caused. Accept responsibility when it is appropriate. Be issue-aware and solution-focused. Honor your loyal customers and fans. The strength, visibility, and success of your brand depend on them. They are also your best defense against reputation attacks.

When you approach your business communication as an evolving story, co-created with your customers, employees, and fans, you will create greater impact, deeper connections, and faster results. Rewire your brain to be a storyteller, speak your mind and be heard!

About Anastasia

Anastasia Pryanikova, M.A., J.D. is the founder of E-Studio, LLC, a coaching, training and consulting company that translates neuroscience and media psychology insights into tools and solutions in the areas of communication, conflict management, public speaking, presenting, and trans-media storytelling. She is a co-founder of *Bookphoria,* a distance-learning platform that enables authors to turn their books into interactive and engaging online courses and grow their information business and communities of practice.

From a linguist exploring the language of advertising, to a corporate lawyer working internationally, to a U.S. Small Business Administration attorney-advisor counseling small business leaders, Anastasia has been in the business of "changing people's minds" to facilitate high-stake conversations and decisions across borders, cultures, and industries.

Anastasia is a speaker and a Certified World Class Speaking Coach, trained by Craig Valentine, World Champion of Public Speaking for Toastmasters International. She helps business leaders step into the spotlight and create greater impact, connection and action through public speaking. As a self-proclaimed tech-geek, Anastasia also explores how technology and social media can boost influence, visibility and strengthen human connection. She helps business leaders find their virtual voice and develop brain-captivating content for various trans-media channels: videos, webinars, information products, social media and e-learning.

Anastasia shares her tips on brain-friendly public speaking and presenting under pressure and in the spotlight at: http://brainalchemist.com.

CHAPTER 6

THE 401(k) TAX SAVINGS MYTH

BY ANDREW SCHADE CFP, CHFC, CASL, RHU, REBC, EA

For years I have been hearing everyone from advisors to compliance officers preach about the amazing 401(k), the 'tax savings' vehicle. It seems like every morning when I turn on the radio, I hear an ad from an association of accountants expounding upon saving into 401(k)'s. In fact, I even had compliance officers tell me that if I wasn't recommending to clients that they use their 401(k) before I recommend other investment vehicles, that I was not in compliance and was not doing what was right for the client. Quite frankly I am sick of being inundated by the masses that continue to push 401(k)'s under the heading of 'tax savings'. Now, please understand, I do not think that 401(k)'s are bad, nor do I think that saving into a 401(k) is wrong. My problem is with the myth of 'tax savings' that are received from saving into a 401(k). You see saving money into a 401(k) does not, I repeat does not, save you money on taxes. What it truly does is **defer** the tax associated with the income that was placed in the 401(k) in that tax year into the future. There are two potential problems with that, first no one knows what future tax rates will be, and second it can be difficult to know what income level someone will have in the future in the year that the deferred tax bill is recognized. In this chapter we will analyze those two potential problems, demonstrate that in some cases utilizing a 401(k) will almost certainly be harmful to an investor from a tax standpoint, and discuss strategies so that you have a better understanding of how to implement tax planning into your retirement plans.

To address the first potential problem of future tax rates you must have an understanding of historical tax rates. One of my favorite questions to ask my clients when they are new to working with me is 'where do you think tax rates are at today from a historical standpoint? Do you think they are high, low, or somewhere in between.' The answer I get to that question is all over the board but usually, somewhere in between or high wins out. So if that was your answer you are like most people I have worked with. The next question I ask them is 'do you think taxes are likely to stay the same, go up, or go lower in the future?' Usually after laughter at the thought that taxes could go down, the overwhelming answer I receive to that question is go up. After asking these questions I explain to the client that we have some of the lowest tax brackets that we have ever had in the history of this country. I then tell them that I agree with the answer to the second question that I think tax rates will likely go up in the future and I base that belief on the budget projections offered to us by the United States Congressional Budget Office which project them to increase as well. When you take these two items into account you will begin to see what I mean by the myth of 'tax savings' in the 401(k). Now let me give you an example of what I mean.

First let's examine a married couple that earns $44,500 per year has 2 children and utilizes the standard deduction. Let's assume that this couple does not save into a 401(k) and has no other adjustments to income, and therefore their Adjusted Gross Income (AGI) equals their earned income. Their tax calculation in 2012 would look as follows:

AGI (Adjusted Gross Income)	$44,500
(Less) Standard Deduction	$11,900
(Less) Personal Exemptions: 4 (2 adults, 2 children)	$15,200
Equals Taxable Income	$17,400

Taxable income of $17,400 filing married jointly would place this couple in the 10% tax bracket as of 2012. This is before they put any money into a 401(k). Now if the couple saves into the 401(k) they **defer** the tax associated with the amount placed into the 401(k) into a future year at their marginal tax rate of 10%. Had the government decided to let the tax brackets revert to their previous levels from 2001 or increases tax rates as the congressional budget office projects, there is a real possibility that this couple could be in a higher marginal tax bracket when they withdraw the money (and growth on the money) that they saved into their 401(k). If that couple is in a higher bracket, say the 15% bracket which would more historically be the norm, the client would have paid 50% more in tax on those dollars saved into the 401(k) than had they not saved the money into a 401(k) and invested it into say a Roth 401(k) or Roth IRA. To illustrate this concept consider the following math:

Contribution into 401(k)	$2,000
Tax at 10%	$200
Future distribution	$2000
Tax at 15%	$300
Tax of $200 V. Tax of $300	$100 increase
% increase $100/$200	50%

This example clearly illustrates how there is a good chance that a couple taking this course of action would actually be worse off for utilizing their 401(k) instead of say a Roth IRA or Roth 401(k). Now keep in mind in this example I assumed there was no employer match offered in the 401(k), if there is a match that obviously impacts the equation. The point of this example is to illustrate how a future tax bracket increase could put someone in a higher tax bracket and thus the tax they **defer** could be less than the tax they would end up paying in the future. It is important to realize that rising future tax brackets can impact anyone!

Next let's consider the second potential problem that I mentioned that your income may be different in the future than it is now. Another question that I ask my clients when I work with them for financial planning is, 'Do you think that your income is likely to stay the same, go up, or go down over time?' Previous to October of 2008 the answer I got from this question was almost always go up. Particularly if I asked the question this way, 'If you received no pay raises over the next 5 years would you likely stay at the same employer or would you look for a different job?' The answer to that question was almost always 'look for a new job.' Given the impact of the events of 2008 and the downturn of the economy I no longer ask that question simply because now you have an abundance of unemployed or underemployed people, and many people are happy just to have a job. This timeframe crucially illustrates the impact of future changes in income.

For this example let's revisit the couple from example one, but with a few changes. The couple is still married has 2 children and files married jointly. Now let's assume the couple was making $120,000, but because one of them lost their job and was forced to take a pay cut now they make $95,000. Before the pay cut this couple was in the 25% marginal tax bracket, math as follows:

AGI (Adjusted Gross Income)	$120,000
(Less) Standard Deduction	$11,900
(Less) Personal Exemption (4 two adults, two children)	$15,200
Equals Taxable Income	$92,900

$92,900 using 2012 tax rates would have placed this couple in the 25% tax bracket. After the pay cut, the client is in the 15%, marginal bracket:

AGI (Adjusted Gross Income)	$95,000
(Less) Standard Deduction	$11,900
(Less) Personal Exemption (4 two adults, two children)	$15,200
Equals Taxable Income	$67,900

$67,900 using 2012 tax rates would place this couple in the 15% tax bracket. This couple was **deferring** at 25% but now would be deferring at 15%. Is utilizing the 401(k) the right decision for this couple? The answer is it depends on many factors. Will the underemployed spouse return to a higher income? What income level does the couple plan to live on in retirement? Will that amount be more or less than what they are living on now? The reality is that this couple could end up being in a higher tax bracket in the future and particularly in retirement than they are in under the current reduced pay situation. If that happens their situation could end up looking similar to the couple from the first example, a higher tax bill than necessary.

Given the potential problems that can arise from the 'tax savings' myth associated with using 401(k)'s how do you go about planning for retirement and successfully navigate the tax pitfalls that can happen. Here I will provide some tips that you can utilize to improve your chance for success.Know your current marginal tax bracket. If you do not know your marginal tax bracket it is difficult to construct a game plan around tax rate changes.

If you don't know your marginal tax bracket, ask your tax preparer. While your tax preparer may not know this number by memory for your situation, they should be able to look at your return and tell you.

Review your marginal tax bracket annually. Keep in mind that your tax bracket may change due to increases or decreases in income or because of future tax rate changes from the government.

Review your marginal tax bracket well before the end of the calendar year. There is very little that can be done from a tax-planning standpoint at the time you prepare your return. Therefore it is vital that you project your income for the year during the calendar year. For example, at the time you file your return for 2013, begin projecting numbers for 2014. (You can start by using the 2013 numbers and adjust for any changes you anticipate for 2014.)

Decide for yourself where you think tax rates will go in the future. If you (or your professional) do not have an opinion on this you are unlikely to have success.

Determine how much income you will need in the future for retirement. Compare that amount to what tax bracket you are in today. If that amount would put you in the same or higher tax bracket today, if tax rates go up even slightly you will pay more taxcs in the future by **deferring** the associated tax today.

If you do not feel confident in your ability to execute complex strategies on your own you are not alone. While it is very common to utilize a tax professional keep in mind that many tax professionals are only providing preparation services. They often do not provide any real tax planning strategies. Do not assume that because you have a good preparer that they are implementing any strategies for you from a planning standpoint. If you are unsure, ask them. If they say they are doing forward planning for you ask them for an example. Ask them about your marginal tax bracket and what tax bracket they think you will be in down the road. Chances are if they are not doing planning they will not have an answer. In addition, if you only see them once a year at tax time, they are not likely doing any tax planning.

As an alternative, some people will rely upon their financial advisor for forward-looking tax advice. If this is your case and you are not sure if they are doing forward-looking tax planning for you ask them similar questions. Ask them for a copy of the projections that they have run to show you what tax bracket you would be in and how their strategies have impacted your tax situation. In addition, ask them what their background with taxes is. Many financial advisors will indicate that they are keeping taxes in mind for their clients when really they have a limited background, or no background at all in taxes.

About Andrew

Andrew Schade is President and founder of Phoenix Advisors, LLC. A one-man band of financial planners, Andrew holds a myriad of distinctions including: Certified Financial Planner (CFP), Chartered Financial Consultant (ChFC), Chartered Advisor Senior Living (CASL), Registered Health Underwriter (RHU), Registered Employee Benefits Consultant (REBC), and Enrolled Agent(EA). He received two Bachelor's Degrees, Business Administration and Economics, from Alma College.

Andrew's satisfied clients would say his dedication brings the best of many aspects of financial planning under one roof. In fact, the book *America's Select Financial Advisors 2013 The Professionals of Financial Planning,* recognized Andrew's contribution to his field.

Andrew is a member of the prestigious Theophilus C. Abbot Society, a philanthropic organization at Michigan State University. Members of the Theophilus C. Abbot Society, according to Michigan State University, "continue Abbot's efforts by providing a critical financial edge necessary to maintain a high level of innovation in academic as well as non-academic areas of the University."

In addition to his philanthropic involvement at Michigan State University, Andrew is a co-founder of the charitable foundation Friends Fur-Ever. The mission of this organization is to help dog owners whose life events would otherwise force them to give up their dog by acting as a temporary or permanent home and when possible reunite them. This organization looks to help many different groups including the elderly, chronically or terminally Ill, and military members.

Contact Andrew Schade at: AS@PhxAdvisors.com

CHAPTER 7

KNOW YOUR DAM NUMBERS

BY CHAD CELI

Did you know a dam less than a quarter mile long can stop 247 square miles of surface water? The relatively small Hoover Dam is a remarkable example of leverage; a small dam controlling a large body of water.

I'd like you to think of the large body of water as potential new clients waiting to come into your business. All of these new clients are being held back by one small dam. I believe many businesses today are stuck at the "dam" because they don't know how much they can spend to "buy" new clients; and thus restrict the number of new clients. The DAM Number is a simple formula created to make marketing decisions easier and more effective. This is the one number that, once fully understood, can crack open the DAM and flood you with new business. It can take you from **limited to limitless** overnight. Your DAM Number is the single most important ACTIONABLE number you need to know to grow your business.

What's happening without knowing your *DAM Number*?

- Marketing decisions are made from the gut and results suffer
- Businesses aren't able to routinely "buy" new client opportunities and growth is limited
- Businesses are at the mercy of referrals for growth
- Businesses aren't able to attract enough new clients

KILLING A SACRED COW...

The Dam Number was created to help businesses grow. Before we continue, may I ask you to kill a sacred cow? Many business owners make marketing decisions based on a long-standing sacred cow: the percentage based model. I suggest reconsidering this model. In a percentage-based model, marketing budgets are created annually based on percentage of gross revenues (e.g., company revenues of $1,000,000...7% for marketing is $70,000). Each industry tends to follow their own range of *acceptable* percentages. The percentage model is broken for three reasons:

1) It lacks accountability for what happens to the budget. You can meet budget and generate ZERO new clients.

2) It's restrictive and doesn't allow for exponential growth. Opportunities are easily missed when new budgets need to be approved.

3) Its useless for a new business or business that wants to grow faster than industry competitors. If you want to double your business in 12 months you may need a much higher percentage of current revenues.

The DAM Number requires a paradigm shift away from the percentage-based model. It is nontraditional, performance-based and not for everyone. If you use your DAM Number it will empower your business for growth.

NOW, WHAT IS YOUR DAM NUMBER?

Your DAM Number is the **most** you could spend to acquire a new client based on the current cash flow and the average lifetime value of a client (LTV). The core essence of marketing is how much you are willing to pay to acquire a client. How well you compete comes down to how much you can afford to pay. If you don't know how much you're able to spend to "buy" new relationships, you're at a huge disadvantage in a hyper competitive world. Most people spend all their time and energy determining the least amount of money they can spend on marketing. The most successful businesses have determined their DAM Number and spend their time and energy on what they need to spend in order to grow as fast as they want. See the difference? The closer you allow your acquisition budget to get to your DAM, the more potential you have to flood your business with new clients.

Based on my experience with over 117 different industries, your DAM Number should be at least 11% of the average lifetime value of a client. If your DAM can't reach 11% of LTV that means you're undercapitalized or fixed expenses are drowning the business model.

This isn't brain science and it doesn't need to be complicated for any business. There's only one DAM number you need to know. First, you'll need to calculate your "Average Lifetime Value" (or LTV per client).

Average Lifetime Value Formula:

(Average Transaction $) x (Incremental Gross Margin %) x

(Average Frequency Per Year) x (Industry Average Lifespan in Years) = LTV

Example:
Let's say you own company A. The average transaction is $1,000. Your gross margins average 60% so you make $600 (before overhead) on each transaction. The average buyer makes a purchase five times a year and buys for 5 years. The average lifetime value would be $15,000.

($1,000) x (.60) = $600 x (5) x (5) = **$15,000 (LTV)**

Insert your numbers:

_____(transaction) x_____(margin) = $____(avg. profit)

x ___(transactions) x __(years)= $_____ (LTV)

This basic calculation will suffice for over 95% of all businesses. For a more advanced calculation of your average lifetime value (LTV) look into referral rates, retention rates, discount rates, client segmentation or contact a marketing expert.

EXERCISE: Ask ten employees or colleagues, "What is the average lifetime value of a client?" My guess is they will all have different answers.

When a business owner first calculates their LTV number they often don't know what to do with it. Many owners have asked, "How does this change my marketing?" They needed a simple way to interpret and apply the LTV number. Hence, the DAM number was born. It makes the average lifetime value of a client ACTIONABLE.

In order to calculate your DAM Number, you must have a decent understanding of your cash flow. Based on cash flow and the incremental revenue generated from the first transaction of a new client, what is the most you could spend to acquire a new client?

Insert your LTV number below to calculate your minimum DAM Number:

_____(LTV) x .11 = $_____ (Your DAM Number)

From our example above, the average client lifetime value of a client for company A is $15,000. The DAM "minimum" would be $1,650 (11% of $15,000). This means company A could spend $1,650 to acquire an undetermined number of new clients at that marketing investment. In contrast to spending $40,000 on marketing and hoping to acquire new clients, the DAM Number is actionable and specific.

Although not always obvious, there are highly calculated numbers at work all around you, every day, and in every industry. Have you ever been offered FREE Roundtrip Airfare if you listened to a two hour presentation from a timeshare company? Have you been offered a first month FREE for a product or service? Opened an account at a bank that offered $50 when you opened a new free checking account? All of these scenarios are similar in that they understand the average lifetime value of a customer and they spend money up front to acquire a new relationship (i.e., a new client). When the bank gives you $50, it is because they know you're worth an average of $1,350. Numbers drive their marketing and sales efforts. Let your gut decide what's for lunch today, not how you should spend your marketing dollars.

ARE YOU STUCK AT THE DAM?

ARE YOU STUCK ON THE NUMBERS? Some business owners don't know the numbers of their business well enough, and therefore, have difficulty calculating their average lifetime value number. Without knowing how much a client relationship is really worth owners rarely spend enough to be competitive. What should you do when you don't have the real numbers? Guess. That's right. Take the numbers you do have and make a conservative estimate of the missing numbers. It's better to have conservative LTV and DAM numbers than no numbers at all. If you don't know the numbers of your business, you don't really *know* your business.

ARE YOU STUCK DOING INSTITUTIONAL ADVERTISING? John Wanamaker, the father of modern marketing and founder of America's first Department Store, notoriously said, "I know that half of my advertising doesn't work. The problem is, I don't know which half." Some business owners spend their marketing dollars on "institutional" advertising (i.e., TV, radio, print with no direct response) and can't track how much it cost to generate a lead or new client. If this is you, divide your entire monthly marketing budget by the number of new clients generated in a month (excluding referrals). This will give you a rough idea of your cost per acquisition (cost to acquire one new client). Start using more direct response marketing vehicles. Unless you're Proctor & Gamble, it's too expensive to generate awareness without a trackable response.

ARE YOU STUCK ON AVERAGE? Some business owners don't trust the mathematical principle of averages. They won't agree on an actionable DAM Number because they don't believe EVERY new client will be worth the lifetime value. They are correct (of course) BUT that is the point to leveraging the law of averages. It's not "**All Clients** Lifetime Value," it is the "**Average** Lifetime Value." You must be willing to ACT AS IF every new client opportunity is worth the average lifetime value; if not, you're the most vulnerable to lose business to competitors and the mostly likely to have poor new client conversion rates. This may sound simple in concept, however, 80% of businesses don't apply this principle.

YOUR DAM NUMBER AT WORK FOR YOU...

Want more referrals? What has grown your business more than anything? "Referrals" is the most frequent reply from business owners across the board. Do you have a systematic referral program that helps generate referrals consistently? Often, a business will have no referral program or a very weak one in place while spending 10 to 100 times the amount in marketing dollars to acquire a new client. I call this the *Referral Gap*: The gap between what you spend to acquire "strangers" and generating referrals from existing clients. By knowing your DAM Number you can close the *Referral Gap* and spend more to attract and acquire referrals. If you're spending $500 to acquire a new client via advertising, why wouldn't you be willing to spend at least the same amount to receive a referral? (Hint: referrals statistically spend more, are less likely to haggle about price, and are more likely to refer others.)

Need more new clients? One of the most common and most expensive mistakes I see in businesses is a weak first time offer. Today, attention is a scarce resource and it can be challenging to get people to respond to something new or different. Businesses can't afford to make weak offers and lose business. A previous client of ours had an average lifetime value over $120,000 and the owner was concerned about offering a $50 gift card for first time clients. Once I convinced him of his real DAM Number, the offer was approved and response rates tripled overnight. Avoid the expensive mistake of short-term transactional thinking and create an irresistibly strong first-time offer.

EXERCISE: List the marketing channel or activity currently being executed and it's respective cost to acquire a client. (i.e., Direct Sales, Telemarketing, Referral Systems, Joint Ventures, Direct Mail, Advertising, Endorsements, Strategic Alliances, Database Reactivation, Sponsorships.)

Channel or Activity	Cost	# New Clients	Cost per Acquisition
_____	$_____	_____	$_____
_____	$_____	_____	$_____
_____	$_____	_____	$_____
_____	$_____	_____	$_____
_____	$_____	_____	$_____

Note: if you've had trouble thinking of five different ways you're generating new business, review your DAM Number and consider new channels for growth. Also, consider the idea that you will gain many more new clients if you are able to spend more money in each channel.

How do you know how much to spend on advertising or marketing? How do you formulate that number? A random percentage of gross revenues? A gut feeling of what should be allocated? I recommend you make marketing decisions based on the numbers of your business. One of the most important numbers of any business is the average lifetime value of a client. Calculate your DAM Number to make your average lifetime value actionable information. Use your DAM Number to make marketing decisions easier and more effective. Your DAM Number will forever change your perspective on marketing and can open up a flood of new clients.

Chances are if you're reading this book and have calculated your DAM Number you're ahead of 95% of your competitors and destined for success. Congratulations!

About Chad

President Obama, Princess Grace, Ralph Lauren, Phil Collins, Steve Jobs, Tom Cruise, Steve Martin and Oprah…What does Chad Celi have in common with these celebrities? Chad Celi and Steve Martin are both members of MENSA, the international high IQ society. Chad was the first non-celebrity to receive the FAB Award of Excellence; past recipients include Princess Grace and Liza Minnelli. Both Chad and Oprah have walked on fire with Tony Robbins. Chad Celi and Bill Gates both decided to drop out of college to pursue their dreams. During the world premiere of *The Others*, Chad interviewed Tom Cruise on the red carpet. Similar to Ralph Lauren, Chad has also had a cover feature in *VOGUE* magazine. While taping the Maurizio Costanzo Show in Italy, Chad Celi shared the stage with Phil Collins and Alanis Morissette. President Obama did receive more on-air time, however, Chad has also been interviewed by Matt Lauer on NBC's *The Today Show*.

In 2009, Chad founded Reset Strategies based on a dramatic trend happening in the market: the death of traditional marketing. He noticed old marketing methods and approaches were no longer generating enough ROI and formed his company to help businesses "reset" their marketing strategies. Reset Strategies helps businesses grow without traditional advertising and they guarantee a 3 to 1 Return On Investment. Reset Strategies is based in Louisville, Kentucky. Chad Celi and his "reset" approach have been seen nationally on NBC, ABC, CBS and FOX affiliates and seen in *Fast Company, Entrepreneur, Inc.,* and *The Wall Street Journal* (www.ResetStrategies.com).

Chad is happily married to his wife Stacy, and together, they are proud co-creators of three energetic children.

CHAPTER 8

HOW TO CHOOSE YOUR IDEAL FINANCIAL ADVISOR

BY P. CHRISTOPHER MUSIC

Who should you listen to regarding financial advice?

With rampant TV shows and commercials, magazine articles and ads, newspapers, gurus or other sources of opinions, it's confusing to say the least.

Many people approach financial matters in one of two ways:

1) Working with a professional in the financial industry (perhaps having a non-optimal experience), or

2) Purchasing financial products directly from the providers (considered the "do-it-yourself" approach) promoted to save money while actually costing a fortune.

If you have had a bad experience, I understand. So have I (more than most) and I've been a professional in the subject for more than 20 years. The unfortunate reality is that each one of us is responsible for our own financial results and experience. We choose our own advisors, and if the result is bad, then the choice is bad. We must learn to make better choices from whom we take our advice. As a consumer, you should feel confident that you are receiving substantial value for the fees you pay.

Because of this dilemma, I decided to outline the ideal financial experience I wanted to have for my own household based on my experience and education. In fact, I have spent two decades discovering an entire financial planning system based on results, and found that other small business owners wanted to have that same experience.

The first step to achieving "ideal" financial success is to find your "ideal" financial advisor. I developed a rather simple interview process to assist a small business owner in finding the correct advisor to help him achieve a more optimal financial condition while he pursues his passion.

Choosing a financial advisor can be frustrating and downright scary. You must understand that you will want to choose only ONE primary advisor and follow his advice. To choose more than one primary advisor has proven time and time again to be disastrous since the conflicting opinions and guidance from more than one advisor will cripple your ability to be certain in your decisions, and will therefore prevent necessary action being taken to improve your financial condition. This primary financial advisor will act as a general contractor to coordinate most of the financial planning and implementation with other professionals in each specialty.

To choose a primary advisor, I have created a list of questions to help you. First, ask each of these questions of yourself so you are clear in what YOU require in an Ideal Financial Advisor. Then, ask potential candidates the same questions so that you can compare your requirements with those you interview. With this method you can confidently recognize and choose the correct advisor for you and your family.

QUESTION #1:
ARE YOU OBLIGATED TO ACT IN A FIDUCIARY CAPACITY IN YOUR RELATIONSHIP WITH ME AND HOW DO YOU DEFINE THE FIDUCIARY STANDARD?

In the world of financial advice, there are two basic standards by which an advisor may operate—the suitability standard or the fiduciary standard.

Advisors who are licensed for insurance or licensed to sell investment products (called Registered Representatives) are held to a suitability standard. This means that if your advisor has these licenses only, then he will give advice that is considered incidental to the service provided, such as a life insurance policy or investment product. "Suitable" means that the investment or insurance product will meet your needs and be acceptable, but will not necessarily be in your best interest.

Conversely, a fiduciary standard is a relationship where one acts at all times in the best interest of the client. Registered Investment Advisors (RIA) and Certified Financial Planners® (CFP®) are held to this standard, as well as insurance agents and Registered Representatives who are also RIAs or CFPs. Anyone acting as a fiduciary would also be obligated to disclose conflicts of interest that may interfere with what is considered to be "in the client's best interest."

But how does the advisor define his fiduciary standard? How does he define "in the client's best interest?" This is going to vary from advisor to advisor based on what he believes is his fiduciary role and his knowledge of financial planning technology. Not all advisors are the same when it comes to how this standard is interpreted; there will actually be a wide variation amongst financial professionals.

First, you must decide to what standard your Ideal Advisor would adhere: Suitability or Fiduciary?

Then, you will have to decide how you define what is in YOUR best interest. You will have to evaluate the different results each advisor provides and determine whether they are what you consider part of your ideal experience.

For me, I would not work with an advisor who did not act as a fiduciary and define "the client's best interest" as the manifested progress towards a definable optimum financial condition in all areas of my lifetime financial experience.

QUESTION #2:
WHAT OBJECTIVE RESULT CAN I EXPECT TO EXPERIENCE ONCE I RECEIVE YOUR SERVICE?

What will be the real world manifestation of the implementation of his advice if you follow it?

In my experience, the vast majority of financial professionals have never really defined the exact measurable results they are intending to achieve with their clients. Asking hundreds of them over the years has led me to note lack of consensus, and PR nonsense such as: "I help clients achieve their financial objectives," which is useless since it is a statement of a purpose (why), not an end result that can be measured objectively (what).

To address this problem, let's start with the apparent intended end-results of different professionals:

1. Insurance agent: the sale of a suitable insurance policy to effectively transfer risk from the client to the insurance company.

2. Registered Representative: the sale of a suitable investment product within the agreed-upon risk tolerance of the investor.

3. Registered Investment Advisor (or portfolio manager): a well-managed portfolio to achieve the best possible returns while minimizing risk in alignment with the account holder's risk tolerance.

4. Financial Planner or Advisor: A delivered financial planning process (whether written or not) to assist clients in implementing effective strategies to achieve their financial objectives.

As you can see, each specialty within the financial services industry has its own end-results, whether they have been specifically defined or not, and they will vary with each individual you consult. This creates a wide divergence of possible financial outcomes.

We all know that financial professionals will engage in advice and activity that compensates them. This is what all professionals do, and cannot be faulted. But they should have a well-defined and specific end-result you expect to experience if everyone does their part. Only then do you have some prediction of what you can expect by implementing their programs. Only hire those professionals who can provide results you want to achieve.

I would want an advisor who can give me a detailed and specific outline of the objective results I can expect to achieve.

QUESTION #3:
HOW DO YOU OBJECTIVELY MEASURE
THE RESULTS OF YOUR SERVICES?

Have the advisor explain what metrics will be used to determine whether his product has been achieved. These should be statistical and financial calculations that are compared from year to year to determine progress toward the defined end-result. These calculations should go well beyond rates of return or net worth, since these are only two minor results that should be achieved with a complete financial plan.

I would expect to have several metrics that accurately measure ALL aspects of my financial experience, not just one or two specific areas.

QUESTION #4:
DO YOU HAVE A WRITTEN FINANCIAL PLAN FOR YOUR HOUSEHOLD? IF SO, CAN I SEE THE PLAN BINDER?

Anyone who does financial planning for others should have himself as his first client. He should have his own written financial plan and be implementing it in a manner consistent with the advice he gives his clients. He should be able to produce the plan binder upon request. This is a matter of integrity and an indicator that the advisor believes in the value of his services enough to do what is in his own best interest.

A financial plan will cover all aspects of one's financial experience. There is a difference between a financial plan and a financial proposal. A plan would be a "series of actions worked out beforehand to accomplish a known objective," whereas a proposal is "the act of offering or suggesting something for acceptance." These two concepts are confused since many financial "plans" are actually "proposals" for insurance and investment products. Because most advisors do not receive compensation to assist clients in achieving other objectives--such as debt elimination-- they do not get done.

My financial advisor would have a full, written comprehensive plan for himself, similar to the type he offers to clients.

QUESTION #5:
DO YOU SPECIALIZE IN THE TYPE OF CLIENTS UNIQUE TO MY INDUSTRY OR PROFESSION?

There is a major difference in the quality of service between advisors who specialize with a particular type of client and those who specialize in financial products for anyone who will buy them. When a financial advisor specializes with a specific type of client, such as private practice professionals, he learns nuances about those industries that lead to synergistic results well above the average outcomes gained from advisors who do not specialize. Often, advisors will gain additional training and education in business management, transition planning or benefits programs unique to that industry to incorporate in the financial plan.

My ideal advisor would have his own practice and have many clients who are in my industry. Ideally, he would have had training and experience in starting and transitioning out of his own business in the past.

QUESTION #6:
DO YOU OWN THE SAME (OR VERY SIMILAR) INVESTMENT AND INSURANCE SERVICES THAT YOU ARE RECOMMENDING TO ME?

Anyone who gives investment advice or sells financial products should own them himself. If he is acting in his own best interest, then it would stand to reason that the recommendations he is promoting to you are the same as what he owns (within certain parameters such as age, tax brackets, etc.). If not, then that may be an indicator that the advisor is not convinced that the recommendations he is promoting are the best available.

My advisor would own the same products and services that he suggests for me.

QUESTION #7:
WHAT SERVICES DO YOU PROVIDE TO EDUCATE ME ON FINANCIAL AND ECONOMIC MATTERS SO I CAN HAVE A MORE SUCCESSFUL FINANCIAL EXPERIENCE?

A financial advisor is a specialist in financial and economic matters. In order to successfully partner with you, he has the responsibility to educate you in simple, easily understood terms. The more training you have on the basic principles of financial prosperity and confidence in your application of them, the more you will enjoy a successful lifetime financial experience.

My advisor would engage in educational processes to place me in a position of greater confidence and certainty in my financial decisions. He writes books and provides seminars on proven knowledge and strategies.

After you have interviewed the potential advisor and are satisfied that you have the complete and accurate answers to these seven questions, compare his responses with what you desire in your Ideal Advisor.

Then ask yourself the following questions:

1. Can I trust this advisor to act in my best interest based on his definition of fiduciary responsibility?

2. Do I agree with his financial planning philosophy and system enough to follow through with his recommendations over a long period of time?

3. Do I feel confident that he understands my unique needs such as my personal goals, my business challenges and the type of financial experience I want?

4. Do I really believe that he has the knowledge, resources, experience and competence to actually help me and my family achieve our financial objectives?

When you can answer "yes" to these four questions, then you have potentially found your Ideal Advisor. Commit to working with him as a partner to get the results you want.

It is my hope that you use this process to help you have a truly successful financial experience.

To learn more, please visit: www.IdealFinancialAdvisor.com to help you in your search.

Happy Hunting!

About Christopher

P. Christopher Music®, also known as The Financial Prosperity Coach™, is a best-selling author and personal financial expert. He has been seen on NBC, CBS, ABC and FOX affiliates around the country as well as *Newsweek, Forbes* and various healthcare industry publications.

Christopher is known for asking the question, "How does a private practice professional have a successful and positive financial experience while he lives his art?" Frustrated with the unpredictable and sometimes disastrous outcomes from inconsistent financial advice, he founded the subject of Econologics®, Results-Based Financial Planning® and Results-Based Transition Planning™ to standardize and codify the next evolution in financial planning results for America's professional households.

Christopher is the Founder of the Econologics Institute, a financial education company providing books, audio courses and seminars on the subject. He is also President of Econologics Financial Advisors, a Registered Investment Advisor, serving the financial prosperity needs of private practice professionals nationwide through the implementation of the *Econologics Road Map® for Professionals* financial plan.

Christopher is a 20-year veteran of the financial planning profession and the author of industry-specific *Financial Success Guides* for Private Practice Physical Therapists, Veterinarians, Optometrists and Dentists. He also created the *Private Practice Millionaire®* audio program with best-selling author of the *E-Myth*, Mr. Michael Gerber.

To learn more about P. Christopher Music, The Financial Prosperity Coach, visit: www.Econologics.com or join us on our blog site: www.PrivatePracticeMillionaire.com. For additional information, visit: www.IdealFinancialAdvisor.com.

CHAPTER 9

7-STEPS TO FINANCIAL ABUNDANCE

BY DAVEN SHARMA, CPA, CERTIFIED FINANCIAL PLANNER™

Flashback to November 1984 – A PANAM Airways flight from Nairobi, Kenya lands at JFK carrying scores of passengers headed to the immigration lines. Many of them will choose to adopt USA as their future permanent home. One such immigrant is of East Indian descent whose final destination is Los Angeles, CA. After clearing immigration and customs, he is advised to go to another terminal to catch his next flight. Being new to the area, he is somewhat unsure and a NY City cab driver catches his bewildered look. The cabbie claims that the next terminal is quite far and it will cost $100 for the transport. The immigrant refuses as he landed with only $20 in his pocket. The cabbie then agrees to transport him for just $20 because he would like to help the newcomer. To the immigrant's surprise, the ride is over in less than 2 minutes. Somewhat wiser and $20 poorer, the immigrant finally gets on the next flight, still ecstatic, as his dream to be in the land of opportunities and opulence has finally come true. In case you are wondering, yes, this is my story.

Today, less than 5% of households in America are affluent despite the fact that this is *the* land of opportunities. We define affluent as someone with over $1 million in investable assets, excluding their primary home. A steady decline in interest rates over the past many years has unnerved even the wealthy about having sufficient income in their golden years to sustain their current lifestyle.

Getting back to my story, I found gainful employment, pursued higher education and got married, almost all at the same time. I also started saving money and, like most others, decided that investing in the stock market is the way to go. My investments didn't go anywhere at first but then Black Monday of October 1987 changed it all. The damage from that day must have shown on my face as my colleague, who was also a close friend, inquired if everything was all right. "Of course not," I replied. "It seems like my dream to achieve financial success is already turning into a nightmare." He laughed at my story, which only made me scream - "I have lost thousands of dollars and all you can do is laugh." "I am laughing at your thought process, not at your loss," he replied. "What do you mean?" I asked. "My friend, if you just follow the crowd, all you will get is what they get," was the reply. "Pray explain," I said. "I am not the best person as I am still learning, but I will put you in touch with my mentor Mr. Yin," he suggested. "Go meet him with an open mind, and see if he can guide you." I called Mr. Yin and made an appointment for the upcoming Saturday.

I arrive at his house the next Saturday, which was in a very nice suburb of Los Angeles. He greets me at the door and invites me to come inside. My first reaction upon meeting him was that of being surrounded by peace and serenity. He then introduces me to his wife and tells me that they have been married for over 50 years. His wife smiles and welcomes me to their home. She then offers me tea, and politely leaves the room. Now I am at the disposal of My Yin. To make me comfortable, he briefly tells me about his family – he and his wife are the only people living in that large house. He wants to downsize, but his wife doesn't part with her memories of living in that house. Their kids are now grown up and have moved away. One is practicing law and the other one is a professor at a well-known University.

Then he inquires about my family and I bring him up to date with what I have done thus far with my life. I also told him about the money I lost in the market and how I felt. He smiles and then asks me a question – What do you think I was earning just before I retired? I guessed a number based upon where he lived, and this time he laughs heartily. "I wish," he says. "Your number is three times higher!" The shock shows on my face and I ask – "How could you afford to put your kids through college, own such a beautiful home, and still retire comfortably? Surely you must have invested very wisely in the market, and I hope you will share your secret with me."

He says he will ask a few questions before he starts sharing his wisdom with me:

Mr. Yin – Tell me exactly what are you trying to achieve?

    D.S. – I want to be rich.

Mr. Yin - How do you define rich?

    D.S. – I don't know exactly– maybe One million dollars, maybe more.

Mr. Yin - And how do you plan to go about becoming rich?

    D.S. – By investing my money wisely in the market so I can benefit from compounded returns.

Mr. Yin – And how has that worked thus far?

    D.S. – Not so good, especially after black Monday. Sometimes I feel financially I am back to square one - the day I landed in this country.

Mr. Yin – So what you want from me?

    D.S. – Show me the right way to invest in the markets so I can grow my money faster and reach my goal.

It suddenly occurs to me that he wasn't happy with my answer and he says without any hesitation

Mr. Yin – If that's what you want from me, you have come to the wrong place. I can't help you.

    D.S. – I am sorry if I misunderstood. My friend mentioned that you could help me achieve financial success similar to how you have done for yourself.

Mr. Yin (smiles and says) – I am not refusing to help you. All I am trying to say is that your idea about achieving wealth is ALL backwards. He then asks me – Do you know the meaning of insanity?

D.S. – You mean madness?

Mr. Yin – That's one definition, but here's another one – it is doing the same thing over and over again and expecting different results.

I smile at this and he continues.

Mr. Yin – To reach your destination, you should walk in the right direction. You will never make it if you are headed the wrong way, no matter how fast you run.

My respect for Mr. Yin went up one notch upon hearing these words of wisdom, and I was looking forward to more.

D.S. – Please show me the right way, Mr. Yin.

Mr. Yin – Let's have some lunch before we start.

Soon Mrs. Yin served us with a wonderful home-cooked meal after which we resumed our conversation.

Mr. Yin continued – Let me start by asking - how did you get here this morning?

D.S. – Since I had your address, I looked up the map, identified the best route, noted it down on a piece of paper, and used it as a guide to reach your home.

Mr. Yin – Did you get lost along the way?

D.S. – Yes, once or twice I took the wrong turn, but since I had the map with me I was able to get back on track without too much trouble.

Mr. Yin – Now where is your road map to achieve financial success?

And it hits me; I am trying to get somewhere without any roadmap. I am embarrassed so I look down.

Mr. Yin – You are not alone son, most people in this world are trying to attain financial success, but they have no road map to guide them.

D.S. – Mr. Yin, I completely agree with you. We plan for little things such as a short trip, our vacation, etc., but we completely fail to plan for the most important thing in our life. Now, I see it as, ***those who fail to plan simply plan to fail.*** Now please tell me how to go about creating a plan.

Mr. Yin – A financial plan is very similar to the roadmap you created to get to my place, just the goals are different. To create a financial plan, you must establish your goals. Can you think of some goals that are related to financial matters?

D.S. – Sure I can, like getting rich, growing my money.

Mr. Yin – NO, you got it wrong again. Getting rich cannot be a goal as there is no way to measure it. Growing your money cannot be a goal as it is a journey without purpose. Do you remember anything you learnt about setting goals?

My light bulb goes on! Of course I now remember the SMART process - a goal should have five key elements - Specific, Measurable, Attainable, Relevant and Time measured. Thus far I was just chasing dreams, not goals.

D.S. – Mr. Yin, I think I understand what you are trying to tell me. My goals should be specific, such as putting money aside to buy a house, sending my kids to college, planning for my retirement, etc.

Mr. Yin – Exactly that's what I mean, start by putting together your goals. Then it will be a simple mathematical process of allocating your income towards expenses as well as savings for the future to meet your goals. Be aware that if you spend too much today, you won't have enough left to meet your future goals. If that happens, you may not be able to buy the house of your dreams; your kids may not be able to go to college, or your golden years may be so miserable that you wish you were dead rather than alive.

D.S. – You are absolutely right, now I can see the bigger picture of creating a financial plan to succeed. But creating a plan by itself does not guarantee success, right?

Mr. Yin – You got it. Creating a plan is just the first step. The bigger challenge is to start implementing what the plan tells you to do, and then monitor it continuously. Once in a while you may find that you are not hitting your targets due to forces outside of your control, such as the stock market going down, but if you take a long-term approach, things should work out just fine.

D.S. – It sounds so easy, but I am sure there is lot more to it. Please take me through those steps as well.

Mr. Yin – Once you have gone through the process of creating your plan, the next important step is to invest your savings in the right places. How do you think it should be done?

D.S. – I think I should invest my savings in the stock market to grow them fast.

Mr. Yin - You seem to be a smart person, but you surprise me with your foolish answers! Let me ask the question a different way. Let's say you are planning to save $50,000 for down payment to buy a house in the near future and you invest that money in stock market. Just when you are ready to buy the house, the stock market takes a nosedive and you lose half of your money. What happens to the goal of buying the house?

D.S. – Yes, that could happen in which case I may have to delay buying the house.

Mr. Yin – Exactly my point. Always remember, your investments should match your goal. In other words, you should match long-term goals with long-term investments and short-term goals with short-term investments. The match between your investments and your goals is like a marriage.

D.S. – Everything is now making perfect sense. What other things I should be aware of?

Mr. Yin – You should always be aware of the risks that can derail you from your plan as we are continuously surrounded by risks. Just getting here was risky because there are lots of crazy drivers on the road. Make sure you understand all the risks and take steps to mitigate them so that a bad occurrence just doesn't end up killing your plan. Now it is time for me to take my nap. Please go home and think about what we discussed today. Come back if you need to and we'll continue with our discussion.

I went back to his house a few more times and he taught me everything he knew about preserving and steadily growing wealth over time. He imparted his most valuable lesson at our last meeting in which he taught me how to achieve a right balance between life (which includes health, relationships and values) and wealth. Only a perfect balance between the two will allow one to lead an abundant and serene life.

The knowledge that I gleaned from Mr. Yin, as well as from many other mentors, lead to the development of a system that I call **7-Steps to Financial Abundance**.

Here's a summary of the system, and I hope I will be able to convert this into a book for the benefit of those who are serious about achieving financial abundance. Here I present you with the 7-Steps:

1. Have a lifetime financial plan which incorporates your goals, timelines, income, expenses and investments. Let this be your guiding path.

2. Manage your expenses – It's not what you make, but what you keep.

3. Start saving early and on a regular basis - As Warren Buffet says - "Spend what's left after saving, and not the other way around."

4. Invest properly - Make sure your investments are commensurate with your planned objectives. Fear and greed are the worst enemies when it comes to investments. Don't hesitate to work with a professional if you are not sure that you can handle it right. Here's what the editor of Money magazine said as his editorial – "To get smart about your money, **you can follow advice from brilliant people or make your own mistakes.** As one who has done it both ways, I can tell you, the former is cheaper."

5. Tax Planning – Today the Federal debt is close to $17 trillion, and unfunded liabilities related to Medicare, Social Security, etc. exceed $90 trillion (source: www.usdebtclock.org), which translates to a deficit of over $1,000,000 per taxpayer. Is there any other way to pay for this other than raising taxes?

6. Manage Risk – Always remember Murphy's Law - "If something can go wrong, it will."

7. Estate Planning & Charitable Giving - Don't let others dictate how your estate will be distributed, and last, but not least, be charitable. Charity comes in many forms, and in closing I share this wonderful quote –

The simplest acts of kindness are by far more powerful
than a thousand heads bowing in prayer.
~ Mahatma Gandhi.

About Daven

Daven Sharma, well-known developer of **7-Steps to Financial Abundance,** is an educator, author and a financial planning expert in the San Francisco Bay area. His CPA firm, Davis & Company, provides tax and accounting services to individuals and small businesses, while his financial planning firm, Strategic Advisors, Inc., provides wealth management and wealth preservation services to its clients.

Daven considers himself to be a holistic fiduciary advisor. His **7-Steps** system touches each and every facet of his clients' financial life, not just their investments. He helps in creating a lifetime financial plan that helps to identify strengths, weaknesses, opportunities and threats specific to each person, and from there, recommends how to put that plan into action by capitalizing on those strengths and eliminating any potential threats along the way.

As an educator, Daven teaches his concept of **7-Steps to Financial Abundance** to his radio listeners as well to those who attend his seminars and webinars held throughout the year. He strongly believes in having a good balance between creating wealth and enjoying life.

He maintains his own balance between work and enjoyment by spending time with his wife, two daughters and newly-rescued puppy, Lilah.

To learn more about **Daven Sharma** and **7-Steps to Financial Abundance** visit: www.abundanceadviser.com, or send an email to: info@mysevensteps.com.

CHAPTER 10

DOES YOUR LOVE LIFE SUPPORT YOUR SUCCESS?

BY KRISTA WHITE

Here's the secret to success; are you ready for it? It's love. That's right. Love. You're probably asking yourself how it could possibly be that your love life has anything to do with the success of your business, right? In fact, you may consider yourself to be married to your work and be perfectly happy with that arrangement. First of all, I get it. My career is a tremendous part of my life and I work exclusively with people who describe themselves as "Type A" – driven, and success-oriented. Let's face it – success is no accident. It's something you work hard at, invest in, and continuously strive for. But here's the thing – being married to your work (and not a person) actually has an incredibly harmful effect on your bottom line whether you realize it or not.

Everyone has bad days. When you are married to your work, where do you go to recharge? Does plowing through another five hours give you a fresh perspective? Of course it doesn't. Having a stable, positive relationship provides you with a place to go to refuel and enjoy yourself on both the good days and the bad. Being in a healthy relationship also has a tendency to improve your mood, boost confidence, and put a little extra pep in your step. In fact, studies show supportive relationships contribute to longevity and even wisdom! (Ackerman, 2012)

Now, the key here is that it's a *good* relationship. Bad relationships, on the other hand, tend to be distracting. Much like other unresolved

101

issues, your thoughts will wander to them and focus on the aspects that just aren't quite working. They affect your mood, and in turn, your interactions with your clients and colleagues. They also have a nasty tendency to leech your time and energy, leaving you even more exhausted than you would be with no relationship at all. And well... with no relationship at all, you are missing out on a stable foundation to support and recharge you day in, day out. I have yet to meet anyone at the top of their game who has not taken the time to hash this part of their life out.

This was especially true of one of my clients, we'll call him Jack. He had earned a good living for himself when he came to me. He was an entrepreneur, clearly a bright man who had put in a lot of hard work into building his business from the ground up. He was like many of us in that he found himself working a lot. Jack was very deeply invested in building his business. It wasn't unusual for him to call me from his office at odd hours over the weekend or for me to get messages from him late at night when he was heading home from the office with just enough time to sleep and do it again the following day. Jack clearly loved what he did, but he initially came to me because he realized there was a certain element missing from his life. He enjoyed being a workaholic, but wanted a companion. As he put it, he wanted that first phone call – that person you immediately call when something happens – good or bad.

Jack had a lot going for him. He could have strolled into a bar and just picked a woman up, but he was looking for something more substantial than just *some* woman for a night. Jack had already been through a lot. A few years back, business had been great for him. He was on track to have a great year. However, as his business was really starting to take off, his relationship began to sour. His girlfriend began to feel she was second fiddle and Jack seemed to become a different person. The negative feelings in his relationship spilled into the way he communicated with everyone. He became closed-off and found the coldness of his relationship creeping into the way he spoke to his employees and even clients. Ultimately, in a nasty turn of events their relationship ended. Jack was noticeably affected by the breakup, but he did what most people do. He threw himself deeper into his work. The problem was, now, even with all these extra hours he was putting into his business, it started to decline. Naturally, he was puzzled and frustrated by the fact that what twelve months ago had been a prosperous business on track to complete success, was now struggling to make ends meet. Nearing burn out, he came to me.

As I got to know Jack, I saw his business was directly affected by his relationships. When his love life was good, his business was good. When things started to head south in his love life, his business went down with it. Clearly this was no way to live life. I asked Jack what he felt he was missing in previous relationships. He said he thought other women weren't entirely understanding of what it took to make a business work. He felt his exes had never really been on his team and seemed to feel *threatened* by his business. I introduced him to a woman, we'll call her Jill. Jill was stunning. She had long brown hair and a slender build. Like Jack, she could have easily strolled into a bar and met *some guy*, but that wasn't what she wanted. Jill had trouble meeting the right types of men. Often times, despite her sunny disposition and great sense of humor, men seemed to be intimidated by her success. She also owned her own business and could not only respect, but truly appreciate the effort that it takes to be a successful entrepreneur. It was a hit. I got calls from each of them around 10 pm the night of their first date. They seemed to click and had already scheduled a second date for later that week. These first few dates quickly turned to months and then years. Then one early spring morning I got a call from Jack.

Jack was calling to report that things were going well with Jill. In fact, they had just returned from a week in the Bahamas. Now, if you know Jack, you know that it's unheard of for him to take a few days off, let alone an entire week. He told me Jill was the love of his life and to top it off, business had never been better for either of them. In fact, he was projecting doubled profits the following year.

Now, based on what I've seen in working with clients like Jack, there are essentially 5 key steps to landing yourself the perfect partner to support you in your professional success:

1) Life is a Balancing Act.
   Surely this isn't the first time you're hearing this, but if you haven't set aside the time to do it yet, consider this your wake up call. You will not reach your full potential if you do not take care of the basics first. Finding a good work/life balance can change both your

personal life and your business for the better. For many people spending enough time at work isn't really the problem. Instead, the challenge is your personal life. How do you put enough time in at the office while maintaining any sort of social life? How can you justify it when there is so much to be done? Many people don't and that's where the problems start. When your "balance" is too business-heavy, you may be spending more time working, but the quality of your work will be much poorer. It is absolutely imperative that you take a moment to step back and reexamine how you are spending your time before you do anything else. This has proven to be beneficial for even my most successful clients. This helps eliminate burnout and makes life more rewarding to boot. Naturally, this also makes you more productive and gives you something even better to work for, making your office hours more fruitful and your away hours more enjoyable.

The best way to achieve this is to compartmentalize your life. Everything from emails to dating should be scheduled for a specific time of the day (and only addressed at that time of day). It is truly incredible how much more time you will have in your day when you do this. Stop responding to emails as they come in. Instead, schedule a specific time to read and respond. Don't open it if you don't have time to deal with it. Set aside a specific time for meetings (by appointment only), and another for dating (when you can truly focus on your goals, battle plan, and heck, maybe even meet someone). You will be amazed by how much time you get back when you take this approach.

2) Focus on yourself.

After compartmentalizing your life and striking a comfortable balance between work and play, you will likely find yourself with more time than you're used to having. The key here is to figure out how to get the most out of that time. Before you can bring another person into your life, you need to be content with your life and confident that you will have a place for them in your already busy schedule. I've met far too many successful, intelligent businessmen and women who simply attempt to work and squeeze in a date or two and believe it will all work out to be something resembling a successful life.

Instead, treat your personal life as you would your business and your ideal mate as your target client. Would you simply go out in search of your ideal client without a business plan? Of course not. You would take the time to work out a solid business model with something uniquely appealing that fits the needs of your ideal client. Treat your personal life the same way as you would your business (minus the testimonials from "previous clients").

First things first, you need to be happy with your life as an individual. If you're looking for someone else to come into your life and make you happy, it will never work. The same rings true in business. Nobody else is going to make things happen for you so take the time now to create a life you love. If you've always wanted to take sailing lessons, now is the time. Want to run a marathon? Start training. Build the life you want and the rest will fall into place.

3) What do you want in a partner?

After creating a life (not just career) you can be proud of, the next step is considering what you most want in a partner and then, what *they* might be looking for in a partner. Most of us have no trouble coming up with a long list of all the qualities a partner could/should possess but take a moment and consider what on that list is truly most important. Aside from chemistry, I recommend giving extra consideration to someone with a good head on their shoulders who will be a supportive, positive force in your life. Look for someone with complementary goals and a similar lifestyle. The more of the "big picture" you share, the more likely you will be to complement each other and work well together long-term.

4) Be proactive.

So here you are, you have a great life and you know what you want. You're just looking for someone to share it with. Of course, sitting idly by and waiting for your ideal partner isn't going to get you anywhere. It's time to get proactive. The main ways singles go about trying to meet someone are what I like to call frogs – fix-ups, pick-ups, and everyday encounters.

The "kiss a lot of frogs" theory essentially builds on the old sales mentality that it's just a numbers game. This is the same idea behind online dating and speed dating, only you're kissing a lot of frogs from your computer or kissing a lot of frogs fast. The trouble is this can be a time suck and you never really know if the person is who they claim to be.

"Fix ups" rely on your friends and family members to fix you up with people they know. The trouble is this can be a somewhat limited pool and be somewhat uncomfortable for everyone involved if things don't work out.

Then there are "pick-ups." Perhaps you've heard of men who call themselves "Pick Up Artists?" This option relies on creating some really good lines to pick a woman up, usually in the bar. The trouble with this option is it just doesn't work – not on the right types of people at least.

Then, there are "everyday encounters." This technique relies on meeting someone in everyday life – perhaps at the office or Starbucks. Now, while your love life is in direct correlation to the success of your career, this is not to say you should *mix* business with pleasure. I've seen it happen to lots of successful businessmen and women. You spend a lot of time at the office so it's somewhat natural to look to the people around you for potential dates, but regardless of company policy, dating colleagues or employees is a minefield. If things don't work out, you're still forced to see this person day after day, and you could even be hit with a sexual harassment lawsuit. Heartbreak and legal issues aside, this technique is also entirely unpredictable.

Lastly, there's the professional plan where you work with an expert Matchmaker. This is in much the same way you would work with a real estate agent when buying a house to refine your search and get some guidance. A good Matchmaker will also take care of scheduling the dates to save you time. If you go this route, look for a Matchmaker with a big client base who guarantees you dates and uses your feedback in the matchmaking process.

5) Reinvest.
Just like your business, once you've landed your dream partner, the work doesn't end here. If you had a successful quarter, surely you wouldn't just kick your feet back and stop improving. You would keep going to continue to have even better quarters. Your relationship works the same way. You need to continuously reinvest in it to get the most out of it and truly reap the rewards. Oh – and don't forget to enjoy yourself a little along the way!

About Krista

Krista White, better known as "The Professional's Matchmaker" is the president of the Matchmaking company, *It's Just Lunch,* located in Washington D.C. She has been a successful Matchmaker for several years working for a company that has set up over two million dates for busy professionals.

Her clients include multi-millionaires, politicians, high-ranking State Department officials, professional athletes, and ambassadors to foreign nations, all of whom she has helped find success and fulfillment in their love lives.

Krista grew up in a multi-cultural family, this experience translated to a unique understanding and perspective into the way that different communication styles can affect relationships. It was this keen understanding of relationships that took her down the path to be one of the best-known Matchmakers in the country.

Her passion for matchmaking and helping people understand relationships led her to the decision to become a Certified Matchmaker (CMM) as well as a Certified Professional Coach (CPC).

Krista has been featured as an expert in *The Wall Street Journal* as well as ABC, CBS, NBC and Fox Network affiliates.

Learn more about Krista at: KristaWhiteMatchmaker.com.

CHAPTER 11

SUCCESS AS A YOUNG ENTREPRENEUR

BY ELIZABETH ROOK

My father has had an extremely successful career as an Allstate Agent for over 30 years. I guess you could say I was born into the insurance business. I can remember being a little girl, sitting in a huge conference room, spinning around in the desk chair and pretending to write insurance. It wasn't until college that I actually started working for my dad. It was just a part time job to help pay my rent and car note. I was bored to tears being stuck in an office all day while my friends were hanging by the pool. Between the paper applications and policy information, the insurance business was a snooze fest. I grew up in a small town where my dad was practically a local celebrity. My opinion of his business started to change. I realized that he was not just an insurance salesman; he was actually providing a service. I was intrigued by the amount of respect people had for my father but never in a million years would I have dreamed I would follow in his footsteps.

In 2000, my dad asked me to come to work for him full time and manage his new second location. It wasn't until then that I actually took an interest in my job. I started going out "calling on businesses" and attending networking meetings. I did everything I could to meet people from other business who could send me referrals. One of the biggest challenges I have faced over the years is with people not taking me seriously. I don't know what was worse, that I was young or that I worked for my dad. Working with family wasn't always peaches and

109

cream. The whole situation gave me a fierce determination to prove myself. The more people underestimated me the harder I worked. I studied all of our policies and underwriting guidelines. I listened to my dad talk to customers and memorized what he said verbatim. I practiced, studied and practiced some more. It took me several long years to earn my father's respect, but we became a great team. After the purchase of his second location, we tripled the size of his agencies. We won multiple company sales awards every year including the 2011 Allstate Agency of the Year in Tennessee.

GROWING MY BUSINESS

Now here I am 16 years later with my own agency, which I started from scratch. I have continued as a family owned and operated business. We are located in a suburb just outside of Memphis in Lakeland, Tennessee. We also recently opened a second location in Covington, Tennessee. My cousin, Benjamin Rook, whom I previously worked with for five years at Allstate thankfully came with me. Our agency primarily represents the Erie Insurance Company, which I cannot say enough great things about. However, we are independent agents, which allows us to have direct contracts with multiple companies. Being independent gives us the ability to find the best company based on what is most important to the customer, whether it be price, service, stability, or a combination of all three.

HERE ARE 14 TIPS TO HELP YOU
ON YOUR ROAD TO SUCCESS:

1) Your Reputation is Priceless, Don't Damage It

There are so many factors that can make or break you in business. Your reputation plays a significant role in the customers search in finding a company and agent they can trust. Over time, your reputation is the most valuable currency you have in business. It's the invisible key that either opens or closes doors of professional opportunity. Especially in an age where everything is forever recorded and accessible, <u>your reputation has to be guarded</u> like the most sacred treasure.

2) Network, Network, Network

In business, it really is all about who you know. Knowing the right people is what gets you ahead in business. Surround yourself with successful and positive people. If you are surrounded by people who are meeting their goals, it will help motivate you to achieve your own objectives. Regardless of how busy you are, you need to make time for networking. There is no such thing as too many connections. Take advantage of the opportunity to attend trade shows, conferences and meetings. Network with other insurance professionals in your field. Meet and stay connected to lots of folks, and invest your time developing as many of those relationships as possible. Begin networking with local businesses that complement your insurance business. Be sure to leave plenty of contact literature behind in case people have follow-up questions.

3) Community Involvement

My dad taught me the importance of giving back to your local community. We are heavily involved with the local schools and athletic programs – as well as many other non-profits such as volunteering for the Red Cross. I estimate that 75% of our marketing budget goes directly to schools, athletic programs, churches, and other nonprofits. The rest of our budget is spent on networking with other local business owners, direct mail and ads in our local newspapers. You are more likely to receive referrals when people see you as more than an insurance agent and see you out participating in events.

4) Captive versus Independent Agent

I started my career as a captive insurance agent. If anyone is just starting out as an insurance agent, a captive company is the way to go. Some captive insurance companies include Nationwide, Allstate, State Farm and Farm Bureau. As with any job, there are pros and cons. Here on some of the advantages: The companies usually provide free on-the-job training to the agents and their staff. There are already established systems in place needed to run your agency. Another huge plus is that you don't need a large marketing budget since companies already spend a small fortune on advertising. The companies can even negotiate your local marketing opportunities which reduce the cost. Here are a few of the disadvantages: You can only sell the insurance that is offered by your company. As a small business owner, you basically have little to no control over what products you can sell. At any point the company you represent can stop selling a particular line of business, which can result in loss of clientele. Whereas being an independent agent allows you to have contracts with several companies. When you're an IC, you're your own boss, with all of the risks and rewards that entails. You can choose how, when, and where to work, for as much or as little time as you want. If you plan to start your own independent insurance agency, you need knowledge and access to plenty of liquid capital.

5) Don't sell on price

It does not matter what company you decide to work for, your customers will always be able to find insurance cheaper somewhere else. I understand that pricing will always play a huge part in the sales process, but if you honestly believe people buy on price alone then you are mistaken. Oftentimes, people don't realize how important insurance is until they need it or worse when they need insurance and don't have it. This is where you, as the agent, come in. Since insurance is not a tangible item that you can purchase and take home with you, you need to remember you are actually selling yourself. You are selling your superior customer service.

6) Talk Less, Listen More

A lot of complaints about insurance agents are that they're overly persistent. I learned early on that high pressure sales are not my thing. Luckily there is another way to do business without compromising your integrity. To succeed in the insurance industry, you must love your job and believe in the products you are selling. You cannot be just an agent. You must be a sales professional – which means making the customer's needs primary. Instead of collecting information and spitting out figures, we ask questions about their lifestyle, family, and concerns for the future. Understand that each situation is different. Before you can make proper recommendations you need to know what exactly your client is looking for.

7) Find a Mentor

Find an experienced and successful agent with similar values to mirror yourself after. I am sure whoever you choose will be flattered that you asked. I was fortunate enough to have my father as my mentor. He was able to teach me things that can only be learned by working out in the field.

8) Create a Standard Operating Procedure

Successful people live disciplined lives and set their priorities. They don't procrastinate. They are busy, productive and proactive.

Systems will help you establish credibility and will help you make fewer mistakes. In a business that revolves around multi-tasking and paperwork, organization should be a top priority. If you need help getting your agency running smoothly, I highly recommend Joe Hagen's <u>Freedom Through Systems™ Program for Insurance Agency Owners</u>.

9) Become an Expert

Know your strengths and work on your weaknesses. Devote some time each day to improving your <u>sales and marketing</u> techniques. There are so many different formats available. You can attend webinars, read business and marketing books or take college refresher courses. A few years ago, I was struggling with speaking in front of groups. I needed help so I took a public-speaking class at the local college and it made all the difference in the world.

10) Follow up after the sale

You have earned your client's trust when they decided to have their insurance written by you. You can maintain that trust by keeping in touch with them regularly. Handwrite thank you cards and always ask for referrals. I cannot stress this enough! Your clients can also be a source of future clients. Create a customer referral program that offers some sort of incentive for your existing customers to refer new customers to you. Things such as gift cards work really well. Don't just take referrals, give them also. It helps strengthen your connections and will come in handy in the future. Word of mouth advertising is free, and referrals have a better closing ratio than cold-call telemarketing.

11) Be Accessible

With the advancements in technology, communication and accessibility is more important than ever before. A work day no longer fits between the hours of 9:00 am – 5:00 pm. This generation has become more of a phone call, email and text message society. I am always working. Not only do I not want to miss out on a sale, but I also want to be the first point of contact in case someone needs to file a claim. Otherwise, they might as well be insured with an 800 number.

12) Brand Yourself

Your personal branding campaign should be primarily centered on the goal of marketing yourself as a celebrity within your industry. The key phrase here is "within your industry." Establish yourself as a go-to resource in your community for all things insurance. That involves branding yourself both as an expert and as an *interesting* individual. Why interesting? Because it's not good enough simply to be considered good at what you do, you also need to be memorable. You need to stick in the minds of potential clients, so that when they need your services, you are the first person they think of.

13) Social Media

Now, making an unforgettable first impression *in-person* is no longer the only way to establish your brand. Another great way to build relationships and brand yourself is through social media. You can connect in real time with clients, colleagues and friends; and build relationships across the globe. This will form stronger relationships with customers as well as getting your name out to potential clients. Keep the content interesting and unique. Remember your clients want to do business with insurance professionals they trust. Facebook and Google Business Pages are good for reminding your friends about what you do for a living. LinkedIn is for networking with other business professionals. I have also seen quite a few insurance professionals with YouTube channels and blogs. You can use these sites to announce upcoming promotions and events.

14) Maintain confidence in your abilities, relax and enjoy the ride

Regardless of your career path, there will always be roadblocks and distractions along the way. To survive in the competitive world of business, you have to be able to deal with rejection and still remain optimistic. My final piece of advice is to read or listen to the book *Think and Grow Rich* by Napoleon Hill. It completely changed my perspective on life and hopefully it will help you as well.

About Elizabeth

At the age of 34, Elizabeth Rook has become one of Memphis's most successful businesswomen in the insurance industry. She attributes her success to having worked with and being mentored by her father, Ron Rook, for over 15 years. Her father was an extremely successful insurance agent, who owned two of the most successful Allstate Agencies in the country. She was involved in the sales, management and marketing of their family business and learned a tremendous amount about every aspect of the insurance industry from him.

After leaving Allstate at the end of 2012, Elizabeth decided to branch out and open her own company, Elizabeth Rook Insurance. Although it was definitely a leap of faith, she believes that her partnership with Erie Insurance Company has been her best career move to date. She opened a second location in her first year with Erie Insurance. She has recruited some of the most knowledgeable and successful insurance agents in the Memphis Area. Her agency services multiple lines of insurance, including home, auto, life and all types of commercial policies. She has won dozens of business and insurance awards throughout the years. She was awarded Small Business Woman of the Year at the age of 29. Considering she started her insurance agency from scratch, her proudest achievement so far was being awarded "New Erie Agent of the Year - 2013."

Elizabeth also understands the importance of volunteering and giving back to her local community. Being a mother of two young daughters, Taylor and Jaime, she is extremely passionate about education and helping children that are less fortunate. She is a Red Cross Volunteer and her company makes significant financial contributions to the local schools systems and athletic programs. Elizabeth and her team members are also heavily involved with many organizations focused on building strong businesses throughout the community. The purpose of her agents are to be respected professionals and trusted advisors.

"My family and I grew up in a small town about 30 miles outside of Memphis, Tennessee. Here in the south, I was raised to mind my manners, respect my elders and have a genuine, down-to-earth attitude. Basically it is just Southern Hospitality. I take pride in the fact that the majority of my business comes directly from referrals. When people tell their friends, family and colleagues about you, it's one of the best compliments your business can get."

For more information about Elizabeth Rook Insurance you may call 901-867-SAVE or visit:
www.rookagency.com
www.facebook.com/rookinsurance
www.linkedin.com/in/rookinsurance
www.twitter.com/rookinsurance

CHAPTER 12

COLLECTING YOUR WAY TO SUCCESS

BY ERIC J. CHRISTESON, PHD, DBA

Money. No matter what someone else might say, it's still about money. Finding it. Getting it. Keeping it.

Perhaps nothing is more frustrating or counter-productive to a business leader than worry over the cash flow of their business. When the individual elements of a business are successful—sales, development, production—the business should be thriving. All too often, however, seemingly successful businesses lament their cash flow issues. The knee jerk reactions include investigating production to look for any lagging there, pushing partners to increase their community presense and bring additional contacts to the company, and hiring additional salespeople to bring more business to the table. What are infrequent are businesses that analyze their collection processes, and hire additional collection staff to shore up their bottom line. Too often, successful businesses produce a product or service, sell that product or service, bill for the product or service and there the process stops. Even successful businesses leave out one critical element, collection; they do not follow up on clients who pay late or who do not pay at all.

Every year, successful businesses write off money owed to them to "get it off their books" so they can focus on what they do best— manufacturing, selling or even mainstream lending. Writing off those balances is equivalent to working for free. It is equivalent to leaving tons of money on the table during negotiations. It is equivalent to paying workers to produce nothing. I know of no business leaders who would willingly leave that money on the table, work free or pay employees to produce nothing but receive pay regardless. Why, then, do those same business leaders thwart their own success by not collecting the money that is owed to them? In *Victory, Persuasively Separating People from Money,* we discussed the morals, ethics and motivations of collections, and here now we'll explore the infrastructure of collections for these business leaders and some more techniques. Simply put, they are not natural collectors or they do not know how to hire effective collectors to improve their business's bottom line or even "there's just no skin in the game" to keep the adrenaline moving in a profit centered direction.

If invoicing for products and services are the lifeblood of any business, then collection is the transfusion that keeps the business alive when invoices fail to deliver payment. Many business owners just lack experience or training in collections. There are key items for which to look when hiring a collector, which I will share with you. Knowing whom to hire is only half the equation, however. While most excellent collectors need little management, the business owner or manager supervising the collector benefits from some basic knowledge of collection techniques. Here is the ultimate guide for collecting your way to success, honed during years of experience breaking the cycle of unintentionally donating your goods or services.

HIRING A COLLECTOR

For the untrained owner or manager, hiring an excellent collector can be as difficult as discerning the difference between a diamond and a cubic zirconia without a jeweler's loop. Just as the jeweler has specific indicators to tell him he is looking at a diamond, there are nine points the educated manager will look for in hiring a collector. During the interviewing process, the manager should strive for a candidate who meets at least five of the nine requirements. After hiring a qualified candidate, the manager or owner can then assist the collector in developing the other four traits. Here are nine indicators of a qualified collector:

Obtain a college graduate when possible. Their degree should be in a subject area that requires excellent command of language.

Obtain past examples of resourcefulness. You are looking for ways in which the collector has taken approaches that are different from the norm.

Obtain past examples of where she or he listened well and then helped somebody. These are examples that will demonstrate the collector's effectiveness at relating to debtors and developing rapport.

Obtain a few imaginative approaches (not necessarily correct) about how the collector would collect if you gave him a telephone right now.

Test his or her knowledge of policies and procedures on those approaches.

Observe enthusiasm and energy as he or she sells his or her talents during the interview.

Obtain a quality answer to the question, "What would be your ambitions in our company?"

Look for a bit of cockiness and braggadocio. These are good traits for any collector.

Explain that collecting is a high-pressure job. Judge the quality of his or her answer to, "How well can you handle pressure?"

The next step after hiring the right candidate for collections is to help them to develop the character traits below. Most candidates will possess some of the eleven key traits, but the manager can help bring out the best in the collector. With hard work and the right tools, you will be managing an outstanding collections team that achieves better cash flow for your already successful business.

PROFILE OF A COLLECTOR – CHARACTER TRAITS

There are eleven key traits owners and managers should look for in their collectors. Most candidates will not possess all eleven, but if you find six or more, you can bet you have found an excellent candidate.

A collector should be **empathetic**; they should understand and be sensitive to the debtor's position, but should still move for "payment in full today." They should be **imaginative**. An effective collector constantly develops better than average collection approaches.

119

An excellent collector is **resourceful**; he or she reviews files quickly yet thoroughly. He or she discerns key points on which to focus with the debtor. The collector should be **intelligent** and able to, quickly and completely, absorb training policies and procedures.

The collector should be **eloquent** with a strong command of written and spoken language. The collector, when speaking, should make few grammatical errors.

Your collector should be **energetic**. You are looking for the type of person who will move quickly and purposefully even in the last hour of the day. He or she should be **ambitious** and should be the type of person who desires and expects promotions, at reasonable intervals, when work is well done.

Cocky collectors get things done. They should be confident and assertive and dominate without being arrogant. And the superior collector will be **enthusiastic**. They will love to collect, to get "on a roll," when telephoning debtors. They brag about their ability to collect.

The collector will be **results oriented**, consistently collecting more dollars than the average collector. This collector will make a greater than average number of phone calls per day and a consistently higher than average number of debtor contacts per day. Finally, the collector is **controlled**. This person thrives on pressure or at the very least does not succumb from pressure.

Business owners and managers should observe collectors closely and question them relevant to these traits to discern where they excel and where they could improve. If a collector does not qualify for six or more of the eleven traits, a manager should assist him or her to come up to speed.

Competent collectors are not easy to supervise, as each has his or her own methods. However, competent collectors are easy to manage, when you let them pursue entrepreneurial instincts within your policy guidelines. Think of collectors as the completion of a sales cycle. Your collectors make sure that your hard work does not go unpaid and ensures the viability of your business.

STANDARDS OF COLLECTORS' CONDUCT

Collecting, when performed properly, is a highly professional skill. So, help your collectors establish high standards of conduct. Try the acronym **"DECK"** - **D**ignity, **E**loquence, **C**ompetitive, and **K**nowledgeable.

DIGNITY comes in two packages: the collector's dignity manifested in the ability to remain calm under emotional conditions and the dignity of the debtor. The collector earns his PhD (preserve human dignity) by responding to colorful words and phrases with firm payment demands not laced with invective.

ELOQUENCE is mastery of the language. Collecting utilizes only two skills, writing and speaking. By reading omnivorously and looking up words not understood, the collector masters language and dominates without arrogance.

COMPETITIVE means the collector must be, and know that he is, the best of all the collectors from other organizations contacting the debtor. The business' bottom line depends on the collector separating the debtor from money *before* his competition does.

KNOWLEDGE means the collector will know his organization, will be able to solve any complaint with transferring the call, and then will collect in full.

While keeping watch over collectors to help them grow into better collectors is desirable, most qualified collectors work better when they have less supervision. Creative collectors require wider authority than do other employees.

GIVING WIDE AUTHORITY TO QUALIFIED COLLECTORS

Tell your collectors to use their authorities over you. Be assured that when your collectors understand the four dimensions of authority, there will be no question as to who is the manager. You are.

The first authority is position. The first authority is yours exclusively; the buck must stop somewhere. The other three authorities belong to the collectors. Their first authority is competence. Every owner or manager should be inclined to approve the ideas of their competent collectors. The collectors' second authority is character. You want to go along with people who do not lie to you or steal from you. A competent collector of high character will and should quite often gain your approvals of his or her ideas. Their last authority is personality. By itself, it means nothing. When combined with competence and character, the use of this collector's personality makes it very difficult for you to say no.

The effective manager won't *appear* to be the boss. That manager will give enough freedom to the collector that the collector may well wonder, "Who is really the boss?"

You will always know the boss is you.

How will a business owner receive respect as the boss of the collections department if that boss has no collections skills himself? Every collections manager must possess some basic knowledge of the collections process, starting with collections telephone calls.

PLANNING AND CONTROLLING COLLECTIONS TELEPHONE CALLS

Each collection telephone call has three phases: the statement, the response, and the rebuttal. The statement phase is what the collector says to the debtor and it has five steps: 1) identify the debtor, 2) identify yourself, 3) ask for payment in full today, 4) solve the problem, 5) and when you cannot collect payment in full today, follow up on time.

The second phase, response, is what the debtor says back to the collector. The response is the reason why the debtor has not paid the bill or cannot pay in full today. An example for commercial collecting might be, "Our customers are not paying us."

And third, the rebuttal is the collector's response back to the debtor to circumvent their response. Any payment proposal made in this phase will be based on the data collected that answer questions beginning with "Who, what, when, where, why or how." Such questions do not elicit 'yes' or 'no' answers and will extract data needed to make an effective proposal. When enough data has been extracted by the collector, the words for the payment proposal will already be internalized. For example, if the debtor answers the question "When will you have the money?" with the response, "When my clients pay their invoices on the 15th," the collector will have a payment proposal on the tip of his

COLLECTING YOUR WAY TO SUCCESS

tongue. (The technique is called, "Stimulus, Pause, Response" or **SPR**) The collector's response must be, "Then let's schedule a payment for the 16th of the month."

All collectors are different; ask your collectors to experiment with the statement-response-rebuttal approach, then to modify it to fit their own collections personality. Your cash flow will improve rapidly. However, what should a collector do if this approach fails?

IMPLEMENTING LATE COLLECTION TELEPHONE CALLS

After two failed attempts with the *statement-response-rebuttal* approach, the collector has already exhausted that approach's effectiveness. Another call using the same approach would likely draw similar excuses and become a wasteful repetition of history. The collector should change tactics and employ the late-collection technique.

Plan the late collection call using the acronym **SPRA—Situation, Proposal, Reason, Action**. Plan the call with a few key words to answer these questions:

1. What is the **S**ituation here? The question gets right down to business.
2. What shall be the **P**roposal to the debtor? Be very specific in the proposing of a plan.
3. What is the best **R**eason why the debtor should do what the collector proposes? It is necessary to note that the reason MUST come from the debtor's viewpoint.
4. What **A**ction does the collector desire of the debtor? Action is the payment commitment that the debtor must make. Know the commitment you want before phoning the debtor. There is an old adage, "If you don't know where you are going, any road will get you there." In this situation, not knowing where you are going will likely only elongate the discussion.

The second part of Action is what the collector will commit after the debtor commits. Normally, this will be the collector's plan for following up.

After completing the SPRA call, follow up to make sure the debtor keeps the commitment made, and of course, the collector must follow up with his commitment. The SPRA call should rarely exceed one minute.

Business owners will like the improved cash flow batting average of this one-minute telephone call. Even with standard breaks during the day, an organized and empowered collector will be able to complete an abundance of collection calls in any given workday. There are some tips to keep calls focused and short.

TALK-OFFS MAKE SHORTER
COLLECTIONS PHONE CALLS

The standard length of a collection call is one minute; however, not every call must be completed in one minute. When the collector believes a solid payment arrangement can be made, of course he or she will need to hang-on and spend extra time. Nevertheless, when working toward a one-minute standard, the collector will usually not exceed that time.

The debtor will make excuses and the debtor will try to steer the discussion into any area other than the payment arrangement. Payment arrangement is the only matter the collector wants to discuss. When the discussion moves away from the payment arrangement, instruct your collectors to move in with the "Talk-Off."

The "Talk-Off" will return the discussion to the appropriate topic. For example, one "Talk-Off" would be, "We understand your position, Mr. Jones, and we have covered that before. Our job now is to work out a payment of your balance." Tell your collectors to develop six or eight of their own "Talk-Offs" and to review them with you. Collectors are more likely to use what they invent and which feel natural to them, and not the ones that you give to them. Shorter telephone discussions lead to more debtor contacts and faster improvement of cash flow.

No matter how successfully you fill the economic pool of any business with increased sales or faster production, you will continually bail a sinking ship unless you first plug the holes left by uncollected receivables. With the right collector, dialing approximately 200 debtors per day and talking with debtors and doing little else, increased profitability and increased cash flow truly are just a phone call away.

About Eric

Eric J. Christeson, CPA, MBA, PhD, DBA founded Dynamic Interface Systems Corporation (DISC) in 1982. As Chairman of the Board, Eric has spearheaded a team effort to cultivate strong sales and earnings growth while ensuring stability and long-term survival by acquiring or developing easy-to-learn, affordable, technologically-advanced products to assist the financial lending industry.

Prior to leading DISC, Eric spent twenty years in senior financial and line management positions in both small and Fortune 100 companies. During his tenure as CFO of a troubled, high-tech electronics firm, Eric restructured and refinanced the firm that then regained its NASDAQ listing and subsequent acceptance on the American Stock Exchange (AMEX). His additional experiences include controller of the $400-million division of a Fortune 100 company and several years as a contractor with the U.S. Department of Defense.

While in the U.S. Air Force, Eric obtained a Top Secret Cryptographic "codeword" Clearance. He has a B.A. degree in Russian from Syracuse University, a B.S. degree in Accounting from San Jose State University, and an M.B.A. with a concentration in Marketing also from San Jose. Dr. Christeson's Ph.D. in Economics and D.B.A. in Marketing Management both were conferred by Canterbury Christ Church University near London, England.

Despite a work ethic and schedule that would make lesser men cry "Uncle," in 2004 Eric was met at the door by his wife and his son as he arrived home from the office. He was greeted with the words, "Alex wants to join the Cub Scouts, dear." Not one to shy away from a challenge, Eric began what he then-called his "second full-time job" as leader of a 160-youth Cub Scout pack for the Boy Scouts of America. Of his experiences in Boy Scouting, too numerous to mention, Eric says, "Scouting has changed my life forever, just as Scouting has changed the lives of boys everywhere forever."

As often happens when one excels at one's job, the Boy Scouts soon asked Eric to build a district leadership team as District Chairman—comprised of 6,000 youth and 2,500 adult leaders, for finance, training, membership, advancement, OA, camping and many more committees. He recently received the Silver Beaver Award from the Boy Scouts of America; "The Silver Beaver Award is made for service of exceptional character to boyhood by registered Scouters, Cubbers, and Explorer leaders..." Eric sums up his Boy Scouting experience by stating, "Nothing is more rewarding than watching a group of kids coming up the trail with smiling, dusty faces."

In his free time outside of work and volunteering in Boy Scouting, Eric sits on the Board of Directors for several other organizations. He and his family have been quiet, contributing members of the Unity Church of Unity Village, Missouri for the past 12 years.

CHAPTER 13

THE MILLIONAIRE REAL ESTATE INVESTOR *MAKEOVER*™!

BY DWAN BENT-TWYFORD

When the latest economic crash began, it was a bloodbath for homeowners as well as real estate investors. People were losing their homes to foreclosure at record speed, while many investors lost their entire business and net-worth. I personally know many investors who did not survive. Now that things are slowly looking up, people are wondering back into the streets looking to invest. Most have no clue where or how to begin. Fortunately, I am here to share how you can makeover your finances and become part of the richest asset class in America – A Wealthy Real Estate Investor!

There are many so-called "real estate gurus" on the scene now that it must be frightening to be a young real estate investor or someone who has lost it all. Most of these people showed-up on the scene *during* the crash, selling you do-it-in-your-sleep programs that didn't work and setting many of you back even further than you already were.

With over 20 years of experience and surviving several difficult markets, I feel I am well-equipped to lead you down the quickest path to real estate investing millions! Steve, himself, says that real estate investing is still the largest asset class that produces more new millionaires every year than any other. Why not join us!

Since the crash did you know:

- There are approximately 10 million people in some stage of late payments or foreclosure right now.
- Over 4 million foreclosures have been completed.
- 1.4 million people will file bankruptcy *this* year – most to avoid the foreclosure sale of their home.
- Hundreds of thousands of millionaires have lost their status.

The good news: America is expected to *ADD* five million *NEW* millionaires in the next *FIVE* years. Five million! **Who would like to be one of them?**

Bottom line: There is a lot of opportunity to "become" or "re-become" a millionaire real estate investor right now. All you need is a proven system that has sustained several economic up and down turns and still works, which I just happen to have.

Real estate investing is simple when you have a plan. For example: I wholesale or "flip" properties, buy single family homes for rentals, and rehab one here and there to stay sharp. In other words: Flipping properties feeds me, rentals will allow me to retire someday, and rehabbing is just plain fun!

Most new investors have this bright idea that they want to buy a "fixer-upper" and "flip" it for a profit. They don't have a long-term game plan and that is often why they fail. To become a successful real estate investor it is important to treat this like a business…**not a hobby!**

I'm going to share my proven **Three-Step Real Estate Investing System** that will change your financial life and make you a millionaire real estate investor!

1. **Wholesale** Flips
2. **Rehab** Fix and Flips
3. **Rentals** for Long-Term Wealth

I. WHOLESALE FLIP

After being a part of many up and down markets, I can say, without hesitation, that wholesaling or **"flipping"** a property is the absolute best place to start. I prefer to do Wholesale Flips because I never have to touch a hammer to the property, yet I still average **$30,000 per deal**!

Let's look at wholesaling on a smaller scale:

- You go to the grocery store and buy food; that store bought the food for less and then sold it to you for more.
- The clothes you are wearing right now were bought by a store for less than you paid for them.

Our entire economic system is built on wholesaling – buying something for less and selling it to another for MORE! It is how the entire world works – we sell stuff. What I am going to teach you to do is to sell houses just like the store sells groceries. The only difference is that we have a higher price tag.

So, how does one begin to wholesale or "flip" a house? We start with a homeowner facing foreclosure who is looking for *YOU* to help them so that they can put this nightmare behind them and get a fresh start.

With millions facing foreclosure it is easy to find homeowners: Craigslist, Facebook, Internet Marketing, Bandit Signs, Public Records at the Courthouse – Foreclosure, Divorce, Probate, and Evictions. Tell everyone you know that you are a real estate investor and see if they know anyone who needs help, talk to people you work with, leave cards at the dry cleaners, flyers on grocery store bulletin boards, doctor's offices, any place that you go! Foreclosures are everywhere!

> **ARV – what the house is worth if you fixed it up to current market standards. Most forcclosures need a lot of TLC.**

Once the homeowners call you it is time to get down to business. The most important factor in any real estate transaction is: **What do they owe against the property versus what you can sell it to a Rehabber/ Landlord for.** You make your money when you *BUY* the property, not when you sell it. If you pay too much up-front that does not mean that you can sell it for more at the end.

➤ REPEAT AFTER ME UNTIL THIS BECOMES
PART OF YOUR VOCABULARY:
I BUY LOW and I SELL LOW!

Here is an example:

The average house costs $200,000. Using that number you want to buy the property for one-half of its "after repaired value" (ARV) or $100,000. Since you are going to **Flip** this property you need to sell it to a Rehabber who will do a "Rehab Fix & Flip" or a Landlord who will keep it for a "Long-Term Rental."

- Rehabbers will pay 60% to 65% of the ARV while a landlord will pay 70% to 75% of the ARV.

In this scenario you would pay $100,000 for the property – **Remember, it is a foreclosure.**

- You could **FLIP** it to a rehabber for $120,000 to $130,000 (60% to 65%) making you a net profit of $20,000 to $30,000!

- You could **FLIP** it to a Landlord for $140,000 to $150,000 (70% to 75%) making you a net profit of $40,000 to $50,000!

"But Dwan, how do I buy a property for 50% of the value when everyone is upside down?" **It's easy, you do a short sale®** -- meaning you contact the bank, ask if the bank will accept less than what is owed against this foreclosure, and then **FLIP** it to your Rehabber/Landlord for *MORE* – making a profit for yourself immediately!

Flipping Instructions:

- The homeowners have contacted you.

- Set a meeting and get the property under contract:
  - Use a "board approved" real estate sales contract – which you can find online.
  - Name the homeowners as the sellers and you as the buyer.
  - Make the sales price low enough so that you can **Flip** it to another investor.

- Find a Rehabber or Landlord to sell the property to:
  - Put a "For Sale By Owner" (FSBO) sign in the yard.
  - Attend a local REIA meeting (look online) to meet other investors.
  - Run an ad on Craigslist.

- Get the Rehabber/Landlord to agree to buy the property for more than you are paying for it.

- Contact a "Title Agency" to do the closing – Google one in your area and ask them if they are "Investor Friendly." If they say no keep calling until one says yes, as they will handle 100% of the closing for you.
- Set a closing date.
- The Rehabber/Landlord comes with CASH in hand.
- You leave with a HUGE paycheck and you NEVER owned the property or used one dime of your own money!

Flipping properties is fantastic, easy to do with proper instruction, and will make you a millionaire just like it did me!

II. REHAB FIX & FLIP

As I mentioned, I started as a rehabber. Unless you know how to fix stuff I don't recommend starting here. Fix & Flips are a blast and can make you some hefty paychecks if you know what you are doing. When I look back at my start I am amazed I made any money at all…☺!

Rehab Instructions:

- Find a homeowner using methods described in the **Wholesale Flip** section.
- You will do a **Fix & Flip** instead of a straight **Flip.**
- You find the same property as above that has an ARV of $200,000 and buy it for $100,000. because you called the bank and did a **Short Sale®**.
- You use your own cash to buy the property or find a "hard-money" lender.
- You close on the property.
- You **Fix** it up.
- You **Flip** it for a huge profit.

If you bought the property for $100,000 and spent $25,000 on the fix-up, you would make a profit of $75,000 when you sell it to a retail buyer!

When doing a **Fix & Flip** pay attention to *TWO* main areas of the house:

- **The Bathroom and The Kitchen**

In most cases, a husband and wife will be looking at the house. Do not kid yourself...the wife makes the decision as to whether they buy the house!

The wife wants to imagine herself in a nice tub, candles lit, relaxing after a hard day, in a new kitchen with all the bells and whistles, and not looking at how much work needs to be done. If you are on a limited budget, spend most of it in the kitchen and bathrooms. I used to fix-up houses as if I was going to live there. I soon learned that I was always going over budget.

> ➤ REPEAT AFTER ME UNTIL THIS BECOMES
> PART OF YOUR VOCABULARY:
> **I AM NOT GOING TO LIVE HERE!**

For new Fix and Flippers let me give you two valuable tips:

- Most home improvement stores will assist you using a computer program that will lay-out a new design for the bathroom/kitchen. Simply take the measurements, include where the windows and door are, and the computer will redesign the rooms for you.

- When you decide which cabinets to use, buy the less expensive cabinets for the base, sides and back and buy a more expensive cabinet door for the front. This way the cabinets will look more luxurious and expensive while you will have saved a ton of money to use in another part of the house.

I want to share two kitchens I did on a **very** limited budget.

Go to: www.Investors*Edge*University.com/Successonomics for the before and after pictures.

> Simply repositioning appliances and putting new cabinets make a small kitchen look fantastic!

It doesn't need to cost an arm and a leg to **Fix & Flip** a property. It just takes some planning and learning how to shop on a budget.

III. RENTALS

The path to long-term wealth. While I love to **Flip** properties, I also realize that six-months off work means six-months with no income. When you Flip properties you create a job for yourself. While it is a fun job that doesn't feel like work, it is still a job.

In order for you to actually retire you need to buy rentals, pay them off, and have passive income. I buy single-family homes that I rent to people in the Section 8 program. People have mixed emotions about Section 8 tenants, but YOU get to pick the tenant – *not the government!*

> **Section 8 is a government run program whereby the government pays the rent directly to YOU!**
>
> **It is always on-time and the check always clears!**

MUST FOLLOW TIP:

- When prospective tenants fill out a rental application tell them it will take a few days to process the application. Later that night show up at their current residence **UNANNOUNCED** and tell them that you are there for the final step of the rental process and that you need to see the property in which they currently live.

If they won't let you see the property they automatically fail the rental process and their application is denied. If they tell you things are a mess because they are packing assure them that you are not basing your decision on the clutter. You simply need to "inspect" the property. There is a HUGE difference between moving clutter and filth. If the house is nasty, this is exactly what your rental will look like in 90 days *NO MATTER* what they say!

Look in the refrigerator, in the microwave, under the beds, inspect the carpet, see if they have changed the air conditioning filters, look at the bathtub for rings, the floors for deep-rooted dirt…really inspect. If you have to rehab your properties between tenants you will never become a successful landlord. Ask me how I learned this?

Personal Example: I had a family come to one of my properties and fill out a rental application. Jackie showed up in a Jaguar, had five kids wearing their Sunday best, and the kids used "Yes Ma'am and No Ma'am" during the entire process. I went against my own rule and decided not to do the home inspection because the family seemed perfect. The voice in my head kept telling me to inspect their property and don't break my own rule. Reluctantly, I showed up at her door the next evening. Thank God I did!! As I stood at the front door ready to enter the property a cockroach fell off the door-jam **into my hair!** The trash had not been carried 10 feet to the curb for weeks and had actual maggots crawling in the torn-open bags, the bathroom was enough to make me gag…needless to say she failed the rental application.

I choose to buy single-family homes to give people a sense of ownership: A fenced-in yard where their kids can play, I allow a small dog or cat, I buy three bedroom/two bath houses in nice areas, and I provide a safe environment for the family. The longer your tenants stay, the more money you make!

Buy rentals at no more than 65% of the current market value. For Example: Purchase a $100,000 home for $65,000 and leave the equity in the property. Using this example, if you owned 25 rentals at 65% of the value when the market crash began in 2008, where would you be right now?

RIGHT…you would be sitting on 25 properties that STILL have equity! The market fell as low as 30% in some areas. Even if you had lost 30% of your value you would still have equity in all of your rentals and would be sitting pretty.

Over time, let's say you buy 25 rental properties that each rent for $1,000 a month. Once they are paid off you now have a passive income of $25,000 a month which equates to $300,000 a year! NOT BAD!

Say you mistakenly listen to another guru who convinces you to pull out your equity to buy more rentals. You now own 50 rentals, but each of them has a mortgage. You make $350 on each rental because they are mortgaged. Your income is now $17,500 and you own 50 rentals – which is twice the expense, twice the repairs, twice the worry and less monthly income. Why would you do that?

Friends, the bottom line is that there are a TON of deals out there right this very minute. It is up to YOU to take the first step and make it happen. I have given you THREE SOLID real estate investing techniques that will put anyone on the path to financial freedom, including you!

MY FINAL THOUGHTS

- Find a great mentor – me!
- Don't try to reinvent the wheel.
- Learn from someone who has done it, still does it, and has brought others up behind them.
- Enjoy the business and your new-found success.
- Share your knowledge with others and help them change their lives, too!
- May God Bless and Reward You Always.

About Dwan

Dwan Bent-Twyford, America's Most Sought-After Real Estate Investor™, started as a broke, single mom who had been fired from Denny's. Now divorced, having no formal education, and no job skills, she was at a major crossroad in her life.

After licking her wounds, Dwan made one decision that changed her life forever: **She decided that she was not going to raise her daughter in the daycare system.** She had waited until she was almost 30 to have a child and planned to be a stay-at-home mom. With that dream now shattered, she set out looking for something she could do from home and raise her daughter herself. As fate would have it, she discovered **real estate investing!**

She began as a naïve rehabber who thought rehabbing and decorating were the same thing. Having cleaned-up and painted her first property she soon realized she possessed no further rehab skills and the property was still a mess: Everything was ugly and outdated. With no money to hire help, Dwan began taking The Home Depot "how to" classes and finished her first rehab herself. She sold that property four days after it was completed, made $22,000 on her first deal, and never looked back!

As she began flipping and rehabbing foreclosures she discovered that some of the properties had no equity. Curious, she started calling banks to see if they would take less than what was owed on some of the foreclosures she was finding and to her surprise the banks said **YES!**

Realizing she had uncovered an industry yet to be built, she quickly trademarked the term **"Short Sales®"**, wrote the very *FIRST* training program on short sales (way back in the early 90's) for real estate investors, and helped found this money-making segment of the real estate investing industry. That discovery dubbed her the term "Queen of Short Sales®" and helped her climb to the top of the real estate investing industry.

Having flipped over 2,000 deals and trained countless students, Dwan is well qualified to show you the ropes as well. She has written two best-sellers: *Short Sale Pre-Foreclosure Investing* and *How to Sell a House When It's Worth Less Than the Mortgage.*

She now heads up "The Investors Edge University" - A company that specializes in training new and seasoned investors in a wide range of real estate investing techniques through live workshops, weekly webinars, a membership site, seminars, and much more.

She is a highly sought-after celebrity expert and has been featured on Fox & Friends, MSNBC, Naomi's Good Morning, Colorado & Company, and hundreds of other TV, radio, and print medias.

She has also spoken on stages with Donald Trump, Robert Kiyosaki, Suze Orman, Tony Robbins, and more! When Steve Forbes discovered what a hidden treasure Dwan was, he could not resist asking her to share her vast knowledge with you!

Her goal never changes – to make a difference in the lives of others! God Bless…

For more information on Dwan Bent-Twyford, please visit her site at:
www.Investors*Edge*University.com

CHAPTER 14

SURVIVE TO THRIVE

BY ERIC PENARANDA

It was a beautiful 95 degree summer day in Orlando, not a cloud in the sky, sun shining bright, basically the perfect day to start my career as a full time commercial real estate broker. I landed an excellent position with an international firm specializing in commercial real estate. My commute included a half mile walk to the downtown office wearing a suit and tie. The year is 2009; the Great Recession was well underway and happens to be the most catastrophic time period for commercial real estate in recent history.

The salary was zero; 100% of revenue was created by commission through effecting real estate transactions, so I eat only what I kill. My medical benefits included Dayquil and vitamin C boost packets conveniently located in the office kitchen. The perks were a phone, desk, some pens and air conditioning.

Sound dreadful? At the time, sure it was painful. Would I trade this experience for a cushy job, perks and not a worry in the world? Absolutely not.

The truth is prior to 2009, I held an incredible position developing real estate; my resume and project portfolio looked incredible on paper. My career seemed at the time to be headed for greatness and I could only look forward, yet I never took a moment to look around and understand the fundamentals of my success.

During the sudden and rather abrupt financial climate change I found myself in disbelief, how on earth could development and construction cease to exist? Within a very short window my world changed from thriving to surviving.

SURVIVAL MODE.....

So why did I walk to work? The moment my short term income quickly reduced to zero I made a very important decision to define wants and needs, so I didn't need to spend $125 per month for a parking space. This mentality continued through every aspect of my daily life, walking though the grocery store I would literally look at certain foods and question, "Do I really need this?" Turns out I managed to reduce my weekly grocery bill to less than $20, yet ate reasonably healthy. To save gas on the weekends, I rode my bike practically every place that wouldn't frown upon gym clothes drenched in sweat.

Looking back, I learned the true fundamentals of survival not necessarily in terms of fending off wolves with a campfire; it was mainly about finding the true foundation of daily living which will sustain not only health and happiness but also the rate at which cash burns. This is an incredibly important concept to understand when starting a business; profits are not realized until certain thresholds are met. A basic concept yes, but identifying the capital burn between return gaps will help measure the true mode of survival.

Survival doesn't require that you have to live in hindsight or pity the moment, it means understanding future requirements and effectively managing assets to not only outlive the period of survival, but to build a foundation that will sustain prosperity.

HURRICANE PRICES ARE PURE ECONOMICS....

October 23, 2005, living in Delray Beach Florida, the local news weather team and I seemed convinced that Hurricane Wilma would be a non-event for the East Coast of South Florida. With Wilma lingering just North of Key West, I checked into bed around 10pm. Roughly 4 hours later I suddenly woke to what sounded like a freight train outside my window. As I walked outside it seemed something was very wrong, my suspicions were verified when I watched a piece of roofing material dangle in the air then quickly track towards my direction. While I ran for cover I quickly turned to watch the debris smash into my window, if that were not enough the power went down shortly after.

I later discovered that Wilma took a quick Easterly direction and absolutely pounded South Florida. Since we were not expecting such a destructive storm of course nobody was prepared, including myself. I had quarter of a tank of gas, two used batteries and a refrigerator of food that was quickly going bad. I drove to the local store to gather supplies and found a sea of people with the same idea, yet there seemed to be such anger in the air. The store was charging $20 per battery, $40 per buffet burner and nearly an arm or a leg for edible food. People were enraged and felt gouged; many purchased the bare essentials and went about their business. After gathering the minimal necessities myself, I noticed on my way out a man with several generators for sale at what seemed to be an astronomical price of $5,000, but was it? Driving home I noticed a gas station with at least 100 cars in line and a handmade sign which read "10 Gallon max for $100", a police officer was on the scene managing about a dozen angry buyers.

Many felt gouged and taken advantage of during a crisis. Several protested unfair pricing and purchase limits. The reality is this event exposed the true fundamentals of economics. As we all know, the law of supply and demand has a direct correlation to price. As demand rises or supply falls, then prices will rise. Unfortunately hurricanes subject unusual changes to supply and demand which of course drive the value of essential goods to exponential levels. Let's dig deeper, drastic changes in demand can create a supply problem especially during events which interrupt the replenishment chain. Prior to Wilma's landfall, some decided to stock up on supplies. It was reported that many stores were extremely limited in survival materials. The problem here is, without price adjustment, these individuals purchased more than their needs required which lead to significant shortages.

To illustrate the impact of unexpected demand change without price adjustment, consider two scenarios:

A family of four is looking for batteries, flashlights and non-perishable food. When they arrive at the store it seems supplies are reasonably priced so naturally they purchase a flashlight for each member of the family, the required batteries and a stockpile for reserves. Also, they stock up with a food supply to last two weeks. Another family arrives at the store, batteries and flashlights are sold out and food is limited to perishable items.

Consider the same family seeking supplies, when they arrive at the store it appears prices are 10 times the typical market value for all goods. This spike in cost requires the family to consider what they actually need. Are 4 flashlights and a massive stockpile of batteries needed? Is it necessary to buy 2 weeks' worth of food? Due to price increases, demand is managed to sustain supply to meet the needs of the next family.

The exponential increase in price of goods during a hurricane or any natural disaster may appear to be gouging the local population. However, rapid increase in price is a small price to pay for an adequate supply of essential goods.

EMOTION CREATES COMMOTION....

The sun goes up and the sun goes down every day, you can set your clock by it. Certain seasons the sun is further from or closer to earth, we know this through the study of cyclical patterns. Consider another cyclical pattern, if winter is coming then naturally prices or cold weather clothing rises and conversely prices drop during summer. The same is true for purchasing a car, certain time periods throughout the year automotive manufacturers provide fairly aggressive discounts to move inventory. Opportunity exists if you study patterns, understand the fundamentals and control emotional buying.

Let's review the fundamentals of the most recent Great Recession. Real Estate maintains sustainability by progressing through time at natural limits; low, mid and high. In the early 2000's, America experienced a rapid increase in intrinsic real estate value well above the natural high water mark of natural inflation. Like building Legos the perceived value of property rose at an increasing rate according to related comparable transactions. The problem is that perception turned into emotion. The moment I knew we were headed for trouble was during a conversation with a residential broker during a property tour in 2005. She said with a sense of urgency, "If you act quickly and your offer is high enough, buying this property will be the equivalent of buying a winning lottery ticket."

While the thought of buying a winning lottery ticket sounds wonderful, the fundamentals of price relative to value over decades of historical patterns pointed to one conclusion, we are headed for a brick wall. Now, this is the moment of opportunity. As Baron Rothschild once said, "Buy when there's blood in the streets." With real estate values set to take a steep decline, investors with adequate liquid capital seized the ability to capture assets at severely depressed prices.

If hindsight is 20/20 then learn, adapt and grow your ability to capitalize on upcoming trends. Jim Cramer once gave us an excellent opportunity indicator; he identified a correlation between stock trends and news. When a single news outlet is reporting on upward trends in value chances are it's a good buy. When three or more news stations are reporting on the same news the window of opportunity has likely closed. Here is a similar real estate example, when individuals with zero experience in residential or commercial investments suddenly become developers or "flippers" chances are the trend is at the end of its run.

As untrained individuals enter a complex field, common mistakes can be catastrophic. Consider an investment on a 20,000 square foot industrial building. In South Orlando this property would cost roughly $65.00 per square foot to produce. As a Net, Net, Net return, the base rent for this facility could range in the $4.50 - $5.00 per square foot range depending on function and location. Generally an acceptable capitalization rate would be 7%, considering low estimated rent the building value would be $1,285,714. If an untrained investor purchases the property for $2,000,000 the investment would never make sense because the natural base rate could not achieve equilibrium given the market parameters.

Emotional actions will not allow you to experience the true purpose of the decision. Just like the sun and seasonal patterns trends can be found in almost any aspect of life and business — if everyone else is making the same investment then position ahead of the cyclical top end and prepare for the shift.

As I started my career at the absolute bottom of the market I learned to make decisions based on fact not emotion. Surviving on rice and frozen chicken taught me the importance of identifying the most important elements of my business, and that acting on emotion clouds the ability to differentiate between wants and needs.

Study historical trends and stick to the fundamentals to eliminate the tendency to make emotional decisions. Anticipate changes in market conditions and look to adjust strategy to capitalize on foreseeable opportunities.

About Eric

Eric is a native Floridian raised in Tampa while being surrounded by the Development and Construction Industry through the family business. He is blessed with his loving wife Lindsay and two amazing pups Marley and Cooper. Eric is a graduate of The University of North Florida, where he received a Bachelor of Science in Construction and Real Estate Development.

Currently, Eric is the Director of Leasing for the Orlando portfolio of DCT Industrial where he specializes in leasing, development and acquisition of industrial properties in the Central Florida commercial real estate market. Prior to joining DCT Industrial, Eric provided leasing services for over 4 million square feet of industrial real estate from 2009 to 2013. From 2001 to 2009 he developed and constructed over 3 million square feet of real estate and successfully negotiated over $500 million in project contracts. Eric was also recently featured in Newsweek Magazine as one of America's PremierExperts®.

As an innovative entrepreneur, Eric also owns and operates a seasonal Christmas tree business in Winter Park, Florida, whereby he has successfully built and maintained a brand that is well known for delivering a quality product with a focus on superior service.

If you would like more information about Eric Penaranda, or would like to discuss commercial real estate in any market, visit: www.EricPenaranda.com or call him at: 407-222-2424.

CHAPTER 15

THE BEST STORY WINS: FOUR WINNING WAYS TO SOUP UP YOUR BRAND STORY

BY NICK NANTON AND JW DICKS

When it comes to competition, it seems like common sense: whoever is the best at what they do wins, correct?

Well, actually, *in*correct. Think about how many contests you've witnessed – such as employees jockeying for promotions, candidates campaigning for government offices, even attorneys battling it out in criminal trials – where the outcome seemed completely unfair to you and many other people. As a matter of fact, the results may have seemed to signify that facts didn't matter.

Of course, that's not always the case. In many instances, the results of a competition are completely fact-based, such as sporting events and academic exams. But when competitions are left to people's individual judgments, when there is no clear benchmark to base a decision on, anything can happen – and frequently does!

The question then becomes – what are people using to make their judgments when it's not a black and white numbers game? What causes them to lean one way or the other when they have to choose which person to back?

The answer to that question was recently confirmed to us once again when a client came to us and told us he was getting killed in his particular market by a competitor. We asked, "Why? Is your competition really that much better?"

"No," he said, "but he's got a better *story*."

We're big on storytelling – or as we like to call it, StorySelling – because we know, when it comes to business success, *whoever has the best story wins*. That's why having a strong story in place is essential to powering up a personal brand.

In this chapter, we'll prove it – and we'll also give you some very profitable advice on how to be sure your brand story hits the number one spot in your particular industry!

AND THE OSCAR GOES TO...

One of the most highly-anticipated and publicized "contests" is the annual Academy Awards in Hollywood. And the most coveted prizes are the Best Actor and the Best Actress statuettes – because, let's face it, most of us go to the movies to see movie *stars*, which is why the first question we usually ask about one is, "Who's in it?"

Now, of course, you would think that the only criteria for winning a best acting award is who actually gave the best performance. That criteria, however, is far from being clear, since all the nominated actors competing against each other are playing very different roles that require very different talents.

That's why many actors disparage the Oscars, saying they would only be fair if each nominee had to play the exact same part, and the Academy could judge which one played it best. Instead, it's left with having to decide contests like the one it faced in 2013: Did Daniel Day-Lewis play Lincoln better than Denzel Washington played a pilot with a drinking problem or than Bradley Cooper played a manic-depressive?

So how *do* these things get decided? Again, it's *who has the best story*.

Dr. Todd Winther blogged on a disability website a few weeks before the 2012 Oscar ceremony took place and predicted, "Based on past history,

Meryl Streep is assured of winning the Best Actress Oscar this year for her portrayal of Margaret Thatcher in *The Iron Lady."*

Guess what? That's *exactly* what happened – but what past history was Winther referring to? He was merely citing the statistical fact that actors who portray real-life characters with some kind of physical or mental disability usually win the Oscar. In this case, Meryl Streep played the former English Prime Minister Margaret Thatcher, who suffered from dementia in her later years.

Why would this matter? Because it makes for *the most powerful story.* Just two years before, Colin Firth won his Oscar for portraying an English monarch with a severe stuttering problem in *The King's Speech* - a different kind of British head of state, but the same kind of situation.

In other words, audiences get so caught up in narratives about real-life people with either a lot of power or a lot of talent (think Jamie Foxx in *Ray*) who must deal with physical or mental limitations, that *voters reward the actor for the power of the story more than the actual performance.*

STORYSELLING THROUGHOUT SOCIETY

Now, there are numerous other high-profile examples of this kind of StorySelling (whether intentional or not) working their magic. For instance, in a political campaign, one candidate will generally have a story that resonates more strongly with the voters than the other. That candidate will win, even if he has significant scandals in his or her past.

Take the recent case of Mark Sanford, who, when he was governor of South Carolina, had a very public affair with an Argentine woman and a very messy divorce from his wife. Two years later, he prevailed over his opponent when he ran for Congress, because his conservative StorySelling mattered more than his personal peccadillos. (And this isn't unique to conservatives – remember how many extramarital scandals Bill Clinton weathered?)

Then there's the matter of the O.J. Simpson trial back in the '90's. *Every single fact* pointed to Simpson's guilt in the murders of his wife and a friend of hers – and yet, he was found innocent, because his defense team *told the best story* – and it was the story the jury wanted to believe.

Why do stories many times trump facts? Well, there are many significant scientific findings that explain this phenomenon (you can check out our new book on StorySelling to find out more), but, suffice it to say that our brains are conditioned to listen more to *stories* than facts – it's how we process the world around us so it makes sense to us.

Now, that doesn't mean that we can get away with misrepresenting ourselves and our businesses. Besides the issue of the importance of personal integrity, telling an untrue story does catch up to you over the long haul and generally blows your brand story to smithereens. If Mark Sanford, for example, started voting as a liberal instead of a conservative, he would violate his brand story – and the constituents who put him into office would end up hopping mad!

What it does mean, however, is that when you create a brand story that's authentic *and* uses proven, effective story-telling tools, you set yourself up for success.

HOW TO CREATE "THE GREATEST STORY EVER SOLD"

As we noted, StorySelling is really a science – and if your brand story ticks off one or more of the right boxes, you're able to make it both influential and profitable. Your brand will gain power, your audience will grow and conversions to sales will become much easier.

In the remainder of the chapter, we're going to offer you some of the most powerful ingredients you can add to your brand to make sure it outstrips your competition's. Without further ado, here are our 4 Winning Ways to give your brand story the edge in the marketplace.

WINNING WAY #1:
REFLECT INCREDIBLE ACHIEVEMENT

Donald Trump, of course, can give us all a master class in personal branding (and he probably will, but it'll cost you!). His StorySelling is all about his own mammoth personal success, which allows him to have the best of everything, including gold-plated furnishings. This, in turn, makes others believe he has the secret to *their* success as well as his own – so they're eager to buy his books, watch his TV shows and attend his seminars in order to find out more about what that secret is all about (and put it to work for themselves).

When you're the living embodiment of incredible achievement, people are naturally attracted to you, because that achievement is *inspiring* to them and they want to share in your reflected glory. Also, they feel that, because you've accomplished great things, you, like Donald Trump, have secrets to impart to them. Obviously, this type of StorySelling works best when you're selling coaching and informational products that are centered around concepts you teach, but it can also work from a product/marketing standpoint too. Think of how many star athletes are used to sell sneakers, grooming products, etc. — even though it's obvious that's not where their expertise lies!

Of course, incredible achievement can be reflected in many other ways as well. You may have an amazing rags-to-riches story that will inspire your followers, or you may have overcome a physical disability or other overwhelming circumstances that might have prevented others from achieving what you did. These are also important to weave into your brand story, because it distinguishes you from your competitors and also raises your profile sky-high.

WINNING WAY #2:
GIVE YOUR AUDIENCE WHAT THEY WANT

Remember Mr. Goodwrench? General Motors, one of America's most time-honored brands, used that advertising gimmick as a way to reassure customers that their cars would receive repairs and maintenance from people who were nice and competent at their jobs. "Goodwrench" was a name, albeit an imaginary one, that conjured up both those qualities. Mr. BadWrench might fix your car, but he might also be mean or rip you off. Mr. GoodSpatula, of course, isn't a guy you'd let near your car, but maybe you'd let him make you an omelet.

Anyway, Mr. Goodwrench was a GM advertising mainstay for almost 40 years, before he was sent to the scrap heap two or three years ago – so he obviously made for a winning long-term brand story. That's because, even though he was a mythical creature, Mr. Goodwrench made GM customers feel as though they would get what they want out of the guy.

Now, you probably don't want to legally change your name to Mr. GreatCoach or Ms. RealEstateRiches...but there's no reason why you can't create a brand story that matches up with what your potential customers want out of you. Zappos built a billion dollar business out of providing incredible customer service; even though you could buy the shoes they sold pretty much anywhere else, they worked so hard to fulfill their customers' needs that their brand story took off and their revenues followed suit.

So think about the NUMBER ONE thing prospective buyers might want from you – and work out a way to make that a vital part of your brand story. It creates an irresistible incentive for your leads to check you out further.

WINNING WAY #3:
MAGNIFY A MAGNETIC PERSONALITY

Back in 1988, the top two comedians in the U.S. couldn't have been more different. One was Jeff Foxworthy, the "You Might Be a Redneck" guy who to this day still has a giant career as TV host and stand-up comedian. The other was Andrew "Dice" Clay, an incredibly controversial "Jersey Guy" who based his routine on X-rated sexual material; although his star has diminished considerably, his acting and comedy careers are still going strong and he earned acclaim for his role in the recent Woody Allen movie, *Blue Jasmine*.

Again, these two guys were worlds apart in their approach. One had a large, dedicated rural Southern audience, the other had a huge urban following, particularly in New York and New Jersey. What they had in common, however, was much more important and much more integral to their brand story: their *personalities*. Both of them took existing aspects of who they were and blew them up big enough to fill up a stage - as well as the seats in front of that stage.

This is another trait common to the StorySelling of such familiar personal brand legends as Richard Branson and the aforementioned Donald Trump; they take the aspects of their personalities that people find the most exciting, focus on them and make them larger than life in the process. Nobody wants to see Richard Branson in a long, boring business meeting, although he undoubtedly participates in them. Nobody wants to see Donald Trump act concerned that he won't succeed at something, even though, privately, the man probably does fret a bit from time-to-time like we all do. So people rarely, if ever, see those sides of these two business titans – they make sure of it!

The important thing to remember about this particular Winning Way is that you should *build on an existing part of your personality*. You'll come across as a lot more authentic if you're leveraging a part of yourself that's already there instead of creating an outrageous character from whole cloth.

WINNING WAY #4:
LEAD WITH YOUR EDGE

Okay, so you want to establish your brand story as the best. Well, then... simply make being the best your brand story.

Brands as diverse as Jaguar, Ritz-Carlton and Neiman-Marcus all make it a point to position themselves as superior to the vast majority of their competition; yes, they can sometimes come across as snobby for that reason, but, on the other hand, they exert a strong attraction to those who can afford to patronize them. Since these brands are perceived as superior, those who buy from them also feel superior as well!

Of course, if you take the luxury brand approach in your StorySelling, your products and services also have to be premium quality; otherwise there's a distinct disconnect between what you're saying and what you're selling. Ultimately, as in any instance when your StorySelling isn't authentic, that will cause a breakdown of your brand's narrative.

Another thing to note is that, in order to implement this particular Winning Way, you don't have to go the luxury brand route; you can also focus on some essential element of your business that's better than your competitors. Apple's brand story has always practiced this Winning Way as an integral part of its brand story, because it markets itself as an overall superior choice to the competition (which is usually Microsoft).

One of their most successful stabs at this kind of StorySelling came in a series of simple and impactful TV ads that were so effective in delivering their message, the campaign continued for three years. The commercials featured actor Justin Long, representing an Apple Mac computer, squaring off against comedian John Hodgman, representing a Windows PC. Each touted the benefits of his product, with the Mac, naturally, always coming out the winner. Both personalities accurately reflected the consumers' view of the brands, making it feel both authentic and credible.

Positioning your brand as better than the competition is nothing new; it's essential to most marketing. However, when you incorporate some of the Winning Ways we've discussed in this chapter into your brand story, you continually reinforce that superiority with customers and prospects alike as a matter of course. Whoever has the best story wins, whether it's in business, politics or the Oscars – so make sure you're the one who always walks away with the biggest prize.

About Nick

An Emmy Award Winning Director and Producer, Nick Nanton, Esq., is known as the Top Agent to Celebrity Experts around the world for his role in developing and marketing business and professional experts, through personal branding, media, marketing and PR. Nick is recognized as the nation's leading expert on personal branding as Fast Company Magazine's Expert Blogger on the subject and lectures regularly on the topic at major universities around the world. His book *Celebrity Branding You®*, while an easy and informative read, has also been used as a text book at the University level.

The CEO and Chief StoryTeller at The Dicks + Nanton Celebrity Branding Agency, an international agency with more than 1800 clients in 33 countries, Nick is an award winning director, producer and songwriter who has worked on everything from large scale events to television shows with the likes of Steve Forbes, Brian Tracy, Jack Canfield (*The Secret*, Creator of the *Chicken Soup for the Soul* Series), Michael E. Gerber, Tom Hopkins, Dan Kennedy and many more.

Nick is recognized as one of the top thought-leaders in the business world and has co-authored 30 best-selling books alongside Brian Tracy, Jack Canfield, Dan Kennedy, Dr. Ivan Misner (Founder of BNI), Jay Conrad Levinson (Author of the Guerilla Marketing Series), Super Agent Leigh Steinberg and many others, including the breakthrough hit *Celebrity Branding You!®*.

Nick has led the marketing and PR campaigns that have driven more than 1000 authors to Best-Seller status. Nick has been seen in *USA Today, The Wall Street Journal, Newsweek, BusinessWeek, Inc. Magazine, The New York Times, Entrepreneur®️ Magazine, Forbes,* FastCompany.com and has appeared on ABC, NBC, CBS, and FOX television affiliates around the country, as well as CNN, FOX News, CNBC, and MSNBC from coast to coast.

Nick is a member of the Florida Bar, holds a JD from the University Of Florida Levin College Of Law, as well as a BSBA in Finance from the University of Florida's Warrington College of Business. Nick is a voting member of The National Academy of Recording Arts & Sciences (NARAS, Home to The GRAMMYs), a member of The National Academy of Television Arts & Sciences (Home to the Emmy Awards), co-founder of the National Academy of Best-Selling Authors, a 16-time Telly Award winner, and spends his spare time working with Young Life, Downtown Credo Orlando, Entrepreneurs International and rooting for the Florida Gators with his wife Kristina and their three children, Brock, Bowen and Addison.

Learn more at www.NickNanton.com and:
www.CelebrityBrandingAgency.com

About JW

JW Dicks, Esq., is America's foremost authority on using personal branding for business development. He has created some of the most successful brand and marketing campaigns for business and professional clients to make them the credible celebrity experts in their field and build multi-million dollar businesses using their recognized status.

JW Dicks has started, bought, built, and sold a large number of businesses over his 39-year career and developed a loyal international following as a business attorney, author, speaker, consultant, and business experts' coach. He not only practices what he preaches by using his strategies to build his own businesses, he also applies those same concepts to help clients grow their business or professional practice the ways he does.

JW has been extensively quoted in such national media as *USA Today*, the *Wall Street Journal, Newsweek, Inc.*, Forbes.com, CNBC.com, and *Fortune Small Business*. His television appearances include ABC, NBC, CBS and FOX affiliate stations around the country. He is the resident branding expert for *Fast Company*'s internationally syndicated blog and is the publisher of *Celebrity Expert Insider*, a monthly newsletter targeting business and brand building strategies.

JW has written over 22 books, including numerous best-sellers, and has been inducted into the National Academy of Best-Selling Authors. JW is married to Linda, his wife of 39 years, and they have two daughters, two granddaughters and two Yorkies. JW is a 6th generation Floridian and splits his time between his home in Orlando and beach house on the Florida west coast.

CHAPTER 16

WOULD YOU BE A CLIENT OF YOUR BUSINESS?

BY JAIME WESTENBARGER

I would like to start by describing to you the moment I knew I needed to do something different than I was doing at the time. By different, I don't mean the industry I was working in, as I had realized a few years earlier that I had truly found the financial services field, and specifically the job of being a financial advisor, to be my true passion. No, what I mean is the moment I realized I needed to do it at a different company and do it in a different way. I had been with the company I was working for at the time for a few years, and had started to make a successful career as a financial advisor. The moment came while sitting in the car of my manager, the man I was truly trying to be like, when we had an enlightening conversation. He probably doesn't even remember it, but it struck me in both its boldness and how wrong it made me feel about a career I had come to love. What did he say, you ask? He told me he was paying $995 a month for the car payment on his new Cadillac, and when I responded shocked by that lofty sum, he spoke the seven words that would launch me on my trajectory that brought me to where I am today. He said, "That's why we keep selling more policies."

That was it! It wasn't some statement of challenge, and not some infinite wisdom from a great teacher, just the realization that he saw our clients as customers. Customers in my mind are people you sell things to, clients are those you advise and consult. Now mind you, he did not say anything wrong. You may be surprised that most financial transactions are considered sales in the financial industry. He also wasn't saying we should sell anything to anyone. He just had broken down the job that I was finding a real career in as nothing more than a sales job, and I couldn't stomach that. How could your life's dreams for retirement, college savings and more, be influenced, or even determined by what someone sold you? What if my mom or grandma had met the wrong salesman or bought the wrong thing? How could that be the determining factor in successful retirement?

So with my head full of wonderful ideas of how I could do things better, I started my own company in October 2006 determined to do it better. Anyone that tells you the first few years of any new business is a good time, is not being truthful with you. It is *exciting* indeed, but also very stressful. You stress about everything: clients, rent, family, money, etc. etc. Fortunately for me in 2006-2007, my first full year in business for myself, the one thing I didn't stress about was the stock market. It was roaring and people were happy. Business was growing, slowly, but growing and I was looking forward to a great 2008. Now I will explain to everyone reading this what happened in 2008 -- just in case you don't own a television or were out of the country. Beginning in late 2007 and through all of the 2008, the market fell. Then it fell some more. Banks, companies, eventually even countries hung on the brink of ruin. To say it was petrifying to be in the financial industry at this time would have been a huge understatement. Some estimates are there were over 10,000 financial advisors that left the industry during this time.

Every morning brought more bad news and uncertainty, but one thing I noticed was that I wasn't losing clients. We talked, they stayed. This was unusual. As I would talk to other advisors, many of them were hemorrhaging clients and here I was not losing a *single one*. As the end of 2008 approached, I was actually gaining clients and increasing revenue. The clients I had were referring their friends and relatives, and by early 2009, I had to transition into a larger office space and hire a full-time staff person. So what was the magic that I had? What was the secret to my success? How did I continue to grow during one of the worst recessions our country has ever seen? I found it broke down to three things that I was doing that I now know many others weren't. I didn't at the time do them because I saw them as the keys to success. I just did them because that is who I am. These are three things I still do today, and they are the foundation of how I have grown my single man, small office company, into a four office, multi-state financial services firm with over $100 million in assets and more than $1 million in annual fees projected for 2014.

Even if you are not in the financial services industry, I think you will find these apply to all markets. I realize although they may seem like simple thoughts, maybe even common sense, they are not common at all. Take a step back and look at your business now, or the businesses you choose to work with and ask yourself if these principles are present. You may be surprised they are not.

1. <u>RUN YOUR COMPANY AS IF YOU WERE A CLIENT</u>

This is my version of the golden rule. We know we should always treat others as we would like to be treated, but how often do our companies truly reflect that? I wanted to create a company that I would want to be a client of. In my business that meant doing some things that were somewhat out of the ordinary. The first one I discovered when asking a new client, we will call him John, why he was looking for a new advisor. John said he didn't have many complaints, except for one. John's current advisor never called him back on time. He would take two or three days to return phone calls. Now I am sure John's advisor knew the question wasn't life or death and figured there were more important things he needed to do first, but to his clients it only illustrated one thing. John, the client, just wasn't that important to him. When we run our company as if we are the client, we naturally do things differently. We put ourselves in the shoes of our clients, the lifeblood of our business and we see things as they would. This drives everything we do. If we are going to implement a new strategy or a new marketing plan, or even change our website, we always take the client's perspective into consideration.

In 2011 I needed to move my office. We had grown and needed much more square footage. The downtown area of my city had really grown and was becoming the hot spot to be. I really thought moving downtown would be great and honestly I really wanted to be down there. When I sat down and looked at the location from my client's viewpoint, my thought process changed. It is often difficult to find parking downtown and it can be confusing to locate a building if you aren't familiar with downtown Grand Rapids. Many of our clients are older or retired and they may have to walk a much greater distance to reach our offices. Once

I looked at it from this viewpoint, I knew I had to keep my company in the suburbs. I found a great office space on a main road, with a big sign and front row parking. My clients have to walk approximately 50 yards from their car to my conference room and they love it. In the last year I have had two new clients tell me the reason they were looking for a new advisor is because their current one was downtown.

I eventually took this idea to the next level. I now provide to all clients of FHF a client Bill of Rights (email me and I will send you a copy). It tells them what we expect of them as clients and what they should expect from us. It has been a huge hit. It covers everything from full disclosure of fees, to 24-hour return calls promises. Most importantly though, it tells my clients that I value them and I want to always provide the best service possible. They truly are first for both myself and my company.

2. <u>BE BRAVE. DO WHAT EVERYONE ELSE IS AFRAID TO DO, IF IT IS WHAT IS RIGHT FOR YOUR CLIENT</u>

The definition of insanity is doing the same thing over and over again but expecting different results. In business I think there is a similar insanity that happens when companies do the same things their competition does, but expect they will do better than them. Why would a prospective client even bother talking to you if you are no different than your competition? The only exception to this is of course price, but I want to be a good value, not the cheapest. BIG DIFFERENCE!

For my industry, there can be a herd mentality. If you keep saying what everyone else is saying than you will never be alone and wrong. If you're wrong, so will everyone else be so you won't stand out. Well sometimes we have to be brave, because it is what is right for our clients, and be confident that by taking that step forward, we will stand out, but in a good way.

The opportunity for this came for me in 2008. If you have any kind of investments, you have heard things like: "you should buy and hold," "investments always come back," or "if you sell when things are going down you won't be able to tell when to come back in." The common thought is to have a balanced portfolio and ride the wave. I never liked this philosophy. While it is sound in principle, it is also very rarely followed by clients. They never want to lose money so they fight the idea of holding until they have lost more than they can stomach and they sell. Usually this is at the worst time and they may never recover. Think about your own investments and how you felt in 2008 and you will see what I mean. It is why the average investor came out so much worse than the overall market, because they panic and sell or because they buy when it is too late.

So I developed a different way of doing things, something that would help ease the fear of my clients during unpredictable times, and help them capture more upside return in the good times – because they would be invested. Now the point of this was not to teach you how to invest or even get you to invest with me – so I won't go into great detail. What I will tell you is my clients are more engaged and less afraid. Don't get me wrong, I don't have some magical formula and my clients can lose money just like everyone else. What I do different is give them a plan for all market conditions. They know what to expect. The reason I do this is simple. It is because if I were a client, that is what I would want as I mentioned in the previous step, but also because it is what my clients need and I wasn't afraid to be different than everyone else. Imagine how this simple idea could change the way you do business and help you retain more clients.

3. <u>NEVER STOP LEARNING AND GROWING</u>

I warned you these were not crazy ideas you've never heard of. Hopefully I have clearly illustrated my philosophy to make you realize you're not doing them. Obviously we have all heard the saying: we need to never stop learning. We should always be growing. I think this becomes another of those ideas that we all know but don't necessarily implement, but it can be very powerful in driving your business to the next level. I am always exposing myself to opportunities to grow, both professionally and personally. Sometimes you have to go back to step two and be brave to do it, but it will always pay dividends to your career, your company and your clients.

In 2008 I had an opportunity to be interviewed on the radio about what was happening in the market. After the interview, someone from the station approached me about doing a weekly show on the weekends about money. Now anyone that knows me will tell you I don't have a problem talking. Most would say it is easier to get me to talk than to get me to stop, but the radio was different. This was something I was unfamiliar with and a big learning curve. I could have easily declined the invitation and not thought another thing about it, but I was so incredibly driven and interested in learning, I accepted.

My first show was nothing short of a disaster. I was really bad at knowing how to go to a commercial and I said, "Um or uh" at least 100 times. I am sure anyone that tuned in never came back to listen again. The next few weeks it somewhat improved, and I started to get a real flow of how things work. Today my show is nationally syndicated and I am featured on numerous other programs across the country. Radio and television studios are like my second home. Had I never taken the opportunity to learn new things, this would have never happened. This chapter in this book is a perfect example. As you read this you may think it is great or you may hate it. I'm not sure because I have never done this before. I am not a professional writer. Hopefully it is not too bad, but I guarantee the next one will be better and someday you will buy a book I wrote and never know a small chapter in a Steve Forbes book was where it all began.

I hope you find many ideas on how to be great in this book. I hope some of them come from this chapter I have written. If you remember nothing else that you've read, just remember to be brave and be different, and treat your clients as if you were one, and never stop learning. You will be a better person for it. Your clients will be better for it. And you will build a better business because of it.

About Jaime

When Jaime Westenbarger bought his first stock while still in High School, he was unaware of the large influence that the purchase would have on his future. Always interested in finance and economics, Jaime enrolled at The University of Michigan shortly after completing his service to our country in the United States Marine Corps. In 1999, he officially entered the financial services industry and worked in a number of capacities including, but not limited to, managing a team of financial advisors until he decided in 2006 it was time to build his own company, Forest Hills Financial, Inc. Although the entrepreneurial spirit was partially responsible for the endeavor, it was also driven by his desire to create a company he would want to be a client of. His concern lay in the belief that the financial industry was focused more on sales goals than in truly helping the client, and resulted in the founding of Forest Hills Financial, Inc. in 2006.

Since starting Forest Hills Financial, Inc. in a small one-person office in 2006, Jaime Westenbarger has turned the financial world on its head. Through his nationally-syndicated radio show, *The Keeping Your Money Show,* he has helped thousands of people filter through the salespeople of the financial services world and focus on the information that actually matters. Jaime's style of simple explanations of complex problems helped grow his business in only seven years to include clients in 15 states, advisors in four offices, and *The Keeping Your Money Show* continuing to grow its listening audience. Forest Hills Financial, Inc. was able to grow revenue over 300% during one of the most devastating recessions in recent memory. Additionally the company continues to develop in size and influence in the financial community on a local, state and even national level.

Jaime resides with his amazing wife, Hillary and their two children in the Forest Hills community of Grand Rapids, Michigan.

Jaime can be contacted through his website at: www.myfhf.com. You can also see show times and stations in your area for *The Keeping Your Money Show* at: www. Keepingyourmoney.com.

CHAPTER 17

WORK TOWARDS A HEALTHY, ENGAGED AND FINANCIALLY INDEPENDENT RETIREMENT

BY CARL A. BARNOWSKI

What's your retirement going to be like? Much different from your parents I'm sure. Will you be able to spend relaxing, carefree afternoons out on the golf course, or will you come up short financially and have to cut back on life's pleasures? As many retirees have discovered, it's no fun facing a financial shortfall in retirement. Remember the good old days when your banker managed your checking, savings, and CDs and you got a toaster for opening a new account? You also had your "insurance guy" to take care of your home, auto, life, and health policies. If your finances were doing well and you felt ready to invest, you got in touch with "your guy" the broker. You trusted these people because they were each experts in their own fields; they knew their clients' needs, they understood the products they were selling, and they provided top-notch customer service to you and your family. These days, the financial services industry is a selling machine with no shortage of products to sell. When I used to call financial advisors as a wholesaler, I consistently heard that they weren't looking for more products to sell, but for more people to whom they could sell. Over the last 10-15 years, the financial services industry has become clogged with salespeople scrapping for the next sale and most of them have increased the scope of their product lines to avoid leaving any money on the table for the next guy. Brokers today are licensed to sell insurance products and insurance salespeople are licensed to sell securities. But do they really know enough about all those products to be able to advise and serve their customers? Some may, but most do not, and that answer is what prompted me to found Barnowski Financial Group.

At the Barnowski Financial Group, we have positioned ourselves as retirement income specialists, and only offer our clients 100% insured products that are risk-free. We also provide each client a complimentary Social Security Optimization service that helps them to understand the ins and outs of when and how to start drawing on that benefit – so that its reward is maximized. I founded the Barnowski Financial Group with three primary goals:

1. To preserve my clients' capital to ensure it lasted their lifetime.

2. To positively impact the financial industry by creating a safe, transparent, and interactive environment for my clients.

3. To provide a level of service and understanding that alleviated stress and worry from my clients and their families, and allowed them to enjoy the security provided by the products I had to offer.

Over the last 20 years, we've all seen a lot of changes in the economy and most of us have experienced some sort of significant change in our lifestyles. Many Boomers are starting to feel the financial squeeze of joining the Sandwich Generation – as they begin to take on caring for their aging parents while also working to help their children get through college. Suddenly, you're in your sixties (or very nearly there) and your stress levels are higher than ever as you realize that retirement may be further away than you'd originally planned—or it's no longer even an option because you have been providing for everyone else. If you're in your forties or fifties, you still have time to plan and time to make changes, but you probably see your membership in the Sandwich Generation as inevitable.

Regardless of your age, there are plenty of things I advise people to do to help alleviate the stress that goes hand in hand with financial unease:

- Consider working a little bit longer than you had planned.

- Take a long, honest look at your expenses – and then trim them.

- Encourage your children to explore every option for college financial aid, especially options that don't require repayment such as merit grants and scholarships.

- If you are, or soon may be, taking care of aging parents, use their assets to finance their care for as long as possible.

- Plan ahead and consider what it will cost if Mom or Dad comes to live with you, or if Junior comes home after college and needs to live with you while he finds a job. Suddenly the empty nest is filling up again and that's going to cost more money.

- Put yourself first. The only person who can save for *your* retirement is *you*. Get your financial house in order before you try to take on the needs of your parents or your adult children. Debt to personal disposable income is the best calculation you can use to assess your financial situation, and may be calculated rather obviously by comparing your debt to your income.

My personal definition of retirement is: "The point in your life where work is optional; play and leisure time are affordable." With that in mind, I know there are many Baby Boomers who are reassessing their retirement plans, accepting that they'll have to work past the traditional retirement age of 65 years. Some are even considering the advantages of a phased or gradual retirement to help provide continued income. 60% of the Boomers are concerned that personal debt will be a challenge and will be a factor in preventing a retirement that allows them to stop working completely. They are also facing concerns about the ongoing effects of economic volatility with the possibility of significant inflation, rising health-care and long term care costs and longer life expectancy. On top of those concerns, let's throw in future reductions in pension benefits and the increased age of qualification for Social Security benefits. We seem to be looking at a Perfect Storm, but one that has been brewing for many, many years.

Many Boomers and seniors have unfulfilled dreams and desires that they should be able to start pursuing as they age. Some may decide to re-direct their lives either towards voluntary and charitable enterprises or to begin new careers, moving towards the passion that has always been dormant but can now be realized. With increased longevity and overall improved level of health, Boomers have the time and energy to pursue new avenues and reach their goals. With their experience and the wisdom of age, Baby Boomers still have much to give, even in their later years. Indeed, yesterday, I read an article stating that many businesses prefer hiring seniors as they have the wisdom of their years and a better work ethic than some of the younger generation. Boomers or Seniors who do continue working or who do get involved are able to avoid some of the more negative effects that often accompany full retirement: depression, feeling a loss of self, or withdrawal from social interaction, to name a few. Gradual retirement allows an individual to come to terms with a changing status while also allowing time to adjust to a reduced income and an assessment of future needs. The free time someone gains through gradual retirement also provides a great opportunity to reassess one's life path. Finally, there is time to step off the Hamster Wheel of Life, as you are no longer driven by the time and financial commitments of family. Re-evaluation of a life needs time for thought and a phased retirement offers the luxury of having time to reflect on life and plan for the future.

I mentioned above that my personal definition of retirement is: "The point in your life where work is optional while play and leisure time are affordable." I created the Annuity Safe Zone® within Premier Annuity Source with that definition in mind. At Barnowski Financial Group we believe it is important to focus not just on the money but on the whole person—their family, their lifestyle, their needs, and their wants. We like to promote "The Four Biggies," and, although our expertise (as you'll soon understand) falls quite obviously under Biggie #4, each of these Biggies is intertwined because without one you probably won't have the others.

WHAT MAKES BOOMERS SLEEP WELL AT NIGHT? I CALL THEM THE FOUR BIGGIES

After spending 22 years in the financial services industry and interviewing thousands of retirees I've boiled it down to four basics that if you think about it, without one, you probably are going to suffer a loss in at least one if not more, of the others. So what are the FOUR Biggies?

1. **Good Health** – My grandmother used to say… "If you don't have your health, you don't have much." Maintaining your health as you age will not only prolong your life, but also make your years in retirement more active and enjoyable.

2. **Mobility** – If you don't have your health, one of the important things that you give up is your ability to be mobile, whether that means having to give up your driver's license or something as simple as getting out and taking a walk.

3. **Socialization** – If you lose your ability to stay mobile, more than likely you will also forfeit your option to socialize. Socialization is key to maintaining your physical and mental stimulation as well as adding balance to your life through activity.

4. **Sustainable Income for life** – This means that every morning, every week and every year you wake up knowing without a doubt in your mind that you will have adequate funds and an income stream to last you your entire lifespan. Knowing this not only alleviates stress, it also gives you avenues to the best health care and medical treatment – which brings you full circle back to #1.

HOW TO CAPTURE THE ELUSIVE SUSTAINABLE INCOME FOR LIFE... AND PEACE OF MIND

A recent study by the U.S. Census Bureau revealed that 45 percent of Americans feel that Social Security and Medicare will be a major source of their retirement survival. Only about 15 per cent of those surveyed said they had any investments to prepare for life after 65. What this means is that, with regards to Social Security... you have to get it right.

There are only three ways of generating sustainable income for life with any sort of guarantee and a cost of living increase. In order to maximize and ensure your income stream, it's critical to get each one of these dialed in and optimized:

1. **Social Security** – The prospect of retirement is becoming an increasing concern for many baby boomers who often file for Social Security benefits as early as possible in order to secure their finances. In fact, 72% currently drawing Social Security started early, the first chance they could – at age 62 – not knowing that if they waited they could increase their benefit by 45% if they waited until after age 65 or a whopping 98% if they were able to postpone until age 70. However, patience and professional guidance can help boomers avoid financial mistakes and make sound investments so they can retire comfortably. Getting this right is critical in order to squeeze every dime possible out of this benefit that you worked so hard to acquire.

Common mistakes Boomers make when filing for Social Security Benefits:

- **Filing for Benefits Too Early**: Although a person can begin receiving Social Security benefits at age 62, this is generally not a wise move, barring extreme financial or medical hardship. There is often a significant difference between early Social Security benefits and the amount you can receive at retirement age or beyond, as benefits that are cashed in early are only worth a fraction of what you have earned. In addition, once you have applied for benefits, the rate becomes fixed and can only be increased by an estimated cost of living adjustment. Conversely, filing for Social Security after your full retirement age nets you an additional percentage for each year you wait, which provides a much more favorable return than most other investment strategies could.

- **Following the Advice of Non-Experts**: Well-meaning friends and family may try to convince you to pursue certain avenues for retirement, but you must remind yourself that it is easy to know what to do when someone else's money is at stake. Your best course of action is to seek out a financial expert who specializes in Social Security planning with in-depth knowledge of benefits optimization. This will ensure that you can get the most out of your benefits, striking the ideal balance between the amount of money you receive and the amount of time you must wait for it.

2. **Pensions** – Few people realize this, but back in the 1980's 80% of the United States workforce had a pension plan. That number has shrunk to a mere 40% offering instead a 401(k). Converting this asset to your own pension plan requires some planning and can be the largest investment besides your home that you will ever make, but it can be done. If you are lucky enough to have a pension plan, it's critical to understand the risks of doing so once you are retired since you often have a choice to leave those funds alone in lieu of an income stream or take it in a lump sum. It's important to know that if your company pension plan fails, you won't necessarily end up without any retirement income. Most traditional pension plans, but not 401(k)s, are insured by the Pension Benefit Guaranty Corporation up to certain annual limits. The maximum annual

guarantee for a 65-year-old retiree whose pension plan ends in 2013 will be $57,477.24, up from $55,840.92 in 2012.

3. **Annuities** – With the unstable economy still a major factor in investments, retirement planning is a bigger challenge than ever. However, financial advisers and analysts are increasingly turning to annuities as the answer to this instability. The investment safety offered by annuities is a welcomed guarantee in such a volatile market, making annuities the best option for many retirees. There are a number of benefits to owning an annuity, including asset preservation and safe appreciation as well as giving you a guaranteed income for life. Annuities are safe, secure investments offering a guaranteed minimum rate of return. Although they will never make you rich, they are ideal for asset preservation and safe appreciation, and can become supplemental security income, the only vehicle that will fill your income gap on an insured basis.

The concept of retiring, giving up that regular paycheck and interacting on a daily basis with coworkers, can be a stressful transition. The environment, economics and strategies have changed significantly over the last decade or so and unfortunately, the financial services industry is lagging in its response to the needs of the Boomer generation. There is a massive difference between accumulating wealth and financial assets and transitioning those assets in the fourth quarter of your life to an income stream that will last a lifetime. My opinion is that eliminating doubts, question marks and uncertainty not only adds to your quality of life, it also gives you the confidence to Plan Smart… Retire Right… and Sleep Well!

About Carl

Upon graduating from Purdue University, Carl A. Barnowski found he had a passion for developing new approaches that would equip Baby Boomers with financial security at a time when many of that generation had little to no retirement plan in place.

At a time when many of his peers were singularly focused on helping only themselves, Carl was hard at work developing new ways for pre-retirement Boomers to achieve access to the Four Biggies: Good Health, Mobility, Socialization, and Guaranteed Income for Life. For Carl, the first three Biggies were directly impacted by the fourth. With Guaranteed Income for Life secured, retirees would be better able to enjoy Good Health, Mobility, and Socialization because, unlike so many other Americans, their financial futures wouldn't require them to "work until they drop." In 1992, he established a financial advisory firm that educated his clients and provided access to carefully-researched investment products that would allow them to enjoy the Four Biggies.

Promoting this approach through weekly speaking engagements around the country, as well as through appearances on World Business Review on CNBC, Carl relocated his family from Indianapolis to West Palm Beach, FL in 2002. It was there that he founded Premier Annuity Source, LLC, a media company whose sole purpose is to positively impact the financial industry by creating a safe, transparent and interactive environment for principal-protected annuity contract holders. He has since established four Premier Annuity Source locations: Circle City Annuity Source, Inc. (Indianapolis, IN); South Florida Annuity Source, Inc. (Palm Beach, FL); Gulf Coast Annuity Source, Inc. (Sarasota, FL); and Kansas City Annuity Source, Inc. (Kansas City, MO).

Carl was enjoying the success of his endeavors, but knew that that his vision of innovation beyond the familiar was going to require him to make a more profound impact on local and global levels. This desire to serve led to the 2011 founding of Premier Annuity Source Foundation, Inc. Directors and advisors in the Foundation supply their time and efforts for no pay thus ensuring that all proceeds go directly to organizations in need. The funds they distribute are derived from a percentage of revenue received in the form of franchising fees, royalties, commission over-rides, and bonuses paid out from offices nationwide.

In 2013, Carl founded Barnowski Financial Group, thus allowing him to further broaden the scope of his vision to serve not just the financial needs of individuals, but to provide them with education and access to resources that would ensure their enjoyment of all Four Biggies. He continues to promote change in the financial services industry as a whole.

Still living in West Palm Beach, FL, Carl balances his professional and family life with dedication and commitment. When he's not working to help others succeed, you will find him at his sons' baseball and football games, or cheering for his daughter's volleyball team. His passion for life and his commitment to making a positive difference in people's lives continues to develop as he branches out into new endeavors.

CHAPTER 18

SUCCESS UNDER ATTACK IN AMERICA — THE 3 BIGGEST THREATS

BY CURVIN MILLER

I can imagine over the past few years you've experienced ups and downs, financially and emotionally, and that has caused stress in your life. On the flipside, I am sure you have a lot to be grateful for. Where you are today is a result of the cumulative decisions you've made. I know it sounds heavy, but think back 5, 10 and 15 years, and how one decision could have changed where you are now.

So in a book about success, I questioned, what is success? As you know, success doesn't come easy. As an advocate who represents successful, self-made millionaires, my definition is based on the single belief that if I don't do everything in my power to help you craft a personal strategy that addresses major risks and problems, then you may struggle with success in retirement. My goal today (and moving forward) is to help Americans succeed in an environment where success is under attack and portrayed as something to be ashamed of.

You are retiring in an uncertain time. For the first time in our history, our country is experiencing serious growing pains. We are broke. According to Stan Collendar, one of the world's leading experts on the U.S. budget and congressional budget process, "Social Security is projected to be out of money by 2035 and, even worse, Medicare by 2018." Turning your head and pretending that the monster doesn't exist will lead to pain

175

– emotional and financial. There's not a quick fix as <u>this is the NEW normal</u>.

The good news is that successful people are made in good times and in bad times. So, it has nothing to do with the "times" as long as you possess the right knowledge and take the right action.

THE 3 BIGGEST THREATS TO YOUR SUCCESS

1. HIGHER TAXES

2. INFLATION

3. WRONG KIND OF DIVERSIFICATION

> *"The surest way to accumulate wealth is to not pay tax on income you are not using"*
>
> -John D. Rockefeller

1. ***HIGHER TAXES*** - It's what's left *after tax* that counts. The less you give to the government, the more for you and your loved family.

I have a multi-millionaire client who had been extremely active in following his investments for years before our initial meeting, yet he never considered a proactive strategy that addressed advanced tax planning as a part of his financial planning (most disturbing to me that no one, including his financial planner at a major brokerage firm, and tax preparer, ever taught him the importance of having a complementary strategy).

I asked him when the last time his advisor asked to see a copy of his tax return. Silence. It was at this moment that I literally watched a light bulb go on above his head. Let me tell you a dirty little secret: There are two sets of tax laws in this country, one for the informed and one for the uninformed. And guess who pays more tax? Investment performance, as it is marketed by the financial services industry, is typically the perceived measure of success (or failure) of an investment. The key word is perceived, not what is real. Real returns are after tax. What made a bigger impression on him is that he could potentially increase his real return (and income needed to support his retirement), if he invested in a tax-efficient way or utilized tax-reduction strategies.

Why is this story so important? Because the trend in the USA is to higher taxes. It is the new normal. Mark my words; you will see additional tax increases in future years. How else are we going to pay for 17 trillion of current debt and a projected $67.7 trillion in future unfunded liabilities (source: Fiscal Year 2012 Financial Report of the United States Government, US Dept. of Treasury, January 17th, 2013) over the next 20 years without raising taxes? Of course this assumes we don't file bankruptcy sooner. According to the American Tax Payer Relief Act of 2012 (ATRA), in 2013 there were 3 new tax laws...that create 7 new ways taxes are affected...based on 3 different income levels...figured 4 different ways. This is the beginning.

Why are you in the crosshairs? It's because your largest asset is your retirement account (IRA, 401(k), 403(b), TSP, etc.). This money has never been taxed and when you need it, it will be taxed in this rising US tax environment, *leaving you and your family with less.*

If you agree with me that it's only what's after tax that counts, what are you doing to TODAY to protect yourself in the future?

I continually train with a Jedi IRA master named Ed Slott, CPA, who is considered by Wall Street Journal to be one of the best possible sources of IRA advice. By attending Master Elite IRA Advisor training conferences twice a year, we dissect the tax code and learn how to apply it to our high net worth clients' money. Why would any sane individual keep a copy of section 590 in his nightstand and continually study the tax code?

Because being informed gives you an advantage over others who aren't paying attention.

No one is above the law, no one is below the law, every person is held to the same letter of the law, but whoever is informed, succeeds. Amateur hour is over in the financial industry. It's time to graduate to the big leagues. Find an advisor with the skills to manage your hard-earned dough with taxes in mind.

2. *INFLATION -* It's hard to argue that there is an absence of leadership in Washington. Inflation is a debt problem that will cause future pain. It's not because of growth. Here's why:

I could get technical and talk about money supply multiplied by velocity defining inflation, but I will spare you and get to the point: It means your money buys less. A gallon of milk will cost $20 as opposed to $4. This is really bad if you are retired, relying on a fixed income to pay the bills and supplementing that income with your savings. If your assets are not insulated from this "hidden tax", you could run out of money quickly in retirement.

I am surprised people in Washington are not paying closer attention to past instances of inflation. Citizens of Germany in the 1920's (Weimar Republic) and Zimbabwe in 2007-2008 can tell you all about the evils of inflation. Can you imagine buying food with wheelbarrow full of cash? Can you imagine having a $10 trillion dollar bill in your wallet that is worth less that $20 today? Why is the US running the printing presses at full speed, trying to "quantitatively ease" our pains and conjuring up ideas of minting trillion dollar platinum proof coins to solve our budget problems? It's like a drug addict who keeps using and making excuses for why he can't quit. I believe the end result will not be good.

We currently borrow .42 cents for every dollar we have to spend (Spending to GDP Ratio = - 42.5% — June 2013, USDebtClock.org). If you look at other examples of inflation throughout world history, you will find a common theme: poor understanding of debits and credits and paying the bills? Why would the USA be any different?

Do you have investments that will keep pace and fight inflation or ones that will run the other way when inflation becomes real? Long-term bonds and other fixed income investments will suffer the most in an inflationary environment, as we've seen in the past. Stocks and equities tend to do well in moderate inflation, but contrary to popular belief, could be awful in high inflationary times. Every dog has his day. Case in point in the late 80's; not only did we have a stock market crash, but also a bond market crash at the same time due to inflation.

Other investments may do very well. Investments like opportunistic private real estate (important to have the right sectors here), secured floating income, natural resource exploration investments for accredited investors and trend-following managed futures are designed to stare inflation square in the eyes and fight. Understand that this is war (war for your lifestyle) and you need to have the right artillery if you plan to win. All investments, of course, have pros, cons and strings attached, but I believe an allocation of 20-30% to non-correlated investments will give you a far better chance in a government-induced inflationary environment.

> *"Every economic disaster during the last 100 years has its origins in bad government economic policies, from the Smoot-Hawley Tariff, which triggered the Great Depression, to the Federal Reserve's excessive printing of money, which brought us the Great Inflation of the 1970's and the recent housing bubble.*
>
> - Steve Forbes

3. ***THE WRONG KIND OF DIVERSIFICATION*** - What if one of the most fundamental rules of investing that once worked, may be broken now?

   I meet with around a hundred of the brightest, most successful people each year who are concerned about the amount of risk they have in their investments. I hear, "I can't afford to go through another 2008"…or on the other side, "I eat risk for breakfast and truly thought I was diversified in 2008."

You are always told that the market goes up over time (what I call Buy, Hold and Pray Investing), but after looking at your statements and you wonder why your money is still worth what it was years ago.

Even though you may have diversified sectors and fund types, having all of your money in the market can subject you to loss by events and occurrences that are outside of your control. Rick Santelli, daily commentator for CNBC, likes to call these occurrences "Tape Bombs", but simply put, they are daily events like world news from China / Europe / North Korea, flash crashes, terrorist acts, natural disasters and so on. These events can cause unexpected volatility in the markets.

I get it, when there's uncertainty, we as humans tend to sell our winners and losers based on an emotional feeling we have. This is natural human behavior. If you are nervous about losing your retirement savings, there are 76 million Baby Boomers possibly thinking the same thing. Don't get caught in the herd. Unfortunately, when you invest in mutual funds or other correlated investments, you become the herd. The sell decisions of others can force you to unknowingly sell a portion of your assets at the wrong time, thus dragging down the value of your investments.

True diversification is that of multiple asset classes that are not correlated with each other. The wealthiest endowments, institutions and people utilize this investment concept.

Years ago, we integrated this concept of true diversification for our high net worth clients. We refer to this concept as *building* your Fiscal House™. The beauty of this strategy is its sophisticated simplicity. If you can't conceptually understand it, then how do you ever plan to sleep at night?

So, visualize your dream home. What characteristics does it have: A solid foundation, sturdy, well-insulated walls, and a one-of-a kind roof? You want this high-end home to withstand powerful storms and provide years of entertainment and comfort. Don't you want the same for your portfolio and retirement? Something you can count on when the perfect storm hits?

So let's build yours:

ROOF: These Investments are defined as money that you can lose due to forces outside of your control (and your advisor's control); like the "tape bombs" discussed above. The opportunity for higher returns exists in the roof, but you also take the most risk here (high liquidity here too).

The rule in determining how much you should have in the roof is based upon a simple formula called the <u>Prudent Investor Rule</u>:

1. Take the number 100
2. Subtract your age
3. What's left equals the maximum percentage of your money you should have in the Roof

Examples include: Mutual Funds, Equities, ETFs, Hedge Funds, etc. The key here is that Buy, Hold and Pray doesn't work in today's markets, rather, you must be proactive in this 24-hour news, information-packed world today.

WALLS: These are alternative, non-market-correlated investments. You want them to be well insulated from the unexpected storms that impact the roof. I look for three key characteristics here:

1. Not market correlated

2. Emphasis on cash flow and dividends

3. Tend to be inflation protected

    *BONUS – Potential Tax Efficiency

Examples include: Opportunistic Private Real Estate, Secured Floating Income, Trend Following Managed Futures and Natural Resource Exploration Investments. The key here is that hard assets tend to back these investments as collateral, thus there is some insulation against market volatility and an emphasis on inflation protection.

FOUNDATION: Here is the salt of the earth, contractually guaranteed stuff that will be there for you when you need it, especially for income. Ever heard a good defense is sometimes better than a good offense. I can imagine that you may feel this way if you're transitioning into retirement. In a very uncertain world, the foundation provides certainty and is critical for your peace of mind.

Examples include: bank CDs, US Treasuries and Fixed / Hybrid Annuities among others. The key here is to have a contract between you and strong institutions that will protect your money. Interest earned can vary depending on how long you hold the investment. Also important to consider methods in which interest is paid.

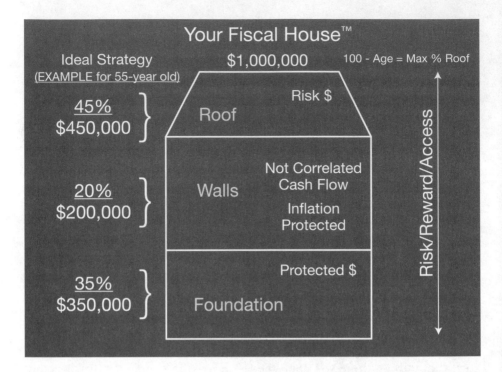

Well there you have it. The three biggest threats to your success. Any one of them could derail your future plans, but combined with others, could create more certain problems. You only get one chance to be successful in retirement. Don't be the person who looks into the rearview mirror with regret and wishes things had turned out differently if only you would have trusted what you knew was right. There is plenty of hype out there. I ultimately, do not care what you invest your hard earned dollars in, as long as there is a plan to address the above threats and your personal concerns. There are thousands of options for investments, but there is only one WHY. Why is it you invest the way you do? What are you hoping to accomplish by holding a particular investment? Why is it important to you?

Living a successful retirement is different than thinking about a successful retirement. It's not going to be easy. You must find the right advice-giver who can coordinate a team of professionals to help you get it right the first time. I sincerely wish you the best.

About Curvin

Curvin E. Miller IV, CRPC has been Vice President for 9 years of Russell & Company - Total Wealth Management in Dayton, OH. He is a contributor to various national financial programs and publications, including CNBC, Fox Business, *Forbes* and *Financial Advisor* Magazine.

He was a keynote speaker in Times Square, NYC in June of 2013 at the Success in the New Economy Summit along with Steve Forbes. Curvin hosts live educational events throughout the year where he teaches members of his community on various topics relating to retirement planning, including the impact of taxes, inflation, lack of true diversification, and ways to create comprehensive income plans.

Curvin hosts Retirement Rescue Radio every Saturday at 1 pm on WHIO News Talk Radio, 95.7 FM and AM 1290 (RescueYourRetirementRadio.com). He also hosts *Retiring Well*, seen Sunday's on FOX 45, Sunday's at 10 am.

Curvin was recipient of the Top Forty Professionals Under 40 by the Dayton Business Journal in 2010. Curvin is a frequent contributor to the Dayton Daily News and has also been a special guest on WDTN Channel 2 and FOX 45 in Dayton, OH, as well as WLWT Channel 5 and Local 12 WKRC-TV in Cincinnati discussing Retirement Planning, Taxes, Roth Conversions and Social Security.

Curvin's firm was the subject of a documentary produced by an Emmy award-winning producer called, *Filling the Financial Gap* and aired on the Bio Channel in Fall of 2012.

Curvin has been a member of the Ed Slott's Master Elite IRA Advisor group since 2007, is a registered representative through Kalos Capital, Inc., is an investment advisor representative (IAR) through Kalos Management, Inc. and is a Chartered Retirement Planning Counselor designee (CRPC®) through the College of Financial Planning.

He is married to his wife, Emily and they live in Beavercreek, OH. They have two awesome, little boys together, Curvin V and Colin. The Miller family is also active in Southbrook Christian Church in Miamisburg, OH.

For more information visit the website: www.TotalWealthAdvice.com.

CHAPTER 19

LEADERSHIP THRU PASSION: YOUR CRITICAL KEY TO SUCCESS IN THE NEW ECONOMY

BY GARY LEVESQUE

Leadership: *a process of <u>social influence</u> in which one person can enlist the aid and <u>support</u> of others in the accomplishment of a common <u>task.</u>*

Passion: *(from the Latin verb patī meaning to suffer) a term applied to a very strong feeling about a person or thing. Passion is an intense <u>emotion</u>, compelling feeling, enthusiasm, or <u>desire</u> for something.*

Government spending is out of control. Until recently, stimulus money was being injected into the market at a rate of $85 Billion (with a "B") per month while record numbers of people were unable to find work or receive adequate medical care. And that's just in the United States. What's the solution to this dilemma? Most free market experts would agree we should let the business world do what it does best – let Entrepreneurs provide ingenious solutions to otherwise complex problems. Government agencies should get out of the way. Small business owners will lead us out of this crazy situation. As an Entrepreneur you can be part of that solution. The question is now, "How do you stand out in a sea of competitors?"

Do you have an unfair advantage that puts you at the top of the heap in your niche? What is it that makes you attract new clients and customers at a faster rate than your competition? What is the one single thing that keeps bringing your customers coming back to you for repeat purchases? Do you know what makes you stand out from your competition in today's economy?

If you couldn't answer these questions with ease until now then you are in luck. The answer is quite simple. It may surprise you to learn how inexpensive it is to launch yourself past your competitors with what you are about to learn. Now the title of this chapter may give away the secret at first, … or so you may think.

Before we start you will want to know why you should listen to me? The answer is that I want to help you become part of the economic solution. Simply put, this text will help you make a lot more money than you thought possible and will leave your competition far behind you. Applying this simple principle will make you a Leader in your field and as a Leader you must have respect in order to be successful. You can either Demand respect, or Command respect. Applying what you learn here will help you Command respect from your competition as well as your peers.

Why should you care? Success in the New Economy depends on a variety of factors from having sound economics to picking the proper niche, hiring the right people at the right time for the right job, communicating the right message to the right target market, etc., etc., etc. The list can appear to be endless. The one key factor to "Successonomics" that you must pay close attention to is *the art of standing apart* from your competition. If you don't find a way to stand out in the middle of the crowd, your business will not survive the long haul in a competitive market. The information age gives consumers more than what they need in terms of content. Your job will be to "sell" them on the idea that you are the best to provide what they need and Lead them to Success.

In essence, you should care because your business survival may depend on it. This one simple key to your success will make you more money than you could imagine and leave your competition in the dust all in a single stroke. It comes down to basic sales dominance by the "Attract don't sell" mentality. We sell ourselves, our goods/services in order to make a profit but today's client/ customer or patient relies on having established a relationship with you in order to feel comfortable and confident enough to come back for repeat business.

Today's savvy consumer wants you to show them you care. They want to see your *Passion* – THAT is the key to your Success in the New Economy. Your *Passion* for the audience you serve will attract the right client to you instead of you having to chase down and work the prospect who may not necessarily relate to you on the level needed for them to make that purchase.

By letting your *Passion* shine through in your business you will naturally attract the right niche client while having unconnected prospects "self-select" themselves out. Those who don't relate to your product on the emotional level we are talking about should be ignored/passed over and your efforts should be focused on the hyper-responsive prospects who engage you because of your passion. The results will amaze you. Your economics will naturally become efficient, because you will no longer be wasting time and money on those difficult potential buyers who were going to take a lot of effort to convert. You will be "lowering the fruit on the branches" versus having to climb up there yourself.

By allowing yourself to show your passion, you will become known by clients for being real, and being real is what many consumers are seeking these days. But what does this have to do with "Success in the New Economy" and why listen to me? Well, I am also an Entrepreneur and I've learned a few things throughout my 20+ years in small business. From hustling for gigs as a DJ in my early days to now educating soon-to-be-retiring (or recently retired) military persons how to start a business with absolutely no previous business experience, I have found the one true thing that helps you standout in the market. "Your *Passion* will set you FREE!" You MUST let your *Passion* shine through for others to see. The results will simply amaze you. Showing your *Passion* will make you a Leader in your field.

There are many books published on the topic of Leadership. It is a skill to be developed over time -- and acquired with experience -- as you progress through you career. Whether you're a seasoned businessperson or still an employee looking to make that leap to becoming an Entrepreneur, you have the ability to *Lead*. You will find volumes upon volumes of free readings in the library and on the Internet regarding leadership. But those tomes will not explain to you how to be yourself in order to grow a profitable business.

As you invest time in your own education, you are seeking for that key piece of knowledge that will make you stand apart from your competition. You can spend money to acquire an education. You may even hire someone with the knowledge you lack to do a certain job for you. Those are resources you dedicate to acquiring renewable assets. The one and only non-renewable asset everyone possesses is TIME, and you want to know your time is spent effectively and efficiently when you invest it in something. Fear not my friend! Your time spent here will be well worth it for you.

If you have carefully selected and researched your business and the surrounding markets, you will have studied competitors and peers alike. You will have chosen a business that speaks to you and one that you can dedicate yourself to on a full time basis. To survive in business you must have a true passion for the niche you have chosen. It is that passion that you will need to harness and let shine through in everything you do, everything you write, everything you create for your business. From Mission Statements to Marketing Messages and everything in between. Your *Passion* is your key to success because when things start to go wrong, it will be your Passion that will keep your customers coming to you.

YES, you heard me! It is your *Passion* that will keep your customers buying from you. Your *Passion* will not only keep you going when times are tough, it will keep your employees motivated as you lead them out of that rough patch. It will faithfully keep your clients coming back. Why?!? Because your *Passion* will reveal parts of your personality and that will build relationships with your leads, prospects and customers (new or existing).

In today's information age, it is increasingly difficult to nurture meaningful relationships. The nature of business makes it even more difficult because we are taking money from people in a transaction. It's nothing to be ashamed of but having to pay money adds a certain level of expectation on behalf of the one paying it. Having an established relationship prior to taking any money will make the exchange much easier to do. You must build a relationship with your prospects and clients, and work hard at nurturing that relationship. Letting your *Passion* shine in everything you do will create a bond and affinity to your client.

Even though we are always "selling" ourselves, in terms of business, you should concentrate on "attracting vs. selling." Whether you realise it or not, you are constantly selling your ideas, your image, yourself. You want others to like you and your brand. Mark Zuckerberg from Facebook got that part absolutely right – people want to be liked!

When people like you they take interest in you. They will listen to you – you'll have their attention. When you have their attention, you want to show them part of your true self and that is where the *Passion* comes in. That *Passion* will naturally attract those who share your interest, and push away those who do not. By doing so, you will be separating yourself from the competition as you acquire better-qualified clients and more of them. Any existing clients you currently have will be able to provide testimonials on your behalf and that will in turn attract even more new clients, and the cycle goes on and on.

So who can benefit from using this simple technique? Entrepreneurs who want to make money and have more freedom because of the flood of reliable customers you will have lined up at your door (think Apple during the latest iPhone release). It's also for those of us who are NOT that good at putting on "face" for that proverbial sales pitch we need to make. Not everyone is comfortable making that sales pitch. In reality, displaying real *Passion* should be for all Entrepreneurs because attracting that ideal client is so much more cost efficient than chasing after questionable ones. Statistics show it is 7 times more costly to acquire new customers than it is to retain one. Building that affinity allows you to keep that customer you acquired for longer periods of time, causing them to buy more over their lifetime thus raising their final customer value. This will allow you to spend more to acquire customers in the first place (but that is an entirely different topic).

So when should you start showing that new found *Passion* of yours? The BEST time to start is always NOW! Let your true colours shine through. It is essential for you to relate to your niche as soon as possible because nobody wants to deal with a robot. Your visible *Passion* will create stronger bonds with your Team and your clients. It will also allow you to command more in fees because of that strong bond. The "Know, Like & Trust" (KLT) factor will be exponentially higher with you showing your *Passion* as your prospects relate directly to you to become clients. That is why I refer to KLT as BLT (not the sandwich) for "Bond, Like & Trust." That bond will allow you to make mistakes if that ever happens. That same bond will also allow you to try out new material, products and services on your clients because they know what you are passionate about. If your stuff is good, they will let you know, if it isn't, they will let you know. Your bond will give you the flexibility you need to grow your customer relationship and THAT is where your customer's true value is found. Your customer is the ONLY true asset you have in your business.

Who else is talking about "Leadership thru *Passion?*" While watching some episodes of the Dragon's Den and the Shark Tank recently, I observed that the one thing "Sharks & Dragons" look for in deciding whether to support a Business owner's new venture or not, is the owner's *Passion*. Knowing your numbers is critical, but the one intangible is that *Passion*. Mark Cuban, Kevin O'Leary and Barbara Corcoran have all commented on that fact. When I met Mrs. Corcoran in Orlando this past year, she mentioned that very point to me. It was commented directly to me that my Passion for helping retiring military personnel become Entrepreneurs after they hang up the uniform is what people appreciate. My *Passion* attracted them to me. They asked me to tell them more about what I do, and that is the beginning of the relationship.

So now what should you do with this little secret. First, start sharing your passion with others immediately. Show your true colours in your copywriting. When you hire new staff, make certain they understand what your *Passion* is and how it drives everything in your business. When you interview new prospects you should engage them more openly. They will appreciate your candor. If not, they walk away. You will have reduced the time wasted on someone who wasn't going to buy from you, and can then focus on the next prospect in your sales funnel.

Next, eliminate the "vanilla" in your business. **STOP BEING BORING!!!** There is enough boring garbage out there for those who want it, and your clients do NOT want that crap. They want to relate to you and share your passion. You are providing them a service for their money. Show them you genuinely care. If you don't, they will figure it out and shop elsewhere.

Finally, go back to the start of your business and rewrite your Mission Statement. More importantly, post that message everywhere! In your boardroom, on your computer screen, in the lunch room, by your phone and at your front counter or in the waiting area of your office. Tell the entire world what you do and why it drives you to be so passionate about it. The bonds you create and the quality of customer you will have from that point on will be so much more valuable to you and your company. If you build, it they will come. If you're passionate, they will run to you. Remember that you are in business to make money. Your customers know that already. Bond with them. Have them like you. Learn to *Trust* each other because of the affinity you have built by sharing that *Passion*. You will be commanding "Leadership thru Passion" and that will definitely be a key to your Success in the New Economy. That will be part of your Successonomics!

About Gary

Gary Levesque is one of Canada's top Business Consultants, a Best-Selling Author, and the founder of Entrepreneur Soldier, an organization dedicated to assisting retiring Military personnel return to civilian life by empowering them to grow successful businesses. As a 24-year veteran of the Royal Canadian Air Force, and as an accomplished business consultant, Gary has a unique skill set which fuels his life's passion: helping Soldiers. Gary is also known as the creator of the Marketing Sniper System — which helps business owners zero in on their ideal business targets quickly.

A graduate of the Royal Military College of Canada in Business back in 2000, he also studied Economics in Quebec City in the 80's, Commerce & Trade in Halifax, NS during the 90's and Marketing in Kingston, ON and Winnipeg, MB in the early 2000's. Known as a problem solver throughout his military career, Gary has taken his knowledge and experience from both his military and business lives in order to thoroughly analyze his successes (and failures), and brought to life simple and effective business systems that entrepreneurs of all experience levels can implement.

He has spent much of his business career proving his theories in the small business world. During the last three years, with the help of some of his millionaire friends, Gary has been assembling a multitude of business lessons into specific courses. Many of these courses are aimed at helping the NEW businessperson with little to no business experience. Gary has created a building block approach to business systems for folks just like him.

Today, his passion for marketing drives him to seek out the best techniques in the industry and boil them down — so the layperson can use and implement them quickly to maximize return on Investment (ROI). Gary teaches a course entitled "Leadership thru Passion: An Emotional key to Success!" combining his experience as a military trained leader and instructor. His personal journey is no different than anyone else's – filled with ups and downs…successes and failures. Through that journey he has developed a unique approach to simplifying problems down to 1 or 2 basic factors… and then conquering them.

As the first Canadian Certified Business Advisor for Glazer-Kennedy Inner Circle (GKIC), Gary is a results-driven individual who now teaches No B.S. business practices in Victoria, BC. When he isn't teaching marketing or studying the markets for advanced techniques, Gary can be found spending time with his wife Lisa and their two dogs once he is off the ice from playing hockey in the winter, or golfing in the summer.

To learn more visit our site at: www.EntrepreneurSoldier.com, or send us an email at: info@EntrepreneurSoldier.com

CHAPTER 20

FREEDOM TO PROFIT: UNLEASHING THE POWER OF PEOPLE, OUR REAL ADVANTAGE

BY GAYLE E. ABBOTT

The challenge we are facing in the new economy is:

> How do organizations and people move to a whole new level of meaningful, productive, innovative contribution and a higher level of consciousness?

Companies may seem like abstract structures but they are really just people. And, people provide the greatest opportunities and create the greatest complexity for organizations. How people show up and how organizations lead and engage with people make the real difference in achieving short and long term success for the organization, individual, economy and society.

We are on a journey which is requiring us to go to a higher level of consciousness. While there are "bright spots" of real forward movement, issues still to be addressed include:

- How do we more broadly and effectively engage, tap into, and harness the most prevalent natural resource we have – the human being?

- How do we move beyond limiting tendencies such as ego, judgmentalism, limited vision, complacency, criticism, controlling others, self-centeredness, inattention, self-righteousness?
- How do we more effectively see and tap into the potential that exists in each person as a unique individual?
- How do we work together and value each other more?
- How do we go to higher levels of consciousness and proficiency so we can more effectively contribute to achieving practical, real results that truly make this world a better place?

It is time for individuals and organizations to look through a new lens – to view themselves objectively in terms of how they're actually showing up and to carefully evaluate what they're truly capable of. I know some of you may want to stop reading at this point but I encourage you to keep an open mind.

If we look at every advancement throughout history – they all go back to a person or group of people who:

- saw a problem or opportunity
- had a vision for something better
- weren't afraid to look at or do things differently
- created and got results through determination, decisiveness, action and persistence

The people who led us to our current level of evolution challenged the *status quo*, did things in new and different ways, used their minds and leveraged their individual freedoms despite obstacles put in their way. Although many wouldn't admit it, they were also guided and took action based on listening to their inner voice. For example, when you dig deep into the founders of the U.S., you see how their actions and decisions were guided by a higher level of consciousness. They were ahead of their times, had a vision and were willing to do what it took to ensure individual freedoms and create a place where people could use their insights and talents for creating a better world. Yes they had limitations but they also had vision. They knew where to push, where to "plant the seeds" and where to let go and let things evolve on the universe's timeline.

Just as we evolved in the past, now is the time to evolve to the next level. We still have more we can do to move to a higher level of consciousness and better tap into the immense power of the human being – our greatest natural resource. This is the surest and most guaranteed path for achieving a strong and enduring economy and society.

We have done many things which have blocked and stymied human capacity (e.g., controlling or constantly criticizing, enabling, taking away their pride, implementing rigid structures, creating excessive rules). Now we need to find more ways to leverage individual capacities and help people tap into their true potential.

I work with a lot of really bright, talented individuals but I still see opportunities to go to even greater levels of contribution and effectiveness. I see individuals stuck in their own way. They fight, albeit sometimes subtly, to maintain the status quo or hold on to their turf or they "ostracize" or attack those who bring new or different ideas. As a result, they aren't as effective as they could be in letting go, and letting themselves or others come up with ideas, approaches and solutions, which could move things to the next level. And yes, given the way the human brain works, they are usually very effective in rationalizing why.

Digging deeper I've found that the reasons for being stuck or operating at a lower level are bountiful and varied – it may be experiences with a boss, a parent or in school – but the thread is the same – the individual has gifts, talents and potential they haven't tap into or stopped believing in just to get along. In fact, I'll never forget the moment I was working with a group and a light bulb went off! How could we expect people to suddenly be creative, innovative and empowered in the work place when for the most part, (and there are exceptions happening today), our education system, entry level jobs and in fact, society in general, create a very structured environment and rewards those who fit in and don't "color outside the lines."

I'm not by any means advocating mass chaos. There is a place for rules, but when we go too far, when we create too much structure and rote, then we fail to develop and access the real talents and potential of individuals. When we label children who do, learn or see things differently, who can't sit still or have avid curiosity outside the structure as disrupters, we squash some of their inherent potential. This all spills over into the workplace and subsequently the economy.

How many who actively contributed to building, evolving and expanding the economy and world, were individuals who resisted the status quo, who didn't fit the mold or structure, who saw or did things differently? They were the ones who saw an opportunity or problem and had the vision to create something different and better – to innovate and approach things in different ways. They didn't just follow others or implement "best practices" but looked outside the box. Consider just a few who made significant impacts on business or society by doing and seeing things differently – Edison, Einstein, Franklin, Carnegie, Gutenberg, Gates, Jobs, Dyson, King. And yet, despite the examples of these individuals, we continue to proceed for the most part in the way we always have—often only reacting when a crisis hits.

While we bemoan crisis of any kind, some of the greatest strides in companies, society and human evolution have come as a result of it. Why? Because crisis forces us out of our complacency. We have no choice but to do something different, to find a path we wouldn't have consciously followed if we had stayed safe and been left to our own devices.

All the changes and challenges that have been ushering in the new economy, (and they have been occurring on a variety of fronts), are merely there to break us out of our comfort zone, to get us to go way beyond where we've been and provide an opportunity for us to really step back and look at the possibilities.

So what is it going to take to survive and thrive in the new economy?

1. **Make friends with change.** Do it in ways you haven't done or experienced before. Understand—change is part of the process of your evolution as a human being. You can consciously choose to evolve and break through your own limiting barriers or you can be forced to change when the proverbial brick wall falls on you --- the loss of a job, the failure of a company, a wake-up call illness, financial setbacks, divorce, death of a spouse and the list goes on… When we don't evolve we stay stuck and fail to leverage or experience our true potential. Individuals I have worked with who have made the greatest advances and contributions have continued

to learn and grow even when it wasn't comfortable. They have been open to hearing the tough stuff and taking action even when it wasn't easy. Change is not an easy or natural phenomenon and as humans we are much more comfortable staying in the status quo. Now is the time to "step off the cliff" and see where you can really go.

2. **Unlock the creativity and innovation within.** Yes, there are those who are held up as wildly creative and innovative but there are so many more people, who due to subconscious programming, have the capacity but don't recognize it or use it. Look beyond the box and find your inner creativity. Tapping into this creativity and innovation can bring about a new future and economy not even conceived of at this time.

3. **Increase your use of discernment and "critical" thinking.** Ask tough questions. Dig deep. Assess what's real and what isn't. Listen to your inner voice. Don't automatically accept what someone else says. Use your brain and intuition at new levels and in new ways.

4. **Objectively assess and look at your organization through a new lens.** Organizations are people and people are organizations. If you lead a company, now is the time to objectively look at yourself and your organization to honestly assess where you are and what you could be doing to better leverage the individual talents and capacities that come together to create and deliver your products, services and, ultimately, your profitability. This often requires some real paradigm shifts on the part of individuals in management and leadership. It requires conscious acting on the fact that organizations are people and people are more complex than any piece of equipment or spreadsheet. Over the last 30 plus years, I've seen many organizations lose profitability and competitive edge or even fail, especially when times are changing, because leaders got lost in ego, complacency, hubris, or listening only to the "yes people" who said what they wanted to hear. Other contributing factors included doing the wrong things at the wrong time, rationalizing the status quo, ignoring the "little" signs, pursuing "quick fixes," not using critical thinking and being a follower. Companies that create enduring success:

a. Create their own authentic culture.

b. Ensure clarity and alignment.

c. Leverage and develop the talents of their people.

d. Take full accountability for their actions and results instead of spending their time complaining or attacking others who are succeeding.

e. Continually do critical thinking and engage in meaningful and deliberative discussions.

f. Consistently innovate and identify ways to go to new levels of productivity and contribution.

g. Understand and actively act on the fact that people are the business. They know that every advance or misstep by a company is really only one made by a person or group of people.

With that in mind, successful companies make the time and effort, which can be uncomfortable, to determine the best way to unlock the real potential of people. They hold leaders and managers accountable for developing and engaging people as opposed to creating fearful, robotic, unengaged, insecure people who aren't contributing to their full capacity. They set the bar higher instead of dropping to the lowest common denominator. They understand that many a person has become disengaged and unproductive because of being mismanaged. They have high expectations for their managers as developers of people.

Identify ways your company can more effectively unleash and engage the hearts, minds and capacity of the people who make up your organization. Recognize the impact of people on your sustainable profitability. Help your managers become more effective in their role as coaches and developers of people. Hold them accountable for doing so.

5. **Increase your own individual self-awareness and awareness of others.** Assess yourself with brutal honesty. More importantly, take real substantive action based on that awareness. In the new economy, you are going to need to tap more deeply into your inner power and take greater responsibility for going to higher levels of consciousness and effectiveness yourself. We have found that as humans we often need multiple insights in different ways, at

different times to truly become aware. Even the most successful individuals have untapped opportunities and potential to grow and become even better so they can contribute at even higher levels. While "behavioral style" assessments, which help people understand how they do what they do and how they are seen by others abound, they only scratch the surface. Insights from them moved us to where we are today. However, to move to the next level we have to be willing to move beyond the quick and easy to real substantive understanding—which only comes by going deeper. It's about becoming objectively aware of our acumen, cognitive valuing processes, emotional intelligence, beliefs, life purpose, destiny, and other more esoteric factors. More fully tap into the true potential that lies within you. Learn those things you're here to learn so you don't repeat them. Fulfill your purpose.

6. **Make sure you aren't unconsciously getting in your own way.** We consistently see the impact of beliefs or paradigms when we see individuals or companies that are not meeting their objectives, struggling, trying to transition, unclear on direction, or failing. Research has indicated that 95% of our conscious actions are actually driven by our subconscious and unconscious beliefs. That means that we show up, take actions, solve problems and make decisions based on things we're not even aware are influencing us. And this is where it gets interesting–our beliefs, that we're not even consciously aware of, limit fulfilling our true potential and achieving what we're here to achieve. We unknowingly sabotage ourselves in some areas of our life as a result of beliefs we don't even know we have. The good news is – today we have the methodologies to identify those beliefs, and then, using techniques that tap into our super-conscious, quickly and rapidly change one within 10 to 30 minutes. Get out of your own way. Stop letting limiting beliefs keep you unknowingly stuck. Create, at a super-conscious level, a new set of empowering beliefs.

7. **Move past fear into confidence.** You have the resources within you to tackle the challenges that come your way. Only by finding your inner strength and moving past "fear" can you make the full contribution of which you're capable. Fear in many daily situations is only in our head. Do something, even if only baby steps. You're

still moving forward. And, with each step and victory you'll become more confident and have more success.

There are so many ways to succeed in the new economy. Join those individuals who are on track for bringing about authentic change. Ask yourself:

- Am I ready to take the next step, to find out what my real destiny and potential are, to contribute at a whole new level?
- What am I capable of that I don't even consciously know or recognize at this time?
- What are others around me capable of–which I'm not recognizing?
- What unconscious or subconscious beliefs might I have that are limiting me?
- What's my next step?

The world around you is constantly whispering insights to you. Listen for that whisper, become aware of the subtle signals and see how much more of the human potential you can tap into.

About Gayle

Gayle Abbott, President and CEO, Strategic Alignment Partners, Inc. and Mind Soul Academy works with boards of directors, executives, leaders, high potentials and teams to fulfill more of their potential and facilitate their achieving their strategic initiatives and practical performance results. She is passionate about helping people and organizations move to new levels on their journey. In doing this, she uses her sixth sense, practical business techniques and tools, the esoteric sciences and her expertise in people, communication, critical thinking, practical results and business strategy and execution to help move individuals and organizations to the next level of performance. She is an entrepreneur and leader who has run a successful company for over 20 years.

She is a co-author in two best-selling books, *Think and Grow Rich Today* and *New Rules of Success.* She has been on America's Premier Experts which aired on ABC, NBC, CBS and Fox and was in the August 2013 Edition of Fast Company. She has previously been quoted in several articles in CBS *MoneyWatch,* businessnewsdaily. com and *CEO Update* and had an article on Competencies in the magazine, *Dollars and Sense.* She previously co-authored *Deflecting Workplace Violence.*

Ms. Abbott speaks on such topics as:

- Success Doesn't Wear A Watch
- Mind Your P's and You – CEO Strategies for the New Economy
- Increase Your Profitability and Leverage Your Time: Keys to Grow Your Business
- Strategic Alignment for Increased Productivity and ROI
- Achieving Your Summit: Strategies for Personal and Career SuccessSelecting and Retaining Top Performing Talent in a Competitive Market
- Using Competencies to Develop and Get Better Results through People
- It's Not What You Know but What You Do
- Increasing Your Leadership Effectiveness"

Ms. Abbott has served as an adjunct faculty member at Marymount University and American University. She has her BA from American University and her MBA from Loyola College. She is a certified Growth Curve Strategist and is TriMetrix® HD certified and Emotional Quotient certified.

Ms. Abbott has won several awards for outstanding leadership the Lodestar Award and Alumni Recognition Award from American University. She has been listed in: *Who's Who in America, Who's Who in the South and Southwest, Who's Who in Finance and Industry* and *Who's Who in American Women.*

On her journey she has experienced extensive personal growth and achieved her successes to this point by seeing the opportunities in and overcoming a variety of life challenges–such as the bad manager, divorce, being widowed unexpectedly, and financial challenges to name a few. She has learned that while we are continually learning and growing that if we leverage our gifts and get on the right path for ourselves there's no end to the possibilities of what we can do and contribute.

A few of her other passions include spending time with her daughter and their two Husky's, travel, reading, visiting museums, and being outdoors whether by the water, in the woods or by the mountains.

CHAPTER 21

RETIREMENT SUCCESS IN THE NEW ECONOMY

BY GREG TAYLOR

I was recently asked to teach a class to a group of people who were retired or within five years of retirement. Before I began my class I asked what were their primary goals and concerns as they began this new phase of their lives. One gentleman spoke up that he didn't want the government to have a hand in his retirement. A dear lady mentioned that she was very concerned with the prospect of a long-term illness taking away the family savings. Another said that her biggest concern was the possibility of outliving what she had saved for her retirement. One person after another chimed in with great concerns such as Obamacare, taxes and our national debt. The thing that stood out to me as I listened, was that these people had so many concerns that they didn't allow themselves to even think about the goals and dreams that they have for retirement. Welcome to the New Economy.

This New Economy brings with it some challenges that previous generations never had to face. Who would have believed that America would have over 17 trillion dollars of debt and would continue to borrow or print money that it did not have in order to increase that debt. National healthcare never seemed possible and social security actually seemed to be secure. If you listen to many of the doom and gloom hosts of national radio and television talk shows you may begin to think that there is no hope for America or for you. But I am one that likes to view things from the positive side. I still believe the glass is half-full. Oftentimes, the difference between success and failure is based on the preparation we make to achieve success. In other words, *we can stumble into failure but we must plan to succeed.* If we are to be able to properly plan, we must understand the rules of the game.

Just two days ago a lady came to meet with me after hearing my radio show. As we began, I asked as I always do, "what concerns or goals do have that you would like to discuss today? She said, "Greg, the reason I am here today is because I need hope. I have listened to so many people that have me too scared to do anything. I would like to take a trip to Asheville, North Carolina but I am afraid that Obama will enact Marshall Law and I won't be able to get back home." She had done some good things financially to be able to enjoy retirement but lacked the confidence to feel comfortable. I told her that fear and doubt come when we do not have a plan to succeed. I finished the meeting by giving this dear lady an outline of how we would provide income she could not outlive with an income plan and how we would protect her from the next 2008 with an investment plan. Needless to say, she was thrilled.

CROSS OVER THE LINE

The reason so many retirees are fearful about their retirement is because they keep getting the same old tired and worn out answers to their concerns, such as, "hang in there" or "it always comes back." The problem with that type of thinking is that it doesn't address the fundamental shift that has occurred in your life called "retirement." *If you are going to succeed in this new stage of your life in this New Economy, you must cross over the line from the Accumulation Specialist to the Preservation and Income Specialist.* You have to know that the rules of the game have changed and now you need a new specialist on your team.

UNDERSTANDING THE RULES

As I mentioned in my book *Winning Retirement*, retirement is a game changer and we must understand what the rules are and how to properly play the game if we truly want to come out as a winner. The rules of investing and taking risks drastically change when we retire. The Rule of 100 is a gauge on how much risk you should be taking. You simply subtract your age from 100 and the balance is approximately the maximum percentage of risk you should take with your retirement savings. Now that you have an idea of how much risk you can take with your retirement savings, you need to understand the rules of who should be helping you as you take these risks.

IT TAKES A TEAM

I don't believe there is any one person who has all the answers you need to make your retirement a success. You need to surround yourself with a team. The person that got you **to** retirement (Accumulation Specialist) is usually not the best one to get you **through** retirement (Preservation and Income Specialist). The preservation specialist surrounds himself with a different team, a team that has many distinct differences. You have saved and accumulated and now it's time for you to enjoy the fruits of your labor. It is also time that you get rewarded for your success.

INSTITUTIONAL VS. RETAIL

If you have ever purchased a product from a wholesale club or shopped for a discount then you understand the value of saving money. If you are a young investor contributing $50 per month towards your IRA account, you are glad to have the opportunity to invest with a professional money manager through a mutual fund. Even though the fees may be higher than other instruments, you get to take advantage of the expertise of that manager. If you have saved hundreds of thousands of dollars for your retirement, you have earned the opportunity to no longer pay retail. The "too big to fail" retail brokerage system is essentially the process of packaging goods and services that can be sold to the general public. The retail financial industry predominantly distributes its products through a broker. For brokering the transaction, they generally get paid a commission. In many cases the commission they receive depends upon the benefit of the product to the company that manufactured the financial product – the more the company makes, the higher the commission.

I met with a family last week that heard my plea to get a Risk/Cost analysis of their portfolio. We discovered that they were paying nearly 3% annually in retail fees plus $15 for every trade. Institutional management will cut the annual fees nearly in half and cut the cost of trades to $1. How can you expect success in this economy if you continue to allow yourself to pay retail?

FIDUCIARY VS. SUITABILITY

These two words *fiduciary* and *suitability* are critical in understanding the motivation behind the person offering you financial products or advice. A broker has a suitability standard, which allows him to offer products by the company he represents and get paid a commission as a percentage of the money invested. The fiduciary advisor must offer the "best advice" based upon the needs of the individual client. The advisor receives a quarterly fee as a percentage of assets under advisement. This fiduciary standard requires the advice to be in the best interest of the client including the disclosure of possible conflicts of interest. In a way, when a broker checks the suitability of a potential buyer, they are measuring how much financial product can be sold, not the needs of the investor. If the markets only went up we would not have to be as careful about the costs and whether or not someone has your best interest at heart. I believe many people were left unattended in 2008 because there was no fiduciary standard to uphold. Success in the New Economy requires that we do our due diligence to make sure we have the right advisor.

PUTTING IT ALL TOGETHER

Having a successful retirement is not only about how you invest your money or who is advising you along the path. You must have every phase of your retirement covered. Just as in football where the offense can be great, but if the defense doesn't do well you can still lose the game, the same holds true of your retirement. The coach, the quarterback and the receivers can be on the same page, but if the offensive line doesn't block you will not achieve success. Your retirement is no different -- all the areas must be covered. You must have a plan in place that will protect you if an unexpected healthcare crisis comes or if the stock market crashes…a plan that will protect you from avoidable taxes and excessive fees…a plan that will make sure that the people you love receive what you leave behind and not the government, the court system or some attorney.

Do not let politics, national debt, taxes or anything else that is out of your control spoil your fun. Retirement doesn't have to be a burden, …get a plan in place, …determine your goals and go have the time of your life.

About Greg

Greg Taylor is a retirement coach, specializing in complete retirement planning and asset preservation for families and retirees. He is the founder and CEO of Legacy Retirement Group, LLC, serving Central and Northern Ohio.

Greg has been helping families and retirees reach their goals for over 20 years – building a reputation among clients and colleagues as a personally-engaged problem solver. Working together with his team of attorneys, tax and insurance professionals, advisors and caregivers, Greg's approach is inclusive, transparent and education-based.

Greg has been featured in *The Wall Street Journal, Yahoo Finance, Market Watch,* and *USA Today.* Greg has been seen on Fox, NBC, ABC and CBS as a Consumer Advocate. He educates people throughout Ohio each week on the Financial Safari radio show and is a weekly guest on Daytime Columbus. Greg is also the author of the Best Selling book, *Winning Retirement.*

Taylor is a member of many distinguished organizations. He was named "Advisor of the Year" by a national industry organization for his commitment to client education and perseverance in reaching out and assisting Ohio's retirees with their planning needs. Greg assists retirees and those transitioning into retirement in developing a comprehensive plan so that their savings will last the rest of their lives and beyond, protected from excessive taxes, inflation and the high cost of healthcare.

CHAPTER 22

EMPOWER YOURSELF:
TAKE ACTION!

BY STEVEN NETZEL

Like most of the North American population, I was born and raised in a small town – central Iowa to be more specific. My parents had their hands full with six children and both of them worked more than one job at all times to put food on the table, clothes on our backs and a roof over our heads. From my earliest memories, I watched my parents' example of hard work unfold before me as a natural way of life. Needless to say, I inherited that great mid-western work ethic and it has served me well.

After high school graduation, I was fortunate to be able to attend the University of Northern Iowa to play football. That worked out great until a severe sports injury sidelined my athletic career. But, while in college I became interested in aviation, leading me to fly airplanes and become very knowledgeable in many aspects related to aircraft. As a result, I was offered a position in the commercial airline industry with Lockheed in Albuquerque, New Mexico where I relocated.

However, after only six months in this position, I gravitated toward a career in financial services and I've never looked back. It was in that change in career paths that I discovered my passion for working with people in ways to better their lives.

After several years away from my geographical roots, I was presented with the opportunity to join the Principal Financial Group. I accepted the offer and purposefully began to focus my attention on learning from every person I met. I have learned much from studying the successful as well as those that have fallen short of achieving their financial goals.

In 2004, I, along with my family, made a decision to move to Arizona where we currently reside. I didn't know anyone here and didn't have any clients or any assets under management. It was a new adventure. In a very short period of time, my business began to flourish and has continuously grown year after year. In eight short years, I have earned the trust of over 400 households and have hundreds of millions in assets under management now for those clients.

Over the course of more than twenty years, I have had the privilege of helping thousands of people develop balanced and sound financial portfolios and have become one of the regularly recognized full-service Financial Advisors in Arizona. In this chapter, I would like to share with you some of the principles that have guided me to success, as well as the general financial strategy I use with my clients to help them have a prosperous retirement.

LESSONS IN SUCCESS - WHAT NOT TO DO

People often ask who I learned the most from, and my answer often surprises them. I believe I learned the most from people who made their way to their retirement years, but didn't have enough money to sustain them through retirement. While you can learn a great deal from people that have been successful, I have found you can also learn a significant amount from people that have not been as successful as others. Often the lessons from this segment of the population are related to "what not to do." I would submit to you that knowing what not to do can be as valuable as knowing what to do.

In a very brief synopsis, this is what I discovered from the less successful:

1. They always seem to have been in a situation where they could blame someone else.

2. They were not disciplined in a savings GOAL!

3. They bought a lot of items on credit when they truly could not afford them.

4. They seemed to have low self-esteem.

5. They didn't stick it out when the going got tough.

You know the old saying, "When the going gets tough, the tough get going." While it has become somewhat of a cliché over the years, there is a great deal of truth to this phrase and it can be a key to success in every aspect of our lives.

The five characteristics I have identified above are what not to do when planning your financial future. But, let's focus on what you can do to experience success.

LESSONS IN SUCCESS - PRINCIPLES THAT HAVE GUIDED MY SUCCESS

In addition to the example of an extremely strong work ethic from my parents and learning from the mistakes of others, I believe my success has been based on the following 7 principles:

1.) Look at every person as an individual because no two people are alike.

People are very important to business. Without people, my business would not exist. I determined very early in my career that I would treat every person with kindness, professionalism and the respect they deserve. Each person's needs are different just as each person has their own individuality. It's very important to recognize the distinction between people. Without this understanding it is easy to become impatient and intolerant. That only results in hard feelings and a lack of desire to do your best for your client. However, if you view each person as a unique individual and respond accordingly, your business relationship can flourish.

2.) Work only with people you like and respect (it goes both ways).

I don't set financial limits on who I will work with, but it is extremely important to me to work with people that I like and who like me. If you are going to build a long-term business, you have to get along with your clients or customers. It can't be just a transactional-based relationship. If you get along with the people with whom you are working and you place as a top priority helping your client first and foremost, then you will have a good client relationship that allows you to build a solid business. This has been a key point to my success.

3.) Don't ever focus on money!

If money is your main motivation, you probably are not going to do well in business.

4.) Always do what is best for the client.

Instead of focusing on money, place your focus on doing what is best for your client or customer. In any business, sometimes what is best for the customer isn't always what is most lucrative for the business owner. But that's OK. What is lucrative for the business owner doesn't matter. What matters is that you do what is in the best interest of your customer. This principle transcends any industry. When you focus on what is best for your customer the other components of your business will fall into place.

5.) Treat others the way you wish to be treated yourself.

I am very aware that I'm not better than anyone else and I don't try to present myself in that way. I treat my clients as I would want to be treated and this goes a long way in developing mutual respect and trust. I am constantly building relationships with my clients. The way I know they trust me is by watching them refer their family and friends to me. That's the greatest testimony of trust that can be given. I also let my clients know how much I appreciate them. Not just in words, but I invite them to special events that are held specifically in appreciation of my clients.

6.) My clients work hard for everything they have; I owe it to them to work just as hard for them.

I never allow myself to lose sight of how hard my clients have worked to get to the place they are in life. Obviously, some have achieved greater financial success than others, but each one has demonstrated a dedicated work ethic and I believe it's my responsibility to show them the same work ethic when it comes to the work I do for them. My clients know I will do everything within my power to help them continue their successful financial journey.

7.) Protect the client's principle first; focus on income second.

In my business, protecting what my clients have worked for their entire life, their principal, is foremost in importance. My clients know that is my first order of business and they have a great deal of appreciation for that. Knowing their principal is being protected is my first goal and a great trust builder for our relationship. Investing can result in a loss of principal, so making guaranteed statements is not possible. But, it is always best practice to constantly do everything possible to protect the client's principal.

LESSONS IN SUCCESS- PLANNING FOR THE FUTURE

Planning for the future requires very specific and well-planned direction. I would like to give you a road map to assist you in your own planning process for a successful future and retirement. From my perspective, when planning for a goal we have to start at the end and work our way to the beginning so we can accurately identify the steps needed to get from where you are today to where you want to be in the future.

Example: Mr. Z wants to retire with $10,000 per month of income.

How much does Mr. Z need to save over his working years to achieve that goal? When answering that question it is imperative to make sure the goal is achievable. If it is not possible, then the end goal must be adjusted or Mr. Z has to find an additional source of income.

Assuming Mr. Z has been successful in the accumulation phase of his retirement plan, let's look at an overall plan for his retirement years. It is imperative to establish a realistic budget for the retirement phase of life. You will want to add up all your fixed income assets such as Social Security, pension plans, Defined Benefit Plans, Business buy-out, etc. Then deduct all your fixed liabilities such as food, utilities, home, auto, recreation, etc. It's also a very good idea to account for unexpected expenses because we know things don't always go as planned.

STEP ONE - FOUNDATION

When you have determined the amount of additional money you will need to accommodate your desired lifestyle, you will want to deposit enough money into a Fixed, Indexed or Single Premium Immediate Annuity (SPIA} with an income rider to cover the short fall between your fixed assets and your fixed liabilities. This will establish the important foundation to assure a worry-free retirement based on the claims paying ability of the insurance company backing the annuity contract.

STEP TWO - ALTERNATIVES

Traditional Securities investments typically fall under the general categories of bonds, preferred stock and common stock. It is highly important to understand the potential volatility of Traded Securities and make well thought-out decisions about these alternatives. You worked hard for your money and you want to take the appropriate steps to keep it as long as possible. Although many alternative investments are **NOT** liquid, they can offer a great point of diversification to a portfolio. Examples of these alternative investments include Real Estate Investment Trusts (REIT}, BDC's, Notes, Equipment Leasing Trusts, Oil and Gas to name a few. Many of these require qualification to invest.

STEP THREE - STOCK MARKET

The two best things about the stock market are that it is liquid and it offers a great opportunity to smart investors. I say it is liquid because you can get into the market one day and get out the next day. Your investment is not locked in for a specified period of time. The "opportunity" factor is the ability for your investment to grow. Again, a word of caution, there is also the potential for loss in the market. That's why it is so important that you choose investments wisely and preferably with the assistance of a qualified financial advisor.

Broadly speaking, investment strategy has three different categories: Liquid, Safe and High Rate of Return. The chart below illustrates the differences.

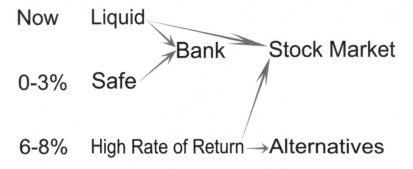

LESSONS IN SUCCESS - TAKING ACTION

One thing that definitively separates the successful from the non-successful is the "Taking Action" step. If you want to achieve a particular financial goal in life, you must take action sooner rather than later. It doesn't matter if you are still in the accumulation phase or already in retirement. If you don't have a specific and formal financial planning strategy in place, you should immediately find a qualified retirement advisor and get a plan in motion. The reason many people don't have enough money to last them throughout their retirement is because they didn't take the time to implement a strategic and disciplined plan. As with almost anything in life, the earlier you start your plan the more successful you will become. I strongly encourage you to not leave your financial future at risk. Now is the time to take action. Be proactive! Your financial success depends upon it!

About Steven

Steven M. Netzel is a well-known speaker in the Phoenix Valley. He is Founder and President of Netzel Financial, Full Service Financial Advisors. Netzel Financial is a firm that focuses on helping both pre-retirees and retirees avoid the most common financial mistakes.

As a Full Service Financial Advisor, Steve has provided objective, comprehensive and independent advice to his valued clients, helping them to preserve their assets, increase their income and reduce their taxes.

Steve is a member of the National Ethics Association, The Better Business Bureau of Central and Northern Arizona, Sun Lakes Rotary and the Chandler Chamber of Commerce. These trainings and accreditations are important when looking for quality advice.

Steven M. Netzel was noticed as one of the "Financial Trendsetters" in the December 17th, 2012 issue of Newsweek, and also recognized as a "Financial Trendsetter" in the June 5th, 2013 issue of the USA Today and in the June 5th, 2013 issue in *The Wall Street Journal*.

Steve can be heard on *KFNX News Talk Radio* 1100 on the AM dial. Steve co-authored and published a book with Brian Tracy.

In addition to being a Valley resident, Steve is also involved in his community and his church.

10450 E. Riggs Road, Suite 101, Chandler, AZ 85248

Tel: 480.219.0657

info@NetzelFinancial.com

CHAPTER 23

NEGOTIATING WITH INFLUENCE AND PERSUASION

BY FRANK VELAZQUEZ

Negotiating is a common fact of life. It can take place in a corporate setting and beyond, because we all negotiate something with someone every day. We are negotiating when trying to decide where to go out for dinner. We are negotiating when we discuss a performance evaluation and salary with the boss. We also negotiate when we go out to buy a big-ticket item like a car, a house and home appliances. These are just examples of ways we try to influence others to agree with our choices, our demands in order to meet an objective in mind. That objective can be to buy a car at the lowest possible price, with as many extras as possible, with the lowest interest possible. Think about all the other instances you have tried to influence, persuade and negotiate with others in your daily life.

I love negotiating, but I have also learned that there are many people who dislike, and some even fear, negotiating. Some of the common factors that make people dislike or fear negotiating include: the fear of confrontation, the fear of feeling rejected or disliked, the thought of losing something they really want or need, not knowing enough about the industry in which they are negotiating, feeling inadequate to negotiate. But the reality is that negotiating can be fun, can bring great satisfaction and can be quite rewarding. It all boils down to understanding the negotiating process, and knowing how to approach and take control of the negotiation.

Negotiating was not always fun and easy for me. As a teenager, I went through a number of tough experiences dealing with car dealer crooks who took advantage of me. They would overcharge me for car repairs, and there was a time when they even added installed accessories that I never ordered in order to bring up the bill. I remember one time I took my used car to the dealer for some repairs, and when I went to pick it up, they had "fixed" the car, and installed brand new hubcaps, new floor mats, and other things, which quickly added to the bill. However, the one experience that really opened my eyes and changed me forever was when I was manipulated into buying a new car that I could not afford. At the time, I had so many problems and car expenses with my old car, that I was desperate to find a reliable alternative, and the car salesman noticed. He started by building rapport and finding common ground with me. Then he took me to test drive the car. This is a powerful tool for car salespeople as it involves all the senses of the potential client: the smell of a new car, feeling the comfort of a new steering wheel and car seats, the great state-of-the-art stereo system, and to top it all off, the car salesman persuading me about the great feeling of driving this great looking car home.

Having signed all the paperwork, I left the dealership and next day I went to buy full cover insurance for the new car. This is when I realized that I could not afford the new car payment plus full cover insurance. I went back to the car dealer trying to cancel the contract (I had not taken possession of the car yet, because they needed proof of insurance), but neither the salesperson nor the manager were anywhere to be found. Now I had a new car contract, but no car, (I needed proof of insurance before car could be taken off the lot), my old car I had traded-in, so it was in their possession. So, I consulted with an attorney, and he said there was nothing to be done, because I had signed a contract. So, here is how the story ends…

The bank disapproved the loan the dealer had processed for me, and I was able to go back to pick up my old car. These were key experiences, life lessons that taught me first, to never sign a contract without reading and fully understanding it (what a novel idea), and secondly, to never again allow anyone to take advantage of me. This whole experience motivated me to learn more about influencing, persuasion and negotiation techniques.

Mastering the art and science of negotiation can make the entire difference in the success of a business. When used as part of the buying process, a good negotiated deal can increase a business' margins and profits. Buying at best price can also give you an advantage over your competition. For sellers it can translate into maximizing the yields and revenue a company can command for their products.

So in this chapter, I simplify and share what I have discovered in this fascinating field – successfully negotiating and closing deals in over 30 countries around the world. I also apply some techniques that I have developed and tested as an avid student and researcher in the fields of accelerated learning, holistic health, human potential, media/communications and innovation engineering.

So, let's begin by defining some of the core concepts…

   1. Influencing is about getting others to experience (see, hear, feel) an issue as you want them to experience it.

   2. Persuading is about getting the other party to agree to your desired outcome.

   3. Negotiating encompasses:
   a. Defining your objectives and ultimate goals
   b. Understanding the other party's needs, pain points and…

… using influence and persuasion to match the others needs with your objectives/offer to reach a satisfactory agreement between the parties.

So when engaging in the negotiating process, here are the basic steps that I take:

Step 1: Get into the right Mindset
First, start by getting into a winning mental attitude. This process is about managing the emotions that drive you to success. By doing this, you already have an advantage over the others as you enter the negotiation in a superior mental state. Prior to this you should have identified (individually and with your team, if applicable), clearly defined objectives and a clear image of what you want to achieve. Once your objectives and goals have been defined, it will be time to mentally rehearse the entire process, imagining the outcome of the negotiation in

your mind a few times prior to your first encounter with the other party.

Step 2: Research and Preparation

Time to do some prep-work to get to know your opponent. This is the time to explore and define their wants and needs, their pain points and weaknesses, and to identify their key negotiating players. Your formal research can be enhanced/validated by gathering additional intelligence informally. This can be over a meal, at a sports event, or some other setting where you can gather your observations when most people tend to lower their guards. Identify their Strengths, Weaknesses, Opportunities and Threats and use a chart similar to the one below to compare and match their SWOT (Strengths, Weaknesses, Opportunities and Threats) chart to yours.

SWOT ANALYSIS			
STRENGTHS		**WEAKNESSES**	
Ours	Theirs	Ours	Theirs
OPPORTUNITIES		**THREATS**	
Ours	Theirs	Ours	Theirs
ACTION 1:			
ACTION 2:			

This analysis is important in order to have an awareness of both sides' power traits and vulnerability – so that you can play to your strengths.

- Your strengths can work hard for you, especially if you control a unique product/service the other party really wants/needs or can't live without.
- Know your position and stay grounded.

- Put yourself in their shoes in trying to understand their posture and in trying to anticipate their next move.

Step 3: Subliminal Strategy

Designing a strategy that's uniquely targeted to influence and persuade the other party in order to reach your goals.

Strategy elements can include:

- Roles - Assign who will lead your team, who will be the good guy, the bad guy, the mediator, etc. and try to identify roles of the other party.
- Territory - Your turf, theirs or neutral location.
- Seating plan and Positioning.
- Sensory Influence.
- Light levels.
- Room temperature and comfort.
- Presentation materials and others.
- Position Power (Authority and Expert Credentials).

All of the elements listed above can be strategically crafted and executed to consciously and sub-consciously influence and persuade the outcome of a negotiation.

Step 4: Build the Affinity Link

People like to conduct business with others they like and are like them. So it's important to build the emotional bridge. Here are a few tips to build the affinity link:

- Establish common ground. Find things in common at the business, professional and personal levels.
- Pay attention intently. Listen well. Lean forward. Make eye contact. Make everyone feel important.
- Build Rapport. Match body posture, Voice pitch and Tonality.

Step 5: Strategy Implementation

Once a common ground is well established, it becomes easier to move the other party towards meeting your negotiation objectives.

Here are some of the *Influence* and *Persuasion* tactics that can be used to move towards attaining your negotiation goals:

- Magnify the elements and benefits in your offer in order to further increase the desire for your products and/or services.

- Illustrate the losses they could sustain if no agreement was achieved.

- Use Smart Arguments that are strategically planned. They are convincing, carry some common sense and have the potential to lead the other party to say "Yes" to your requests.

- Reciprocity tactic: Give in order to receive. Be ready to identify concessions that you can live with, which can facilitate reaching a compromise. Plan a concession point for each critical issue so that you can keep control of the process as it moves forward. This tactic also works with physical gifts of various sorts, entertaining, and so on.

- Overwhelm tactic: You can influence the other party to give into your requests through consistency, repetition and standing firm on no-compromising issues. For the skilled negotiator, this tactic tends to wear people out mentally and it gets people to give-in to your requests. (More effective if concessions have already been granted.)

- Reputation and Affiliation tactic: Many companies are willing to "sacrifice" their margins by offering their products and services at prices that are below what they charge the bulk of their customers. They do it in order to be able to link their company to their customer's brand.
  In cases like this, the customer's name carries a positive reputation and brand recognition that the vendor can then present as a reference to new and potential customers. Evaluate whether or not this is relevant to any of the parties involved in the negotiation, and use it to move the negotiation forward.

- Urgency, Scarcity and "Too Good of a Deal" tactics: Deadlines, shortages and "too good of a deal to pass" are techniques that can create an almost irrational effect on the decision maker. While people focus on these factors, other critical elements that could have been considered get overshadowed and the targeted individual tends to agree and give-in order not to lose the deal.

While there are different types of negotiations, there are common elements to all, so in summary:

- Begin with the right state of mind and with the end in mind.

- Have a clear picture of the expected outcome of the negotiation.

- Plan, Plan, Plan. Plan your strategy with elements that can produce the most impact consciously and subconsciously.

- Know everything you can about the other party. Try to anticipate their arguments and moves.

- Build rapport. Find things in common. Build common ground. Connect at a more human level, putting pride aside. Treat others with dignity and respect. Treat people as they would want to be treated.

- Keep your objective in mind at all times.

- Keep your opponent at close distance. Know what they are up to at all times.

- Practice, practice, practice on a day-to-day basis so that you can discover and notice the techniques most effective for you.

Negotiating with Influence and Persuasion is about using a variety of communication tactics that get people to agree and keeping the process fluid and moving forward towards the achievement of key goals and objectives – with the ultimate goal of building long-term collaborative partnerships and creating value for all stakeholders.

About Frank

Frank Velazquez is an Executive Advisor, Author, Lecturer/ Speaker and Entrepreneur.

With over 20 years of International Business Management and Training Experience, Frank's passion is to research, teach and coach teams and individuals on how to successfully achieve their business and personal goals easier and faster.

Frank holds a Masters degree in Education and Leadership with an Emphasis in Corporate Training from New York University and a Bachelor's degree in Hospitality Management from Florida International University. Other studies include: Innovation Engineering, Film and Television Production, Alternative Medicine, NLP and Human Design Engineering.

Frank is a former college professor, actor and model. Frank's other interests and hobbies include exercising, travel, learning and charity work.

Frank has served on the boards of a graduate university as well as on one of the largest humanitarian organizations in the world.

For more information on Frank Velazquez's programs, please visit: www.FrankVelazquez.com

CHAPTER 24

DEBUNKING THE WALL STREET MYTHS OF INVESTING

BY LEE HYDER

Over the course of the past 23 years, my career as a Financial Wealth Coach has evolved quite a bit. Technology, especially the Internet, has revolutionized the way we do research and invest. With trends toward globalization of financial markets, 24-hour news coverage, and hundreds of cable TV channels to choose from, sifting through the endless amount of conflicting information makes finding accurate financial information a daunting, if not impossible, task for the average investor. Today, more than ever, there is an infinite amount of self-serving and conflicting information every time you open the newspaper, turn on the TV, or go online. Some "experts" want you to believe that all of this easy access to free and unlimited information is a good thing. They even use tired expressions like "knowledge is power" and provide massive amounts of confusing and often useless, self-serving information. Ultimately, the end result is often more confusion, which frustrates the would-be investor into giving up in believing that they will ever have the peace of mind they long for so desperately.

While the availability of public financial data is there to help us make better and smarter decisions, often it has the opposite effect. Just watch self-professed financial gurus like Jim Cramer shriek obscure tips and recommendations, while a cacophony of bells, horns and other crazy noises are simultaneously going on. This scene may seem to be an appropriate representation of the world of financial investment advice to the eyes and ears of the inexperienced investor. As sad as that is, it's even more tragic when people use his predictions and others like him, as the sole basis for their investment decisions. Ask yourself, if your personal financial advisor acted like Jim Cramer, would you listen to them or take their recommendations seriously? Another popular personal finance personality is Suze Orman. On her television show, *The Suze Orman Show*, you can call in and explain your entire financial situation in two minutes or less and she will immediately either "grant you permission" (or not) to spend your money on what you were asking her advice on. Jim Cramer and Suze Orman are just two of the many financial personalities that dupe many people into thinking they are providing sound financial advice, when really it's just entertainment at best. Do not be fooled into thinking it's anything else.

Many people wanting sound, financial advice on what to do with their money often look to these financial icons on TV, radio, Internet blogs and other readily available media outlets. Unfortunately, these celebrities are given more credit than they deserve. I don't mean to pick on any one individual, they all are equally guilty of trying to convince the public that they possess the acumen of the Dalai Lama when it comes to investing. Additionally, they often overlook or ignore the true costs and risks of their financial recommendations, leaving the helpless investor to discover it for himself some time later, when it's too late. We have become a society that is star-struck by celebrities who thrive on the expense of others. Simply put, advice is easy to give when you don't have to be correct, or have to deal with the consequences.

For most of my 23-year career, I have worked in the retirement planning field with both pre-retirees, nearing their retirement, and current retirees, trying to stay on sound financial footing in their twilight years. Most clients come to me looking for a second opinion and reassurance on their portfolio. Their main concerns are finding ways to avoid and manage risk, determine and reduce hidden fees, and more importantly, understanding why their returns repeatedly fall disappointingly short of their expectations. As a Wealth Coach, I am continuously disappointed with the generic investment advice that most of my clients receive from their financial advisors. Most of the strategies I see that are utilized by most other advisors are nothing more than a combination of mind-numbing selection of "their" stocks and/or mutual fund selections, track record investing, and market timing. None of these options seem to give my clients any assurance that their money is being invested wisely, thus, I have never been comfortable with exposing them to the stock market under these restrictions. You may be asking yourself, "Isn't investing all about picking specific stocks and mutual funds, determining when to buy and sell them? Furthermore, shouldn't past performance be a good indicator of future performance?" If that sounds over-speculative then chances are you're right! The seemingly narrow scope of investment options and strategies for the average person is not by accident. I believe this is because the financial industry does not have any real incentive in offering anything else. As a matter of fact, they are highly compensated in trying to keep you buying and selling their latest and best "hot stock" of the week for you to invest in. If that doesn't sound like a trip to Vegas, what does? In the past, the average investor has been used as a pawn for the various schemes of Wall Street. If we look back to the financial crisis of 2008 as a barometer of current Wall Street attitudes, between the mortgage-backed securities and credit default swaps scandal, not much has changed.

Financial misdirection is not all deliberate; sometimes it's inadvertently given by well-meaning advisors whom themselves have been given bad or self-serving advice and/or training. Much of this is the result of the financial dogma, force-fed to entry-level advisors who begin with clients of average income, then work their way up their career. I witnessed this first hand when I began my career as a wealth coach. During trainings, they would boast, "our research department really knows how to pick tomorrow's winners today!" and "Now go call your clients and tell them this is a great time to buy because our research department thinks it's a bargain ready to make a move!" Almost reminiscent of the 'snake oil' salesmen hawking their wares on the Atlantic City boardwalk, isn't it? The training seemed more appropriate for a used car salesman rather than a financial advisor, but it continues to this day. You know this is true. Haven't we all gotten that phone call from our broker or advisor telling us he has identified a great opportunity for us to take advantage of? And aren't we lucky he's only sharing it with us?

Let me share with you what I learned after 23 years in the financial industry. Many of my peers won't like what I am about to share with you, because it will arm you with what you need to know, to be able to ask the hard questions of the person giving you financial advice. I learned that there was a much smarter way to invest based on academic research, instead of speculating and gambling with your money. The process dates back to the 1950's, and allows one to be a successful investor without stock-picking, market-timing, or gambling with your money. In 1950, the world laughed at these strategies. Today the world has stopped laughing because history has proven these points to be true. The results invariably were greater market returns with less risk and enhanced client satisfaction. This epiphany profoundly changed my career because I realized I could finally help families find that peace of mind that had escaped them for years. For many of my clients, a comfortable retirement was not so far-fetched anymore. All this could be accomplished without excessive client risk, arbitrary stock picking, or perilous market timing.

FINANCIAL WEALTH COACHING VERSUS TRADITIONAL FINANCIAL PLANNING

Often times, investors will disregard their intuition and defer to the advice of a financial advisor under the assumption that he or she is an "expert" in the field. The simple truth is that many financial advisors do not make their clients' needs their highest priority. Instead, many of them place the needs of the firm, as well as their own, as their highest priority, to the detriment of the clients' financial future. Furthermore, most advisors I have come across are quick to let an investor make an emotional knee-jerk-based decision in reaction to short-term market fluctuations. This "rookie" mistake is wrongly ignored to appease the client and maintain the flow of monthly fees for the advisor. I believe financial coaching provides greater service and value to investors.

Financial Wealth Coaching is no different from its traditional athletic counterpart. Everyone can think of an individual who has inspired them. This person may have also been a coach, teacher, or pastor. We look to these individuals for guidance because of their wisdom, leadership, and because they cared enough to teach us. I hope you are thinking of someone right now who fits the criteria of a good coach. The same qualities that attracted you to that person should be present in your financial advisor. A good coach understands the needs of his or her players and will not bully or intimidate them; nor should any financial advisor – it's your money, not theirs. Education and involvement of the investor is crucial for effective wealth coaching.

SOME VARIABLES AN INVESTOR SHOULD KNOW ABOUT THEIR INVESTMENTS ARE:

CAP exposure, Needless and Invisible Fees, Diversification, Portfolio Overlap, Portfolio Turnover and Rebalancing Triggers. When talking to my clients for the first time, I am always surprised to learn how little they understand about their portfolio. I find most clients that come to me are completely ignorant of crucial information relative to the health of their portfolio. Standard Deviation is the term used to measure the risk in a person's investments. If you are asking yourself, "What is standard deviation?" then you need to have a discussion with whoever manages your portfolio. Simply put, a portfolio earning 10% with a standard deviation of 20 is twice as volatile as a portfolio earning the same 10% with a standard deviation of 10. To base one's investments solely off subjective words like "risky, moderate, conservative and/or safe" is very dangerous, because these words simply mean different things to all of us. Math, science, and standard deviation are a universal language.

Fees are another aspect of many investors' portfolio. They usually have no true understanding of what they are actually paying – as if it doesn't matter. I'm dumbfounded every time a client says to me "I don't know what the fees are, I just look at the bottom line." I don't think anyone would be comfortable buying gas at a gas station without knowing what they're being charged per gallon, just as long as they're leaving with a full tank. As an example illustrating how quickly fees can erode returns, recently, I showed a family that came to see me that they were paying approximately $21,000 in fees a year on a $700,000 portfolio, and worse yet, these fees didn't even appear on their statements! Needless to say, upon realizing they were paying 3% per year they were less than pleased. Reducing your fees is an easy and painless way of immediately increasing returns. I hope you are wondering about your fees?

To summarize, most people assume that being a successful investor requires omnipotent powers of prediction only held by a financial advisor or a famous TV host. Being a successful investor doesn't have to be as hard as the financial industry and Wall Street would lead you to believe. They have a vested interest to convince you that you are not capable of doing their job or really understanding what they are talking about, so you're told, " just trust me, don't worry." According to the financial research firm, Dalbar Inc., markets return more than the average investor actually receives. Returns come from the market and not from the manager or advice of any one advisor. Moreover, CNN Money found approximately 79% of money managers consistently fail to surpass the S&P 500. This subpar performance can be attributed to common investor behaviors versus portfolio problems. These investor dysfunctional behaviors are found in market timing, hyperactive stock picking, short holding periods and ignoring portfolio fees. Most investors, including some professionals, underperform the market because they are overly invested in US large cap stocks (SP 500) instead of being in a truly globally-diversified portfolio. You can't achieve market returns if you are overly weighted in small sectors of the entire market and not fully invested in the global markets and many uncorrelated asset classes.

To be a successful investor, you should focus on the following basic guidelines:

1) Invest in Equities
Own the entire market, not just a small selection of sectors of the market. Too many clients come to me with an overabundance of large cap stocks (S&P 500) and the result is an overall diminished effect on returns.

2) Be Globally invested
Most people think by investing in only a handful of countries is sufficient diversification, however, it's not. Your portfolio should have DOZENS of countries represented (ours contain over 40). This is the only way to avoid a potential pitfall, should a nation's economy suffer some unforeseen calamity, such as a natural disaster or financial collapse. The economic crisis in Europe, especially in Greece and Italy, serve as a great example, as well as our own tech and housing bubble.

3) Pay attention to Fees
Be sure you are aware of all fees, not just the ones you know about. Make sure every dollar is accounted for. Remember, reducing fees is very easy (and satisfying) way to increase returns.

4) Understand True Diversification and Risk Assessment
The minimum amount of holdings needed for true diversification,

I believe, is at least 10,000 or more. Our portfolios have just under 13,000 holdings in over 40 countries with more than 18 asset classes. True diversification will also make risky market timing unnecessary, because investments are thoroughly spread out. Additionally, you should evaluate your portfolio quarterly to determine if rebalancing is needed. Rebalancing is more about being sure your portfolio doesn't drift out of your acceptable risk tolerance. Most importantly of all, do not succumb to emotional whims when investing. Impulsive investing is a cardinal mistake in the financial world and chances are, you'll be doing more harm than good.

If you can't answer 'yes, I know' to the following questions concerning your portfolio, you need a Portfolio MRI and a second opinion:

- What you are actually paying in all fees.
- How diversified your portfolio is or isn't.
- What your portfolio "Standard Deviation" is (risk number).
- How much portfolio overlap and turnover is going on in your portfolio.
- How many holdings are in your portfolio.
- If you can increase returns and reduce risk at the same time.

I hope you were able to answer all the above questions. We used to believe what we don't know won't hurt us. I don't believe anyone still believes that today. Do you?

About Lee

For over 23 years, Lee Hyder has been helping families in Northeastern Ohio navigate the dangerous and confusing waters of financial and retirement planning through his Wealth Coaching Advisory Practice. Lee's approach, design and implementation to all of his custom strategies are engineered around each and every family's unique circumstances.

There are not two identical situations when dealing with people, so there can be no two identical solutions when trying to solve a family's retirement puzzle. Lee says, "I've seen way too many people get pushed into buying financial products from some commission-hungry advisor using fear to motivate and persuade their client into taking action." Lee believes in educating each and every client so they thoroughly understand the ever-changing world we live in today and all the options available to them. Consumer education and awareness are so important to Lee that he has started teaching retirement planning courses at many of Akron's colleges and universities. In an ongoing effort to keep his clients informed, Lee also conducts educational classes at least every six weeks for his clients to keep them up to date on current world affairs and necessary portfolio information. Lee has been seen on NBC TV and heard coast-to-coast on radio shows, and quoted in newspapers and magazines. Lee has been a sought-after advisor at many national meetings where he has been a platform speaker in sharing his unique and refreshing client focused approach to marketing, customer service, and practice-building strategies.

Lee and his wife, Lizzi, love hosting fun and exciting client appreciation events throughout the year. Lee says the best part of his job is hanging out with his clients outside the office. Lee says, "I love the ability to help total strangers find peace of mind about their financial futures and turn total strangers into lifelong friends." As Lee is writing this, he is planning their second client appreciation seven day Caribbean Cruise leaving from Puerto Rico in March of 2014.

Lee is married to an incredible woman, Lizzi, who is a successful business woman in her own right. Lizzi helps women start their own Arbonne businesses. Lee's son, Codi, is following in dad's footsteps and is also in the financial industry at a local bank. Lee's daughter, Jessi, is a yoga instructor in New York, and more importantly, a new mother to Lee and Lizzi's first grandchild, Julian. Lee says, "Now, I understand the excitement I have seen for years in all my clients' eyes when they talk endlessly about their grandkids." When not working, Lee and Lizzi can be found riding roller coasters at Cedar Point at their beach home in Sandusky or visiting National Parks.

Lee can be reached at:
Tel: 330-836-7800
Email: lee@leehyder.com
Website: www.leehyder.com

Lee Hyder offers investment advice through Signature Investments, Inc., A Registered Investment Advisor, 6500 Poe Ave, Suite 110, Dayton, OH 45414, 937-890-1988. Lee Hyder & Associates and Signature Investments, Inc. are unaffiliated.Local office: 1655 West Market St #445 Akron, Oh 44313/ 330-836-7800

CHAPTER 25

THE FOUR MONEY MISTAKES IN YOUR BLIND SPOT

BY KYLE WINKFIELD

Suppose you're in your car driving down the highway and you want to change lanes. You turn on your blinker, check your mirrors, see that it's all clear, and begin to move into the left hand lane. In the process, you hear a blaring horn honk. You jump back into your lane. You look 15 degrees over your left shoulder and you notice a car that you didn't see before when you checked your mirrors. Did this car come out of nowhere? No. Anyone who drives a car knows that every car has a blind spot. This vehicle was in your blind spot until you were alerted of its presence via horn honk. So what does this have to do with personal finance? There's what we believe and then there's reality. In this example, you believed that there was no car in the left hand lane, but in reality, it was there the whole time. The same principle applies to personal finance. There's what you know and there's what you don't know. When you study affluent individuals, you can pick at the minutiae of what makes them different from everyone else but at the end of the day, what truly makes them different is their knowledge - they know something that you don't know.

So if something you thought to be true about money turned out not to be true, when would you like to know? If you're like my client Joe, you'd want to know as soon as possible.

I met Joe and his wife Mary a few years ago during a seminar. They were in their late 40s with two young teenage children, residing in the Maryland suburbs. With an annual combined income of $240,000, $750,000 in savings, $1.3 million in mortgage debt and $65,000 in vehicle loans, Joe and Mary were most concerned about their ability to fund college for their children and also have a comfortable, stress-free retirement. For most people, Joe and Mary seem to be on the right path; they were saving 10% of their income annually, maxing out Joe's 401k, investing in a few non-qualified accounts and responsibly managing their debts, including sending extra mortgage payments to the bank as often as possible. So why were they seeking help?

Joe and Mary had been receiving advice from a traditional financial planner and while that relationship had netted them a modest nest egg, they had the feeling that something was in their blind spot. That's where I come in; I teach my clients how to understand the impact of their financial decisions over the long haul, in turn, teaching them how to be aware of those blind spots and subsequently make wise financial decisions. Experience shows that if people understood the long-term impact of their decisions, they would almost always choose differently. Your most valuable assets are time and cash flow, especially when it comes to retirement preparedness, but these are the most overlooked and/or mismanaged assets when it comes to traditional financial planning. Typical financial advisors spend their time pushing products and can often be heard asking, "how much do you have?" "where is it?" and "what rate of return are you getting?" No matter how you answer, they almost always respond "bring it to me and I can do better." Unfortunately they're not having conversations about how to optimize cash flow or discussing long-term impact; ultimately they're selling a product to collect their fee. While many fee-based products can be good investments, failing to effectively strategize and analyze the big picture with long-term goals and real numbers will more often than not leave the consumer hearing multiple horn honks on their road to retirement.

So now let's focus on the four major money mistakes that most people (including Joe and Mary) are unwittingly committing:

1. Paying off the mortgage
2. Contributing to a qualified plan over and above a match (or at all)
3. Creating consumer debt

4. Owning non-qualified investments

MISTAKE #1: PAYING OFF THE MORTGAGE

Let's say that you're in the market to buy a house that costs $300,000 and you have the cash to pay for the house outright. A good strategy to consider would be to pay cash and have no mortgage. The right strategy would be to obtain a mortgage, maintain control of the cash, and utilize a strategy that allows you to safely compound interest on that $300,000 (after your down payment of course). Let me explain:

Assuming a 30 year fixed rate mortgage at 4% interest, the payment for a $240,000 mortgage (assuming a 20% down payment of $60,000) would be $1,146 (including principal and interest). Assuming a federal tax bracket of 28%, your net after-tax payment would be $996 and your net cost to borrow goes from 4% to 2.8% due to the mortgage interest deduction. Let's now say that you could invest your $240,000 at 4% compounding over 30 years (coincidentally the same term as your mortgage); your account balance would be $795,000. The difference between the total cost of your mortgage of 30 years ($358,698) and what your investment is worth ($795,240) is $436,542...in your favor.

If you had paid cash for the house, you would have lost the opportunity to earn compounding interest on your money because you would have given it to the bank in exchange for the house. In the right scenario, you maintain control of your cash, earn compounding interest, and have your house as long as you are fine with using your cash flow to make the mortgage payment...which by the way also earns you a tax deduction. What would you prefer? If you said that you prefer to have your house paid in full, then you most likely don't mind eating Raman Noodles once a day during retirement. If you said you'd like to optimize your cash flow by maintaining control of your cash in order to pursue other opportunities and/or handle emergencies, then you are one step closer to dining at Ruth's Chris a few nights a month during retirement. Relinquishing control of your money for the psychological achievement of having your home paid off is a money mistake that most people make without realizing the lost opportunity cost of such decision. In the right scenario where you maintain control of your cash, in the event that you had to pay off your mortgage, you would not only have the means to do so (in this case, twice over), but you would also have the liquidity to do so. See when you give the bank all of your money, you have to ask for it back when you need it for something, and they decide how much you get and how much they want to be paid for the privilege of allowing you access to your money. This is not liquidity and this is not control. When you maintain control of your cash and properly apply the principles of compounding interest, you win on both counts. At the end of the day, you want to maintain control over your assets.

If by working together I could help you create a strategy in which your home could be paid for (as opposed to paid off) in a fraction of the time while simultaneously giving you complete control of the principal of that real estate, would that be a conversation you'd want to have?

MISTAKE #2: CONTRIBUTING TO A QUALIFIED PLAN OVER AND ABOVE THE MATCH (OR AT ALL)

Your qualified retirement plan ranks just behind your home as one of your biggest assets. Time and cash flow are your most valuable assets, but most often your home and qualified plan are your "largest." While qualified plans such as your 401k might be a good decision, I do not want to recommend a good plan for you; I want to recommend the right plan for you. When it comes to qualified plans I have two questions for you:

1. Do you know what tax bracket you will be in 15-20 years from now?
2. Do you know what tax deductions you will have 15-20 years from now?

The point of putting money away for the future is so that you can have a future similar to your present. Does it make any sense to put money in an account whose sole benefit is tax deferral when you do not have any idea what you are deferring to? When qualified plans were introduced, we were all told that they were a sound investment because "you will be in a lower tax bracket when you are older." Is that really true? Do you want to be in a lower tax bracket? Bear in mind that tax brackets are a function of your income – a lower tax bracket means a lower income. Subsequently, when you take distributions from a qualified plan, you will be charged ordinary income tax. So what exactly is the benefit of a qualified plan?

If you're not saving at all, the benefit of a qualified plan is that you can set up an automatic withdrawal from your paycheck and at least there's something saved somewhere. There's also the benefit of dedicating those pre-tax dollars to the account. But what many of us fail to remember is that we aren't avoiding taxes, or saving money on taxes somehow, we are simply deferring taxes. When qualified plans first entered the arena, we were told that qualified plans were the way to go because you can stash pre-tax dollars away now and pay our taxes later when we retire, because we'll be in a lower tax bracket. Really?

Qualified plans defer the tax and they defer the tax calculation – that's it. What's another word for defer? Postpone or delay. The truth is, if you own a qualified plan, you own a tax-delayed account, and with our country's skyrocketing debt and unfunded liabilities (Medicare, prescription drug coverage and Medicaid, amounting to approximately $127 trillion dollars as of September 15th 2013) what are we delaying these taxes to? Most likely we are delaying them to higher tax rates. Face it - tax income is the only income source that our government has, and it's got bills to pay. If you are delaying paying taxes, chances are you are delaying now to pay more later. Does that make any sense? The bottom line is, the government controls tax brackets and tax deductions, thus they control your retirement in the form of your qualified plan. So if you are depending upon your qualified plan for retirement, you are putting money in an account that you have no control over. In essence, Uncle Sam has a tax lien against your retirement. So when you put money in a qualified plan, whose retirement are you really planning, yours or Uncle Sam's?

Not to mention, you can't touch your money in a qualified plan without penalty until the age of 59 ½. What if an opportunity or an emergency happened along that requires cash? What if you want to use some of the funds to pay for the kids' college, can you? So WHOSE MONEY IS IT REALLY?

Let's take this further. The largest deduction you can take on your taxes is your mortgage interest, yet "they" tell you to hurry up and pay off your house. So then you get to retirement and your house is paid off (therefore, no deduction), your kids have moved out (no deduction), and you have all of your money in tax-delayed accounts. You've done everything "they" told you to do. Then you go to pull your money out of your qualified accounts and the withdrawal is taxed as income (and don't forget, taxes are going up). You have no deductions and your savings are getting hammered by taxes. Does that make any sense?

So, if by working together, I can create a strategy that allows you to accumulate money for retirement in a tax-free environment while also providing you with liquidity, safety and access to your money without penalty, would that be a conversation you'd want to have?

MISTAKE #3: CREATING CONSUMER DEBT

This is one area in which all financial advisors agree – eliminate your debt. However it's so hard to go through life in America and not accrue any debt. What most advisors aren't doing is showing you how to more effectively manage your cash flow such that you do not become a victim of our consumer-driven country. This is because most financial planners themselves don't know how to most effectively manage cash flow. The most they'll talk to you about is a budget and let's be real, budgets are like diets, no one likes them and very few stick to them.

Knowing this, I created an advanced cash flow strategy called the Wealth Accelerator. It is a strategy that allows people to manage their cash flow in such an efficient and effective manner that they are able to eliminate consumer debt in a fraction of the time and get their real estate paid for in 1/2 to 1/3 of the time. It's just that simple.

So if by working together we could utilize the Wealth Accelerator approach to eliminate your debt, get your real estate paid for and redirect the interest you were going to pay the financial institutions and the cash flow you were giving away to creditors, and put it in an account that you own and control, all without spending any extra money or affecting your current standard of living, would that be a conversation you'd want to have?

MISTAKE #4: OWNING NON-QUALIFIED INVESTMENTS

First let's define what a non-qualified investment is so that we're all on the same page. It's money that you have already paid taxes on once (at the ordinary income tax rate) and you decide to use it to purchase investments (mutual funds, equities, etc). The benefits of a non-qualified investment include liquidity and the potential for growth. The benefits start to dim when every April 15th, you're forking over "penalties" (a.k.a. taxes) for your growth (a.k.a. success).

Suppose you're going to invest $5,000 in a non- qualified account annually and you're receiving 9% interest on the money. Your earnings for that year amount to $450.00. Depending upon your tax bracket, if you did this for 18 years where would you be? If you consider the chart

Compounding Interest With Taxes

Year	Annual Deposit	BOY	Annual "1099" (9%)	Annual Tax Due
1	$5000	$5000	450	-135
2	$5000	$10,450	941	-282
3	$5000	$16,391	1,475	-443
4	$5000	$22,866	2,058	-617
5	$5000	$29,924	2,963	-808
6	$5000	$37,617	3,386	-1,016
7	$5000	$46,002	4,140	-1,242
8	$5000	$55,142	4,963	-1,489
9	$5000	$65,105	5,859	-1,758
10	$5000	$75,965	6,837	-2,051
11	$5000	$87,801	7,902	-2,371
12	$5000	$100,704	9,603	-2,719
13	$5000	$114,767	10,329	-3,099
14	$5000	$130,096	11,709	-3,513
15	$5000	$146,805	13,212	-3,964
16	$5000	$165,017	14,852	-4,455
17	$5000	$184,869	16,638	-4,991
18	**$5000**	$206,507	18,586	**-5,576**

(inset), at year 18, you're paying more in taxes than you are actually contributing to your investment. Investing and growing is always a good thing, but in this particular environment, the tax man always wants to be paid and ultimately it's to your detriment. When you think about paying taxes, keep in mind the lost opportunity cost of those tax dollars; what could you have made on those dollars if you'd kept them and invested them elsewhere?

If in working together, we could create a strategy that would give you the compounding growth that you enjoy of the market without the tax pain and the associated lost opportunity cost, would that be a conversation you'd want to have?

ADDRESSING THOSE BLIND SPOTS

So now that you've seen what's hiding in those blind spots, what to do for Joe and Mary? When I analyzed their current plan, we found that if they stayed on the same path, by the age of 76, they would be out of money. Considering our life expectancies take us way beyond 76 these days, that was a problem for them.

Retirement Ready Or Not

5.00% / 3.00% Increase ROR	$2,000/month $24,000/year Save More	Work Longer Age 67	$30,102/month $361,222/year Spend Less	3% Inflation
Present Projection			**Revised Projection**	
Account Balance	Annual Withdrawal Plus DBs	Age	Account Balance	PV of Annual WD Plus DBs
$2,826,532	$361,222	67	$2,826,532	$200,000
$2,578,289	$372,059	68	$2,578,289	$200,000
$2,311,855	$383,221	69	$2,311,855	$200,000
$2,026,350	$394,717	70	$2,026,350	$200,000
$1,720,859	$406,559	71	$1,720,859	$200,000
$1,394,427	$418,756	72	$1,394,427	$200,000
$1,046,062	$431,318	73	$1,046,062	$200,000
$674,729	$444,258	74	$674,729	$200,000
$279,352	$457,586	75	$279,352	$200,000
$0	$334,234	76	$0	$141,831
$0	**$55,706**	**77**	$0	**$22,950**
$0	$56,542	78	$0	$22,616

Instead of discussing budgeting or locating new investments for them to try, we took the more comprehensive approach. We looked at their cash flow, current liabilities, and monthly expenses and identified their wealth transfers. What is a wealth transfer? It is money that you are unknowingly and unnecessarily giving away to a third party or organization that does not care about you or your family's financial security and independence. There are five major places where people transfer away their wealth:

1. Income taxes (when, how, and if you pay them)
2. Real Estate (how you pay for and manage it)
3. Qualified retirement plan contributions over and above a company match
4. Interest on non-deductible debt
5. Higher education expenses

Most individuals and families will lose more money in wealth transfers than they will ever accumulate in savings, predominately because of financial decisions with pitfalls lurking in those blind spots. Each financial decision incurs an opportunity cost, jeopardizing the ability to optimize every dollar earned. Identifying wealth transfers and subsequently using strategies to more efficiently and effectively eliminate them without impacting the current standard of living was the right plan for Joe and Mary.

Then we redirected the dollars that would have been sent to creditors or otherwise "lost" and picked a savings strategy that would capitalize on the benefits of compounding interest in a tax- free environment while also allowing for market gains and minimizing or eliminating the pitfalls of the market. In doing so, we designed a plan for them that paid off their primary home's mortgage in 16 years, created cash flow for the kids' college via a wealth acceleration strategy, increased their net worth by over $1 million, and lowered their wealth transfers by over $800,000. We accomplished all of this without changing the family's lifestyle.

What could your financial future look like if you knew what was in your blind spots?

About Kyle

Kyle Winkfield, ChFEBC℠ is the Founder, President & CEO of The Winkfield Group, a personal retirement planning firm headquartered in Rockville, MD. He is a leading retirement advisor who has spent more than 10 years helping hard-working Americans grow wealth through cutting-edge financial strategies.

Kyle has shared his knowledge and experience in the financial services industry in various public forums including as a featured syndicated radio personality; and, his insights and advisory advocacies have been quoted in several widely-distributed publications, including Black Enterprise Magazine.

The Early Years

In 2000, Kyle began pursuing his dream of helping individuals and families achieve financial independence by joining American Express Financial Advisors. Not satisfied with some of the financial tools and retirement planning techniques that American Express Financial Advisors and many financial planning companies use, he decided to create his own company focusing on many families' biggest need, paying for college.

In 2001 Kyle co-founded the American College Funding Association with the goal of assisting working class families in the Washington DC metro area achieve the goal of higher education, with a focus on helping families learn how to make college affordable for their children.

Making A Difference

In 2007, Kyle established Infinite Wealth later becoming The Winkfield Group, which focuses on common sense strategies for retirement planning and financial independence. He is quickly building a loyal clientele of individuals and families throughout the Washington, DC area. His local success has allowed Kyle to grow his business into a multi-state operation with offices in Atlanta, Georgia, Norfolk-Hampton Roads, VA & Denver, Colorado. Kyle also provides training and mentorship to over 70 independent advisors across the country.

Building Wealth for the American Family

Kyle works hard to produce financial systems and strategies that build wealth for the average American family. He educates families on how to more efficiently manage their cash flow so as to recapture money of which they are unnecessarily losing control. Kyle also prepares his clients for stress-free retirements by teaching them how to accumulate wealth more efficiently and more safely – using compound interest strategies in a tax-advantageous environment.

For the past 10 years, he has helped hundreds of families live the American dream, build wealth and secure a comfortable lifestyle deep into their golden years. Kyle is a member of the National Association of Insurance and Financial Advisors and the Financial Planners Association. He also currently serves on the Business and Industry Committee for Frederick Memorial Hospital.

A Native Washingtonian, Kyle and his wife Ashley reside in suburban Maryland and they welcomed a baby boy to their family on June 7th.

CHAPTER 26

THE SEEDS OF MY SUCCESS

BY LANCE DRURY

I've had a lot of success in my life and a great deal for which to be grateful. I've been blessed with a good family, the best friends, the dream team for co-workers, the greatest adventures, romancing a Russian princess in the Caribbean and the Crimea, the best childhood you could ever imagine, writing books, having meaningful work, going to number one on Amazon, appearing on all the major networks and Fox, featured in USA today, delivering a keynote speech with Steve Forbes in NYC, and the list goes on and on. But the real seeds of my success were laid a long time ago.

I remember my Great Aunt Ethel. She was my second mother, my mentor, and my fairy godmother all rolled into one. She loved me and supported me at a time in my life when I needed her great love and support. When I would complain about what a rough time I was having, she would say to me, "That's no hill for a stepper." In other words, that's not an obstacle that should stop someone like me. She gave me my profession. I think she always regretted not becoming an attorney herself and she instilled that desire in me. After my parents divorced, I would walk my cocker spaniel to the other side of town to see her every Friday night. And on those Friday nights, she allowed me to escape from my emotional pain, and created a magical world for me--a world of politics, of glamour, of movies, of celebrities, and most of all, reminiscing about her days in Santa Barbara. She brought California,

Hedda Hopper, the Rose Bowl Parade and the glorious coast to me. She didn't mince her words. She was an independent woman before women talked about being independent. She walked the talk, and I loved her very much.

I remember my Father. My father wanted to name me Lancelot, but my mother thought that was going a little too far. I lived in my father's world when I was a child. He took me with him everywhere---to work on the railroad (even at night), to the Legion Hall, to Pete Jokerst's meat market on Main Street. I know people and places in my hometown that others my age don't remember simply because my father shared his world with me. He had a wonderful voice. He would sing me to sleep at night and would always sing about great love. To this day, I can still picture him on the side of my bed singing "Danny Boy" or "Nature Boy" to me. He taught me about integrity, and principle, and doing my best no matter what I did with my life. But I think the most important thing he taught me was this, "Son, don't ever worry about being liked, worry about being respected, because with respect comes love." My father was quite a character---boisterous, opinionated, and yet generous to a fault. You never forgot him once you met him. To me, he's the biggest man I have ever known. And as Martin Amis said of his father on the day he died, it was "the day the clocks go back. For I am you and you are me."

But most of all, I remember my Mother. My mother spent 20 hours on the operating table having me because I knew there would be too many old German broads I would have to tangle with in my life. My first living memory is hiding behind her skirt when the guns went off during a military parade. I can even remember the wooden rocking chair in which my mother spent countless hours rocking me. I can remember exactly what that chair looked like; every grain of wood is etched into my mind.

My Mother was a typical '50s housewife---quiet, reserved, and loyal. But, I remember how excited she was about John Kennedy and the 1960 election. I was sick with mumps or measles or chicken pox, but I had her wake me up to see the Inaugural Ball.

I was much more attached to my Father in my early childhood, but my Mother's true greatness as a person came to light after my parent's divorce. I was always rebellious, but I became very rebellious after my parent's divorce. I felt I had failed miserably — I couldn't be there for my Father who was alone, and all I seemed to be able to do was inflict emotional pain on my Mother. As our next door neighbor said to my Mother, "You've got one big problem. All your children have their Father's disposition." My siblings were as independent, hard-headed and opinionated as I, but I caused my Mother much more grief than they. I was kicked out of Catholic high school twice, only to be reinstated and there was talk of sending me to a military school.

We were very poor, and we had no car the entire time I was at home. My Mother never went out, never dated, because she devoted her entire life to her children. However, she never disparaged my Father to me and she never discouraged me from seeing him. With no monies, but with a home filled with love and devotion, she raised a doctor, a lawyer, and an engineer.

In my work, I often am a part of child custody battles, and when I see how some of these children are used as pawns by their parents, I realize how fortunate I was to have my Mother's presence in my life.

Several years ago, I gave her a book written by Rick Bragg called "All Over but the Shoutin'." It was the story of growing up poor in Alabama with a mother who devoted her life to her children. One particular passage in that book reminds me of my difficult days growing up. "Every life deserves a certain amount of dignity, no matter how poor or damaged the shell that carries it." We were poor, and I was damaged. But the dignity and the grace with which my Mother carried herself during those strenuous times is a lesson that I have learned with the passing of the years. Our Mother gave us dignity, and because of her example, her devotion, her love and her attention, I have been able to achieve more than I ever thought possible. My Mother literally gave her life so her children could succeed.

While I have a penchant for not mincing my words like my Aunt Ethel and my Father, I think my Mother's dignity and grace in the face of great adversity has somewhat softened the hard edges of my demeanor. I have had dark clouds in my life and more may be on the horizon, and I may never be able to realize my fondest dream, but because of the strength, courage and perseverance of my Mother, I will, in the words of Tennyson, continue "to strive, to seek, to find, and not to yield." I will never yield until the last of my days on earth.

The greatest gift my Mother ever gave me was to encourage me to follow my star, even if it took me to the ends of the earth. That is her gift and her legacy to me. And when she dies, I will be in the desert again, but this time she has given me the tools to march on and to honor her memory and her life by doing the best I can possibly do.

My Mother is the finest human being I have ever known and I love her more than anything on this earth. She is my heroine for all time.

Now that's success!

So therein lay the secrets of success that I would pass on to you:

1. Take to heart Great Aunt Ethel's admonition and develop the attitude of "That's no hill for a stepper."

That phrase is an old southern expression meaning, "You can conquer that hill or that mountain." It's not too big for you! Many times people get intimidated by hills or obstacles that get in their way. But successful people don't!

A very old author, Orison Swett Marden, once said, "Obstacles are like wild animals. They are cowards, but they will bluff you if they can. If they see you are afraid of them they are liable to spring upon you; but if you look them squarely in the eye, they will slink out of sight."

You may think that's a great line, but you will think it's even greater when you know more about the life of Mr. Marden. You see Marden was a hotel owner who had been quite successful, but lost his business during the deep depression of the 1890's. With very little money, but lots of time, he decided to write a book. He took a room above a livery stable and worked night and day on his manuscript. The evening he finished the final page he decided to go out to a small café for dinner. While he was dining the livery stable caught fire and burned to the ground. His entire manuscript of over 1,000 pages was destroyed. An entire year's worth of work literally went up in flames.

Although overwhelmed by the situation, he immediately started writing again. One year later he had re-written his personal development book only to be turned down by multiple publishers. They thought no one would read a book like that during the third year of the depression. After moving to Chicago he was introduced to another publisher who read the book and said, "This is exactly what people should be reading in the middle of the depression or at any other time." The book, *Pushing to the Front*, became a wild success and was read by people like Henry Ford, Thomas Edison, Harvey Firestone and J.P. Morgan. Marden went on to write more than twenty other inspirational books.

You see, the loss of an entire year's worth of work and a 1,000 page manuscript was "no hill for a stepper" like Orison Swett Marden. He was a definite "stepper." It isn't surprising that he also said, "There are two essential requirements for success. The first is "go-at-it-iveness" and the second is "stick-to-it-iveness."

2. Remember the advice of my father and understand that "It is better to be respected than liked, because with respect comes love."

Almost everyone wants to be liked. But, successful people aren't always liked. In fact, many successful people are hated by countless others for various reasons. However, successful people are usually highly respected. One of the most important characteristics that results in success is to have clarity of purpose. Clarity of purpose will lead to specific direction and definitive decisions. This is where the break occurs between being liked and being respected. Many times people will not like you because of the decisions you make. But, if your decisions lead to the success, the same people that didn't like you will now respect you.

Obviously, respect is something that must be earned. Unfortunately, the journey you take to earn respect will result in people not liking you. But, that's OK. Tough decisions don't always make friends. If it is a decision that affects someone's status, money or power in a negative way, they most assuredly won't like you and they will be confident you made the wrong decision.

It takes a very confident person to make difficult decisions and tough calls on a day-to-day basis. But over time, if you treat everyone fairly and explain your rationale clearly, you will earn the respect of others. In the end, if your decisions were right and result in a positive outcome, you will not only be respected, you will also be loved. You will have to be tough skinned and you will have to learn to live with the doubters, naysayers and grumblers, but you will be a good leader. You will be someone who has clarity of purpose and the earned respect of others.

3. Live out the words of Rick Bragg. "Every life deserves a certain amount of dignity, no matter how poor or damaged the shell that carries it."

It doesn't matter where you've come from or the level of your social status. It doesn't matter if you have been damaged by a difficult past. The reality is that every life deserves a certain amount of dignity. Someone who is homeless deserves the same amount of respect and ethical treatment as someone who lives in a mansion. I grew up in humble circumstances, but there was definitely dignity in my household. My mother carried herself with dignity. It isn't a matter of money; it's a matter of personal perspective.

Not only should each of us feel this way about ourselves, but we must also extend this same emotion to others we encounter. We must not only allow them to retain and display their own dignity, but we must treat them with the dignity they deserve. Michael J. Fox said it well, "One's dignity may be assaulted, vandalized and cruelly mocked, but it can never be taken away unless it is surrendered."

4. Put into practice the encouragement of my mother to: "Follow your star, even if it takes you to the ends of the earth."

I think everyone has a star to follow – a dream, an ambition, something to which you aspire. Some stars are more lofty than others. People who do take the initiative to follow their star grow to be more independent and learn that they can make a difference all by themselves.

Regret can be a terrible thing. Again, I think of my Aunt Ethel and her lost ambition to become a lawyer and the regret that I sensed in her life. While she did inspire me to take that life path, she could only experience that aspiration vicariously through me. She never was able to personally experience the sense of accomplishment to pass the state bar, to win the first court case, and to understand the great sense of fulfillment of helping others through difficult times in their lives.

Don't live in regret. Take charge of your ambition. Defeat the internal doubt. Follow your star even if it takes you to the ends of the earth.

As Dylan Thomas said, "Do not go gently into that deep night, rage, rage against the dying of the light." May your journey to success be ever meaningful and always fulfilling.

About Lance

As a Missouri native, Lance Drury possesses that unique quality only present in those who choose to live their lives in the state of their birth — a complete and personal investment in the lives of the people of his community. He was born and raised in Ste. Genevieve, Missouri and moved back to the area 22 years ago. By creating a local presence in Ste. Genevieve, Columbia, and Southeast Missouri, Lance brings 28 years of legal experience to the area.

Lance has an undergraduate degree in political science and economics, a law degree, and an MBA from Washington University in St. Louis with an emphasis in finance. Lance is also the best-selling co-author of the legal book, *Protect and Defend: Proven Strategies from America's Leading Attorneys to help you Protect and Defend Your Business, Family and Wealth.*

Learn more about Lance Drury at: www.LanceDruryLaw.com

CHAPTER 27

UNDERSTANDING THAT SUCCESS COMES FROM WHO YOU ARE – NOT WHAT YOU DO

BY GREG ROLLETT

We are taught from an early age to go to school, get good grades and the skills and education you receive will help you to get a good job. Then you are told to go to graduate school, get your doctorate, your MBA… all to help you advance your career!

But the advice they never give you is to work on yourself, your personality, your relationships and to showcase who you are.

We focus on test scores and lab results. We then tie credential into credential and start adding letters to the back of our names. Next thing you know we are in the real world. Thrown to the wolves in the mean streets of business.

And none of those credentials matter when it's you against the world. What matters is how you relate to the person on the other end of your conversation. How you connect. How you get in tune with their emotional needs at that specific moment in time.

For all good business is done based on who we are, not necessarily what we do.

All doctors go to medical school. All pass state board exams. But not all doctors are created equal. They have different beliefs. Different values. Different systems and processes. Different styles. Different backgrounds.

Each factors into the acquisition and retention of a patient. And if you were a doctor, just relying on the fact that you have your shiny degree hanging on the wall, you are going to keep spinning around and around in circles losing clients to the new lowest price doctor with credentials.

I want you to focus on something much more important. I want you to focus on who you are. Not what you do.

And I want you to focus on the top of the food chain, not the bottom.

You see, today's affluent clientele are eager to work with people who are like them. Who relate to them. Who have an affinity or connection to their own life. They understand that most competent people with a certain skill level can perform the task at hand. What they really want is someone they know, like and trust.

They don't want an institution either. They want the person for the job.

Remember those old mafia movies where someone would always shout out, "*I got a guy*?" You want to be that guy. Someone that gets referred. Someone that gets talked about at cocktail parties. Someone who is known for being the only solution for the given situation.

Where no one else even comes up in conversation.

Different success and business mentors have made reference to this type of person before. They might be called a guru or wizard. Others might call them a savior or even an expert.

Legendary marketing and business strategist Jay Abraham has a brilliant strategy based around this theory, called the *Strategy Of Preeminence*, where you are seen as the most trusted advisor for life.

We call this person a Celebrity Expert®. That is someone who combines the marketing and the "be seen everywhere" aura of a celebrity and the knowledge and talents of an expert. You see, being famous for being famous can only get you so far. You need to apply some type of skill or knowledge in order to take that fame and put it to good use.

Thus the Celebrity Expert knows that he needs to share his story of magic powers with the world. Much like how we know the origin stories of our comic book heroes like Superman and Spider-Man, so must everyone in your market know your story.

People remember these stories. I know people that can tell me the entire Bat-Man origin story and have never read one of his comics or seen any of the movies. That is the power of a great story that is told time and time again. It's about the person. There is an emotional connection to a boy whose parents are murdered and seeks vengeance.

Showcasing flaws is also a powerful part of the equation. It's ok to be vulnerable. To pull back the veil. Too often we showcase only the good. We try to manipulate perfect lives through social media. We post status updates only when vacationing in exotic locations or eating fine foods.

But a superhero without flaws ultimately becomes boring. We lose interest. We know what the outcome is going to be. The flaws give the character life… a reason to keep tuning in every week or month. Your own success depends on selling yourself, your personality and your own unique super powers.

YOUR STORY IS THE DRIVER OF NEW SUCCESS IN TODAY'S ECONOMY

Many entrepreneurs and professionals today simply have a fear of sharing their story. They fear they are not unique or distinctive. They feel their story is plain or boring.

That is simply not the case and one of the biggest limiting beliefs to overcome. As humans we all relate on a very primitive level. …Family …Travel …Hometowns …Love …Relationships …Food.

These build the essence of your story. Where you grew up. How you grew up. The schools you went to. The sports teams you root for. Your first love. Your children. By starting on this basic level you start to create a connection that is easy for others to gravitate towards. It starts the conversation. And it continues the conversation.

It's the reason we go to the same barber for 20 years - we keep having that new conversation based on the connection we created the first time we sat in their chair.

It's the reason we go out of our way to the dentist who remembers us, has a child the same age as our own and always has a story to tell.

It's the reason we listen to certain news programs and sportscasters. The reason why we read every book from certain authors and never get into books from other authors. It's why we will watch certain movies before others - because of the story we heard about the actor or the filming of the movie - it's not just the movie itself.

We are drawn to people. And people working together provide the fastest path to success there is:

- One person sharing an idea with another person.

- An introduction or connection made.

- A partnership or joint venture opportunity.

- One person's resources being applied to another's
  ability to implement and act.

But none of this is possible without the two people getting together. And it's never the thing that gets them together. It's the two people connecting.

All too often we fall back to what we do. It's easy to talk about the details of the thing…the features…the benefits. It's harder to find stories and build context. But we remember the stories about the person. We forget facts. It's why 48% of all statistics are made up 63% of the time.

SO HOW CAN YOU FOCUS ON WHO
YOU ARE AND NOT WHAT YOU DO?

By telling your story. And by using media to enhance the visibility of your story.

Every advertisement you write is a place to tell your story, not just what you do. Why do you do what you do? How did it come about? Where did your magic powers come from? What is the story about the first person that you helped?

These are all key elements to share every opportunity you can. It's why I lead every presentation, webinar, interview or video with some rendition of my background in the music industry, which led to starting my first business venture, which spawned my successful ventures today.

I do this for many reasons. The most prevalent is to have some common ground that people will want to talk to me about. It is something they will remember long after I leave the stage or the interview has ended.

They will remember that I was the marketing guy who used to be a rapper in a rock band. They will forget the facts, the tactics, the steps in whatever it is I am talking about. But they won't forget the fact that I was a musician, that I toured the country, that I survived on ramen noodles in the back of a van for weeks, or that my band mates left me hanging out to dry just weeks after I got married to my high school sweetheart.

DO YOU SEE HOW I SNUCK ALL OF THAT INTO THIS CHAPTER?

And even with everything I have written about, it is those interesting tidbits about the author that you will remember above all else. My marketing skills are implied. You assume I can write a great sales letter or ad for you. You assume that I know my stuff. That I have the necessary credentials.

And it's the same in your business. The letters at the end of your name mean nothing to the person making the buying decision. And it will stop you from being successful in today's economy. It will hold you back. It is a belief you need to get over.

Today more than ever, you get paid and hired for who you are and not what you do. And the higher up the ladder of affluence you go, which is where you should be aiming at, the truer it becomes.

I was speaking with a client recently who was working on the marketing for his company. He said that his customers were having a hard time connecting to his product. They had the best specs, the best raw materials, the best formula, the best delivery times – everything you would want from this product.

The immediate problem I saw was that there was no human connection. All of the emails came from the institution. They sounded vanilla. There were no stories, just facts.

I reminded him that we forget facts. And we forget facts fast. But we remember people and stories. I told him to talk about his life. To introduce his daily thoughts and issues into his emails, newsletters and even proposals. I told him to start telling his story about why he started the company and the first customer he helped using his products. The minute he made that adjustment, the difference was clear. The customers had someone to cling onto. They suddenly remembered who he has when the phone rang. And when his sales reps went into the field they were flooded with questions about the CEO of the company and his kids, his trips around the world and about his magic powers.

Sales spiked because of stories, not specs. The specifications were assumed at that point. They were a quick point of negotiation and reassurance as the contract was being signed.

Your business is too important to be forgotten. Especially in today's fickle economy. When price becomes a prospect's only point of reference, you lose. If you don't lose today, you will lose tomorrow. Someone will always come along cheaper and faster. But no one can replace you. Who you are. With the relationships and the connections that you have with your customers, your list, your clients.

The first step is to write down your story. Map it out. Reverse engineer the pieces that you want told and re-told. Simplify the complicated. Create emotional ties. Paint pictures with your words.

After you have your story, start inserting it using media, both online and offline. In your brochures and catalogs, do you tell your story, the story behind the products, or do you just state the facts? If it's the facts, it's time to make a change.

In your social media posts are you just pointing people back to sales pages and product pages? Or are you connecting and sharing things about you? Make the change.

Most importantly, adapt the mindset that you are the biggest asset in your business. You alone have the ability to grow, multiply and expand your operation by sharing more of you…by telling your story and having others tell the tale for you...to build your legend. And it starts today.

Your success depends on who you are, not what you do.

About Greg

Greg Rollett, @gregrollett, is a Best-Selling Author and Marketing Expert who works with experts, authors and entrepreneurs all over the world. He utilizes the power of new media, direct response and personality-driven marketing to attract more clients and to create more freedom in the businesses and lives of his clients.

After creating a successful string of his own educational products and businesses, Greg began helping others in the production and marketing of their own products and services. He now helps his clients through two distinct companies, Celebrity Expert Marketing and the ProductPros.

Greg has written for Mashable, Fast Company, Inc.com, the Huffington Post, AOL, AMEX's Open Forum and others, and continues to share his message helping experts and entrepreneurs grow their business through marketing.

Greg's client list includes Michael Gerber, Brian Tracy, Tom Hopkins, Coca-Cola, Miller Lite and Warner Brothers, along with thousands of entrepreneurs and small-business owners across the world. Greg's work has been featured on FOX News, ABC, NBC, CBS, CNN, *USA Today, Inc Magazine, The Wall Street Journal*, the *Daily Buzz* and more.

Greg loves to challenge the current business environment that constrains people to working 12-hour days during the best portions of their lives. By teaching them to leverage marketing and the power of information, Greg loves to help others create freedom in their businesses that allow them to generate income, make the world a better place, and live a radically-ambitious lifestyle in the process.

A former touring musician, Greg is highly sought after as a speaker, who has spoken all over the world on the subjects of marketing and business building.

If you would like to learn more about Greg and how he can help your business, please contact him directly at: greg@dnagency.com or by calling his office at 877.897.4611.

CHAPTER 28

BRINGING YOUR BRAND STORY TO VIRTUAL LIFE: THE 7 LESSONS OF ONLINE SUCCESSONOMICS

BY LINDSAY DICKS

SuccessOnomics. There's a course we'd all like to walk away from with a 4.0 GPA, right?

Well, If you're looking for a way to get to the head of your industry's class, just open your web browser and start schooling yourself – because the online world is essential to making the grade when it comes to your own success.

Of course, you may not agree. You may not think Facebook, Twitter and even your own website matter that much to your day-to-day business. If that's the case, then I'm sorry to say that you may never be elected President of the United States!

I'll give you a moment to deal with your disappointment – and then ask you to take a look back at the last presidential election in 2012 between incumbent Barack Obama and challenger Mitt Romney. Consider these campaign statistics, compiled three months prior to the actual vote by InternetMarketing.com:

Facebook "Likes": Obama, 27 million, Romney, 2 million

Twitter followers: Obama, 17 million, Romney, 650,000

Instagram followers: Obama, 1.1 million, Romney, 24,000

YouTube channel views: Obama 200 million, Romney 12 millions

Pinterest followers: Obama, 1.1 million, Romney...well, Mitt didn't have a Pinterest page, but *Ann* Romney's page had 7000 followers....

Even accounting for the fact that Obama had a younger group of voters than Romney, the above numerical gaps are nothing short of astounding. Obviously, the Obama team had a much more engaging and dynamic online strategy than the Romney campaign.

But, you say, how much did that strategy contribute to the President's victory? Well, ORI, a market research and strategic business intelligence firm, and The George Washington Graduate School of Political Management teamed up to do some research on just that question.

Their conclusion? *Almost a third* of those polled said social media was moderately to extremely influential in their opinions of the candidates and issues. That influence also counted when it came to the candidates' bottom lines. In terms of dollars and cents, the impact of the Internet is once again very clear: Of likely voters, *77% made their political contributions online.*

In other words, when it comes to where you should focus your marketing, my advice is to "Follow the money!" So, file into my classroom, take your seat and I'll help you do just that – because I'm about to educate you on how to engage in the most profitable kind of online story-telling.

THE IMPORTANCE OF YOUR "VIRTUAL STORY"

The overriding lesson of Online SuccessOnomics is that, in order to make it work for your business, you have to have in place a robust Internet strategy – and the centerpiece of that strategy should, of course, be your brand.

Now, the basis of your brand is your *story*. What makes your business different? What makes *you* different? How are your benefits to potential customers unique and special? All of those elements and more go into creating a narrative that attracts leads, converts them to customers and keeps them buying from you for the foreseeable future.

Elsewhere in this book, you'll learn some inside secrets from my partners at the Dicks-Nanton Celebrity Branding Agency, Nick and Jack, who reveal how to craft a story that's more compelling than your competition's. In this chapter, however, you're going to matriculate to the next level of study – and discover how to effectively *communicate* that story through today's overwhelming number of online tools.

The good news is that, even if you're a single-person entrepreneur, you can still level the playing field against the big boys by telling your brand story via the Internet *consistently and effectively* - by observing what I call "The 7 Lessons of Online SuccessOnomics." These "lessons" are all proven ways to deliver your message across a range of powerful platforms in a memorable and impressive way. So please, read on - and think about how you can use each of them to promote your own specific brand story.

LESSON ONE:
MAJOR IN UNIQUENESS

To begin with, your brand story should stand out from everyone else's – so make sure you tell that story in a different and compelling way that reflects how you want to be perceived. If you want to seem cool and cutting-edge, it's very easy to create some weird and wonderful video "Vines" (find out more about them at Vine.com) with your smartphone that can extend your brand message. If you want to communicate in a more buttoned-down professional manner, think about how you can tell your story through attention-getting LinkedIn content or informative Facebook posts.

This idea of differentiation, of course, extends to your website, which should never look like a generic cookie-cutter creation. Instead, it should reflect the 5 W's - *Who* you are, *What* your business is about, *Why* visitors should buy from you, *Where* you're known and *When* they should act (to which the answer is always, of course, NOW!).

By the way, your uniqueness should be a natural evolution from whatever your basic brand story is. Don't be different just to be different – be different in a way that makes sense for your story!

LESSON TWO:
EDUCATE WITH EVIDENCE

Anyone can tell a story. That doesn't mean the listener has to believe it! As a matter of fact, in this day and age of marketing overkill, most potential customers are more inclined to dismiss rather than believe a brand story.

Don't see that skepticism as a disadvantage – instead, leverage it to your advantage, by providing credible evidence that *your* brand story is true, and put yourself in front of the line when it comes to establishing consumer trust.

Do that by creating and posting legitimate content that supports your story. Authoritative articles and blogs, tweets and status updates that provide relatable and usable information establish you as an authority in your field and draw people to your expertise.

Of course, customer testimonials go a long way towards proving your story. Third party verification (people other than YOU saying you're great) always goes far in terms of backing up your story – especially if you have some case studies with individuals or companies that have a good, well-known reputation that you can share with potential leads.

LESSON THREE:
SHOW *AND* TELL

Many of the hottest new social media sites – Instagram, Pinterest, and Vine – as well as old stand-bys like Flickr and YouTube – put the accent on the visual, either through photos or short videos. With today's overcrowded social media landscape, anyone going through their Facebook or Twitter feed might zip right past your latest post – unless there's a provocative or interesting photo that motivates them to take their finger off the scroll button.

When it comes to telling your brand story, a picture can definitely be worth a thousand words. A photo of you and a happy customer – or your latest and greatest product, accompanied by a caption that entertains and sells – can make each of your statuses and posts a must-see for your following.

Think about what's visually interesting about what you do and what you offer – and also, of course, make sure it fits in with your brand story!

LESSON FOUR:
EXCEL IN PERSONAL CHEMISTRY

Interesting characters are essential to a good story – and since you're presumably the representative of your brand, it's up to you to be that interesting character!

Personal chemistry is the formula that allows you to bond with your customers and prospects. You may think it doesn't matter what you're personally interested in and what you're all about, because, after all, we're talking about your business here, not an eHarmony.com profile! The truth of the matter, however, is you *are* your business – and, as the old maxim has it, *"People buy people."*

So don't be afraid to make jokes or root for your favorite sports team (if you don't have one, the Florida Gators football team is an excellent place to start!). Or, in my case (and as some of you already know), I use Pinterest to share fashion ideas, home décor inspiration, and of course, anything and everything shoe-related!

Of course, when you're getting 'up close and personal,' you should try to avoid topics that might actively alienate some of your potential customers. Otherwise, don't be afraid to be yourself and let your personality out of the box - because nobody likes a story with a boring main character!

LESSON FIVE:
EARN YOUR DEGREE IN CONSISTENCY

Entrepreneurs and business owners are busy people – and that means, unless they have a staff person or department dedicated to doing social media, they can find it hard to *consistently* communicate their brand story.

First of all, because there are so many different social media sites available, you can find yourself jumping from one to the other – and never developing a real following on any one of them. Or, you may only post updated statuses, photos and videos every so often when you have an idea or a few extra minutes – and, because you're so hit-and-miss with those posts, you may fail to engage anyone with your brand story.

That's why you must:

(a) focus your efforts on the social media sites that attract the most people in your specific niche,

(b) regularly update content on those sites by sticking to a schedule, and

(c) make sure your messaging is *consistent* on every platform (in other words, if you act hip and cool on one site and revert to Mr. Suit and Tie on another, it's going to confuse people).

Let me elaborate a little more on the second item in that list – regularly updating content. This isn't as daunting as it might sound; it can involve something as simple as updating your status, but, if you have the time, it can be as elaborate as posting a new blog, article or video. Whatever you choose to do, make sure you're able to carve out the necessary time in your schedule to do it. Even if you have to limit yourself to just five minutes to send out a quick tweet or two, it's better than nothing. Consider it your SuccessOnomics homework!

LESSON SIX:
"ACE" YOUR VIDEO PRODUCTION

I've touched on video a couple of times already in this chapter's curriculum – but it's important enough to feature in its own specific lesson.

As I noted, "people buy people" – and video is the best way to sell yourself! A video featuring you is the next best thing to meeting in person with someone – because the viewer experiences your personality in an immediate and human way. Not only that, but video also gives you the opportunity to demonstrate your expertise, by talking about subject matter that directly relates to your business. That makes for quite a one-two punch!

Probably many of you have heard of Gary Vaynerchuk – he's been profiled in *The New York Times*, and has appeared on such national TV arenas as the CBS and ABC news, as well as on the Conan O'Brien and Ellen DeGeneres shows. Well, he became a national success story mostly because of his online videos.

He began working at his parents' retail wine business in New Jersey while still a teenager – and soon brainstormed ways to boost its revenues to unimaginable heights. First, he gained the necessary expertise; he trained himself in wine-tasting, became an expert and began advising customers on what was a good buy. He rebranded the store as "Wine Library." And he began increasing the store traffic and sales because people sought out his advice and liked his reboot of the business.

But he wanted to take his brand story beyond the borders of New Jersey, so he started selling wine online and – most importantly - began recording a video wine blog, called Winelibrary TV, in 2006. He promoted the video blog and his website endlessly, through YouTube, Facebook and Twitter, until he got Wine Library to the point where sales had increased to 60 million a year – over ten times what it had been making. In the process, Gary also turned himself into an incredibly successful self-help and business advice guru!

That's what the power of video can do when used properly. There's only one major word of caution I have to share when it comes to videos – and that's when their production quality is poor. That can be very damaging to your brand. These days, almost everyone has access to quality equipment, so there is no excuse for posting a video that looks like it was shot on a cellphone 10 years ago and makes you resemble a hostage victim. If you're going to use video to tell your story, which I highly recommend, you have to be sure that you do it right!

LESSON SEVEN:
GRADUATE TO NEW GROWTH

Finally, if you've mastered the first six lessons in this chapter, never feel as though your education is complete. You should always be evolving your brand story and how you tell it online.

A common element in every good story is *growth*. Characters in great stories face challenges, overcome them, and often transform themselves in the process. So don't be afraid to let your audience see you grow. Sure, you don't want to post on Twitter every time something goes wrong with your business… but you can use social media to celebrate your victories and to let people see how you and your business are evolving. And by the way, your slip-ups can be endearing too – sometimes laughing at yourself creates an even stronger bond with your audience.

Also, the Internet landscape keeps changing rapidly. Three or four years ago, nobody had ever heard of Pinterest; now it has, as of this writing, over 70 million users (and, by the way, over 80% of them are women, if that's the demo you're after!). So always look for what the Next Big Thing might be, when it comes to online marketing – and see if it could be a big thing for your branding!

Did I hear the bell? I guess class is over for now – but I encourage you to keep learning on your own (or with my help, if you need it!). As I noted, the online marketing world is one that keeps changing every day – and new opportunities for story-telling are always emerging.

So make sure you engage in continuing education – and school yourself on everything out there that can help you tell your tale in the best way possible.

About Lindsay

Lindsay Dicks helps her clients tell their stories in the online world. Being brought up around a family of marketers, but a product of Generation Y, Lindsay naturally gravitated to the new world of on-line marketing. Lindsay began freelance writing in 2000 and soon after launched her own PR firm that thrived by offering an in-your-face "Guaranteed PR" that was one of the first of its type in the nation.

Lindsay's new media career is centered on her philosophy that "people buy people." Her goal is to help her clients build a relationship with their prospects and customers. Once that relationship is built and they learn to trust them as the expert in their field, then they will do business with them. Lindsay also built a proprietary process that utilizes social media marketing, content marketing and search engine optimization to create online "buzz" for her clients that helps them to convey their business and personal story. Lindsay's clientele span the entire business map and range from doctors and small business owners to Inc 500 CEOs.

Lindsay is a graduate of the University of Florida. She is the CEO of CelebritySites™, an online marketing company specializing in social media and online personal branding. Lindsay is recognized as one of the top online marketing experts in the world and has co-authored more than 25 best-selling books alongside authors such as Brian Tracy, Jack Canfield (creator of the "Chicken Soup for the Soul" series), Dan Kennedy, Robert Allen, Dr. Ivan Misner (founder of BNI), Jay Conrad Levinson (author of the "Guerilla Marketing" series), Leigh Steinberg and many others, including the breakthrough hit *Celebrity Branding You!*

She was also selected as one of America's PremierExperts™ and has been quoted in *Newsweek*, *The Wall Street Journal*, *USA Today*, and *Inc.* magazine as well as featured on NBC, ABC, and CBS television affiliates speaking on social media, search engine optimization and making more money online. Lindsay was also recently brought on FOX 35 News as their Online Marketing Expert.

Lindsay, a national speaker, has shared the stage with some of the top speakers in the world, such as Brian Tracy, Lee Milteer, Ron LeGrand, Arielle Ford, David Bullock, Brian Horn, Peter Shankman and many others. Lindsay was also a Producer on the Emmy-winning film Jacob's Turn.

You can connect with Lindsay at:
Lindsay@CelebritySites.com
www.twitter.com/LindsayMDicks
www.facebook.com/LindsayDicks

CHAPTER 29

BUILDING YOUR EXECUTIVE COACHING EMPIRE

BY JOHNNY TARCICA

When I was 12, I asked a friend at school:

"Why do you answer every question with another question?"

And he said: "Why not?"

At that time I could not recognize he was using intuitive coaching techniques. Actually, many years later, he has become a well-known coaching practitioner making a living by just asking questions.

Of course, not any question, but powerful questions, and people pay him to hear their answers. Awesome I thought.

Everybody Seems to Need a Coach

I was attending a coaching training on the West Coast and we were asked to get our first paying client.

There was some kind of School Principals meeting in the same hotel we were staying, and one of my fellow students got very enthusiastic and offered her services as a coach to one of the school principals.

The school principal said:

"Oh yes, our baseball coach just left the school last week. Please come in on Monday and fill out an application."

When she shared the story with the class, one word came very strong to my mind: The word was "Opportunity."

If a school principal did not have in the top of his mind what a life or career coach could do to help his students, there were two possibilities:

1. - Sport coaches are much more in demand than life or career coaches.

2. - Life and career coaches are just an emerging new discipline that many people have heard of but are not familiar with.

The correct answer is that both are true. Actually, just a couple of years ago, I had a vague understanding regarding what a coach did, or I thought so. Again the same image keeps coming to my mind, every time bigger: *Opportunity, Great Opportunity.*

FOLLOWING THE RULES

In my mid-twenties and then mid-thirties, I was leaving a life designed with what I considered best practices at that moment. I had finished college with my engineering degree. With these credentials I got a job in sales at a plastic manufacturer. Although I enjoyed my salary and the commissions I was making, after some time I realized this was too boring as the conversations with my clients were always the same. In order to get their attention, I had to always bring new jokes and stories to tell.

So I got a new job at a pharmaceutical company. Suddenly I had become the Alka Seltzer Brand Manager. This got me the "Alka Seltzer" nickname that some of my former clients still use when they see me, even after some decades. My life was starting to get better. I traveled through Central America and met very interesting people.

One morning, I arrived to visit the Purchasing Manager of one of the biggest Supermarket Chains in Panama, and learned something I never forgot. As he had so many salesmen that tried to visit him to offer all types of products, he had installed a one-way mirror and an actual Traffic Light outside of his office.

The procedure you had to follow to get into his office was to go in front of the mirror and ring a bell. If he wanted to see you, a Green Light would flash. If you got a Yellow Light you should come another day, and if you got a Red Light, you should try your luck with other potential clients, as he would not let you in at any time. Fortunately for me, I usually got a Green Light.

One of my friends at that time was a retired football player that got a job as the Sales Manager of a well-known Hotel Chain in Costa Rica. The strange path in his career was that he made the jump from Football Player to Hotel Sales Manager.

He told me his story. A friend of his got very enthused to attend a Sales Training Program and invited him to join.

My friend said, "Ok, let's do the following: You will attend this training and meanwhile I will try to get a job as a Sales Manager using the image and prestige I have achieved while being a football player. Then when you finish your training, come to see me, and I will hire you."

And so he did. Both got the jobs they went after. But my friend taught me a very important lesson in my life: To succeed, sometimes you need to break the rules.

As years passed, I realized that: To succeed, you almost always need to break the rules.

LEARN TO IDENTIFY AND DEFEAT YOUR INNER GREMLINS

Many of the Life Coaching Training Systems devote a very important chapter to illustrate how to identify and destroy your Gremlins.

Your Gremlin is your Saboteur.

It is the inner voice that is always saying:

- "You will not succeed."
- "You don´t have the skills."
- "People will not trust you."
- "You are a failure."

Some Saboteurs are cruel and will tell you: "People will laugh at you." There can be several Saboteurs in you working at the same time. Once you learn how to defeat and ignore your inner saboteurs, your life starts to change.

This is the most valuable outcome you can get from Life Coaching Sessions.

HEAR THE VOICE OF YOUR INNER COACH

Can you answer the following questions?

1. Do you like to help people?

2. Do you feel you have acquired valuable experience in your life that you can share with others?

3. Do you like to speak with strangers and let them tell you their life experiences?

4. Do you like to listen with attention to other people just trying to understand what they are communicating, without jumping immediately to interrupt them to impose your ideas?

5. Would you feel proud looking how people are experiencing positive changes in their lives as a result of your intervention?

This was a quick coaching session. Wow. How did it feel?

I guided you through my questions to try to see if you can hear the voice of your Inner Coach. Your Inner Coach, or your Captain, or your Pilot, as different training programs like to call him, is who directs your life and advises you to take wise decisions.

If your Gremlins or Saboteurs are speaking too loud in your mind, there is a possibility that you will not be able to hear your Inner Coach.

One of the great benefits of Coaching Training Programs is that they help you to defeat your Saboteurs and to put your Inner Coach in charge of your life. This is the reason so many people are able to transform their own life after attending Coaching Training.

Now it is your turn:

Close your eyes (really, no kidding) and try to hear the voice of your Inner Coach. If after answering the five questions above, you hear him saying: 'Yes. Go for it.' Then you should consider becoming a Coach, but not just a Regular Coach. You should try to become an Outstanding Coach.

And moreover, you should try to build an Empire with your Coaching Practice – a Practice that will attract many clients and also many other coaches to work with you.

HOW COACHING CAME INTO MY LIFE

After leaving the corporate world, I realized interaction with people was something I enjoyed. I become a consultant but very soon realized that I could not put all the passion where I was not in charge of execution. I realized that when a crisis comes, the first cut in companies' budgets are consultants.

I first heard about coaching in the early 2000s. At that time I was confusing Coaches with Mentors. I learned that a mentor shares his good experiences as lessons you can try to replicate, while a coach just ask questions directing you to find your own answers. Contrary to my first impression, I started to note that coaching produced outstanding and much more long-lasting results than mentoring.

The reason is very simple. Coaching gets you to explore your inner self… to get your own answers…to identify your Life Mission Statement…to understand your beliefs, and most importantly…to learn how to defeat your Saboteurs.

So, always being a fanatic in all I do, I started enrolling in several coaching training programs. After 10 years I continue doing so, usually taking these experiences as a vacation, attending classes in foreign countries and far locations. I leave my cell phone at home, wear T-Shirts, sandals, and let the instructors transport me with their lessons. How enjoyable and enriching these experiences can be.

SOMETHING WAS MISSING

After attending several Coaching Training Programs, I realized something was missing. The missing link was a structured system to provide clients with standardized processes. When you select a doctor, each one has his/her own preference regarding the technique they use to cure you.

A doctor usually follows a pre-defined protocol that consists in a review of your condition, lab exams, diagnosis, treatment and follow up. So, independent of the doctor you select, you will probably get what is outlined above.

With coaches, there are so many tools and techniques, that you will probably get results depending more on the coach you select and the tools and techniques he/she uses, rather than in the following of an established protocol. And this is not bad. If you select the right coach, you can obtain outstanding results.

But how about being able to understand upfront which techniques the coach will use? It is a situation similar to recruiters that interview candidates without a structured competence-based interview model. Candidates will receive a different result depending on who the recruiter was that interviewed them.

With a structured model, all recruiters will follow the same protocol, so results for the candidates will be more predictable.

STANDARDIZING THE UN-STANDARDIZED

Using my engineering skills, I was able to develop a Coaching Framework that will work with any selection of tools and techniques the coach and the client prefer.

At the beginning I did not realize the big impact such a system could introduce to the Coaching industry.

Using the FuturaCOACHING Framework, coaches can deliver Standardized outcomes for their clients.

HOW TO BECOME A FUTURACOACH:

Using a solid framework will provide a blueprint to plan and deliver your Coaching Projects in a standardized and structured manner.

Five steps to create and grow your coaching empire:

1.- Go to Executive and Leadership Coaching

The fastest growing segment in the Coaching Industry is Executive and Leadership Coaching.

Select a precise niche where you have a lot of experience and are familiar with. It makes much more sense to select an area where you worked before rather than trying to explore something completely new.

2.- Use a Solid Framework

This will permit you to reflect a sound professional image and to charge prices that go with the quality you deliver.

3.- Create a Network

You cannot create a "One Person Empire." Sooner than you think about it, you will run out of your own time. You need to have an ongoing program to add additional coaches to your practice.

Corporations like big numbers, and will usually prefer to deal with a well-founded network of coaches than with a one-man show.

4.- Convert your Coaching Practice into a Machine

Start writing books, creating ebooks, create your own tools and all sorts of materials that will acquire a value and you will be able to sell.

5.- Become a Recognized Expert

Becoming a recognized expert will bring you in more business and more fellow coaches that will want to belong to your network.

Participate in events, deliver conferences, and write articles for specialized magazines.

10 COMMON MISTAKES EXECUTIVE COACHES MAKE
(And lose clients and business opportunities as a result)

1.- Being an Uninformed Outsider

Professional clients move inside their natural and self-imposed boundaries. They have their own jargon, keywords and communication style.

The only way to penetrate is to learn how they behave and communicate.

Once you select a niche for your Coaching Practice, it is necessary to make your best efforts to become an insider of the group where your target clients belong and move.

2.- Not knowing WHO your client is and WHAT he wants

You cannot offer a "one size fits all" solution and pretend to become successful – at least not in Executive Coaching.

It is paramount to define the specific niche where you will develop your Coaching Practice. Select a field you are familiar with. Experience and knowing the tools of the trade will provide a significant advantage.

If you know who your potential clients are, where to locate them, and what they want, you have at least started your road to success.

3.- Letting the Client Take the Rhythm

Executive clients are used to structured environments. They want to feel that your coaching sessions have a corporate style. If they feel otherwise, they will start thinking they are wasting their time and you will lose your clients.

4.- Using intuition instead of a Framework

Although Intuition is a much-desired coaching skill, you cannot rely on it to conduct your Executive Coaching Sessions. You need a solid Framework that will provide Structure.

Executive clients like to be treated in a Corporate Style Manner. And every Corporation uses Frameworks for their Processes.

5.- Not Planning the Coaching Project

Executives like to plan. They plan everything, their projects, career, and their whole life. For them coaching is just another Project that needs to be well-planned and organized.

If you do not treat your Coaching Service as a Project, you are speaking a language that is very different to what your client wants to hear.

6.- Not Planning Ahead Coaching Sessions

Delivering poorly-planned Coaching Sessions is the fastest way to disappoint and promptly lose your Executive Clients.

7.- Not Documenting Coaching Sessions

Documenting your Coaching Sessions in an adequate manner is paramount to show to your client the progress that was made later on.

More importantly, this will become a prerequisite for the company to approve extensions or additional budget.

8.- Not defining Precise Outcome GOALS

If your client does not have a clear understanding of the desired outcome goals to be reached with your Coaching Sessions from the beginning, it will be almost impossible for him to make an objective evaluation regarding your service afterwards. You need to define Goals at the beginning, not at the end.

9.- Not using Complementary Resources

There are lots of external resources that can help your client achieve desired goals. Accompanying Coaching Sessions with reading books, viewing videos and sharing articles is the easiest way to establish rapport with your client.

10.- Using a Low Pricing Structure

Corporations hate low-price suppliers for their executive level consumption. It goes against their pride and culture.

They may argue for cents to a carpeting contractor, but will not take seriously a low price offer for Coaching or Consulting. At the Executive Level, they will immediately relate low price to low quality.

About Johnny

Johnny Tarcica is the Founder and CEO of Empleos.Net, a leading Job Portal in the Internet for Latin America. He is also the creator of the FuturaADEP and FuturaDIAV assessments, which include personality, behavioral, desires, interests, attitudes and values tests, used by human resources departments, recruiters, trainers, consultants and coaches all over the world.

Johnny is a well-known entrepreneur, marketer, advertiser, talent acquisition expert, headhunter, international consultant and coach. Wearing so many hats, he has developed multiple relationships in different industries around the globe, with a variety of clients, partners, business associates and friends.

A self-taught software developer, Johnny wrote the first code for: www.empleos. net. He launched the company as a one-man show (himself), and worked his way to becoming one of the best-known and most popular recruiting platforms in Latin America. An avid traveler, he divides his time between creating new software tools and attending conferences and workshops – to make sure he is always current with the new trends.

Always creating and developing new projects, he is also the founder of latinojobs. com, an Internet job portal for the Latino community in the US that was launched in 2013.

Johnny is also an enthusiastic golfer. He plays just for fun, to enjoy life. Many people seek to play with him just as an opportunity to spend four hours of valuable talk and usually sound advice.

Johnny also founded the Happiness Bank for Latin America, where people can open accounts to keep track of their good actions, and include them in their resumes...

In business, he usually over-delivers, besides being extremely flexible and targeted, so it is no wonder his clients love him and love doing business with him. A famous tale of Johnny recounts a prospect client he met on a plane who asked for a service that was not provided at that time, and Johnny created and quoted it. Business was closed before the plane landed.

With so many projects and business ventures, when somebody asks Johnny to define which of them he thinks provide more value to the world, his answer is always FuturaADEP. It consists of an online testing platform that can be easily used for employee training and development, career planning, individual performance coaching and many more uses. This platform has been constructed following worldwide best practices using a multicultural team that provided input to different countries and continents.

If you are interested in starting or expanding a consulting or coaching practice, there is no better tool than FuturaADEP to establish and engage in a long-lasting relationship with your clients and also with your prospects.

Contact Information: For more information and additional resources for Johnny´s latest Executive and Leadership Coaching Framework,
please visit: www.futuracoaching.com

CHAPTER 30

THE ULTIMATE SUCCESS MINDSET— THE 12 ESSENTIAL POWERS TO OVERCOMING ANY CHALLENGING ECONOMY

BY YVONNE DAYAN

The mind is not a vessel to be filled, but a fire to be kindled.

~ Plutarch

What you *aren't* doesn't matter.

Many people define themselves in terms of what they're not. They block themselves from success because they think they're not rich enough, smart enough or as talented as they think they need to be.

None of that matters.

What matters is what you *are* – more specifically, what you *think* you are. You can lift yourself to a whole new level of achievement and attain your definition of success - if you develop the mindset that will allow that achievement to happen.

The kind of mindset I'm talking about enabled artists such as Georgia O'Keefe and Vincent Van Gogh to envision eternal masterpieces. It empowered incredible writers such as Shakespeare, Tolstoy and Steinbeck to put their passions on paper into great works of literature. It drove musical geniuses like Bach, Mozart, Chopin and Debussy to create enduring symphonic masterpieces. It also inspired architectural trailblazers like Frank Gehry and Ieoh Ming Pei to create startling structures that changed how we viewed design, and it drove scientific geniuses like Albert Einstein and Marie Curie to discover scientific breakthroughs that transformed how we view the universe and our own world forever.

Enduring and singular achievements such as these spring from what I call The Ultimate Success Mindset - a way of thinking that spurs you on to endless achievements. In this chapter, I'd like to share 12 Essential Powers I've uncovered that will help YOU do the great things you were born to do.

A VISIONARY ECONOMY

Before I talk about those 12 powers, I'd like to invite you to imagine what could be considered the perfect global economy. There would be an exquisite balance between every country's imports and exports, and all residents of the world would enjoy the fruits of what every nation and culture has to offer.

Each person would play a productive and positive part – with everyone taking on roles that would leverage their individual talents and skills to the fullest. There would be a rich and responsible financial system. Business decisions would be made on the basis on what best served the world and wealth would be used to realize our complete potential in bringing forth an incredible destiny for all. All parts of this ideal economy would work in a positive, productive way – and keep it alive, healthy and continually progressing.

Whether it's an entire world, a country, or a company, or an individual, ongoing success requires *all elements* to work synchronously so that progress can flow forward, unimpeded. However, if only one significant piece gets stuck, stops working, or forgets its real purpose, the whole operation can shut down or stagnate.

You're no different. Your health, relationships, family, wealth, career and spirituality, all need to flow harmoniously together to avoid disrupting your personal path to prosperity.

How do you achieve this ideal? Well, it all starts with your mindset – and I have developed a model for what I believe is the best one possible. The great teachers all tell you *how* to think – not *what* to think. That is the correct path. True Prosperity in any economy comes from developing what I call The Ultimate Success Mindset and allowing it to lead you to your Ultimate Success destination.

DEVELOPING "INSIDE-OUT" SUCCESS

Why is having this mindset so crucial? Because, as you change your inner thinking and your beliefs, you will INEVITABLY change your external outcomes to manifest the success you desire. Your current thoughts will produce your future results.

And the good news doesn't stop there. Your success mindset will continue to inspire and create awesome ideas and opportunities in the future. When you train your "insides" to search for what you want, you will find it – no matter how outside forces might momentarily stand in your way.

However, if you don't develop a success mindset that taps into your inner truth, your success will be delayed, if it comes at all. You'll constantly get in your own way and chase after things that will cause you to feel lost. It's like driving to a new destination with a disabled GPS system – *how can you find an unknown place if you don't have the tools to guide you there?*

You will also be at the mercy of the fluctuations of the world. Without a success mindset, you can too easily lose your center - and you fall prey to the three biggest "dream-killers" out there:

- Becoming fixated on what you lack.
- Repeating past mistakes over and over again.
- Judging yourself by how others judge you.

This Ultimate Success Mindset can help you avoid all that – and show you the way to become the best version of "you" possible.

My own journey to success began when I finally allowed myself to question certain beliefs that were forged from the culture I had grown up in and redefined my role in the world. I took the steps to mentally redefine what success was for *me* – and stepping out of my previous mental "box" was the all-important beginning of mastering my own success and happiness.

Through the following 12 Powers, I'll reveal the process that I used to achieve my Ultimate Success Mindset and empower myself, as well as the tens of thousands of people I've coached over the years. My space is limited here, so I can only touch on each Power briefly – but I will be expanding on these, as well as revealing 9 more essential powers, in a full-length book in the near future.

THE 12 ESSENTIALS POWERS OF MY ULTIMATE SUCCESS MINDSET

#1: The Power to Reprogram Your Mind

There's a difference between *wanting* something and *attracting* that something into your life. Most of us approach our ambitions with that "want" – but don't develop the mental tools to bring that desire into our lives.

In my case, I grew up in a culture where women were not involved in high-level business - and I bought into that very limiting belief. When I finally "reprogrammed" myself, I was able to transform how I felt about myself and to achieve far greater success. It was then, that my father invited me to take over the entire real estate division of his company, and recognized me as a valuable asset to his business. My story illustrates that we need to question our cultural biases. By accepting their limitations, we give our power away.

Affirmations can work wonders in the reprogramming effort. Here are a few you might want to try. Affirm them daily for a month and you'll see how well they work:

- I can do it! I can succeed!

- I am a successful entrepreneur running a fantastic business!

- I have all the knowledge inside me to achieve massive success!

- I can handle and solve any situation that comes my way!

- I add value to my clients and customers lives!

#2: The Power to Focus on What You Want

This power taps into the famous "Law of Attraction," which states that positive brings positive and negative brings negative. Our thoughts are made of energy that actually interacts with the outside world to bring whatever results energy contains. In other words, when you continually focus on why something *won't* work, it probably won't!

Instead, focus on why something *will* work for you and allow yourself to succeed. Meditate on the goals and successes you want to enjoy every day – you'll find your thinking clarified and your results quickly improving.

#3: The Power to "Grow" Your Mind to Bigger and Better Thoughts

An integral part of a success mindset is inviting the expansion of your thought patterns. As I mentioned, I had to expand mine; you also probably have certain "boxes" imposed on your thinking by where you live and what you experienced.

So move out of your comfort zone and open yourself up to new people, new places and new experiences. Work with mentors who have achieved similar things to what you want to achieve and find out their secrets.

And practice big picture thinking – in which a short-term hardship leads to long-term gain. I learned that from my father and brother, two visionaries who instill in their employees that establishing a strong long-term connection with customers is more crucial than making just one momentary sale. They always modeled honor and integrity in their business dealings.

My mother too is a big thinker, she values family as her number one priority and models a life based on principles, making success a wholesome way of life. My family's "big picture thinking" always inspires mine.

#4: The Power to Take Smart Risks

Virginia Rometty, the current CEO of IBM, summed up the wisdom behind this power when she said, "Growth and comfort do not co-exist." In order to achieve, your mindset has to be prepared for the moment when it's time to take a calculated risk.

I live close to a marina, where I like to take walks. In the marina, there is a boat with its name, "Risk and Reward," painted on the side. To me, I see it as the other way around – Reward and Risk! That's because there is a reward hidden in every risk we take. We will either learn from a negative outcome or we will experience the joy of a positive outcome. Either result brings growth and new knowledge – so why not go for it?

#5: The Power to Maintain a Positive Outlook

Positive thinking yields positive results. This is a power that is essential to a success mindset. Negativity breeds doubt not only in yourself, but also in those around you. If you're trying to do a big business deal, and you appear anxious and nervous as you're trying to close it, your would-be partners might not trust you enough to go through with it!

If you don't trust yourself, how can you expect others to? If you don't believe in what you're doing, why should anyone else respect your work? Yes, you must be realistic about the obstacles in your way – but you also must be realistic about the potential to overcome them. There are always positives to find, you just have to look for them!

#6: The Power to Act on Your Own Truth

This power is about training ourselves to choose based on what we want rather than what others want. We get judged and ridiculed sometimes for making choices others don't agree with – but if we don't make choices that line up with our own dreams, our lives are the ones that suffer for it, not those who tell us we're doing the wrong thing.

The Ultimate Success Mindset asks that you learn to listen to your inner voice and allow it to influence your choices. Choices are crucial; as billionaire author J.K. Rowling said, "It is our choices that show what we truly are, far more than our abilities."

The thing about choices is that sometimes we don't even know we're making them, because we communicate important things just in the way we speak or act. Make sure your choices, conscious or unconscious, spring from your personal quest for success. Here is a slogan that has served me well over the years: "Success is a decision, make that choice today. Greatness is a decision, make that choice today." And I did and I still do!

#7: The Power to Live for Possibilities

Success is not defined by outcomes, but on the efforts that you put forth. There is no such thing as "failure," only learning experiences, and negative feedback to change our direction. Just don't quit, and keep living for the possibilities.

There is no real success without failure. Henry Ford failed six times before he prospered with the Model T. Thomas Edison tried 5000 different kinds of filaments until he finally perfected the first practical, commercial light bulb. Don't let failure stop you, let it teach you and continue to be open to the possibility of success in whatever you're doing. Your chance of greatness grows with every disappointment. So always say YES to success!

#8: The Power to Set Your Own Rules for Success – and Live by Them!

Success isn't just about money or buying the best things. Success isn't just about winning. It's about a state of *being* where you feel satisfied with your life as it is and feel grateful about who you are and where you've taken yourself.

You get to set your own rules and goals when it comes to your own personal success – and nobody else should participate in that process, unless you want them to. You define the success you're after – and change it up when you need to (more on that later!). But don't forget you need to adhere to those rules and goals. Discipline your mind, discipline your choices and act on your success strategies.

#9: The Power to Pursue Your Dreams with Passion

Passion and enthusiasm are the fuel that drives us to our success. Successful people are always enthusiastic about what they do – and that enables them to run forward to their goals as though they had the wind at their backs.

A lack of passion in your mindset might indicate that the goals you're pursuing aren't ones you really believe in or want to attain. If you're not pursuing your goals with enthusiasm, meditate on it and make sure those goals really are the right ones for you.

#10: The Power to Be of Service

The more you bring to the table, the more you'll take away from it. The more value you provide, the more you'll create. Don't be afraid to help those around you – and always look for ways to be of service, especially to those in circles you want to be a part of. When your mindset is open to helping others, others will want to help you and you'll feel energized by the positive energy you create.

#11: The Power to Redefine Success as You Grow and Change

When you were seven years old, you may have wanted your own bike. When you were sixteen years old, you may have wanted your own car. And when you were thirty years old, you may have wanted your own house. As we grow and mature, our goals and our ideas about what success means to us change too.

And that's a natural progression. The Ultimate Success Mindset pushes you forward towards new transformations on a continual basis – and you'll want to adjust your goals accordingly as those transformations happen.

#12: The Power to Translate Your Mindset into *ACTION!*

A mindset doesn't mean much if you can't translate it into action that moves you forward. That's why I'm ending this chapter on this particular power. As many a pundit has noticed, positive thinking doesn't mean that much if you don't actually *do* anything to make things happen!

I believe in acting quickly, as valuable ideas are lost if they're not taken advantage of as soon as possible. You lose momentum and the potential for progress – something the Ultimate Success Mindset doesn't appreciate! As the old saying goes, "Luck is when preparation meets opportunity." Your mindset will indeed prepare you for great opportunities – so move fast when you encounter them, before they disappear!

If you'd like to know more about how to create and actualize this "Ultimate Success Mindset," I invite you to find out more by visiting my websites at: www.YvonneDayan.com and www.Imastery.net. In the meantime, I wish you the best of luck in your pursuit of your personal happiness. But remember, luck isn't so essential if you face your future with the right mindset in place!

About Yvonne

A groundbreaking entrepreneur, gifted author and effective corporate trainer, Yvonne Dayan has coached thousands to powerful breakthroughs in their personal growth, emotional well-being and ongoing wealth creation. A sought-after spokesperson in the fields of success and human behavior, she holds several degrees in counseling and psychology as well as a world-renowned reputation for her innovative and effective life and success coaching programs for businesses and individuals.

Yvonne has also had her share of media success; she's been a guest on numerous international TV and radio programs and been featured in various magazine and newspaper articles. She was singled out as one of twenty extraordinary individuals in the 2009 documentary film, *An Anything But Ordinary Journey* and appeared in the Harrison Ford and Kristin Scott-Thomas drama, *Random Hearts.* In 2005, Yvonne produced an acclaimed series of instructional DVDs entitled, *Creating Your Own Fountain of Youth, Bringing Down the Light and Restoring Your Soul to Wholeness,* which focused on how to use our mind-body connections to fuel our passions and heal our lives. She is also the best-selling co-author of the book *Change Agents* with legendary motivational speaker Brian Tracy.

Driven by principle and passion, Yvonne has dedicated her life to empowering others to reach their highest purpose. Her specialty is coaching women through the challenges of modern life and helping them lead their own extraordinary lives. Incorporating her mastery of unique life-changing techniques, Yvonne now holds her new impactful Imastery Seminars and her Tree of Life System in major cities throughout the U.S., Latin America and Europe in both English and Spanish. For over two decades, her seminars, books and videos have helped entrepreneurs, executives, professionals and people from all walks of life experience higher levels of life satisfaction, prosperity, and fulfillment in their professional and personal lives.

CHAPTER 31

THE SECRET INFLUENCE FORMULA

BY JORGE OLSON

Do you know influence is the ultimate secret to success? Yes, you probably did, especially if you have time to think about it. You can read about influence in ancient texts and new and classic self-help books, sales books and even holy books. But did you know influence is not a skill but a superpower? According to history and even Webster's Dictionary, influence is a supernatural power!

Yes, influence is important for business, but did you know influence is also the secret to happiness? It's the key to succeed in the new economy; it's also the key to succeed in life.

You know how this helps others, but, how does it also help you? I would argue that it helps you more than it helps others. You see, when you can create a state of emotional wellbeing, or to be clear, when you make people feel good, those people will want to be with you and they will like you. This will make you in turn feel fulfilled and happy, as the need to be liked and accepted is a primordial instinct.

Is that all? Only happiness? Well, as if this was not the holy grail of life, yes, there is more. You see, the effect of being liked, accepted, loved, and for people to search you out and spend time with you is immediate, but there is another larger, longer effect. When you spread this kind of influence, you position yourself as a leader, an alpha, a person to be respected and many times to be admired. This in turn creates more influence that can also be used in business, in sales, in politics – in other words, to get what you need and what you want. This is why influence is the key to success in business and success in life.

TURNING INFLUENCE ON AND OFF

One of my first and most memorable lessons since I was five years old was "be humble." I learned it at home, in my school and in my church. I also learned "Self Promotion is bad, being unselfish is good. No wonder I wrote the book, *The Unselfish Guide to Self Promotion!*

When I was growing up I went to a private catholic school in Mexico – a very conservative education in a conservative society. Getting attention was not a good thing; on the contrary, you had to be humble and humble equated to being quiet and unassuming. I thought my path in life would be as a missionary in the mountains of Mexico; helping the most neglected and exploited indigenous population in Mexico, up high in the isolated villages covered by tall trees in Chihuahua or Nayarit where no city slicker dares to go.

In school the examples we followed were of Jesus Christ and his mother Mary. The character traits you wanted to develop were: be strong, ethical, loving, and humble. Self Promotion was not part of the curriculum. Influence was not part of the curriculum either, unless you influenced by example.

My mind was so far away from influence and any type of self-promotion that all I wanted was to be a missionary and live with the indigenous population of Mexico. I know what you're thinking: if you're a missionary your job is to influence, to influence people on your religion. Well, not really, the school of thought at my school was not to convert, but to help with social work. Help by building homes and schools for the poorest, to educate and provide love and an example to follow. As I said, self-promotion and influence were far from my mind.

The formula for influence requires that you use "Unselfish Self Promotion" as one of the steps if you want to spread influence outside your immediate social circle. You have to get over the words "Self Promotion" meaning something negative, difficult or even a sin. I know it can be unnatural sometimes. We all know someone that just talks about themselves, their job, their vacations, their kids and how they are so great. That's not self-promotion, that's bragging, or in simpler terms, it's neediness for others' approval.

This is not the self-promotion I'm talking about. Unselfish self-promotion means providing content, information and help. It is spreading what you know will help others using communication tools to do it such as books, articles, speeches, Internet, videos and even mass media.

I discovered the power of influence at a very young age when I found myself listening and learning from people I respected. These could be family members, friends, teachers, or even listening to speeches or by reading. I saw how these people were shaping my thoughts and my character when I was a teenager, and I always told myself since that young age, "I want to learn so I can also teach." I wanted to influence.

As you'll see in this chapter influence is not just selling yourself or your ideas or even products, it's something much more important and deep. Influence has to start within, with change, before it can sprout and be shared with others. Influence can be a gift, it can be learned, and I think it may be a superpower.

IS INFLUENCE A SKILL OR A SUPERPOWER?

—*According to human history, and by definition, influence is a superpower, or supernatural ability.*

Here is the official Webster's Dictionary definition of influence:

Definition 1:

> *a: an ethereal fluid held to flow from the stars and to affect the actions of humans.*

> *b: an emanation of occult power held to derive from star..*

Definition 2:

> *a: an emanation of spiritual or moral force.*

Definition 3:

> *a: the act or power of producing an effect without apparent exertion of force or direct exercise of command.*

> *b: corrupt interference with authority for personal gain.*

Definition 4:

> *a: the power or capacity of causing an effect in indirect or intangible ways.*

Why is influence seen through history as a superpower? My mind can't help but wonder if it's somewhat of a Jedi Mind Trick, where a superpower can make you forget what you're doing or influence your behavior. Influence might not make you forget what you're doing, but it sure can mold, and even change ideas, thoughts, state of mind, emotions and even behavior.

This is why influence can be a superpower. If you can achieve a level of mastery where you can change people's emotions and behavior in a few minutes it can be seen as extraordinary, maybe four hundred years ago it could be seen as a superpower, for sure it was seen as "an emanation of spiritual or moral force" as we see in the definition by Webster. I would like to carry this type of influence and invite you to carry the same torch.

INFLUENCE IS THE KEY TO HAPPINESS!

—Wow, that's a bold statement, but it is true. Influence is one of the main pillars of happiness. It's also one of the main pillars of economic success, or, SuccessOnomics!

I want people to:

- Like me
- Listen to me
- Respect me
- Love me
- Want to be with me
- Give me a job
- Give me a raise and promotion
- Buy from me
- Invest in me and my business

Do any of these points NOT apply to you? Do you want money and business? How about love and friendship? All of these points have one thing in common. You need <u>influence</u> to achieve them. It does not matter if you apply it to your job, your business or your personal life. Influence is a key component in your success and your happiness, because once you exercise your influence it will spread to all areas of your life.

It's very easy to see influence in business; you want to make more money and you need to sell to do it. You sell yourself, a product or a service. If you want a raise you sell yourself, if you're the boss you sell everything! If you're the boss you have to sell the vision, the product, motivate employees, maybe influence investors and customers. It's non-stop influence all day long for entrepreneurs and executives. Now, in your personal life, influence may not be as black and white as in business. After all you don't need to sell anything at home, or do you?

Influence is not just a part of business; as a matter of fact it has to start in your personal life. As we stated earlier, influence is one of our basic survival needs after food and shelter. It is part of our social make-up.

Influence schooling for most of us starts at home as we're growing up. We need attention; we want to be liked, especially if you have siblings and have to fight for attention from parents and other grownups. The same thing goes for parents; you have to influence your kids before somebody else influences them. You want them to do well in school, sports, be ethical, maybe even religious. All of this requires influence, if you have it, you'll succeed in these aspects of family life. If you don't, well, you better have it!

Those influence skills you developed as a child evolve with experience and trial and error. If you're very good at influencing you probably had some formal or informal education on the subject and not just empirical learning. In my case, I've studied influence for a long time. I've studied it in university classes and by reading, courses, conferences and mentoring. There is influence in politics, business, family and other organizations; by oral and written communication, body language and more. Now you might not want to be an "influence scholar," but you do want to dedicate some time to learning this powerful skill or superpower!

HOW DO YOU DEVELOP YOUR INFLUENCE SUPERPOWERS?

—No, you don't have to join a Jedi Knight Temple to learn how to use influence. Influence is acquired with time and molded with knowledge and experience.

Imagine you are a child craving love and attention. Besides food and shelter, the number one thing humans need since we're born is love and attention. As we grow up we have even more needs. We need understanding, we need friends and people to like us and be around us. We want acceptance. These are primitive and basic needs that are embedded in us for survival as social creatures. We all have the need, but we don't all develop the talent and the skills to use this secret formula. The formula I'm referring to is *The Secret Influence Formula*.

Why is influence so important? Those natural impulses we have for attention since the day we're born are the basis for survival. They get us food when we cry, they get our parents to pick us up and give us attention, and later on as children they might get us a toy or a reward. On the other hand if we don't get the attention we need, children or teens might turn to rebellious behavior to get attention. Sometimes even bad attention is better than no attention. All of these attention-gathering activities build our influence skills since we're newborns. If we're good at it or have good parents, teachers and mentors we develop excellent skills we can use in our adult life. If we don't learn them, we'll be at a disadvantage in the workplace, in business and all through our lives.

Influence is getting that attention; it's getting a job, a promotion, an investor or a sale. It's becoming elected to office and being a pillar in your family and community. Influence is also a potential mystical superpower that you can use to change yourself, your family and your community.

The Secret Formula for Influence is very simple. Here is it:

You + Others = Influence

Yes, like most of the great formulas it's simple in concept, but not so simple to apply or follow.

The "**You**" part refers to who you are right now and how to become a better, more evolved person.

The "**Others**" part refers to how to communicate who you are with others and make them better.

Once you achieve these two parts of the equation influence will come by itself. You don't have to look for influence; you don't have to think about it, it will be the direct result of the formula. You will have influence in your family, your business, organization, and in all your social interactions.

Why would others in your social and business circle listen to you and follow you? Why will they call you instead of one of their other friends, colleagues or family members when they have a problem? What makes one person so different from others that makes them the "go-to-person" for everyone, for every reason? This is precisely what the secret formula brings: responsibility and attention. It is all rounded up in one word, influence.

It all starts with **You**. If you are not an example for others, ethical, informed, loving and educated, the formula is a non-starter. You have to be the person that works the most at themselves in every possible way. This includes mind, body and spirit. In other words, sports, exercise, food, learning, religion and all methods of self-improvement are important for your influence formula. Become the person you would like to have around.

Once you work on yourself you need to work on **Others**. You have to make sure others do well, learn and evolve. To achieve this you have to apply some self-promotion, otherwise your ideas, concepts, values will never be known. What do you do for others? You do what you did for yourself. You make them feel liked, comfortable, belonging, and therefore, happy. You can do this quietly one-on-one with people in your family and your tribes (gym, work, clubs, school, etc). If you want to spread out and have more influence you have to apply some self-promotion to your strategy using meetings, blogs, articles, videos and other modern communication strategies.

As you probably determined, *Influence* is much more than a formula, it is a philosophy of life. This philosophy covers the basics of how to live your own life, starting with education and knowledge, but more importantly, it dictates how to live with others, how to interact, and what you should do for others within your own life. If influence is a superpower, it's dormant in most of us.

About Jorge

Jorge S. Olson is President and CEO, Premier Brands Inc. He specializes in building Beverage Companies! Jorge is an international beverage industry expert and builds beverage and consumer goods companies.

Jorge is a dynamic, motivating and humorous storyteller. He has a passion for people, business and life. It is this passion that shines and translates in his stories, books and keynote speeches and conversations.

He will keep you entertained with stories, knowledge, experience and a dynamic pace that will keep you glued to his books. Jorge is funny, inspirational and motivational.

Jorge Olson grew up in Mexico with no running water and no electricity. He managed to land his first CEO position at the young age of 28. By 31, he was a veteran technology and consumer goods executive, consultant and owner of several wholesale distribution companies.

His advice and knowledge is sought after by executives, investors, entrepreneurs and everyday people looking for self-empowerment and growth as well as business advice and expertise. More than 80,000 people subscribe to his newsletters and hundreds of thousands visit his blogs. He's also launched more than 1,000 beverages and consumer goods over the last 12 years.

In his daily work, Jorge gives regular keynote speeches and training sessions on marketing, branding, marketing strategies, influence and self-improvement. He also owns several branding and content companies and consults for C level executives around the world.

Jorge is a social entrepreneur, consultant, writer, keynote speaker and family man. He is passionate about art, business, change and self-improvement.

You can reach Jorge at: www.PremierBrandsInc.com.

CHAPTER 32

THE FAIRY TALE OF RETIREMENT

BY JIM BLACK, MBA, CFP

Good afternoon, what a great conference this has been. The information I have heard so far is incredibly relevant for the world in which we live. I agree with what Steve Forbes said earlier this morning, and believe he has a pretty good grasp on what's happening around us right now.

When I got out of college, I went into the army. When I was in basic training a sergeant drew a circle on the board to explain how to set up a defensive position. As he drew the circle he announced that the full circle was 260 degrees. When I pointed out that a circle actually contained 360 degrees. He yelled back at me and said, "Don't be stupid, this is a <u>small</u> circle."

The sergeant was adamant that his math was correct, but that didn't make it so. Many people enter retirement with a circle that's only 260 degrees. What I'll share with you now, should help you to complete your circle.

My remarks this morning are titled "The Fairytale of Retirement." That title can be interpreted in two ways. First, that the concept of retirement is a fairytale, or second, that you can live your retirement as if it were your own fairytale, your own happily ever after.

My goal this morning is to show you how to make your retirement a fairytale.

If you're like most people, you have spent your entire working life, thinking about what you would do when you retired. You have <u>dreamed</u>, and <u>saved</u>, and <u>sacrificed</u> certain luxuries to be able to spend the rest of your life on vacation. A vacation, that can *easily* last 30 – 40 years.

Last month I took my kids to Washington DC for spring break. In preparation for the trip, I spent countless hours arranging flights, and rental cars, hotels in 3 cities and creating an itinerary that would allow us to see... EVERYTHING. I spent several hours on this project every week for about a month before I had it "nailed down." Its quite possible I spent more time planning the trip than the week we actually spent on vacation.

So lets look at the math. I spent a month planning for a weeklong trip. How much time is necessary to plan the rest of your life?

Last year my first book was published, designed to answer that very question. It's called... *HAPPILY EVER AFTER....Retirement doesn't have to be just a fairytale...* It was written to be a step-by-step guide to truly be able to live your retirement the way you want. I believe that you can indeed have it all in retirement and that it's actually quite simple.

A lot of people come into my office for the first time and tell me they've been trying to have it all, and they are instead on a track to the poor house. I understand the dilemma. We have a stock market that has basically made nothing since 1999, interest rates that are near zero, government debt that has eclipsed 17 trillion dollars and depending upon whose numbers you believe... our inflation is as high as double digits. Anyone looking in from the outside might say there is no way to live the fairy tale that you always dreamed of.

However, before you throw your dreams into the trash, lets talk about what truly matters. I would argue that *none* of the facts that I just shared... actually matter if you know how to manage them. Lets talk about cars for a minute...They all get flats, they run out of gas, they need constant maintenance, however, no one is suggesting that we should abandon our cars. With that same level of care, you too can live your dreams.

Recently, I was approached by a retired athlete who had enjoyed a terrific career in the NFL. He made more money in 10 years than 99% of the world will earn in their lifetime. He should have had plenty of money to live a rational lifestyle for the rest of his life. Unfortunately, he did everything exactly the same way as everyone else in the locker room. During his glory days he bought nice cars, large homes, took exotic vacations and bought pretty much anything else he thought he should have. He spent more money than he earned and when his career was done, so was he. At 30 years old, he retired from the game he loved, and found himself out in the cold, both figurative and literally. Broke and with nowhere else to go, he moved back in with his mother.

Every day, you're faced with the same decisions about money. How should you allocate the precious resources that you've worked so hard to amass? You can save it, or you can spend it. It depends on your goals for retirement, and how much you have already put away.

I have been giving financial advice for over 25 years, and I have discovered a few secrets that the wealthy use to create and increase their fortunes, but seem to be unavailable to the masses. Before I share those secrets, it is important to accept that you truly can have the retirement that you have always dreamed of. Until you allow yourself to dream a little and start making some plans, the rest of what I share with you won't be as powerful as it could be.

I am always stunned when people come into my office and tell me that they have NEVER had independent financial advice. Everything they know about the financial world was taught by a financial salesperson – a great person, but who was compensated to sell them a product. They were referring to their Stockbroker, their insurance agent, the guy at the Bank, and the list goes on.

Imagine for a moment that you knew nothing about cars, and you went into a Honda dealership to learn about cars. The person who spoke with you would spend a great deal of time explaining how the cars on his lot worked. He would find out how much you were willing to spend, and sell you the best car that he had available that most fit your needs. When you told him about what you wanted or needed in your car, you may have described a Toyota, but since he didn't have that option available, he sold you a car he got paid a commission on, instead of sending you to the Toyota dealership across the street.

Unfortunately, the financial world is much the same way. When you sit down with most financial people, they are perfectly happy to tell you all about the products that they sell, but are either unable, or unwilling to take the next step, which is to help <u>you</u> find out what is best for you in <u>your situation</u>, or what goals you are trying to achieve – whether they provide that solution or not. With this limited knowledge, your chance of success decreases dramatically.

Secret #1: You must find a fiduciary to work with, someone who will diagnose your financial health – someone independent and able to give you the advice that you need to succeed. Similar to your visit to a medical doctor, your doctor would never dispense medical advice without a thorough examination, or prescribe drugs or medical procedures without a diagnosis. To do so would be medical malpractice. For that he would lose his license.

However, if you go to a financial salesperson that is exactly what's going to happen. A fiduciary, on the other hand, will spend the time to understand what you need your money to do; they will explain your options, and help you find the ones that are best suited for your situation and your goals.

When I explain this simple secret to most people they always respond the same way… they tell me that they never knew there was any difference between, say, their stockbroker and a fiduciary, and why didn't their stockbroker tell them.

I can only assume why the stockbroker didn't tell them he worked for a large brokerage firm and not necessarily in their best interests, but I can help to sort through the noise. As people are getting more educated on the necessity of working with a fiduciary, many financial salespeople are trying to appear like fiduciaries to their clients…sometimes they're fiduciaries and sometimes they're not. It seems they want their clients to try to guess under which hat they are giving advice. Let me make this easy. If they are charging a fee for their time they are probably acting as fiduciaries, but if they tell you they're giving advice for FREE or being paid by their companies for that, you can bet they're not really fiduciaries, and I would suggest you walk away.

Let me move on to **Secret #2** I want to share with you. Retirement has never been about how much money you have; it has always been about how much money you spend. Let me give you an example. A couple, age 65, spending $80,000 a year including their social security and pension income, might only need about $400,000 in the bank to get the income that they need for the rest of their lives. On the other hand, that same couple spending $150,000 would need a nest egg of nearly $2,000,000.

Any plan you make, to start saving towards retirement, must start with how much money you're spending today and determine how much that will increase from today until the day you retire. Once you have this number, you're halfway home. Once you know how much annual income you will need at retirement, simple math can determine how much needs to be put away. Another point that I want to clarify for you is the concept of retirement itself. Very few of my clients have actually retired in the traditional sense. Yes, they left their full time employment, but they didn't leave the working world. Being in Seattle, I have a number of retired Boeing clients. Many of them when they retired either approached their boss or were approached by their boss, to talk about staying with the company, but cutting back their hours dramatically.

This is a true win/win. Boeing gets to keep a valued employee who already knows the job, but saves a ton of money on salary and benefits, and on the other side, an employee who still wants to maintain their social and intellectual ties, but wants more control of their time gets to stay involved.

To top off this benefit, the employee still has an income stream, although smaller than fulltime work, this income reduces the amount of money the employee needs to have saved before starting to live their dreams. Hence their fairytale can start sooner than they expected.

This point is important because retiring doesn't mean sitting on the porch swing rocking every day until you die. It means taking control of your time, doing the things you want to do, when you want to do them. Having time doesn't mean doing nothing. My clients still want to feel needed and connected socially. They want to be engaged, but simply want to do it on their terms.

Notice to this point, I haven't even talked about any products from the financial world. That is because they are actually much less important than having a plan. The financial salesperson will focus relentlessly on why such a product is necessary or why you can't live without it, but remember that's because that's how they get paid. If you spend hours learning about cars from a car salesman, he will never get paid for that time until he can convince you to buy one of his cars.

Secret #3: The final piece of advice I want to share with you is so simple that you have known it your entire life. Your parents told you this, your friends have said it, heck, even the family dog probably knows this secret, yet everyone still ignores it. Probably because it is the most difficult thing I will ask of you. If you don't remember anything else I said today, if you can remember and follow this final principle, your odds of taking control of your retirement will improve dramatically.

The final secret is this: *"Live below your means."* Simply put… don't spend more money than you make. This is such a problem, such a force of human nature, that there is even a law named after it. It's called Parkinson's Law. The law states that you, and me and every other person on the planet spend to the level of their income – meaning that we spend everything that we make. If you are doing this, there is some comfort in knowing that everyone else is making the same mistake, but more importantly, now that you recognize the problem: STOP! Stop spending beyond your means… stop today, or accept the fact that you will NEVER and I mean NEVER retire – not at 65, not at 70 or 80, or any other age. If you don't stop spending more than you make, you will die sitting at your desk at the office. The easiest solution to this problem is to set up a program to have money automatically withdrawn from your account before you start spending. Many people do this with their 401(k), which is good, but not enough to fund a retirement for 30 years and it will make little difference how much they save if they're running up their credit cards. Be in the minority, be the person who saves even just one penny more than you earn, if you do this, I promise you a happier, more enjoyable, financial life.

I want you to succeed. I have helped hundreds of clients create and implement plans that allow them to enjoy the retirement they always dreamed of, and you can be a part of this fraternity as well. If you'll follow the three secrets I shared with you today, you can have the retirement for which you've always dreamed.

Thank you!

About Jim

A founding partner, Jim Black's responsibilities include all aspects of financial and tax strategy planning. Jim has over 25 years of experience in the financial planning industry, and now devotes his efforts to the distribution-planning arena. His main focus is helping clients to **"Retire"** based on their own terms. For Absolute Returns Solutions, Inc. this means focusing on desired income and estate goals; striving to better assure lifetime income and asset preservation.

Jim has been featured on many TV shows, including ABC, CBS, Fox, NBC and KTCS-PBS in Washington. Jim Black has radio shows on KTTH 770 am "Financial Safari" and has recently published his first book called *HAPPILY EVER AFTER – Retirement Doesn't Have to be a Fairytale* which won the 2012 Quilly Award and has become a best-seller in two categories.

Jim grew up on a farm outside of McMinnville, OR. It was his job to milk the cows every day at 5am and 5pm, giving him the inspiration to go to college. After graduating from Brigham Young University with a degree in international finance, Jim went on to earn his MBA from Willamette University. He served as an officer in the military and ran his first and last marathon. Jim and his wife Ann live in Redmond and have 6 children – from 21 years old to the caboose at 4 years old. Jim enjoys all the activities that go with raising a family – especially scouting, where he has been a scoutmaster for many years.

Jim comments: "If people planned for retirement like they plan a trip: Lets say you and your family of three children want to go to Orlando, Florida and you budgeted $5000 for the trip. If you planned that trip like most people plan their retirement, you would probably only make it as far as Alabama, it would cost you $10,000 and you would have probably lost two of the kids along the way."

CHAPTER 33

FROM THE DITCH TO THE MOON — CAPITALIZING ON THE CREDIT CRASH IN THE NEW ECONOMY

BY ELIZABETH POTTER

Booms and busts are going on all the time. People say there is balance to everything. Believing this to be true, then it would be logical for me to say...the debt collection industry is a spin off of the credit industry.

I don't think I know anyone who <u>has not</u> utilized some form of credit product at one time or another such as credit cards, lines of credit, student loans, mortgages, car loans, the list goes on and on...

Back in 2008 when I first learned about this business, it never really entered my mind about how important credit was to most people in today's society. It seems to me that we live in an *"I WANT IT NOW"* society. Whatever happened to *"Save for a rainy day"* or *"save then spend?"* What a great opportunity for lenders. It opened up the market for new entrants such as payday loans.

The credit card concept was absolutely brilliant! According to Wikipedia, the first credit card* available was the Diners Club Card formed in 1950 by Frank X. McNamara, Ralph Schneider and Matty Simmons. I wonder if they could have imagined how one card could spin off and create so many as there are today. It also created jobs for marketing, incentives, counselling, and collecting. Years ago, I got paid by a focus group to provide feedback to design Wal-Mart's Visa Card. All that from the Diners Club Card.... that's amazing!

Below is the data from the Federal Reserve from June 2013:

Total U.S. credit card debt	$793.1 Billion
Average credit card debt per household	$15,799

Federal Reserve (www.federalreserve.gov)

The opportunity I saw was specializing in credit card debt. Why? Because Credit Cards are important to people. A credit card gives you flexibility in the way you live your life. It can help you with almost anything that may arise for you financially. You can buy groceries, pay for education and buy gas for your car so you can get to work.

There are certain things you can't do if you don't have a credit card such as rent a car or reserve a hotel room. Some even give you added value by tracking expenses for you! On your statement closing date, you know exactly how much you spent on food, entertainment, gas, etc. for that period by a mere glance. More time for the things you enjoy in life! Perhaps spend more time with your family! They give you incentives to use your card and merchants offer the convenience of accepting it. I am one of those who use their card for travel points. The more I use it...the cheaper my travel expenses. I use it for whatever I can instead of cash. I also have more than one...No wonder the number is so high! Forget the old saying: 'manage your money'... you need to add...'manage your credit!'

What do you do when things happen in life? You lose your job, get ill, relationship breaks down...paying your bills can be stressful at the best of times. But at the worst? It's just not that important! Let's face it, when you only have a little money coming in, is paying your bills more important than keeping a roof over your head and food in your belly?

* *http://en.wikipedia.org/wiki/Diners_Club_International

Probably Not!

In 2007, I was diagnosed with an illness that rocked My World! My money train had stopped! I had no money working for me. It was hard enough focusing on getting well. Lucky for me, I got thru my adversity with flying colors. It was enough of a scare that it changed my perspective on life. When I got back to work, I began to pay off my bills and save some money. I gave my money to an investor – only to find out it was a Ponzi scheme and I lost all of my savings! It was then that I committed to myself not only to create a vehicle where my money worked for me, but also because of my illness, I wanted to make a difference in the world. The question was "How can I?"

In early 2009, I met a man named Bill Bartmann. He was speaking at a conference I was attending. Being an Entrepreneur, his outside-the-box thinking grabbed my attention. It was that "inner knowing" moment of "ah-ha!" – becoming a Passive Debt Buyer was exactly the answer to my question of "How can I?" I have one life to live and I was going to make it count!

There are two types of Buyers, one you are considered an Active Buyer whereby you buy and collect on the debt yourself. The second, a Passive Buyer where you buy the debt and give it to a third party collection agency to collect on it for you. There is no upfront fee. They collect on the asset and keep their contingency fee and give you the remainder. You don't even need to look for customers…You just buy them. The challenge is paying the right price.

The problem…millions of people have fallen into default for whatever reason. We know for sure a huge reason is unemployment. Record Unemployment = Record Default…It is the perfect storm for this industry. There is an oversupply of charged-off debt available at steep discounts.

In 2009, LP Credit Resolution (LPCR) was formed and the mission was clear! We were going to help people re-build.

One of my favorite sayings is by Buckminister Fuller: *"YOU NEVER CHANGE THINGS BY FIGHTING THE EXISTING REALITY. TO CHANGE SOMETHING, BUILD A NEW MODEL THAT MAKES THE EXISTING MODEL OBSOLETE."*

This is not a new industry. There are thousands of Debt Buyers and Debt Collector companies in the industry both public and private…however, what if you did it differently?

Being a mom, I do my best not to kick my kids while they are down. Instead, I offer them a hand and pull them up and say, "It's ok! Now how can we fix the problem?" When I say "WE" I do my best not to do the work for them but offer solutions so they can choose what to do next. At times the solutions are simple but sometimes not so easy for either one of us! They, after all, created their problem, and by their fixing it…the result…it built up their self-esteem and they learned from their mistakes.

Bill Bartmann's message made not only ethical sense to me but good business sense as well. These are real people with kids, husbands, wives, etc. They have real problems and need real solutions.

Numerous people have had their lives severely altered and things are just not the same…. I get it! They are already beaten down. The 1996 movie "Jerry Maguire" comes to mind…Especially the words…**"Help me….Help you!"**

In 2011, LPCR moved all of its holdings to CFS2. Not only were we going to help people re-build just like I had to, we were going to do it differently…by treating people with Dignity and Respect!

As a Buyer, I signed the following pledge:

1. We will never attempt any collection efforts on any debt that is beyond the statute of limitations.

2. We will never file a lawsuit for the collection of a credit card debt.

3. We will never charge interest on a credit card debt that was charged-off by the original issuer.

4. We will never attempt to contact the customer by telephone more than two times in any one 24-hour period.

5. We will never re-sell credit accounts to anyone who has not signed this Pledge.

Our Mission as a Group:

To be leaders in the industry with a new model and to create at least 10,000 jobs.

How do I know my customers are being treated this way? Because first of all, as I have gotten to know him over the years, Bill is a man of his word and in my books, if you don't have that... you have nothing.

Secondly, I see many of the thank you letters and stories of recovery from customers working with CFS2. Have you ever heard of a collection agency getting thank you letters? With the industry's bad reputation, this is unheard of!

Thirdly, the awards CFS2 is getting from the business world include the "Code of Ethics Award" – but most importantly, the "Friends of the Consumer Award" was <u>NEVER</u> given to a debt collection company ever in history!

As an Entrepreneur, in my businesses it's all about the customers. You provide a good or service and in exchange you receive money for the value provided. Why then would we not apply the same concept to this business?

If a bank has a customer and that customer has numerous accounts and products everyone is happy! If the customer runs into problems and has only a finite amount of money, they now have to choose what to pay. What if they fall into default with their credit card because it is more important for them to pay for their mortgage till things get better? The bank has to charge it off after a certain period of time because it is no longer a performing asset. Now the collector comes into play. What if that collector is abusive or decides to sue them and pushes them into bankruptcy? Do you think the customer will take it personally? I would! I would be angry at the collector and the bank. I would start looking for ways to do business with another bank. Everyone loses! The customer, the collector and the bank!

In my recent travels I have been approached numerous times by staff of credit card companies promoting their card. I have seen them in airports, large employer staff quarters, malls, on airplanes, etc. In the old days, those promotions usually just came in the mail and now they have gotten more creative.

I have spoken to many people throughout this downturn and the story I heard most often was this…I don't have enough money so I just put them in a hat and pick something to pay. If they are rude to me they don't even get put in the hat! I'm underwater and my credit is shot so who cares. I'm doing the best I can. These people are not bad! They are middle class individuals and being middle class, we know on average it takes two incomes to provide the necessities in life, especially if you have children. What happens if one person in the household stops contributing to the household finances even for a short while? The result is most likely default! What happens if that customer is being treated with dignity and respect? What if they are offered solutions to help them make it better and move forward? What would the results be?

We already know the answer! In business it all starts with the customer! You want repeat business. In my case I want monthly payments just like any other lender. This creates cash flow.

Ask yourself…What is an economy? To me, it is all about people exchanging goods and services with each other for money. Luck is when opportunity and preparation meet!

I once read an article that I never forgot by Bill Gates…

3 Elements in a successful business….

1. You need to have VISION
2. You need to have PATIENCE
3. You need to be able to EXECUTE

Numbers don't lie! As the years go by, I now have enough data to see that by using an agency that operates such as CFS2 has increased the bottom line. They create relationships with my customers and make it a win – win for all of us!

One of my favorite quotes by Socrates: ***"THE SECRET OF CHANGE IS TO FOCUS ALL OF YOUR ENERGY, NOT ON FIGHTING THE OLD, BUT ON BUILDING THE NEW."***

A major debt collection industry reform is underway creating an opportunity to not only help many people, but capitalize in the process.

Lessons Along The Way:

Think Balance .... there are opportunities in every challenge.

Need Help .... hire a Mentor.

Find the Pain .... be the solution.

Be a Leader .... do things differently.

Create the Team .... for the betterment of all.

Investing .... look at the leader and do your due diligence.

Create Wealth .... help more people.

About Elizabeth

Elizabeth Potter brings over 28 years of experience with logistics, production, customer service and financing. She opened her first business in 2006 offering bookkeeping services. In 2008 she expanded as a Professional Organizer specializing in small business. Feedback from clients and realizing a niche for other services, Elizabeth formed a new company Systemized For Play Ltd in July 2010. (www.systemizedforplay.com)

She has a special talent that helps business owners work through their chaos and create simple systems unique to them. She has built a reputation as a reliable, effective, and proactive consultant. Elizabeth has worked with many small business owners by creating systems that help them understand and achieve greater efficiency, profitability and more free time.

Her largest project and passion was formed in 2009. LP Credit Resolution, LLC a credit buying company that specializes in credit card accounts. The company is committed to helping at least 10,000 people re-build their lives by treating them with dignity and respect. Utilizing the resources of CFS2 an outside-the-norm financial recovery agency who in 2013 won the "Friends of the Consumer Award." In June of 2013, Elizabeth was a Keynote Speaker with Steve Forbes at the "Success in the New Economy" summit. (www.lpcreditresolution.com and www.cfstwo.com)

Elizabeth has co-authored two books with Brian Tracy, *Cracking The Success Code* and *Change Agents.* Her contribution to Change Agents won her the "Editor's Choice Award." She is a two-time "Quilly Award" winner and was a guest on the Brian Tracy Show aired on ABC, NBC, CBS and Fox Affiliate stations. She was also in *USA Today* and appeared in the February 2013 issue of *Forbes Magazine.* She is a monthly contributor on the 'Money For Lunch' radio show. (www.moneyforlunch.com)

Elizabeth has trained in the areas of economics, accounting software, business management, sales and marketing. She is a proud member of CEO Space, The Progressive Group For Independent Business (PGIB) and is a member of the Business Development Bank of Canada's View Point Panel.

CHAPTER 34

PASSING ALONG WEALTH TO SUCCEEDING GENERATIONS

BY MICHAEL CANET, JD, LLM

In my first book, the Amazon #1 Best Seller: *Surviving the Perfect Storm*, I told the story of growing up in the foster care system. I spent three years in foster care plus almost another year in a children's shelter. I never lived in one place for more than a year and I actually attended five different high schools - only attending one for a complete year. We were the family that was sponsored for Christmas and church groups took us on "vacation." I joke with friends that my childhood should have been made into an ABC Movie of the Week and a three part one at that!

Well, thirty plus years have now passed and I can tell you that life has definitely turned out better than I could have ever imagined. I am way over educated: undergrad, attended grad school before switching to law school, and even a master's of laws and letters in taxation (for lawyers, a LLM is our advanced degree). I received all sorts of academic honors and awards throughout my college years. I have even have been appointed by the Governor of Maryland to a State Regulatory Board. I host a nationally syndicated TV show, *The Savvy Investor,* as well as a local Baltimore radio show of the same name. I have a very successful Estate, Tax, and Financial Planning firm with four offices in the Baltimore/ Washington corridor. I have reached the top of my profession, and with that success, all the financial rewards that come with the hard work it took to build a successful practice.

I have been married for 25 years and we have been together for over 32 years (my mother was married 5 times and my adopted mother was married 6 – so I wasn't even sure what a long-term marriage would look like). I have two great kids: one off in college doing all those things that college students do as they try to figure out the direction of their lives; and the other is still searching for his meaning of life and it is that search that is my focus in this book.

For parents who have achieved financial success in life, our children face very unique problems. Yes, they have the same teenage angst about self-identity, acne, dating, and just plain trying to figure out who they are. But they also face other pressures that most kids don't. Think about this: my kids traveled the world on vacations; had SUV's and BMW's for their transportation; their senior school trips were to the Galapagos Islands and Barcelona. They both attended private prep schools with fifty to sixty kids per class: my oldest had 53 kids in his graduating class and my youngest had 68. For better or worse (and sometimes I think worse) my kids expect the Ritz Carlton and Four Seasons when they travel. They want limo's picking them up and understand what a dessert fork is and know which glass is theirs at a formal dinner party. My kids had the life that I always wanted for myself and now my wife and I are paying the price for giving them an incredible upbringing.

Neither my wife nor I are Trust Fund Babies (TFB)– we haven't and won't inherit any wealth. Her parents are comfortable but not wealthy and I help support mine. No money coming to us. That isn't true for my kids and unfortunately it has become apparent that my older one expects it to happen and is living his life as if it will happen sooner rather than later. When they were born, there wasn't a handbook on how to raise them, and like most parents, we did what we thought was right. There isn't a handbook for them now either and it is only through having established friendships with adult "trust fund babies" have I come to realize that kids like ours, those children of financially successful people, have special needs of their own.

My friend Gary is a Trust Fund Baby – and I do mean Trust Fund. His grandfather was a very successful businessman and made millions and millions with Carnegie. Growing up, he always knew he was going to inherit a lot of money. For him, his whole life has revolved around money and trying to make more – it takes priority over all things in his life, including his marriage and children. He has done a great job growing the wealth that he was left, but the funny thing is, his grandfather taught him about business and money, but he doesn't talk to his kids about money at all.

As a matter of fact, one day we were having a family meeting and the topic of his sister came up. She has some medical issues, mid-stages of dementia, and requires 'around the clock' attention. His kids were at this meeting and asked questions about her care and the cost of her care. Gary had already told me not to share with the girls that there was a Trust that was paying her bills. He doesn't want them to know that there is money in the family. So here he is, having learned about money from a very successful businessman and having done very well growing that inheritance, and not instilling any of that incredible knowledge onto his own kids. What does he think is going to happen when they inherit $10,000,000 each? This inheritance will have a profound impact on their lives and quite frankly, can destroy it because wealth and money is never discussed in his house.

I know that a sudden inheritance can have a profound and dramatic impact on a person's life. A client of mine, Charlie, died a couple years after we set up his Trusts. He was very charitably-minded so we did some advance planning using Charitable Remainder Trusts (CRT) and Dynasty Trusts. When Charlie set up his CRT's, we did so in a manner that provided Robert, his son, with a sizable stream of income for his life and left a sizable gift to Charlie's favorite charity. In addition to the CRT, we also set up a second Trust for Robert; it was thought that it would be for him only in rare circumstances and for the possibility of future medical expenses, and to benefit Charlie's two grandchildren.

Unlike Gary, Charlie tried to talk to Robert about money. Unfortunately, Robert was never interested and spent most of his life trying to get out from underneath the tall shadow that Charlie cast. Like Gary's grandfather, Charlie was a very successful businessman and made his fortune in railroads. I met Charlie and worked with him during the last 15 years of his life and came to know him fairly well. He had a very strong personality and was quick to voice his opinion – sometimes diplomatically, sometimes not so much. I can imagine that growing up, there was quite a bit of perceived pressure on Robert to achieve that same level of success.

When Charlie died, Robert was surprised to learn that his father had left him over $250,000 a year as an income stream as well as almost $10,000,000 divided between two Dynasty Trusts. What surprised me was how quickly Robert blew through the $250,000 of income. Within the first 6 months of his inheritance, Robert spent almost $150,000 on drugs, alcohol, and a very fast lifestyle. Keep in mind; this is a 50-year old man who has never really held a full-time, long-term job. Dad always bailed him out and always helped him make ends meet. Robert never lived up to what he perceived was his father's expectations. The fact is that in my many conversations with Charlie, all he ever wanted was for Robert to find something he could be happy with. I am not sure that Charlie was able to convey this to Robert and certainly Robert never "heard" Charlie.

To some extent, this is where we find ourselves with our eldest son. We felt like we instilled a respect for money: he always was required to work a job; he had to pay for his gas and cell phone as well as his entertainment. We always spoke about money and explained the costs associated with our lifestyle. But somewhere along the lines, the message was lost, or not conveyed correctly. Just recently I was having a conversation with him about saving for his future. I suggested that he start putting money into a ROTH IRA and that I would match him, dollar for dollar. I went through all the reasons for starting early (he is only 21) and the importance of having enough so that he could retire in a desired comfort level and at a reasonable age. My wife and I were dumbfounded when he explained that he wasn't too worried about saving for his future because he was going to inherit enough from us to take care of him (almost as dumbfounded as when he announced that he wasn't going back to college because it was such a waste of money, after all, you can Google anything you want to know – but that is for another book and another chapter).

For Charlie and Robert, there is a happy ending. After working and talking with Robert for almost three years, he is finally living the life that Charlie envisioned for him and I think to some extent, the life that Robert always wanted but couldn't figure it out until it was too late:

Charlie didn't get to see Robert become the man he is today. Robert went back to school and got his degree in computer animation and graphic design and is actually creating incredible "paintings" on his computer that he then prints in oil onto canvas. I think that given the opportunity, had Charlie spent a little more time on helping Robert figure out what Robert wanted from life – had Charlie given him a little more breathing room, he might have seen the results he always wanted for Robert…for Robert to be happy.

And how does this relate back to Gary. Gary is taking baby steps. The fact that his kids were in the family meeting at all was a huge step for him. Gradually Gary is starting to recognize that leaving money to his kids is a wonderful gift but without teaching them and giving them the necessary skills to handle such a gift, well, it could turn out to be a complete disaster. The fact is that it does require special skills and knowledge to facilitate these steps – and fortunately, Gary was willing to take those steps.

This leads me to John. John isn't a client and neither were his parents. John is an acquaintance I met through a very good friend of mine, Jerry, who is a client and a TFB as well. When I first met John, it turned out to be a small world: his daughter attended school with my son. Over the course of several dinner parties and quite frankly, too much wine for John, his story unfolded. Like many of my TFB clients, John grew up in a life of luxury: private schools, chauffeurs, houses in several states as well as Europe, butlers, maids, and all that really cool stuff we see in the movies (think *Arthur*, the original one with Dudley Moore). Unfortunately for John he has never found himself and like many TFB's who never seem to find their way, his life has resulted in a series of addictions, bad marriages, and a depleting trust. In fact, at Jerry's last dinner party, I learned that John was selling the family home because he needed the money. Here is a man, about 65, having lived "the life" for 65 years and now he is down to selling the family home just so he can make ends meet (he already sold the other real estate).

This leads me back to my own children. If everything continues to go well, they too will be TFB's. I want them to have a comfortable life and I don't want them to worry about retirement or even having enough to get by on during their working years. But more importantly, I want them to understand that my money and wealth won't bring them happiness. They have to find their own success and it doesn't matter where they find it, just find a way to be happy. We can't allow our kids to measure their worth by our accomplishments. They need to understand and know that we are proud of them even if their version of success is different than ours. They are their own people and they will find their way. It is incumbent upon us, as parents, to give them the support and encouragement they need – give them the space and time to figure out life. It will happen.

So how does this relate to *Successonomics*? I am sure there are many great stories of how to make money and where the economy is going – I see them in books and journals all the time. What I don't see is the information we truly need to make sure that our gift to our children and grandchildren is more than just a large Trust Fund full of money. Sure, I could have written about all the tax benefits of CRT's; how to protect your heirs from creditors and greedy spouses; I could even tell you how to establish accounts offshore and live basically tax free. I have a law degree, a tax degree, and I am a financial planner – I could have spent my time and yours addressing these very boring topics – important, but boring. (Have you actually ever read the tax code?) Yes, they are important, but understanding the impact of this gift to our children, understanding how to give this gift and the responsibility that goes along with the gift, well, that is a better story.

Happy Reading!!!!!

About Michael

Michael Canet, JD, LLM is a financial planner and estate-planning attorney specializing in family legacies and is a founding member of Prostatis Financial Advisors Group, LLC.

Canet is the author of the best-selling book, *Surviving the Perfect Storm: How to Create a Financial Plan That Will Withstand Any Crisis*, and has been featured on *The Wall Street Journal, Fox News,* and *USA Today.* He is also host of the nationally syndicated television show, *The Savvy Investor*, and The Savvy Investor radio show on WCBM 680AM. His approach, both on and off The Savvy Investor shows, is distinguished by clear and concise answers that are accessible to the people who need to understand them most: retirees.

You can listen to The Savvy Investor live on WCBM Talk Radio AM 680.

CHAPTER 35

A TEQUILA TRAIN LEADS TO THE DISCOVERY OF UNIQUE TALKING POINTS (UTP)

BY MARC BURTON

Have you ever wanted to know why some businesses are able to increase profits and reduce costs? Able to advertise very little or not at all? To build and retain loyal customers and team members? Many would argue that these outcomes are conflicting and not achievable simultaneously.

I have been lucky to be involved in three businesses that achieved this feat: Mahiki, Whisky Mist and Tonteria are three of London's most famous night spots. We followed certain marketing principles. They are available to anyone and can benefit any business no matter how big or small.

My goal, in writing this chapter, is to explain the three golden principles that anyone can follow in order to achieve unique talking points (UTPs) within their business.

Traditional marketing is growing weaker and less effective by the day. We live in a world where we are bombarded with choice. Our attention spans have shortened. Traditional marketing through advertising has become ineffective. Conventional advertising is ignored. People crave true differentiation. They need 'unique talking points.' The businesses that create 'unique talking points' are the ones that will lead their fields today and in the future.

WHAT IS A UTP? (UNIQUE TALKING POINT)

A unique talking point (UTP) is:

Something that is so unique or different that it compels people to tell others or share it.

In creating unique talking points (UTPs) in your business you will be able to:

- Increase profits and reduce costs dramatically.
- Totally eliminate advertising from your business as your customers and team members will do this for you.
- Help you become the best in your class and achieve long term success.

LAW 1:
BOLDNESS—THE TOY TRAIN AND TEQUILA

Boldness be my friend.
~ William Shakespeare

Boldness is the first principle in creating a UTP.

When developing Tonteria, our Mexican tapas lounge and nightclub in London, we wanted to differentiate the way we served tequila. Guy Pelly and Alain Donabedian, my business partners, suggested we run a toy train on the ceiling of the club to deliver drinks to our guests.

When creating new clubs we have always had a test. If we had friends visiting from overseas for one night, would our venue be so unique that they'd have to visit?

It wasn't easy to get the toy train to fit in the club but through persistence we managed! Before the opening, the press and London crowd were writing and talking about the train. From the opening night onwards, guests quickly fell in love with *The Tonteria Express (The Toy Train)*. They couldn't wait to photograph it with their phones. The train appeared time and time again on Twitter, Facebook, Instagram and was even written about in the US and UK issues of *Vanity Fair* magazine.

The *Tonteria train* is effective because:

1. It is visual and bold. Everyone in the venue can see it.

2. It is unique and surprises people. People have never seen a toy train on the ceiling of a club, delivering shots of tequila.

3. It is consistent, the train is in use every day we are open.

We, like all the other clubs in the world serve tequila shots but as we have done it in a unique fashion. Naturally, guests talk about it and share it. This is an example of a UTP created through boldness.

Other examples of businesses and individuals that used boldness to create unique talking points are:

- The visual white headphones of the Apple iPod made the product stand out from all the other MP3 brands that had black headphones. The bold headphones gave the iPod a UTP.

- Damien Hirst, the richest living artist, rose to fame when he put a 14 foot long tiger shark, immersed in formaldehyde, in a clear tank. He then did a series with other dead animals. This bold statement was surprising and unmissable, creating huge publicity, as people couldn't help talking, writing and arguing about it.

- Tom Eulenberg, the most famous club owner in London (Cirque Le Soir, a favourite of Tom Ford, Rihanna and Justin Bieber), became famous when he started wearing a top hat every night. This bold move created a UTP for Top Hat Tom.

Questions to ask in order to create UTPs through boldness in your business:

- What element of your business could include boldness?

- Is the boldness so unique that when people see it they will automatically want to talk about it, take a picture and share it?

- Can the bold UTP be integrated consistently?

LAW 2:
SIMPLICITY—CHOOSE WISELY AS YOU CAN'T
BE GOOD AT EVERYTHING!

Simplicity is the ultimate sophistication.
~ Leonardo da Vinci

The world is increasing in complexity. We are faced with more choices in every department of our lives. There are millions of websites, thousands of TV channels and even hundreds of toothpastes. In our ever more complex world, simplicity has now become a luxury. Simplicity is rare. Embrace simplicity within your business and this will become one of your most powerful UTPs.

We quickly realised that the popularity of Tonteria was an issue.

The drink service was taking too long. Our bar was small. Guests complained as it reduced their enjoyment. Each cocktail would take a few minutes to make. When someone asked for a mojito, a cosmopolitan and a frozen margarita it would take the barman over ten minutes to make. Each cocktail would take a few minutes of his time.

A friend bought me a copy of Uncommon Service by Frances Frei and Anne Morriss. They explain:

1) You can't be good at everything. It is essential to focus on a few things at which you can be really good. They point out you also need to be really bad at some things.

2) You can reduce costs while simultaneously improving the service.

3) Through bad service design you can undermine the performance of your team.

From reading this book a solution appeared. By offering different cocktails, we had given too much choice to our guests and made life difficult for our bar team. It was impossible to serve all these cocktails quickly.

The solution was to minimise the offering.

We decided to go back to basics. We analysed our vision. We needed to stick to our Mexican roots and focus on tequila. One drink that was becoming known as our signature drink was the frozen margarita. It was quick to make, delicious and a big seller. Another best seller was the mojito. The mojito is rum-based and one of the longest cocktails to make.

The two most important goals were:

a. Significantly reduce the waiting time for drinks at the bar.

b. Stick to our Mexican roots and link to tequila.

We decided to only serve frozen margaritas in various flavours. We were going to be the best at serving frozen margaritas and the worst at serving traditional cocktails, as we wouldn't serve any!

Some of the team didn't think it was going to work. The result has been remarkable.

We have built a UTP as we offer frozen margaritas in various flavours, some of the best in London. It is now quick to get served as it takes an eighth of the time to produce a frozen margarita compared to a traditional cocktail. It has relieved the pressure from the bar team. It is easier for the customer to order as they have less choice. The bar team is able to focus on the interaction with the client as the drinks are easy to make. Guests have more time to dance and socialise. A winning situation for all involved! Just how business should be.

Through focusing on frozen margaritas we were able to create a UTP. In doing this we have been able to become really specialised and good at one thing.

Other examples of businesses using simplification to create UTPs are:

- Burger and Lobster is a restaurant in London that has built up a cult-like following with no advertising. It has been the most talked about restaurant concept in London since it opened in 2012. It is so popular that they have opened four in the last year. They only serve two items, a lobster and a burger. Both are the same price! Through simplification they have been able to source the absolute best ingredients and make the products exceptional.

- Southwest Airlines incorporates simplicity throughout its business. It has achieved a profit every year since it was founded. It was the only major airline to turn a profit in 2002. Southwest has kept their offering simple. They only offer short-haul flights, less than two hours. They fly primarily Boeing 737 planes, they don't serve food, there is no seat selection and they have one maintenance facility. In 1996 Southwest could have opened in hundreds of cities. Instead they opened in just four. By using simplification, Southwest prospered in a notoriously challenging business sector.

- In 2004, Jean Claude Biver turned around Hublot, the luxury watch brand. It became one of the biggest successes in watch industry history. Hublot was sold in 2009 to the LVMH Group. Rick De La Croix, the distributor of Hublot America, explained that one of their most famous Hublot watches was the "All Black" released in 2006. The whole watch is black and is virtually impossible to read! The simple colour choice of the watch turned it from being a functioning watch to a status symbol and fashion accessory. This first limited edition was avant garde in the industry and was later copied by every major brand. Rick told me that when he first wore it men asked if they could buy it from him. The black-on-black colour scheme had never been seen before. Through this unique and counter intuitive colour scheme Hublot used simplification to create a UTP.

Questions to ask in order to create UTPs through simplicity in your business:

- What should you focus on and become the best at?
- What you should you cut out in order to simplify?
- What opportunities do you need to say no to in order to keep things simple?

LAW 3:
INVOLVEMENT—NAMING DRINKS AFTER OUR FAVOURITE CUSTOMERS

You teach me, I forget. You show me, I remember.
You involve me, I understand.
~ Edward O. Wilson

Each day the world becomes more competitive. There are more people and more businesses than ever before competing for our attention. With all these choices people are drawn to businesses that involve them. Involvement gives customers a connection with your business. Involvement leads to loyalty.

At Tonteria, we have always appreciated the huge support of our regular customers. These people not only came regularly but they also keep bringing new groups of people. These people love Tonteria and they share this enthusiasm. This help is invaluable. My business partners Guy Pelly, Alain Donabedian and I discussed ways that we could thank these special people.

We decided that a unique way to thank them was to create a shot in their honour, name it after them and put it on the menu. Below are five examples:

TonteMcnab: Dark rum infused with ginger beer, this dark and storming shot, will take your mind to the next level.

TonteDrake: Café Patron over crushed ice with a head of Baileys, otherwise known as the mini Mexican Guinness.

TonteHoltz: Blue and yellow frozen margarita shot, the colours of the Swedish flag will make sure you're 'ALL IN' for the night.

TonteChrisH: A shot of Herradura reposado for our man from Miami.

TonteFarrow: Frozen margarita shot for this 400 m Champ.

The reaction has been better than we could have ever hoped for. Our regulars were both delighted and surprised. Many didn't believe us at first! When we showed them their shot on the menu for the first time, their expressions were a joy to see. Their first reaction was to take a picture and share it with their friends – as many as possible. To a person our VIPs explained, that it made them feel like they were involved and a part of Tonteria. It is essential to recognise your most important guests.

Other examples of UTPs from other businesses that used involvement are:

- Coca Cola created the 'share a coke with ...' campaign where they put 250 popular names onto the labels of their coke bottles. The effect has been incredible with people looking for their names and the name of their friends and families. As, soon as you see your name, you can't help feeling an emotional connection to the coke brand. It has created huge word-of-mouth interest. People also love to take pictures when they find a bottle with the name of someone they care about.

- Louis Vuitton, the luxury brand, offers a complementary service. You can add your initials to their leather goods. It enables customers to personalise their purchase, making it unique. People feel special seeing their initials on a Louis Vuitton product. It also makes the person look good (social currency) in front of their friends. Through involving the client Louis Vuitton creates a strong emotional bond.

- Nike involves customers by allowing them to customise their shoes through NikeiD. People get to choose every detail of their shoes from colour, to materials, to adding their initials. People enjoy the process in creating their shoes. When they wear them they make sure that everyone knows they are personalised. In doing this they spread the word about NikeiD.

Questions to ask in order to create UTPs through involvement in your business:

- How can you honour your best customers publicly?

- How can you involve your customers?

- Can you give your customers a personalised element to your business that they will appreciate?

Conclusion

UTPs are relevant to all businesses. Giant businesses, tiny businesses, old and new will all need to apply UTPs. UTPs are incredibly effective and they have helped me transform three businesses. Creating UTPs isn't about having huge budgets. It's about being creative, getting inside the mind of your customer and creating unique talking points. *In using UTPs you can become the best in your field, increase productivity, cut costs and build a loyal legion of fans and team members.*

What are you waiting for? Go out and create your own UTPs that will take your business to the next level. Good luck! If I can do it, then you certainly can.

About Marc

Marc Burton, 29 years old, is a Nightlife Entrepreneur – Creator of the 'UTP' business theory and Founder of fashion brand *Decorum LYD*.

Marc was born and raised in London. He was educated at King's College School, Wimbledon and he went on to read and graduate in Economics at the University of Bath.

On graduating, Marc was invited to join the soon-to-be-launched bar and nightclub *Mahiki* as its founder marketing director. Marc helped establish *Mahiki* as London's most famous bar and nightclub. *Mahiki* has been the number one celebrity venue in London for the last eight years. It was the first venue in London to offer sharing cocktails in giant treasure chests and ground breaking cocktails served in actual pineapples and coconuts.

After the success of *Mahiki*, Marc co-founded *Whisky Mist,* the members club on Park Lane in London. *Whisky Mist* immediately became one of the premier venues in London. It has attracted the world's most famous celebrities with everyone from Jay Z, Beyoncé, George Clooney, Cameron Diaz, Rhianna, Kanye West, Madonna, Robert De Niro, Christina Aguilera to British and European Royalty regularly seen in The Mist.

In 2012, Marc sold his equity in *Whisky Mist* and in October 2012 opened *Tonteria,* a Mexican tapas lounge and nightspot on London's Sloane Square. *Tonteria* quickly established itself as one of the top nightspots in London with regular visits from A-list celebrities and the British Royals. *Tonteria* is known for being one of the most exciting and creative nightclubs in the world. Shots of tequila are delivered to the guests by a toy train, situated on the ceiling. Many of the cocktails are served in vessels linked to Mexico such as a Mayan pyramid and Lucha Libre wrestler heads. Guests are entertained throughout the night as the performers and dancers continually change costumes and wear giant masks linked to Mexican characters.

Marc is regularly asked the secrets behind the success and longevity of *Mahiki, Whisky Mist* and *Tonteria*. People are eager to know why the A-list celebrities always flock to these venues, why they are so busy (and profitable) and how the venues became established without a penny being spent on advertising. Marc's driving ambition to creatively innovate and improve his venues lead him to develop UTPs. UTP stands for 'unique talking points' and is a business theory that can be applied by anyone to improve their business no matter how big or small. Marc's goal with UTP is to share his knowledge and help other entrepreneurs achieve success and their business dreams with limited budget and no advertising. The key is to follow the seven principles of UTP. Look out for Marc's forthcoming book, *Unique Talking Points*.

Spectator Business included Marc in their list of the rising stars of the business world in order to find the next generation of entrepreneurs. Marc has been interviewed and appeared in *Vanity Fair, GQ, Tatler, Spectator Business* and *Vogue*.

Marc would love to hear from you and can be reached at:
@DecorumLYD
marc@decorumlyd.com
www.decorumlyd.com
www.tonteria.couk

CHAPTER 36

BEWARE OF FINANCIAL EVAPORATION

BY PETER J. "COACH PETE" D'ARRUDA

*A big part of financial freedom is having your heart
and mind free from worry about the what-ifs of life.*
~ Suze Orman

When it is my turn to tell the bedtime stories in our family, I have a limited, but highly effective arsenal of tales guaranteed to make my daughter's eyelids grow heavy and finally close within 10 minutes. I know nothing of hypnotism, but I am convinced that it is the cadence and the tone with which I read these stories that makes them so sedating. One of Caroline's favorites is *The Little Engine That Could*.

It is the stirring saga of a small, underpowered steam locomotive that bravely volunteered to pull a long train over a high mountain, and could only accomplish the seemingly impossible task by repeating the optimistic chant, "I think I can-I think I can." Sure enough, through hard work and positive thinking, the objective is met, and the little engine emerges a hero. Unfortunately, or fortunately, depending on your point of view, little Caroline usually falls asleep before the part where the little engine proudly chugs into the train yard to the cheers of his railroad pals.

During our accumulation years, while we are still working and saving, we are called upon to haul freight uphill, as it were, in preparing ourselves for retirement. In our younger years, it may be a struggle to chunk away the money we know we ought to save. We are hard wired for having fun. Every cell in our body and every neuron in our brain are thinking of ways to live beyond our means. Then, along comes a family, and our resources seem to be stretched as thin as cheap cellophane. But, like the little engine that could, we give it a go. We chug along. We stick to the program. Then a magic thing happens along the way. Slowly but surely, we get something called momentum. Our capacity to earn becomes greater the more experience we acquire. Our little nest egg begins to grow exponentially – that is – the bigger it gets, the bigger it can get. Because of the beauteous miracle of compound interest, what started slowly picks up speed. We keep pressure in the boiler, we keep our eyes focused on our goal and before long, the Law of Inertia begins to work in our favor. Our money is begetting money, which, in turn, begets more money, until we are at last on top of our personal mountain saying, "I knew I could, I knew I could."

INERTIA AND COMPOUND INTEREST

Galileo, a 17th century scientist, figured out that it's easier to keep something rolling once you have it rolling than it is to get it rolling in the first place. Sir Isaac Newton came along a few years later and named it the Law of Inertia. A body in motion will tend to remain in motion until it is acted upon by an outside force. It's the same way with money. The first few years of accumulating money are the hardest. After that, if we keep on accumulating and investing wisely, it gets easier. Have you ever heard the saying, "the rich get richer?" Well, they weren't just kidding. It's a natural law of economics that the more we have, the faster it grows, especially when compound interest is involved.

THE POWER OF A PENNY

The story is told (fictional, I'm sure) of a job interview where the applicant is offered a job and asked to choose between two pay plans. One compensation plan would pay a straight $1,000 per week. The second plan would pay you a penny per day, doubling every day. That's right…first day on the job nets you a penny. That amount doubles on day two and every day thereafter so that by the end of the first week

340

you have earned a whopping 64 cents. Bad deal, right? Not really. With the penny-doubling-every-day pay plan, you will have earned **over \$5 million** by the end of the month! If you are skeptical of the math, just get out your calculator and a calendar and check it. It's true! In the chart below, a penny is doubling each day for 30 days. By the 30th day you have 536,870,912 pennies. That's a cool \$5,368,709.12.

1	2	4	8	16	32	64
128	256	512	1,024	2,048	4096	8,192
16,384	32,768	65,546	131,072	262,144	524,288	1,048,576
2,079,152	4,194,304	8,388,608	16,777,286	33,554,432	67,105,864	134,217,728
268,435,456	536,870,912					

A penny doubling every day is, in essence, earning 100% interest paid daily. While that is unrealistic, it does well illustrate the value of momentum when it comes to money…how even a small amount, over time, can lead to a surprisingly large growth through the miracle of compound interest.

Albert Einstein is often quoted as saying, "Compound interest is the eighth wonder of the world. He who understands it, earns it. He who does not, pays it." Whether the German-born American physicist actually said that or not is still debated. But it does not negate the truth of the quotation. Compound interest occurs when <u>interest</u> is added to the <u>principal</u>, so that from that moment on, the interest that has been added, also earns interest.

FINANCIAL EVAPORATION

If we are to arrive at a ridiculously reliable retirement income, we must keep our eyes peeled for something called financial evaporation – the slow and often imperceptible disappearance of our assets that occurs when we aren't looking, or aren't looking closely enough. Which brings us to the tadpole story.

Summers were long, hot, and sometimes boring in the little milling community in North Carolina where I grew up. If you've ever seen the old black and white reruns of The Andy Griffith Show, you have a pretty clear idea of the bucolic setting in rural America that comprised my surroundings as a 10-year-old boy. Since my brothers and I did not have much to do, or much to do it with, we invented ways to amuse ourselves. Our favorite play area was a bog near our house where a slow-running creek fed a small swamp. Working like beavers, we dammed up the creek until we had a pond deep enough to swim in.

We boys were intrepid souls. Because we were utterly unaware of them, we were quite unafraid of the dangerous water moccasins that lurked in those waters. A bit further down the food chain were the harmless amphibians with which we shared our aquatic playground. One warm spring day, we discovered in one of the shallow pools near the creek what seemed like millions of little swimmers we would later identify as tadpoles. This was before the Internet and the Discovery channel, so we had no idea what they were at first. We found some jars and scooped up a few scores of the soon-to-be frogs and took them home. Since our mother did not take too kindly to having them inside the house, we found an old dog food bowl outside and made that their new home, putting it well out of the dog's reach, of course.

"Those aren't fish," my father told us, "those are tadpoles. They will turn into frogs in a few weeks…if they live long enough."

I think he knew something about the attention span of young boys.

"I would advise you to keep them out of the hot sun," he warned.

Over the next few days, we checked on our little swimmers, who at the time seemed very happy. We noticed that they were getting a bit fatter and that some of them had developed little paddles that were the beginnings of frog legs.

We had put them in the shade, just like Dad had said. What we did not count on, however, was the shade moving as the sun made its arc across the sky. One morning, after a particularly hot day, we checked on the tadpoles, only to discover that the bowl was bone dry and coated with what looked like small, whip shaped leathery decals stuck to the sides of the bowl. Poor little critters. The heat of the sun had caused the water in the bowl to evaporate, ending any chance our tadpoles had at eventual froghood. Our neighborhood pals who lived next door had better success with their tadpoles. They kept their bowl full of water, and their little tadpoles were still swimming. Overall, I learned the valuable lesson about caring for tadpoles – evaporation happens. In hindsight, we boys should have *repositioned* those tadpoles into a bigger bowl. We should have added water to the bowl. We should have paid more attention.

If we aren't paying attention, the same thing can happen to us in a financial sense. All too often I have seen people build up a nice portfolio that it took decades to acquire. They were counting on these retirement accounts to be there for them when they make their metamorphosis into retirement. Then, evaporation happened. Sizable portions of that reserve disappeared. Was it because they didn't pay enough attention? Did they trust someone else, perhaps a broker, to look after things for them? Did they forget that as they grew older, their risk tolerance would change? Was their ship on autopilot when they should have been tending the wheel? Was their fortune placed in the hands of a financial professional who worked according to some cookie-cutter investing formula that did not take their age into account?

FUTURE PROOFING

The best expression I have heard for making sure that evaporation doesn't erode our retirement savings is **"future proofing."** It reminds me of how we coat something with insulation if we want to weatherproof it. "Future proofing" boils down to something as simple as adhering to one of the oldest rules of investing – the *rule of 100*. Just put a percent sign after your age. That is the amount you should have in a safe place – in the shade – safe from financial evaporation.

Safe does not have to be boring. That precaution will prevent you from risking money you cannot afford to lose. A competent financial advisor will be able to identify for you, programs that are designed specifically for those approaching retirement – income planning programs that replenish the account each year, regardless of outside forces, such as the stock market and world events.

Had we D'Arruda brothers taken the proactive steps of checking on our tadpoles more frequently and refilling their bowl with creek water more often, our tadpoles would have survived metamorphosis. The "set it and forget it" approach may work well in our early years of investing, simply because time is on our side, but as we approach retirement, we have to be proactive with our accounts, if we want them to thrive and grow.

Evaporation takes many forms. It can take the form of unnecessary fees, commissions and needless losses. What's wrong with this statement? "I don't feel bad about my broker losing so much money in my account because everyone else has lost money too." Really? Is that how *you* feel, or is that how you have been programmed to feel? Is the automatic response from your broker one of consolation based on shared experience? When you point out that you pay the same exorbitant fees when your account loses money as you do when it gains, do you receive thorough explanations and solutions? Or do you hear expressions such as:

"Don't feel like the Lone Ranger."

"You're not the only one."

"Everybody's in the same boat."

Don't buy it. Just like those tadpoles that were sensitive to their environment and needed repositioning for their safety, your money needs to be rebalanced and repositioned so that the account won't suffer from either the sunstroke of high risk, or the slow, imperceptible evaporation that comes from unnecessary fees and commissions.

About Pete

Pete D'Arruda (aka Coach Pete), RFC, CTC, is a Financial and Tax Coach. He is host of the nationally-syndicated weekly radio show, The Financial Safari, as well as the author of four books, including *Fine Print Fiasco, Financial Safari, 7 Financial Baby Steps* and *Have you been talking to Financial Aliens?* Themes of these easy readers include helping others avoid being taken advantage of and translating financial jargon for any layman.

He is looked at by many of his peers as an Income Coach and has developed easy-to-understand retirement income strategies such as RetirementAutopilot.com and AnnuityTwister.com.

He has also been seen nationally on CNBC, Fox Business, ABC, NBC, CBS and Fox and in print in publications such as *The Wall Street Journal, Barron's* and *Forbes.* To learn more, visit www.FinancialSafari.com, or call 800-661-7383.

The Right Coach For The Retirement Game

CHAPTER 37

WHAT YOU THINK IS WHAT YOU GET — MAXIMIZE YOUR MINDSET FOR SUCCESS

BY BONNIE G. HANSON

The most important decision we make is whether we believe
we live in a friendly or a hostile universe.
~ Albert Einstein

My comfort zone was fear. I was too young to know anything else, except the unspoken rule that lived within me: People were not to be trusted. An only child, there was no one my size to talk to; not that I would have confided my Secret to anyone even if they were there. My confidants were my animals. They were soft and safe and gave their unconditional love without question or judgment. Constantly on guard, my journey began on the path of Fear.

Although plenty of good happened in my childhood and I had loving parents, *The Threat* covered me like a dark shroud: *"Never tell or I'll kill you and your family."* My thoughts were tinged with *The Lie: "No one will ever believe you."* The possibility that life could turn very dark without notice was my constant reality. Fear and apprehension created the foundation of my universe as I grew up. They were the filter for my thoughts and the courier that unconsciously ushered doubt through every decision and action that I made. Voiceless and alone in my fortress of solitude, I kept quiet to keep safe. The door was closed and would not open again until 40 years later.

You cannot solve a problem with the same thinking that created it.
~ Albert Einstein

On my adult mission to "fix" myself and clear the past from my thinking, I attended hundreds of personal development trainings and events. I read and listened to everything under the sun, studying diligently, trying to gain freedom from the doubt that gripped me. My core limiting belief, "I am not worthy", would not cease. Although I was learning incredible information (building a new foundation), the new tools I gathered seemed to offer only temporary relief . (I was actually healing the deep layers of my wound).

You have to break down to break through.
~ Bob Donnell www.NextLevelLive.com

Despite creating outward success in the financial arena of corporate America mentoring thousands of clients and becoming self-employed a dozen years earlier, my internal emotional life was still raw and unhealed. The Threat and the Lie were still lurking within. Now armed with the ability to be an observer of my thoughts, I began to secretly contemplate, "What if I flipped the light on and exposed them?" At a leadership course in the fall of 2009, I found my opportunity. Weary from the decades of resistance, the white flag was raised and I surrendered. Breaking my vow of silence, I shared my Secret with the class. It was surreal to hear the words come out of my mouth. Trembling and sobbing as I told my story, I shattered the invisible glass walls of the fortress that had isolated me for so long. I returned to my seat and looked down at my newly-freed body. There was no blood. The world did not stop turning. For the very first time, I had owned it and I was free.

ONE EVENT CAN CHANGE YOUR ENTIRE LIFE

*Amplifying what is great within you will accelerate your
life faster than fixing what you think limits you.*
~ www.BrendonBurchard.com

A year later, I attended my first live event hosted by Brendon Burchard, the inaugural meeting of the Expert's Industry Association. Beyond thrilled, I was anxious to see my two mentors, Brendon and Darren Hardy, in person for the first time. I was now an "expert" by association since becoming a member of the EIA organization. "An expert at what? Jack of all trades and master of none…" I let that thought slip by. That part didn't matter yet. (The negative thoughts never leave; we just learn to listen and move past them.) Filled with anticipation, I was immersed in a sea of entrepreneurs and a world of possibility. I felt connected and I knew that I was here for a reason. I belonged. I wasn't searching outside of myself for something any longer. I had changed on the *inside*. By owning the truth, I conquered the gap the lies had created in my integrity.

During the 4-day session of incredible keynotes, I found what I came for. It was Brendon's core message that truly moved me. A powerhouse of energy on stage, he delivers his message fully present and animated: *"Your Voice Matters. Your Life Experience Counts. People Need to Hear Your Story. Everyone Should Write a Book."* Concepts I had never considered for myself until I was introduced to his teachings and life-altering questions, "Did I live? Did I love? Did I matter?"

> *Whether you think you can or you think you can't, you're right.*
> ~ Henry Ford

This mantra of, "Live, Love, Matter" was the theme of Brendon's quest, after he survived a near fatal auto accident at age 19. A successful corporate trainer and speaker, he left the safe zone to pursue his purpose. He went on to decipher the "expert" industry (which he defines as authors, speakers, coaches, seminar leaders, and Internet marketers). In a few short years, he created a legacy of service and contribution by delivering massive value to the marketplace and launching multiple million-dollar brands. I wanted those things. I wanted to live, I wanted to love and I wanted to matter. Experiencing Brendon's story changed the course of my life. For the first time, I felt like it was possible.

THE COMPOUND EFFECT

> *Whoever is controlling your mind is controlling*
> *your life – Take back control!*
> ~ www.DarrenHardy.com

Darren Hardy is a phenomenal man. An accomplished speaker, mentor and author, he is also the publisher of SUCCESS Magazine. As such, he has interviewed mega-stars and some of the most successful people on the planet in virtually every walk of life. He serves the masses by sharing knowledge about success. In a word, Darren's brand *is* Success; however, when he shares his personal story, life did not begin as a fairy tale. Raised by his young single father, a stern football coach, his life was measured and judged by accomplishment and achievement. While these are great attributes, the life of a child trying to measure up and make the cut was quite a challenging one.

Darren's presentation at the EIA contained the perfect visual to illustrate the mind and a journey of personal development (or any instance of change or growth). His keynote was centered on how we can succeed despite the ocean of negativity in our heads, in our culture and in our media. It's a human reflex to focus on the negative. Our brain is engineered in this way to protect us. "Fight, flight or freeze" is hardwired in to keep us alive, not make us successful. "Wow....so I'm just human," I thought.

To have more, you must become more.
Success is something you attract by the person you become.
~ www.JimRohn.com

Darren displays an empty glass to the audience and fills it with clean, clear water. The glass represents "Us" and the incredible brain we are born with: pure, unlimited power. It contains everything we will ever need to create our successes if we use it properly. As we grow, negativity from the outside world seeps in. Darren spoons dirt into the water to represent the thousands of "No's" we hear as a child, the thoughtless comment a parent made, the teasing of siblings or bullying of schoolmates. Add another scoop for the harshness we impose on ourselves and for the judgments we make. He stirs. A spoonful each for the teacher that didn't like your report, the jealous co-worker who made a snide comment and the TV commercial that subconsciously tells you you're not good enough. More debris represents the endless racks of periodicals and news reports that focus their headlines on fear and wrongdoing. Now the glass is full of a dark, muddy brown water, clouded by the negativity swirling within it.

As sludge-filled as our minds may be, the good news is that it's *never* too late. Every moment is a new opportunity to choose. As our thoughts filter through our mindset, our feelings and emotions are generated and from these emotions we choose our actions. Our actions lead to our results and those cumulative results are the situations we face daily. I call this TEARS; making it easy to remember that we can choose to create TEARS of joy or TEARS of sorrow. Consistent actions (or non-actions) turn into our unconscious habits and these conditioned habits *rule* us. Be aware! Thought is the point where we have the power to intervene for ourselves, IF we're paying close attention. When we change our thoughts we can change our lives. A responsible or victim mentality both set in motion the domino effect of the decisions and choices we make. Unchecked habits? Congratulations, your autopilot is now in control of your life and voila! You get what you get. Take back control. Be conscious of your thinking and live by choice, not by default. Every choice and every moment counts.

Continuing his demonstration, Darren raises a pitcher of clear water and pours it into the muddied glass. You have the power – use it! Guard who and what you let into your mind. Be the gatekeeper. Choose optimism. Read positive materials. Stop listening to the constant negative news (if something important happens, you'll find out!). Engage in positive activities and conversations. Listen to empowering audio messages. The people we surround ourselves with are pivotal to the level of success we will attain. Create positive associations or disassociate, if needed. As Darren pours, the contents of the glass clear up. As the positive mixes into the negative, clarity is soon created as light displaces the dark murkiness. The more 'positive' water, the more clarity in the glass until the water is restored, once again, to integrity. As Darren Hardy concludes his presentation, I think, "Someday, I will train with that man. I don't know how. I just know it will happen." My intention was clear and set in motion.

LIFE WILL UNFOLD EXACTLY AS IT'S MEANT TO

Every next level of your life will require the next level of you.
~ Bob Donnell (www.NextLevelLive.com)

While I thought the time following that epic event would be filled with progress, life had other adventures planned. My father had been in poor health, then rapidly declined and became critically ill. He died at home on June 25, 2011. Watching him leave was excruciating for me, but taught me to focus on being totally and completely present in the moment for him. My presence was the only comfort I could offer in those precious final moments to soothe his fear of releasing control and dying. Less than a year later, I lost my home of more than a decade to identity theft, fraud and ultimately foreclosure.

During these difficulties I was filled with gratitude for the guidance of my mentors, Rich German and Bob Donnell, and the knowledge and tools I had accumulated. In the aftermath of these tragedies, I was able to look for the gifts these events held and appreciate the lessons these experiences brought with them. I recognized the distinct pattern of loss, a lesson I had seen so many times in my study of success, as though it were a rite of passage. I took ownership of it all and declared that this was my time! I had hit rock bottom and this was the test of faith to determine if I believed in myself no matter what. I had passed the test. Despite the tragedies, I was now on the path of Freedom. Fear was no longer the ruler of my mind as I made the conscious choice to allow my inner greatness to shine.

THIS IS YOUR TIME

Who do you need to be, to do what you need to do,
so that you can have what you want to have?
~ www.RichGerman.com

I loved every time Rich asked this question on our coaching calls, "Who are you being?" It was so grounding and helped me get out of the cycle of thoughts in my head and back into feeling from my heart. It's easy to go about our business and run purely on the logical mind. However, we are so much more effective and efficient when we take the time to slow down and listen to our bodies, to our intuition and to listen to what is deep within us.

Embrace today. It's a new day and there are no guarantees of another. Set yourself up to win! What do you wish for? Do you have a secret to share? Did something happen to you or not happen for you that still bothers you? Are you waiting for something to happen to validate that you deserve what you want? Are you living up to your own expectations or does your life represent the expectations of others? What do you want out of life or what do you want to contribute? Are you waiting? Stop! You have waited long enough. This is your time.

Questions are such a great tool. Start this ritual. At the end of the day, take a few minutes to sit down and journal. Ask yourself one or two thoughtful questions like, "What are you resisting?" Be painfully honest with your answers. If you don't trust you, nobody else will. This exercise allows the challenges to come up and gives you the opportunity to address them. Pursue excellence, not perfection. Perfection is an excuse to create an incomplete in your life. Just focus on being better than you were yesterday. Comparison to anyone else is futile because there is no one on the planet like you. You are one-of-a-kind!

Want to increase your happiness by 25%? Create a Victory Log. Each day, write down three victories for that day. It can be as simple as, "I did my exercise for the day." When you're having an "off" moment or day, get your Victory Log out and review. In my May 2013 Victory Log I was able to write: I trained with Darren Hardy. Claim what you want! Then take the steps to make it happen.

Be You, Be Phenomenal!
~ www.CliftonAnderson.com

Success is a journey. Be good to yourself. Face your fears. Tell your secrets. Forgive. Heal the past. Live in the present. Focus on your strengths. Be intentional. Take action now. Make mistakes. Learn. Make a difference. Love. Create deep relationships. Do it now! Life is short. Need help? Get a mentor. Be authentically You and you're sure to attract the success you desire.

As we let our own light shine, we unconsciously
allow others to do the same.
~ www.MarianneWilliamson.com

About Bonnie

Bonnie G. Hanson, The Wealth Mindset Mentor, is an author, coach and businesswoman on a mission to empower professionals, creatives and entrepreneurs to thrive by increasing their impact and their income.

An entrepreneur and student of psychology since childhood, she loves working with people to teach them to enhance their mindset and focus their talents to generate powerful results. She brings a contagious passion and creativity to her group and mastermind coaching clients. Bonnie has mentored thousands of clients in finance and life for nearly three decades. Her desire is to accelerate the global shift from Fear to Freedom by empowering others to express their unique gifts, stories and purpose in the world. She holds the vision of a global community who creates personal freedom through the expressions of Love, Compassion and Taking Action.

Bonnie is an advocate for bringing real world experiences to our youth. She dreams of enhancing elementary grade level curriculum to include leadership, financial literacy and personal growth, preparing children to take ownership of their gifts and talents, to embrace an entrepreneurial mindset and become conscious global citizens.

 She enhances the lives of those around her through mentoring and contribution with many non-profit organizations in her community.

Her latest book, *Shatter the Image,* may be found at: www.ShattertheImage.com . To connect to her, visit: www.BonnieGHanson.com or www.WealthMindsetMentor.com .

Bonnie lives in beautiful southern California with her family, enjoying the gorgeous ocean sunsets, photography, art and creative activities, reading, animals, and sports.

CHAPTER 38

BUILDING A REFERRAL PIPELINE

BY CHRISTINE SPRAY

Zig Ziglar said, "You will get all you want in life, if you help enough other people get what they want." I absolutely love this quote and have used it throughout my career. However, I did not know how true it really was until I served in a public accounting business development role. My responsibilities included group network events and one-to-one meetings where you really get to know people and what they do. I loved my role of developing new business for the firm as it allowed me to make friends, help people and be incentivized accordingly.

Have you ever attended network meetings where nothing happened? You meet with referral sources, you have lunch or coffee and spend time talking about what each of you do, then it's, "Well, I will keep you in mind if I think of anyone who needs your services."

…No "second date." No definite plan to interact again. No lead.

Statistically, 84% of new business comes from a relationship with someone you already know. Referrals from your network account for 42%, additional business from existing clients is 21%, and 21% comes from new referrals from existing clients.

If you want to discover the real secrets to building relationships for more business, implement the following best practices:

1. **<u>Develop rapport and trust with everyone you meet.</u>**

   Your rapport-building skills will determine your success and the amount of new business you develop. Everyone develops trust in different ways. Some people trust quite freely. Some are naturally more skeptical and want a person to earn their trust. The way you view trust will govern the way in which you develop relationships in your business. For example, ask a room full of business executives attending a conference, "What does trust mean to you?" and you will get as many different answers as there are people in the room. Most people know their business inside and out and they can explain their services in technical terms all day long. However, when these same people are required to engage in small talk to develop relationships, they often stumble.

2. **<u>Create your 12/12 list to utilize at your one-to-one meetings, so that something does happen.</u>**

   The "first 12" includes twelve key questions. Most people make the mistake of taking the conversation straight to the business card (what you do, who you serve) and wonder why nothing happens. You first need to ask personal questions to build rapport and find synergies in common with one another. Then, you ask questions about the business and end with questions about how you can help them. The conversation might look like this:

Personal Questions

- Where are you from? Where did you grow up?

- Where did you go to college? What was your major?

- What do you do outside of work for fun and balance?

- What part of town do you live in? Tell me about your career and how it progressed to where you are now.

Business Questions

- Tell me about your role and the services of your company.

- Describe your ideal client.

- What differentiates your firm from its competitors?

- Describe a case study of what you actually did for a client.

<u>Help Questions</u>
- Who is your biggest referral source (outside of your clients)?
- Would you like to connect to one another on LinkedIn? I'm happy to introduce you to any of my contacts.
- Would you like me to send you my network list of trade associations in town?
- What can I do for you?

The "second 12" includes a list of twelve ways you can help others. Your list might look something like this:

<u>Twelve Ways to Help Others</u>
- Introduce them to a new business opportunity
- Make introductions on LinkedIn
- Share your network list
- Introduce them to one of their centers of influence
- Host a partnership event
- Make recommendations for service providers
- Send articles on their industry topics
- Add them to your mailing list to receive newsletters
- Identify public-speaking opportunities for them
- Support their community-service endeavors
- Share ideas on best practices for marketing and business development
- Invite them to events that you are attending

3. <u>Create your Trust List.</u>
Take a blank piece of paper and write down every contact that you have not spoken with during the last six months that could be a source for prospects or referrals. These include people who you already know and have built some rapport and "trust" with, rather than going out to a network event and meeting someone for the first time, where it takes longer to build the relationship. Once you have created your list, schedule face-to-face meetings with these individuals if they are local, or conference calls if they are not local. When you reach out

to them to schedule the meeting, all you need to say via phone or email is, "It's been a while since we connected, and I would love the opportunity to meet at your convenience and catch up." Once you get to the meeting or host the call, tell them "I appreciate your relationship because... (why you appreciate them). I want to continue to build our relationship and help you any way I can." Continue the discussion by sharing case studies with one another and discovering ways you can help them. They will likely ask you how they can help you as well. Be ready to share with them how they can help you.

4. Create your Value Proposition.

Your value proposition is also known as your Elevator Statement which should be two sentences or less. We are all asked whether at a trade association event or a party, "What do you do?" When I am asked, I will likely reply by saying, "We are a business growth consulting firm which increases mid-market companies' revenue through proven business development strategies, trainings and coaching." If they said, "Really, tell me more." I would add, "Unlike our competitors, we have been on both sides of the table and know the ins and outs of growing a business."

Your value proposition should include:

- Who you are
- Who you serve
- What you do
- What differentiates you

*If a competitor can introduce themselves with the same thing you are saying, then your value proposition does not have a differentiator.

5. Create your Firm-at-a-Glance.

Print your Firm-at-a-Glance on letterhead and carry a few copies with you in the back of your portfolio to share with referral sources when you meet one-to-one. This document is not meant for prospects or clients; that's what firm brochures are used for.

Here's what to include on your Firm-at-a-Glance:

- Value Proposition
- Target Market

- Private and/or Public Companies
- Decision Maker
- Size of Ideal Client
- Industries
- Demographics
- Triggers
- Differentiators

6. <u>Create your Top 20 Referral Source List.</u>

Take a blank piece of paper and write your name at the top and underneath your name, write Top 20 Referral Source List. Then, write down numbers 1 through 20 down the left hand column. Add everyone to the list who has referred qualified new business to you in the last twelve months whether you won or lost the work. On the list, be sure to include the person's name, title and company on each line. Set a goal to identify and list twenty referral sources within six to twelve months depending on your schedule. Keep this list posted on the wall above your desk or somewhere else where you will see it daily to remind you to help the people on the list, so they don't end up on someone else's top referral list. In addition, when you are meeting other referral sources and they ask you how they can help you, be sure to mention that you would like to meet more people like Jane Doe, President of ABC Corporation on your referral list; they probably know someone like these executives they can introduce you to.

7. <u>Create your own private network group.</u>

Identify a public venue with a private room that doesn't mind taking individual orders and checks. Next, create a list of your top 10-12 centers of influence for your business and an executive in each space that you like and trust who has proven to be a good referral source for you. Reach out to each person individually and invite them to join your group that will meet twice monthly at the XYZ Venue from 11:30am-1:00pm. The purpose of the confidential group will be to provide introductions, referrals and opportunities for each other at each meeting. Every meeting will be focused and productive with a theme of introductions to new business opportunities, referral sources, companies on your target list, and more.

8. <u>Create your Target List.</u>

Use your letterhead and type up a list of 15 target companies you would like to do business with and print several copies out to place in your portfolio. When people ask you how they can help you, be prepared to pull out your Target List. Be sure to update your Target List every 90 days to keep it fresh.

9. <u>Implement a Client Review Process.</u>

Once you implement a Client Review Process, you will gain more new business from your clients themselves or from referrals they make to you. Your current clients are the number one sources of referrals to jumpstart your business. When they see you as a trusted advisor and not just a service provider, they are more likely to refer others to you. Create a list of 10-12 questions to ask your clients in order to gain a better understanding on how your firm is doing in meeting and exceeding their expectations. These questions need to be all about them. Notice the suggested questions below and how far down the list of questions lies the question you really want to know – "Would you enthusiastically recommend us?" You are likely going to know the answer to this question before you even ask it, but it does help pose follow up questions such as "Who can they introduce you to?" or "Can you use their name on future proposals?"

Your questions should include these important points:

Client Review Process Questions

- Reason you chose us? Your expectations?
- Engagement process smooth? Prepared? Adequate client contact?
- Responsive at all levels of communication? Approachable?
- Proactive (questions, lists, ideas, interests)?
- Rate in regards to time management?
- Provide good thought leadership?
- Believe we consistently deliver value?
- Believe we genuinely care about you and your business?
- Often ask us for advice?
- Enthusiastically recommend us?
- Short-term/long-term business challenges and goals?

- Frequently offer unsolicited ideas to add value beyond our services?

People make referrals because they trust you and your business, so it is incumbent that you build trusting relationships. This is where helping others becomes part of the trust-building process. Build relationships outside of your services or the product that you sell. Become a trusted advisor. If a client or prospect knows you only for your service or product, you can lose that client when someone else offers a lower price or when another service provider not only provides a great service for a comparable price, but also helps introduce them to new business or reach other goals. However, if you are a trusted advisor who understands their business and helps them succeed beyond the widgets they purchase from you, they will likely stay with you long-term.

Exceed your clients' expectations by providing them leads, introducing them to other referral sources, inviting them to beneficial community events, identifying speaking opportunities for them and inviting them to client appreciation events where they will meet other clients you serve.

10. Learn to network more successfully.

- *Be the first to arrive.* Most people show up after the event is in full swing. This is actually the most difficult time to meet people. By arriving early, you have the opportunity to pick your spot in the center of the room where others arriving will naturally gather around you. It is far easier and more natural to turn to the person next to you and introduce yourself than it is to arrive late, circle the room full of people and try to engage into deep conversations.

- *Exchange cards selectively.* A pocket full of business cards from random people or businesses with which you lack synergies weighs you down. If someone asks to exchange cards with you, then by all means, do so, but do not feel like you have to request a card from everyone with whom you speak at an event. Asking the right questions about them and their business will uncover synergies to determine if you should exchange business cards. A simple trick to keeping all the cards you ask for separate from all the cards you collected is to put the "warm" cards into one pocket or fold a corner of their card over so you know which ones to follow up with after you get back to your desk.

- *Work the table.* Approach a table that is nearly full with professionals who look like your decision-makers, and ask if the empty seat is taken. If not, put down your things and then, walk around the table and introduce yourself to each person sitting at the table. Then, take your seat and assume the role of table host by creating dialogue with everyone at the table by asking questions like, "Is this your first event?" "Are you a member of this group?" "Have you heard the speaker before?" "Do you know one another?" "What do you each do?" I promise that your tablemates will welcome your assistance at getting to know everyone at the table. Of course, you get to know everyone around the table and can readily discern the ones with whom you have synergies in common. Now you know that the man sitting across the table from you is the best lead at your table, whereas, you might never have known that by speaking only to the two people to your left and right with whom you have nothing in common and little hope of helping each other.

- *Practice appropriate follow up techniques.* 'Strike while the iron is hot' applies to building relationships if you want to exceed expectations. Follow up with people you meet at network events and one-to-one meetings within 24 hours. When following up, thank them for their time and mention that you enjoyed meeting them, remind them where you met, reference one personal and professional element they shared with you, and wrap up with how you can help them.

Ultimately, business development and building an effective pipeline hinge upon distinguishing yourself and your business from your competition by providing your clients, prospects and referral sources with something more than others do. By demonstrating your willingness to develop long-term relationships and identifying how you can assist others outside of your services, you will transition to the role of trusted advisor they cannot do without. Hence, you will get far more than you want when you help others get what they want.

About Christine

Founder & President, Strategic Catalyst, Inc.

Founder & President, National Business Development Association

Chair & National Speaker, Vistage International

Christine Spray is a nationally recognized business development keynote speaker, consultant, trainer and coach. Spray serves as a CEO and business advisor with a passion for helping people and companies grow.

Spray launched Strategic Catalyst, Inc. after working in public accounting and industry in senior leadership roles with start-up, restructuring and growth responsibilities. She recognized that by aligning business goals with marketing, human resource and business development strategies, organizations could leverage new business opportunities for far greater results. With 20 years of experience, Spray has created proven programs for management in the area of new business strategy by implementing Individual Revenue Assessments, Business Development Programs, Strategic Business Development Plans, and Accountability Models.

In addition, Spray launched the National Business Development Association (NBDA) to fill the need for a national trade association to provide best practices to individuals whose primary responsibility is generating business for their organization. NBDA provides a vibrant learning community where members can stay on top of industry trends and continually hone their skills through targeted professional development. Members of NBDA strongly believe in order to be a successful business development professional, you must focus on others and their needs before focusing on yourself. You will find this philosophy at the center of everything that is taught at the NBDA.

Spray also serves as Chair and National Speaker for Vistage International, the world's leading chief executive organization; its affiliates have more than 16,000 members in 16 countries. In her Vistage leadership role, she provides monthly professional development programs and one-on-one coaching for CEOs to help them become better leaders, make better decisions and therefore achieve better results.

As Director of Practice Growth, Director of Business Development, Director of Practice Development, Strategic Sales Director, Vice President of Sales and Marketing and Regional Director of Sales and Operations, Spray has led numerous organizations' efforts in new business development, strategic marketing, employee retention and professional development programs, client relations and operations.

Spray's leadership:

- Founder and President, National Business Development Association
- Chair, Women Energy Network's Advisory Council
- Former Board Member, Women Energy Network
- Former Committee Chair, Emerging Women Leaders
- Former Committee Chair, University of Houston Alumni
- Former President, Association for Accounting Marketing
- Former Co-Chair, Kay Bailey Hutchison Texas Governor Race
- Former Nominating Chair, American Lung Association
- Former Board Member, Houston Health Charities of Texas
- Former Board Member, Houston Strategic Forum
- Former Board Member, MIT Enterprise Forum
- Former Board Member, YMCA Camping Services
- Former Delegate, American Society of Women Accountants
- Former Chairman, Small Business Committee GSWCC
- Former Co-Chair, Shaker Committee GSWCC

Spray's acknowledgements:

- Rookie of the Year, Vistage International
- One of the Entrepreneurs of the Year for 2012, Houston Technology Center
- Top Ambassador, Greater Houston Partnership
- Lifetime Member, Greater Houston Partnership
- Mover & Shaker, Greater Southwest Houston Chamber

Spray holds a Bachelor of Science in Biology from the University of Houston and is a Graduate of Coach University.

CHAPTER 39

MAKING SAVING GLAMOROUS: OLD WORLD IDEAS IN THE NEW ECONOMY

BY DAVID KASSIR, AAMS®, CMFC

Retirement. The Golden Years. A time to enjoy life and live carefree. What a crock! Seriously, how backwards is that? You work for 50 years or more, sweating and fretting at your job, working long hours, missing your children's activities, traveling on your spouse's birthdays and doing little else to invest money for "the future" so that you don't outlive your retirement investments. What about enjoying today a little bit more? What about taking walks with your kids or sitting down to a meal with your family before nine o'clock at night?

At the beginning of my career, I was just like many other working people, like the clients that I meet everyday. I put in long hours and sacrificed time with family and friends. I understood, because of having lived in other countries, that not everyone in the world lived this way with their nose to the grindstone and the constant, nagging fear that they would live retirement in abject poverty if they didn't put the time in now. What would it all mean to retire with wealth if I lost my health and spent precious little time with my family and my friends? I decided to reclaim control over my life; I began a diet, exercised more and hired a prosperity coach to help me move to the next level. I soon realized that the simple principles I was applying to every aspect of my life were especially applicable to personal finance.

From my new vantage point, I saw that the way in which most financial advisors were assisting their clients is wrong. Their philosophies are akin to cleanse diets; they look for quick bursts of activity to offset bad habits or the solutions are so restrictive that they are impossible to sustain long-term. Therefore, people are living and saving for a retirement that they don't really believe they will attain. When I set my life and my business on a different course with my prosperity coach, I realized that habits are the key to any successful outcome. Once a habit is created, usually achieved within a six-month time, the desired outcome is soon to follow. My new habits freed me from worrying about how to squeeze it all in so that I could be a better person, a better spouse, a better investor and a better advisor to my clients. Financial success is but one manifestation of a successful life. We all want to have successful lives. Success is an OUTCOME to a series of habits consistently done. People forget that. They yearn for the idea and the image of success yet fail at setting up the memory muscle and habits to align themselves with their most desired outcome.

Wealth does not equal success. Success encompasses more than creation of wealth. Success is the ability to lead the life you dream of now, not just in retirement. Success means not getting to the end of your life and realizing you missed it. Creating personal wealth becomes a process by which we achieve success.

You can achieve greater success than you ever imagined using age-old principles touted by your great, great grandparents. Success—financial freedom, being able to fly to remote parts of the world, the ability to work at the job you love until you die if you so choose—is really the freedom to do what you want. Successful disciplines create successful lives. We live in the most prosperous country in the world; there is so much you can buy, do and with which to be involved. No wonder so many people suffer from financial stress! Financial stress is a cancer that devours people's lives and relationships. Owning a luxury feels glamorous until the time you must choose between the luxuries and paying for food or an unexpected bill. Let's make saving and other old world economic ideas, glamorous again.

"A penny saved is a penny earned." Attributed to Benjamin Franklin, his version varies slightly from the age-old proverb, "A penny spared is twice got." In essence, you are paid today and you pay forward for tomorrow. Perhaps no phrase better embodies the true American dream. Many have tried to convince us that home ownership is the American dream, but were you to poll immigrants to the United States I do not believe they will tell you that home ownership topped their list of reasons to emigrate to America. In fact, the American dream truly is to achieve financial success as a means to achieve success in all other areas of life. Financial success enables personal freedoms by removing an element of fear that keeps many of us awake at night and enslaved by day. Saving means obtaining wealth, it means setting a goal and measuring achievement.

What gets measured gets mastered. What most people crave when they make impulse purchases with their money is the instant gratification or adrenaline rush that accompanies the purchase. Saving money can provide the same rush when you measure the growth of your bank account and the interest gained. Seeing the results on your computer screen each morning—the weather report for your savings day—can encourage the confidence to save more. This principle is similar to weighing in while dieting or what some call now a lifestyle change. Tracking your positive results provides impetus to continue making progress because of the adrenaline rush it provides.

Never use the word "budget." Some people make the mistake of referring to their savings plan as a "budget." The term budget, however, has a negative connotation similar to "diet," implying the need to do without. When dieting becomes "healthier eating" and working out becomes "strength training or cardiovascular fitness" both sound more appealing. Make saving sound glamorous and more fun! Saving means abundance; it does not mean doing without. You can find serenity with this one discipline.

Before you even select a financial advisor, you can coach yourself through saving at home or at work by utilizing any of the myriad websites at which you can track your financials. See your savings account and your net worth increase daily with the click of a mouse at such websites as: www.mint.com, www.hellowallet.com or www.manilla.com that offer visuals such as bar charts to display your progress. These tools quickly increase your confidence in saving by showing you real results.

Fill your storehouse first. From earliest civilizations, even preceding the use of money as a means of trade, the storehouse served for the putting-aside of prescribed amounts of goods and grains for use later. The fear of not putting up enough to sustain one's family through winter, for example, was a real enough fear that no one wanted to be without stores in reserve. *A good bit of fear creates a margin of safety*; it is healthy. Somewhere long after the advent of coin and monumental hardships like those endured during the Great Depression, Americans seem to have misplaced their fear of not providing for their families by putting up reserves in their storehouses, favoring instead to live paycheck to paycheck, augmented by credit.

Success–A Balancing Act. Living your life waiting to retire before you do anything fun, would be like dieting your entire life and never tasting ice cream or birthday cake. Boring. Success is a balancing act. You can spend the heck out of your money as long as you put a portion of it away. If you earn enough money to purchase a dream home or a dream car for example, who cares if you buy one, as long as you invest in yourself first. Indulge in a little gratification after you put up the stores needed for the future.

> *Life is what happens to you while you're busy making other plans.*
> ~ John Lennon

Harness healthy fear to create a habit. Colonial Americans knew to set aside specific quantities of grains, canned items and dried beans and other foods for harder times. It was easier to measure with specific goals. Therefore, we can learn our first lesson from them; determine how much you would like to save initially in reserve for your family, perhaps a month's salary. Set a goal of achieving that reserve by a specific date as well as how much you will need to save per paycheck to reach that goal. Just as it is easier to achieve a weight loss goal by determining how many pounds you must lose per week to attain the goal; saving will become easier when broken into smaller, more attainable goals.

The banks know that most people lack the discipline to achieve real success. In the absence of disciplined saving there is credit. The banks count on their customers needing to borrow because they have not saved. The only reason that banks are successful is that they know, as human beings, we are much weaker than we think we are.

Wealth creation is a two-sided coin, saving and investing. We begin by just putting aside some money in a savings account or interest-bearing checking account. About six months later, when the client has learned discipline, then we can venture into investing some of the saved money into other financial vehicles. The discipline acquired from saving money carries over into every other facet of a person's life.

Increase Value. Sometimes we focus so much on increasing the value of our retirement portfolios that we forget to increase value in the world around us. Always bring value to your world so that you can earn more, whether you own your own business or work for someone else. In the days before employment contracts and collective bargaining, a person's word was their bond and honor prevailed. Putting forth your best effort for a job well done speaks to your character and discipline and allows you to see success where before you saw failure.

Recognize Real Success when you see it. I know wealthy people who can offer great advice on becoming wealthy. However, when you look at them, they look ten years older than they are, their relationships are suffering, and they take about 10 different prescriptions because their health has deteriorated. If you find yourself over-obsessing solely on the outcome of your wealth you'll be blinded to the life you are living now; it's time to change your strategy.

The Pace of Success. Slow and steady wins the race. Remember when I said that fear can be healthy because it can keep a person on track. Well, too much fear can be financially unhealthy. Fear stoked by the stock market plummets of 2008 and 2009 put many people in shock, causing them to second-guess America and the stock market and generally making them nervous. Many people pulled investment dollars from the market, compounding problems. If you can override your emotions and come back to the table, you will regain what you lost and more. Many of the world's most financially successful have invested money in markets following the crash. They understand that the market always has a tendency to go higher. Life is evolutionary. As humans continue to evolve, there will always be innovations, new technology and biosciences. These will drive the market forward.

Employ a Trusted Advisor. When you feel like you cannot trust your decisions or you cannot get past the financial hurdles before you, a trusted financial advisor serves as your financial psychologist. They help you discern what matters to you, what your goals are, and how best to achieve those goals. Your advisor creates a strategy with you to avoid common financial potholes, like the lottery mentality, as you go about living your life.

Lottery Mentality. Rather than saving a small amount of money each week, people sometimes make the mistake of adopting the lottery mentality. Achieving financial solvency becomes such a daunting task that they begin to think it's more likely that they will win the lottery. So they play the odds with investments they have heard will deliver astronomical returns. If something seems too good to be true, it very likely is. Here your financial advisor will help you assess if a particular investment fits with your goals and the lifestyle you choose to lead. Just like a personal trainer, he will keep you from sabotaging your financial future.

Investing in things for which you have no training or limited knowledge equates to misallocating capital. Investing in a restaurant because you like to eat, or day-trading because you read an article that highlighted the experiences of a lucky few are not sound reasons for supporting such ventures. Why, when you work so hard for your money, would you choose to throw it away on unvetted investments? Swim in your own pond and do not waste time on get-rich-quick business ventures recommended by someone else. Build a plan with your investment advisor and stick to it.

Author Henry David Thoreau who chronicled his time living simply in the woods in his book, *Walden*, experimented living with less – so that he would not when he "…came to die, discover that he had not lived." His belief that if we live for the wrong things perhaps we are not really living, illuminates the intricate balance between living to work for the things we desire, versus living a larger life driven less by things but enjoying a greater satisfaction. My clients desire more from their lives than living for retirement or worse, living paycheck to paycheck. They seek my counsel to eliminate their fear of not living their lives fully on their way to a desired outcome - retirement. Retirement should not be something to live for; retirement is only a time to live to. There is a difference. Your personal finance is your own business. It is the business of living your life. Where **attention goes**, energy flows. Let's make saving glamorous again.

About David

David Kassir had a non-traditional start to his career. He often says he naturally gravitated to his labor of love. As a young man he occupied his mind with his favorite pastime of reading, finding Forbes and other financial magazines the ones he couldn't seem to put down.

One night he stumbled across an ad titled "Stock Market Course" priced at $100. Back then it seemed like a thousand dollars to David, but he made the investment that would lead him into a whole career revolving around investments. By 1994, with the advent of the Internet and E*TRADE, David had saved enough money to buy a desktop and open his own online trading account to continue his self-education. He poured over various investments with charts lining every square inch of his living room and with the recommendation of his father, in 1995, sought a non-paid internship at the renowned firm, Wheat First Butcher & Singer.

After a year of interning while still working nights elsewhere, his mentor Lewis Georges saw David's ambition and took a liking to him. He convinced him to come onboard fulltime. David passed all of the necessary examinations and it wasn't long before he'd realized he'd found his purpose and path to success. In 1997, Wheat First Butcher & Singer merged with First Union Securities, formerly Wachovia (now Wells Fargo Securities), where he was promoted to Vice President.

David was motivated to provide clients with the best possible service, independent research and personalized money management. In 2002, he founded his own investment firm, Georgetown Private Cliente, working in cooperation with Bank of New York and Next Financial Group, Inc.

Over the years, David achieved some of his expansion through the buyout of other firms, and in 2009, Georgetown Private Cliente entered into an agreement to buyout a renowned broker/dealer, Manna Financial Services Corporation, a distinguished investment firm since 1962 with clients throughout the United States. He branded all of his acquisitions as one, and today runs the firm as Manna Capital Management in the Washington, DC metro area.

David's simple beginnings and unwavering enthusiasm for the topic and practice of wealth building has lead him to his dream career, as well as into other ventures such as an investment property management company and a 501(c)3 nonprofit organization – aimed at easing the lives of homeless individuals in the Washington, D.C. metro area.

CHAPTER 40

CUSTOMER "CARE" IS YOUR BEST BET!!!

BY RICK MCFARLAND

In the midst of the Great Depression of the 1930's, there was a man who had a good job at a large grocery chain. Those were the worst economic times in our industrialized history. There was hunger, poverty, and violence – and on top of all that there was a major drought. It was a very trying time for our country and for its people to say the least. Even in those times, however, people still had to get food and goods to survive and live, and having a job at a grocery was pretty secure. That particular industry was still working, although still in very tough times financially. No one would ever think of leaving this type of secure job to start anything new especially in those times.

However, this man, named George, was not satisfied with the way customers and employees were being treated. In those times, most anyone would be lucky just to have a job and did not really care about customer service and/or employee relations. George felt differently. He surmised that having a cleaner, more organized environment would make customers happier and employees feel better about the service they could provide.

So, in 1930, George left his secure job and formed his own little grocery store just down the street. Imagine the conversations with his family and friends. I can easily see them all saying he was crazy and had no clue what he was doing and that he was risking everything. But he had a vision of how his store would look, how it would operate and how it would serve its customers so much better than where he currently worked. His store would set a new standard for cleanliness, beauty and service. And even a higher standard for employee relations by creating profit sharing for all associates.

After a very short time, his associates started calling him Mr. George, and he won the favor of his people and customers and grew from zero to $120,000 by 1934. That's about $2 million in today's dollars. The market spoke and crowned him the winner in that space, and more than 80 years later, the Publix grocery chain is the largest employee-owned supermarket chain in the country with over 160,000 employees and over $27 billion in sales.

We can easily guess that it was not the product he was selling. Lots of stores sold food and consumer goods that people need everyday. We can be pretty sure it was not price as those goods are all commodities and every store was fighting the price game. It had to be something very unique that no one else was doing. First, he got his employees to be fully engaged by making them all partners. Next, he focused on what the customer wanted, which was a clean, well-organized and pleasant environment to shop in. And he treated people fairly. This company has been through every single nasty economic conundrum since 1930. All the crashes, recessions, bubbles and bailouts have not changed this company's mission to serve customers better.

Mr. George was not the only one who saw opportunity in those ridiculously awful times. When the going gets tough, the tough get cooperative. Instead of seeing who could make the tastiest cranberry sauce when consumers were pinching pennies, three cranberry companies pooled their bogs, found success and became Ocean Spray Cranberry. In those same years a small startup named Yellow Pages gave struggling consumers an efficient way for comparison-shopping. Instead of wasting gas or, more often, shoe leather, they could let their fingers do the walking in search of the best deals.

Nearly 60 percent of Fortune 500 companies began business in a bear market. Proctor & Gamble survived the panic of 1837, then the worst recession in our young nation's history, while General Electric came out of the economic chaos of 1872 stronger than ever. The largest insurance companies started in the depression. The largest software companies started in the Carter recession of the 70's. One could even argue that those same companies pulled us out of recession and created new economies and opportunity.

LESSONS FROM THE GREAT DEPRESSION —FOCUS ON CUSTOMER NEEDS

Researching these stories gave me such hope and promise and made me realize what a great life we have today. Technology advances and growth in our country's production have created the largest free economy on the planet. We as Americans today are so very spoiled. In the 1930's, people were waiting in line at the apple cart. Today, even in our worst recession in decades, people are waiting in line at the Apple store! What a contrast in what we call "bad" times today.

I could have chosen a bunch of tech companies, as those are most well known and recent in our memory. But, in fact, we see this happening every year across most industries. As long as we have people on this planet who consume goods and services, and advances in technology keep coming, there will always be a human need, a gap to fill, a market to address. This is the key thing to remember when building a business. Yes, you may have to reboot your entire business, or maybe just a slight change in offering, but the opportunity is there for those who keep a keen eye and their ears open to what customers are saying and what they are demanding.

That's what leads me to discuss this most important topic - Customer Service. This is a topic that is most overstated and abused in market messaging, books and media, yet still goes unsolved or ignored in so many companies across the globe. Why is this? Do companies really believe they can keep growing and making profit by abusing customers? This may be true for a while, but eventually a competitor comes along and offers a better way, an easier or faster way, and "poof" goes the market share. This is true, no matter the size of the company or the size of the market. New ideas, innovations and ways to address customer needs are always around the corner, and entrepreneurs must stay alert so that they may remain in front of the curve.

Technology advancement and proper use of that technology is an important part of success in any business today. It is not just for software companies or technology companies – technology is key for every business that serves customers. Of course, innovation on the product line is what helps create the market interest in a particular offering, but for those companies who don't have a new tech widget and have traditional product or service businesses, they need to use technology to better serve customers. This is what this chapter is about - what technologies are available for this specific purpose and how they may be used to enhance the customer experience with an organization.

For example, let's discuss the front line of the organization - the contact center, sometimes referred to as customer service department. For many companies today, this part of the operation is done by traditional methods (i.e., a call center). Good 'old fashioned' phones on a desk with humans answering calls. That is now a technology that is decades old, but is still useful in today's tech driven world.

Zappos is such a great example. Although they are best known for building a great human culture of great customer service people, it is the technology they have created to help them execute that plan that has taken them to the next level. Desktop tools, web tools, shipping tools, and many other techniques are used to help them deliver the "under-promise and over-deliver" philosophy. Yes, they have over 500 people answering phones, but their customers have access to web tools that make it so easy to do business with them that the customer service becomes a natural extension of the offering not just a call center. After all, people don't buy shoes so they can talk to someone in a service center. They buy them for every reason BUT that. They expect to get great customer service only if a problem or questions arises. In the meantime, the shopping experience itself is so easy and informative that it makes retail stores appear obsolete. Pictures, text, video, simple processing, fast shipping and generous refund policies make this business such a "pleasant" experience that customers return to buy and rave about the company because it is so much fun, and so easy, to interact with.

Even with all the technology they employ they also include one very important feature in their customer service system. And that is "empowerment." They have granted their agents the authority and training to make sure they know how far they can go to help the customer on the other end of the line. This is probably the most important function they have implemented (training and empowerment). They make every single employee go through that training (all the way to the CEO) to ensure everyone in the organization has a complete comprehension of how to treat their customers and make it easy for them to do business with the company.

I believe there is an important message there. The term "easy" is significant. As we all know, people act to gain pleasure and/or avoid pain. It is that simple. So the more pleasure you can bring to the customer experience in your offering, the more people will flock to that business.

"But," you may say, "Zappos has so much business and funding! I cannot afford that type of technology!" So, if you are not a big-time company with a large budget, how can you possibly take advantage of these technologies and compete in your market niche? Oh, have I got great news for you! This so called "expensive technology" is now completely affordable across the board. If you have not been keeping up with what has been going on in this space let me help you.

Traditionally a company would go out and purchase a complete phone system, staff it with people, purchase computers and network and manage that with more people. Then purchase software and training and staff that with even more people. Ugh. However, now you can setup a full help desk and call center with Voice, email and text inside of a day for only a few hundred bucks (i.e., Zendesk.com).

The technology has advanced so rapidly and so cheaply that it has created an entirely new way to start, build and grow a business.

Let's begin by walking through the different examples of how customers like and want to communicate with businesses now and then apply a new technology to address that desire.

1. **Voice**. This is the most common, and in many cases most mismanaged, way of communicating with customers. The phone system is just a simple tool - a hammer *per se*. It works great on nails, but not much else. What is really needed is a way to make that tool smarter and more productive so that before a call even gets to a human, we have half the job done. We all know that ugly service story about calling into a customer service department and a machine (IVR) answers and says, "… please enter your account number followed by the pound sign…" (Sounds more like "pound sand" to me!) Obliging, you enter your

numbers like a good customer, wait on hold, and then finally, once you get to the person, what is the first question out of their mouth? You know this answer. "What is your account number?" AARRGH! What is wrong with these people? I just went through all that, and now you are asking for it again?! Is their phone system that stupid?! Well actually, yes it is. And so are the people who implemented it.

This situation should NEVER happen. Today, the technology exists to make the phone system talk to the database and make sure that the agents have everything they need on their desktops BEFORE you even talk to them. So why do we still face this every single day? I do not have enough space in this venue to detail how this can be fixed, but suffice to say it is not an insurmountable task and in many cases is very simple and inexpensive to implement.

2. **Email**. Oh woe is me! This particular media has become the scourge of our society. How I wish we could go back to Voice or even letters. Call me old fashioned, but my inbox has sucked so much life out of me I feel like I have missed half of my life! Yet, despite my complaining, this media can be a very fast and powerful tool to communicate with customers. And I do mean "communicate," not spam them. I always loved that term because I always get the visual of someone taking a loaf of spam, smearing it in someone's face, and making them eat something they cannot stand. Whew, get that out of my head please - we digress. Today there are excellent tools that can help manage this media for the customer service department and make it easy and fast to solve customer issues and queries. Auto responders and canned messaging can usually take care of half of inbound messages. For the remainder, desktop tools that are integrated with the customer database (just like in the Voice example), can help with the rest.

3. **Text**. Today's up and coming generation would rather text than talk. It amazes me how we have had for quite some time this really cool device called a cell phone that would allow us to talk with anyone from almost anywhere without a landline. Then came the smart phone and no one wants to talk anymore. They wear out their thumbs and tax our brains with so many acronyms that it is almost another language. Well, as customer service advocates, we just have to embrace that. And, of course, we need technology to do that. The main difference in Text vs. Email is that with Text there is a "live" human on the other

end of the line just like with a phone call. Because of this, the tools must react and route the contact quickly just like the ringing of a phone. With a text, there is someone waiting on the other side, and it should be treated as such.

There are a myriad of technologies and software systems available to respond to even the most difficult customer service tasks and environments. And size does not matter anymore. Small companies and large companies can compete on a level ground because of this available technology. I am going to share a fairly popular example of these in order to prove how easy and fast it is to enhance the customer service experience to the level of "pleasant." Let's review what Zendesk has done, including their latest addition of Zendesk Voice. Just for fun I signed up and setup a basic help desk system, a phone number, a menu and call routing system and started taking calls with automated screen pop ups with data within less than 2 hours. Oh, and by the way, I did all of this for less than $100 per month and that includes Voice, Email and Text. No phone system and no expensive servers required! All I needed was my laptop and an Internet connection. Whew!

This is very obvious how exciting this concept is for startups. Now you can setup your entire back office faster than you can drive to the Office Depot and pick up phones. And it is much less expensive. How frightening this must (should) be for established businesses with high overhead and heavy investment in old technology. Even the larger organizations should be acting more like startups. Those companies not embracing this simplicity will fall behind quickly.

Remember that as you grow. Set aside creative time to come up with new and better strategies that allow you to serve your customer base faster and better (not always cheaper). People will pay for a great experience even in commodity markets. From restaurants to hotels to cars to everything in-between, there is always someone who can and will pay more for a better product or better experience.

Regardless of the technology utilized by companies or the status of the economy, we all have goods and services we need every day, as well as many we don't "need" but will purchase anyway because of the experience we get from them. Matching those offerings with a "pleasant" experience will ensure the success of companies and their employees.

Notice I did not use the term "delight" or "wow." Too much idealistic prose has been written already about how a company can somehow control or influence the emotions of a customer and make them "happy" somehow. Frankly, happiness is something that comes from within, and I don't believe organizations can ever hope to sell "happiness." Maybe I have gotten too cynical over the years. But what we can do is provide a "pleasant" experience – one that gets out of the way of the customer and immediately responds to their needs. If doing that makes someone happy then that is a bonus. But for sure we must provide an experience that does not leave them with anything negative about the company or it's offering.

Now, happy employees are a whole other story. I sincerely believe that building a culture where people can gather for a common cause and provide value to others can definitely create a happy state of mind or at least be fulfilling. The technologies discussed here can certainly provide the tools and environment to make it much easier to provide that value and make the service person feel smarter, more valuable and more empowered while working the front line. This is the promise of communications advancements. All of this technology is deliverable today and is being used today; it is not vaporware or fantasyland.

Customer loyalty is also another important benefit of great customer service. Research has shown that for each 10% increase in loyalty, revenue increases 5%. Most of us would work hard for a 5% revenue increase. Loyalty is built over time, and it is built with emotion. That positive emotion comes from positive customer transactions, relationship-building, ongoing communication with the customer and having or doing something unique that sets you apart from your competition. That is exactly what customer service technology can do – make it easy for your company's agents (sales or service) to provide a pleasant customer experience.

Creating a unique experience as well as a pleasant one can also leapfrog your business ahead of the competition. And I am not necessarily speaking of unique products. If you have the ability to create and deliver a very unique (even patentable) product then that is awesome. But most of don't have the resources, money or people to deliver on something that sophisticated and expensive to deploy and support. Many of us just sell "stuff" like the guy down the street. So how do we get unique? The answer lies in the service, the people and a little bit of technology that is easy to use.

For years now, economists have been warning us of this bad economy and how it is the new normal and not going to get better, etc. After all, how could it with all of the government regulation and taxes, etc. currently in place. But the real fact is that we cannot use that as an excuse and depend on someone else to tell us when it is going to get better. As Entrepreneurs we have an obligation to MAKE it better.

Ample opportunity abounds no matter what is going on in the world or with the economy. As long as we have humans with needs and desires, there will be a market for what we do. And if that market happens to disappear, then either find a new one or step aside and work for someone who sees it otherwise. After all, entrepreneurs trying to make it need good, strong, team members to help them. So, if you do not want to be that person who decides to take on the world, at least join someone who has that dream, help them become successful, and you too will enjoy a better "personal" economy.

About Rick

Richard McFarland is a 30-year veteran of building software systems that helps companies better serve their customers. As a seasoned systems designer, best-selling author and leading authority on contact centers in many different industries, he brings a wide range of expertise to each client. Rich is a sought-after resource for bringing multi-media communications and business process automation to the enterprise. He has been featured on Fox News, CNBC, MSNBC, *USA Today* and *Inc. Magazine*. His experience, combined with the latest technologies provided by his company, Voice4net, allows organizations to realize a major return on assets used in the contact center.

His primary mission is to eradicate bad customer service worldwide and create a "pleasant" experience for both customer service staff and customers alike. Thus creating an instant bridge of communications that empowers the end user with easy-to-use tools and toys that make doing business more fun.

To learn more about Richard McFarland and create the best possible service experience for your customers, visit: www.voice4net.com/forbes. Learn how to create a "pleasant" customer experience with your clients – regardless of the industry you are in.

CHAPTER 41

HUNGER

BY RAUL VILLACIS

What is hunger? Not pangs in your stomach for food, but a hunger that will put a family in a boat to row across a sea or ocean, a hunger that will transform an absence of resources into a will so strong it cannot be denied, a hunger so strong that it can push a body beyond normal pain thresholds and physical limits. Hunger directed can take a person from broke to billionaire and anywhere in between. I've been fortunate enough to interview some billionaires, and when asked, they told me that "hunger" was the number one element that contributed to their success.

My parents are immigrants from South America. My mom and dad got married at a young age and had two kids immediately. In Ecuador, there were limited opportunities at that time and their dreams for a better life led them to move to the United States. It wasn't easy for them to leave everything behind. They left my brother who was five years old at that time and me at the age of eight. They arrived in the U.S where they only knew a handful of friends and didn't know how to speak the language in pursuit of a better future – like so many immigrants. They wanted to make enough money to go back to their country and start a business. There were no guarantees that their plan was going to work, but they had an entrepreneurial spirit otherwise they wouldn't have taken the risk. They had limited resources, however they were Hungry for a better life. I often wonder if I would be able to do the same, leave my kids and security to venture to a new land of opportunity. I guess, in a way, that was passed on to me because I have inherited the entrepreneurial spirit to take big risks and live life on my own terms. Someone gave me a gift with a quote that said:

Entrepreneurship is living a few years of your life like most people won't, so you can spend the rest of your life like most people can't.
~ Warren Buffet

So how can we get that hunger in us? That is what I have been searching for, and interviewing some of the most successful people in the world, to find the secrets that made them have the Hunger every day to succeed like most people only dream of. In this chapter, I will share with you the three principles that I've learned that the 'Ultra Successful' have shared with me – that keeps them Hungry even though they achieve more than other people can possibly imagine.

PRINCIPLE NUMBER 1

—The 10X Mindset

Even though some of the billionaires that I interviewed didn't start out their life by saying, I'm going to be a billionaire one day. They had a big vision. Most of them told me that every time they assessed their business, they planned for ways on how to 10X their revenue or return on investments. That was a huge insight for me, because as a small business owner I've always attended seminars and hired consultants with the end goal being to double my business. As I listened to this, I couldn't conceive the idea in my head on how this could be possible? What they taught me was that for an entrepreneur, it is easier to grow 10X than it is to grow 2X because of what happens to your creativity, decision-making and your actions the moment you fix your mindset on a 10X goal. When your mind visualizes the 10X outcome, the emotional commitment and excitement is so much greater than when you are thinking – how can I double my business? You have created an emotional engagement and an intellectual commitment to a vision. Your Hunger meter goes up when you do this. Before when you had the 2X goal your brain was focusing on every aspect of your business and trying to manage everything that came your way so you can accomplish your outcome. Now with a 10X vision, your brain creates a filter because it knows it's impossible to do everything on your own. It forces you to delegate or outsource the things that are only 2X activities and commit to spend time on activities that will 10X your business. Before you would focus on everything that made your company more profitable, but now you are just focusing on what makes your company 10X more profitable by asking questions like: Is this going to make us grow 10X or prevent us from growing 10X? This is the mindset that billionaires have and how they look at their enterprises. It is called the 10x Mindset. Once you have it you will find that you automatically will attract people with the 10X Mindset. These individuals are not playing on the same field as the 2X people. These are the people that have conversations that turn into action plans and immediate implementation. They are more inclined to collaborate and help you if they see that you are committed to a 10X growth, because to them, 2X is just playing small and not worth the effort. If you are going to do something, do it big. In order to continue to be driven and stay hungry, you have to start thinking with a 10X Mindset.

PRINCIPLE NUMBER 2

—Keep an eye on what works and forget about what didn't work.

When I asked one of the billionaires what is the one thing that kills hunger, he says: focusing on the things that didn't work. It is human nature to always think of the worst case scenario and that can be helpful in risk assessment before going into a new venture or making an investment decision, however, it's not helpful when you are second guessing yourself once you made that decision. I've learned that once you make the decision to do something in order to see it through, *you have to focus on the end result and own it*. If you have a shadow of a doubt it will show up in your interaction with others and people will see that you are not confident about the outcome. Confidence is nothing but an emotion, when you believe in yourself you see more potential in what you are doing and put more effort and action behind it. That creates better results and gives you even more confidence to believe in yourself and the cycle of momentum is created.

In the same way when you don't believe in your decision, you are second-guessing the potential – creating less action and producing less results. Focusing on past mistakes or things that didn't work will lead you in a down spiral effect destroying your confidence and killing your momentum and hunger. One of the things I love teaching is how to increase self-esteem and step into your ultimate image. And part of this is acknowledging that the mistakes that you've made are part of the journey. How boring would life be if we never made mistakes and we always got what we wanted?

There is an episode of the of the *Twilight Zone* where a crook dies and goes to heaven and wakes up in a suite in the best casino in Vegas. He looks at his closet and he has the best clothes and jewelry. He has a million dollars in chips on the table with a note that says, "Enjoy your night at the casino, you are a winner." When he goes down to the casino he starts playing the tables and he wins every time. He can't believe his luck and as he is cashing out, two beautiful women approach him and he wakes up the next morning with both of them in his room. Again the next day, he has a million dollars in chips and a note that says, "Enjoy your night at the casino, you are a winner." He goes to gamble and the same thing happens as the night before. He never loses and he makes more money that he knows what to do with it. After 2 weeks of this, you can see that he wakes up frustrated. He looks at his million dollar chips with the note and he doesn't even smile. He goes to the casino to gamble and when the dealer cheers him on as the winner, he yells at him and says, "This is not fair. I always win." The dealer said, "I'm sorry sir, I don't understand. You are not happy that you've won?" He said, "No, this is a mistake. I'm not supposed to be here. I was a bad guy when I was alive, I don't deserve to be here in Heaven. I can't stand winning all the time. I want to go to hell. I deserve to go to hell. I need to speak to the person that is in charge and I want them to clear up this misunderstanding."

The manager comes in at his request and says, "Sir, I believe there is a misunderstanding here." The guy says, "You better believe it, I am not supposed to be in Heaven, I was a crook when I was alive and I want to go to hell. I can't take this anymore." The manager of the casino says, "Yes sir. There is clearly a huge misunderstanding and I'm sorry to tell you that this is not Heaven. This is Hell, so you are exactly where you need to be." Part of being Hungry is knowing that you are going to overcome obstacles and you are going to make mistakes. Don't dwell on them, but keep focusing on the rewards and remember that the harder the struggle, the sweeter the victory.

PRINCIPLE NUMBER 3

—Live in the moment

The Dalai Lama, when asked what surprised him most about humanity he answered, *"Man. Because he sacrifices his health in order to make money. Then he sacrifices money to regain his health. And then he is so anxious about the future that he does not enjoy the present; the result being that he does not live in the present or the future; he lives as if he is never going to die, and then dies having never really lived."*

The ultra successful people that I've had the pleasure to meet have told me that in order to stay hungry, you have to look at every day as if it was the last day and take advantage of every opportunity that comes your way. This doesn't only apply to the opportunity in business, but the opportunity to say thank you to someone or to express your love to your family. I had the pleasure of meeting the Dalai Lama in India and what was most impressive to me was the aura of peace he exuded. You can feel he is a genuine, loving soul that lives every day as if it was his last.

When you are truly present in what you are doing, magic happens. We are so used to living in a culture that is always thinking about tomorrow, and planning your week, month or year, that it's so easy to be distracted from what you can do today to make a real difference. Once I applied this principle, my entire business and personal life changed. I used to have a list of 'to do's' every day, and most of the time I never got to finish all the tasks at the end of the day. This made me feel overwhelmed and disappointed in myself. Now, I choose to live in the present and pick the three things I can do now that will 10X my life, health, business and relationships. Living my life as if it was the last day every day gives me the edge and hunger to do more than the average person. I've made it my mission in life to stay hungry and driven in every aspect in my life.

Life is too short not to enjoy the journey. I can truly say as I'm writing this book, I am happier, healthier, feel closer to God and my family than ever before. By appreciating what a gift it is to wake up every morning, you will start living your life to the fullest every day. I have found that success without fulfillment is ultimate failure. And success to me is living my life totally fulfilled in every aspect and helping people realize that they don't have to have it all to be fulfilled. You just have to have that hunger inside of you that believes that your life is worth living. So why not start living today.

About Raul

Raul is a visionary in a class all his own. As the founder of "The Next Level Experience," a company that assists sales professionals in developing strategies to perform at peak level while building a "raving fan culture," his passion for personal growth has only gotten stronger. His determination and drive are fueled by a constant desire to bring about tangible change – as an entrepreneur and as a man who loves his family.

Raul is in the top 1% of Hispanic Entrepreneurs, making him an iconic role model for all who want to follow in his footsteps. Outside of spending time with his wife and two kids, Raul enjoys traveling around the world attending seminars and Mastermind Groups – where he is hailed as a well-known influential speaker and entrepreneurial coach. After learning from and working with top industry leaders, Raul has decided to record his scope of expertise and share it with anyone who wants to live an excellent life. Following this desire has earned him the title of "Best Selling Author" and "Top Real Estate Sales Expert."

Raul is the CEO of Advantage Realty Group Advisors, a real estate firm based in Connecticut and New York. His company is minority-owned and operated, servicing top financial institutions by finding the best way to market their distressed real estate owned inventory. Raul's work in re-strategizing the real estate portfolios of large financial institutions along with those of the US Government, earned his company the title of "One of the Nation's Top Real Estate Firms" according to *The Wall Street Journal* and *Real Trends Inc.* Raul is the creator of the "Successful Daily Ritual Formula" and the "Formula to take Massive Action" which have become foundations in helping his coaching clients reach the next level in their real estate career.

In addition to his coaching, Raul has consistently sold over $100M a year in real estate. His knowledge of the industry from all angles and his commitment to being mentally prepared for success makes him a unique asset to all Real Estate professionals.

"My mission in life is to help people see their true potential so they can live their ultimate destiny. I believe if you love what you do you will never have to work a day in your life."

For more about Raul Villacis:
www.raulvillacis.com
www.thenextlevelexperience.com

CHAPTER 42

RUNNING YOUR BUSINESS BY THE NUMBERS SHOWS YOU WHAT'S MISSING

BY PETER RENZULLI

Lessons I've learned over the years help small business owners understand how to run their business by the numbers. I dreamed in high school of owning a restaurant, so every elective I took until junior year was home economics. That dream came with a realization that I needed a real understanding of business. While my teacher was supportive of my goals, she pulled me aside to explain the realities of working in the food industry. Besides hard work and apprenticeship-type training, I would need at least a million dollars to open a restaurant. Not being from a wealthy family, I realized that I had to find another way to learn about business so that I could find a way to earn the million dollars. The answer came when my math teacher told me about accounting. My senior year, I chose accounting over cooking to see if accounting was the solution to my million-dollar dilemma. Accounting was an eye-opening experience. Who would have thought that a business could be run using a simple mathematical equation? I was hooked on accounting; I turned down a full scholarship to Johnson and Wales so I could go to Rutgers to study accounting.

While a student at Rutgers, I was fortunate to work for two accounting firms, a small firm and a large international firm. While at the small firm, I learned the basics of accounting and how to apply them to small businesses. At the large international firm, my job was to proofread financial statements and footnotes. I then had to describe the business to a manager or partner based on my understanding of the financial statements. Developing this skill taught me that businesses can, and should, be run by the numbers. From these experiences, I set a new goal. I wanted to own an accounting firm, so I could help small businesses understand how to run their businesses by the numbers and compete with the large companies.

After graduation, I worked as an auditor for Touche Ross, now Deloitte & Touche, and there I further developed my understanding of taxes and how to run businesses by the numbers. I also worked as a controller in the battery division of a large, multi-national conglomerate. During these years, I learned that small businesses were at a disadvantage to large companies. A small business owner can't afford to hire the brain trust that large companies use. As a result, I decided I would open an accounting firm that specialized in helping small business compete. I have helped small businesses grow by the numbers for more than 20 years and have learned some invaluable lessons along the way.

I remember like it was yesterday the first day of owning my own accounting firm. The office was rented, the phones installed, the desk and computer were all set up, and the office supplies were all in the proper cabinet. I arrived at the office at 9:00 am sharp, ready to work. I had forgotten just one thing - I had only one client and nothing to work on that day. My excitement soon turned to panic. Marketing was completely foreign to me. So I did the only thing I knew how to do. I made a list of everyone I knew, about 300 people. I decided to call ten people a day for the next 30 days. Meetings were set up for any time the prospective client wanted to meet - it didn't matter if someone wanted to meet during the day, at night, or over the weekend. After every meeting, I would send thank-you notes, and give myself a report card for how I did on the sales call. Soon enough, I had clients and money was coming in. After two months of opening my new accounting firm, I remembered what my uncle told me, *"You don't have a business until you have a customer."*

One day recently, I learned that Tom, the owner of an auto body shop, was in the hospital and would be there for some time. His business was failing, and his friends and family asked me for help. When I arrived at the auto body shop, it became apparent that there were no systems or procedures in place to service the customers. I then reviewed the shop's numbers; these too proved that the systems in place were inadequate and the shop was losing money every day. They had customers and they were happy with the service and quality of repairs. These happy customers were sending referrals to the shop on a regular basis; but there were no controls or cost accounting to help control each job. I called a meeting with the office manager and the estimator to gather cost accounting data. Early on, the data was depressing. We needed to remind ourselves that we are good at fixing cars and our customers loved us. Every day, we would meet with the shop staff and give them both positive and negative feedback. The shop staff wasn't supportive of the changes at first. But as the business began to turn around and become profitable, everyone jumped on board. At the end of the first two months, the business went from losing money on every job to making money on half of the jobs. It was only a matter of time until we were making money on 95% of the jobs. *Profits and Process go hand-in-hand.*

On another occasion, a friend and client, Bruce, called because he was having difficulty paying his bills. We discussed the numbers and found that he had a great base of customers who paid him. The issue, we realized, was that the customers were being invoiced late. Bruce's lawn-care business was growing and he had great staff providing services for his customers. What he didn't have was help running the back office. As with most business owners, Bruce believed that the only person who could understand and prepare invoices was himself. There was just not enough time in a day to manage the employees and do the paperwork necessary to run the business. He would always say that he would do the paperwork at night when he got home, but many times life got in the way and the paperwork had to wait and wait.

In the end, invoices were mailed to customers 45 to 60 days after services were rendered. Bruce's cash became tighter and tighter because bills had to be paid even though he was not paid. We put a plan in place for my staff to work with Bruce to collect that data necessary to bill on a daily basis and email or mail the invoices on a monthly basis. After two months, we are able to issue monthly invoices by the 2nd or 3rd day of the month. *Go from red to black without selling a thing.*

I have worked with many retailers over the years. Most of them did marginally well, but one in particular is extremely successful. The curiosity got to me and I decided to study why this retailer is so successful. All of my retail clients have good products, loyal customers, and great locations. So what was the difference in their financial success? The answer - understanding inventory and the terms in which they bought it. Most retailers buy their inventory when they think they are low on a product, or increase the items they carry based on what they like.

Not Jack, the owner of a successful paint supply store. Jack uses extensive excel spreadsheets to track his inventory, and spends a good part of his day analyzing the terms the vendors are offering. His orders are based on the facts, what customers want and need, as well as the cost of the product. He also works with his vendors to obtain marketing dollars, which helps reduce sales costs and attract more customers. Jack makes sure that his inventory turns over on a regular basis by advertising regularly and buying what his customers want. Jack increases his profits by buying smart. Many retailers ignore this level of effort because it only improves profitability by 5 to 10%. What those retailers ignore is that 5 to 10% over a million dollars in annual sales is $50,000 to $100,000 in additional revenue. This additional revenue goes to the owner as dividends over multiple years of owning the business. It is no surprise that Jack is the second-generation owner of the business. ***Brilliant Buyers make Profitable Sellers.***

A small business owner with a consulting practice, Steve, asked me to teach him how to run his business by the numbers. To prepare for the meeting, my staff reconstructed five years' worth of financial data, creating balance sheets and income statements. My staff was surprised to discover that this consulting business had not made a profit in those five years! This was the starting point for my meeting with the client. We discussed line-by-line the income statement. I asked him how he priced his product. Steve's explanation was as follows: you take the direct costs associated with providing the service, such as software used by the client, expenses that are related directly to providing service to that client, and you mark it up 20% because that is a fair markup. When I asked him about marketing costs and overhead, he explained that he does not consider those costs in his pricing. Overhead and sales costs, according to this client, are his choice, and the customer should never pay for those expenses. As we proceeded to review the financials, I showed him that he would never make a profit if he does not account for overhead and sales costs in his pricing. It took almost two months to prove the point, when Steve called me excitedly to explain that he finally understood. The next day, he redid his pricing model to include ALL costs. Today, his consulting firm is operating profitably and no longer has cash-flow issues. *Overhead can lead you Underwater.*

I specialize in tax controversy, which means that I represent taxpayers when they do not pay their taxes and negotiate payment plans or offers in compromise (paying a lesser amount of taxes). The common thread with business owners in tax trouble is that they do not pay their taxes so they can pay other bills such as payroll or suppliers. The Internal Revenue Service or a State tax authority can take up to a year to realize that taxes have not been paid and send notices; as a result, a business owner believes she has that time to land the big job and pay the taxes and get ahead. Unfortunately, the big job never comes or, if it does, business owners discover to their dismay that the penalties and interest are so high that they cannot pay off the tax bill. Even after setting up a payment plan, the interest and penalties keep accruing, the business falls further behind and its cash flow is reduced. When a business has a cash-flow problem, it is usually caused by one of the other issues mentioned in the stories above, and cannot be fixed by not paying taxes. In reality, not paying taxes just makes matters worse. *The IRS is not a Venture Capital firm.*

I have come to realize that small businesses face many challenges that they must understand to be successful. The challenges seem so very simple and basic that most business owners take them for granted and often ignore them. Remember, you don't have a business until you have a customer. Profits and process go hand-in-hand. Your cash flow can go from red to black without selling a thing. Brilliant buyers make profitable sellers. Overhead can lead you underwater. The Internal Revenue Service is not a venture capital firm. Managing a business by the numbers requires taking these challenges seriously and devoting time and energy to maintaining accurate records, educating themselves, hiring competent support people and managing them every day.

If a business owner manages their business by the numbers, the business will succeed beyond their wildest dreams.

About Peter

Peter J. Renzulli, C.P.A., has been a go-to senior-level corporate executive in the fields of finance, venture capital, operations, business planning and information technology for more than 20 years. In addition to serving in CFO and upper management roles for private, publicly-traded and entrepreneurial firms in the U.S., Puerto Rico and England, he has taught accounting and taxation courses at numerous colleges, including an ongoing Adjunct Professorship at Rutgers University. Renzulli has also shared his expertise via employee and owner training seminars for the Small Business Administration, and frequently appeared on CNN as a financial matters guru.

Since 2001, he has held the dual role as President & CFO for New Jersey-based Bookkeepers 2 Go, LLC, which provides accounting and tax compliance services for small business owners. In 2013, Renzulli founded a new arm of the company, PerformAccount, which offers full-service back office outsourcing and compliance solutions.

Previously, Renzulli led his own accountancy firm in Bridgewater, N.J.; while he has also been charged with tax, accounting and consulting positions for the likes of Deloitte & Touche; conglomerate Bedminster National, Bedminster Financial and Bedminster Capital; Perform Account; Power Conversion (a subsidiary of British Tire & Rubber); and Kepniss Tufariello & Associates.

Away from the office, he coaches youth hockey to help kids develop life skills while enjoying the competition of athletics; and is a member of the Board of Advisers for Fairview Lake's YMCA Camps in Stillwater, N.J., a state leader in traditional camping, environmental education, and adult and family camping.

Peter Renzulli earned an MBA degree with honors in Marketing and his Bachelor's degree in Accounting from Rutgers University's College School of Business; and is a licensed CPA in New York and New Jersey.

CHAPTER 43

INVESTING IN THE NEW ECONOMY AND BEYOND

BY LAURA H. STOVER

21ST CENTURY FORWARD THINKING

As an investor investing their money in these new economic times, one must not only rely on common sense, but the realization that the era of our parents and grandparents is over—much like the love my grandmother had for her eight track tapes. There are many investment vehicles and tools available today that I find the average novice investor may have little to no concept of. I recently had a conversation with a client who had stated he was 69 years old; his broker had him and his wife invested into a thirty-year bond portfolio. I stopped right there. The client is 69 and invested in 30-year bond durations? I continued to listen thinking why don't Investors realize any long term bond may do very poorly since rates will rise and the bonds will lose value…as bonds have an inverse relationship to interest rates this is how it works. It made no sense. The client proceeded to say my wife liked the rate 6%.

The fact of the matter is returns are a slippery matter in the bond world. A broker may sell you a bond that is paying a coupon or interest rate - of 6%. If interest rates rise, however, and the price of the bond fall by, say, 2%, its total return for the first year - 6% in income less a 2% capital loss - would be only 4%. The client realized they needed a change so they returned to the same broker, who transitioned them out of the bonds and into mutual funds. Now, the client said: *"We did incur a new sales charge and transaction fees for the change however; the dividends and interest we earn should offset that."*

Paying a sales charge on a mutual fund can be considered a 20th Century way to do business...the modern, forward-thinking 21st Century approach often involves fee-based managed money… it's never too late to make a constructive change to a portfolio.

As of June 4, 2013, the ICI estimates mutual funds are an investment vehicle that about 92 million American households are invested in. Many have mutual fund choices in their retirement savings in hopes of having money to sustain their retirements, draw income, fund college plans for the kids. I often meet with clients and ask how many mutual funds do you invest in? Do you have mutual funds invested between Roth IRAs and your company's 401(k) retirement plan? You may be surprised to learn that many of these mutual funds have what we refer to as overlap. There can be a real danger in mutual fund overlap. You may not be as diversified as you think. Owning several funds within a portfolio does not mean you are diversified, especially in a volatile market where we have seen portfolios barely back to even, if that, 5.5 years after one of the worst financial crises of many people's lifetime. Incidentally, The Investment Company Institute found that mutual-fund assets topped $13 trillion in 2012, eclipsing their former record set back in 2007.

WHAT IS MUTUAL FUND OVERLAP?

Overlap occurs when an investor owns two or more mutual funds that hold similar securities. Then, the ***all-your-eggs-in-one-basket*** syndrome can occur. For a simple example, if an investor owns two stock mutual funds and they both invest in many of the same stocks, or own the same positions, the similarities create an effect of reducing the benefits of diversification by increasing exposure to the same stocks, potentially creating an unwanted increase in market risk.

WHAT IS THE DANGER OF
MUTUAL FUNDS OVERLAPPING?

The real danger of mutual fund overlap is that you may not be as diversified as you think you are. This is a real problem especially nearing or in retirement. If you invest in an index fund that mirrors the overall stock market and another actively traded mutual fund, you will most likely have a little bit of overlapping. One of the biggest dangers happens when you have only actively traded mutual funds in your investment portfolio. This can have a negative impact if you are not careful. You need to understand <u>what your mutual funds are investing</u> in to be fully diversified. You do not want all of the mutual funds you invest in to react to changes in the market or economy the same way. You want some of your investments to *zig* when others *zag*.

When a mutual fund does well, investors flock to invest in the investment. I call this the mass-transit-bus theory where everyone hops on board.

Eventually, you wind up with an incredibly large allocation of mutual funds in your investment portfolio. For example, the Fidelity Contra Fund (Ticker Symbol FCNTX) has over $56 billion in total assets invested in the mutual fund. Some of the mutual fund's top holdings include stocks such as Wells Fargo, Walt Disney, Amazon, Coca-Cola, McDonald's, Google, Apple, and others. If you look at many of the other top 25 largest mutual funds, *you will find a lot of other mutual funds holding many of the same company's common stock*. If you dig deeper into the holdings of Growth Fund of America (AGTHX) with its $ 54.8 billion in assets, you will find many of the same names found in the Fidelity Contra Fund such as Google, Amazon, Apple, and others.

If you owned both of these mutual funds in your investing portfolio, you could experience mutual fund overlap where many mutual funds in your portfolio invest in the very same stocks as one another.

To compound that, let's digress for a quick moment and examine fees. Mutual funds can have front end sales loads, back end charges and expense ratios just to name a few. Additionally, there can be many fee turnover ratios that are often not clearly disclosed. Use as an example the Growth Fund of America. The expense ratio for this retail fund is 0.71 basis points vs. Vanguard FTSE Social Index - expense ratio 0.29 basis points. This is the difference of return for virtually the same fund.

Growth Fund of America – YTD = 11.97% vs. No Load Vanguard Index – YTD = 17.0% by comparison 5.75% Front end load A-Share class for the retail fund or 12b-1 fee B-Share class is 0.24 basis points.[*] (*This is on top of the expense ratio for the Growth Fund of America.*)

* Source: Vanguard.com fund comparison website

A possible alternative could be an ETF. ETFs often do not require an investment minimum, so they are accessible to all as long as you have enough to buy at least one share. More importantly this allows smart investors (and money managers) to spread risk among many sectors, and asset classes helping to improve the benefits of diversification. You have full transparency as to what you own; the costs are usually significantly less on the average ETF.

Five to ten years before or during retirement, I think people need a change in their philosophy. This is like mass transit, in other words you're riding the public bus with everyone else during the accumulation phase of investing. Or you are in the mutual fund POOL. Then nearing or in retirement you get in the limo for your accumulated phase of investing. You then transition to separately-managed accounts changing your investment philosophy to preservation and income planning to help keep what in many instances has taken a lifetime of work to accumulate. You change from the mindset of retail high fees, sales loads, and-undisclosed fees, to that of full transparency with institutional fee-based money management under a Fiduciary model – which will be fully transparent and can help provide many intricate investment tools available to help manage your hard- earned dollars. Retail mutual funds internal expenses compared to ETFs are often considerably higher. Of the more than 900 available ETFs listed on Morningstar in 2010, those with the lowest expense ratios charged about 0.10%, while some of those with the highest expenses ran about 1.25%. By comparison, the lowest fund fees range from 0.01% to more than 10% per year. Another expense that should be considered is the product acquisition costs, if any. Mutual funds can often be purchased at NAV, or stripped of any loads, but many (they are often sold by an intermediary) have commissions and loads associated with them, some of which run as high as 8.5%.

Source: http://www.investopedia.com/articles/exchangetradedfunds/08/etf-mutual-fund-difference.asp

There are many tools available today our parents did not have access to. With potential elimination of pensions and questions revolving around social security, is it American's responsibility to fund our own retirements? Nearing retirement or in retirement,I feel this is a lesson we should have learned from the 2008 and 2009 financial crisis. In my opinion, the shift of risk management needs to begin. Acknowledge the impact of risk and volatility. Less than 1% of retail investors purposely build hedged portfolios. Almost all retail investors want downside portfolio protection.

Does the investor have to sacrifice growth of their portfolio?

Investing in this new economy may allow us to lower fees, and manage risk. However, to do this you have to get off the bus (the world of retail) and into the limo (world of institutional fee-based money management). Many retail investors fail to deploy defensive tactics. Why do investors view risk and return so interchangeably? When putting this all together, I realized many investors fail to change their philosophy from the accumulation stage to preservation and income planning when they need to. This is critical, especially if you are five to ten years away from or during retirement.

This change requires forward thinking and evolving from riding the bus as we do during accumulation with everyone else (the world of retail) to getting in the limo nearing and during retirement and utilizing institutional money management.

Look for total return opposed to investment performance. Investing in the new economy, investors have seen much more volatility in the past five and a half years than previously. 21st Century Forward Thinking in the New Economy may involve a *Total Return Approach*; the industry has programmed many investors to compare their portfolio to the benchmark of the S&P 500 Index. So far YTD, the market is up roughly 15%. So many will look at their investment statements and say if my portfolio is not up 15%, my financial advisor has not delivered for me. That is a typical mental exercise many of us do. We use these outside benchmarks that often really do not have any bearing for those who are building a portfolio, or have a financial plan they are comfortable with, because they have created a lifetime income.

What the S&P does should not have any impact on the success of your own financial plan, yet many of us still look at these benchmarks to measure our investment performance. Many investors are taking way too much risk and not reaping the reward they anticipated. This is often revealed when we do a Portfolio Stress Test.

I think it best to be a Benchmark agnostic if a client is seeking 6 or 7% total returns with a low volatility, a low drawdown portfolio may comfortably help meet their goals with an approximate 6 to 7% target and it becomes irrelevant what the S&P 500 does. The focus should be on the targeted returns with the lowest amount of volatility. Implementing a *Total Return Approach* allows you to go down the path of not chasing the market and not worrying about over or under-performing. It can truly become a custom portfolio where you help satisfy your goals and keep comparing your investments to something that is out of your control.

It is in vogue because you have many more options with Institutional Wealth Management. The tools of today are more abundant than during our parents and grandparents era. Our economy and markets have changed dramatically, the past five and a half years is a clear indicator of that.

If you have not adapted a 21st century approach to managing your retirement account, well, do you have a way to play your eight-track tape still? I thought so, best of luck.

About Laura

Laura H. Stover, Wealth Advisor, RFC® and CEO of LS Wealth Management, LLC, has more than a decade of experience working with higher net worth individuals and retirees – which has propelled her to be sought after by the media for her accomplishments. She has been a contributing author to *The Wall Street Journal, Forbes Magazine, FOX Business.com,* and has been featured and interviewed on numerous investment and retirement topics. She is most proud of and is host for *Retirement Talk Radio,* a weekly syndicated talk radio show. The show features national guests and some of the nation's most renowned experts from leading economists, authors, and Hollywood celebrities.

Ms. Stover has been a leading educator on financial topics for many years and has appeared regularly on CBS affiliate *WTOL TV* (Toledo, OH), NBC affiliate *WANE TV 15* (Fort Wayne, IN), and *WNWO* on the *Today Show.* As a recognized authority by the media, Laura has written for the *Toledo Free Press,* the *Toledo Business Journal,* and the *Fort Wayne Journal Gazette.* She was featured in the *Senior Market Advisor Magazine* with her article "2013: The Year of the RMD Tax Bubble." Miss Stover was a keynote speaker alongside Steve Forbes in June 2013 at the *Investing in the New Economy* Summit in New York City. Recognized as one of the nation's top advisors in the area of education; Ms. Stover was a featured speaker for the *2011 SMA Expo* in Las Vegas at the Mandalay Bay, sponsored by Senior Market Advisor Magazine. In 2013, she became an authorized social security instructor with Plan My Benefits, and continues to lead the charge in her local community for educating pre-retirees and retirees on social security.

Ms. Stover attended Huntington University and is currently completing her Masters of Science in Financial Planning. Memberships include that of the International Association of Registered Financial Consultants (RFC), and an Investment Advisor Representative (IAR) with Brookstone Capital Management LLC, An SEC Registered Investment Advisor. Laura is the Founder and CEO of LS Wealth Management LLC based in Bryan, Ohio, and is a fee-based firm. The firm won an award and was recognized for assets under management in 2012 by Brookstone Capital Management LLC, and voted the nation's sixth fastest growing RIA in 2011 by Financial Advisor Magazine.

She is active in her community as well as a philanthropist and advocate with local hospice and cancer assistance programs. She serves as a member of the Bryan Business Advisory Counsel for Bryan City Schools, a contributor and advocate for the Bryan Police Department k-9 unit, a member of the Bryan Area Chamber of

Commerce, and the Bryan Rotary club.

Connect with Laura at:
www.LSWEALTHMANAGEMENT.com
www.Retirementalk.Info
Facebook.com/LSWealthManagement
Tel: 1-855-419-PLAN

CHAPTER 44

PENNIES ON THE DOLLAR:
FACT OR FICTION?

BY NICK NEMETH

If you earn money in any capacity, the Internal Revenue Service (IRS) is destined to get their fair share from you. As an attorney who focuses his practice on tax resolution, I have worked with people from all aspects of the economic spectrum. From high net worth professionals to lower net worth general laborers, people from all walks of life encounter problems with the IRS.

Needless to say, in today's economy, protecting your assets is of paramount importance to you and your family. One of the quickest ways to jeopardize your assets and your overall financial wellbeing is by ignoring an IRS problem. If such a problem arises, immediately seek out experienced legal representation to ensure a manageable problem doesn't cascade into a financial nightmare wherein you find yourself facing levies, garnishments and seizures.

DEALING WITH THE IRS CAN BE INTIMIDATING

When people encounter the relentless daggers of the IRS they often panic. That is a very natural reaction. Let's face it, no one enjoys dealing with the IRS or any other collection agency for that matter. Usually people are not prepared to just write a check for the amount due so they begin to look for someone to help them.

Many people are familiar with the persistent commercials they see on television or hear on the radio for tax resolution companies. These companies are generally not law firms and many don't even have attorneys on staff. Their advertising tactics are slick, engaging and often misleading. They appear on the airwaves nationally so many times that people will remember their name. I'm sure you have seen or heard their commercials many, many times. The FTC and the Attorney Generals from various states have started cracking down on these misleading businesses, but they are still out there. If they get closed down, my guess is that many of them simply change the name of the business and do it all over again.

A lot of people, when they get that letter from the IRS or they realize they are going to have a problem, are enticed to call these national or regional non-attorney tax resolution services. I have known some brilliant people such as doctors, lawyers and engineers that come to me after they have wasted thousands and thousands of dollars on these unscrupulous services because they are the personalities that just want to have it fixed quickly and have someone make it go away. They have seen the television commercials and the organization appears to be reputable. After all, they have been advertising on television for years so they must be legitimate, right? Wrong! People who have an IRS issue will pay these services a lot of money, but in the long run, often don't get the results they need or the representation they deserve.

THE "PENNIES ON THE DOLLAR" FANTASY

What entices people into the grasp of these non-attorney tax resolution businesses are the ads tailored to "pennies on the dollar" resolutions. If you get a letter from the IRS saying you owe them $50,000, of course you are going to want to talk to someone that tells you they can get your problem solved by settling for "pennies on the dollar."

The non-attorney tax resolution companies use a consumer tested sales pitch. There is a reason they talk about "pennies on the dollar." It's because that's what everyone wants to hear. They boast, "We will get rid of all the penalties and interest and help you settle for pennies on the dollar." How many times have you heard that and in how many different ways by how many different companies? And in reality, what more could you possibly want to hear? They are promising they can deliver

EXACTLY what you are looking for. These companies are in essence telling everyone who owes the IRS money that they can resolve their problem through what is termed an "Offer in Compromise." The Offer in Compromise is a legitimate option if you qualify, but not everyone qualifies. Realistically there is no way to know if someone is going to qualify until you've worked together for a few weeks. The commercials you see on television are nothing more than a sales pitch. Anyone can file and request an Offer in Compromise, but the million-dollar question is, "Will it be accepted?"

LOCAL EXPERIENCED TAX RESOLUTION ATTORNEY VS. NATIONAL NON-ATTORNEY TAX RESOLUTION COMPANY

There is a drastic difference when you are dealing with a local, experienced tax attorney who you can sit with face to face versus dealing with some tax resolution company fifteen states away. When I do an initial consult with a potential client by phone or in person, it's a fact-finding mission. What are the specific facts of their case? I need this information so I can establish the direction that will best help my client and determine if it's possible to save them money through an Offer in Compromise solution. Unfortunately, not everyone is a candidate for an Offer in Compromise. If they don't qualify, I explain to them why they don't qualify and we also discuss what other manageable options might exist to resolve their IRS problem. On the other hand, with the non-attorney tax resolution companies advertising on television, it is always a promise to get rid of penalties and interest and they always lead you to believe you will be able to settle for pennies on the dollar. Unfortunately, that is not the reality.

THE REALITY OF THE "PENNIES ON THE DOLLAR" CONCEPT

The Offer in Compromise program is actually one of the most difficult things to accomplish because you're asking the IRS to write off debt. So, you know they are going to do their due diligence when reviewing your case. Again, it's one of the most difficult programs to get accepted.

Additionally, there are different types of offers so you will want an experienced attorney to make sure the type of offer you select is appropriate for your situation. Is it an offer based on "doubt as to collectability?" Is it an offer based on "effective tax administration?" You want to make sure you chose the right one in order to give your Offer the very best chance of acceptance. Additionally, they are going to want a detailed personal financial statement and business financial statement if you operate a business. What are your assets? How much equity is there in those assets? What is your total monthly income? Where is that money going? You want to make sure you present this information in a way that is likely to benefit YOU, not Uncle Sam.

Often these non-attorney tax resolution services make the Offer in Compromise option sound like walking onto a used car lot to purchase a car. You see $8,000 written in shoe polish on the windshield of a vehicle. If you pull $6,000 cash out of your pocket, odds are that the sales person will take $6,000 for the car because he wants that money. Negotiating a settlement with the IRS is not like that. It's formulaic. It's based on equity and asset tables and income and expense tables. And, more importantly, it's based on allowable versus non-allowable expenses.

A lot of people come to me and say, "I'm broke at the end of the month. I barely have $50 to go to a movie with my wife once a month." But, they make $130,000 a year. Well, they have an $800 a month car payment and their mortgage is $2,700 and numerous other expenses that exhaust their paycheck. However, just because they spend all the money they earn on expenses doesn't mean they qualify for an Offer in Compromise. It is important to understand that when you are negotiating with the IRS they are allowed to tell you how much you can spend on a car, how much you can spend on your mortgage and how much you can spend on food. Once they take out all your numbers of what you are spending and replace them with their numbers, they may determine that you have $2,000 to $3,000 of extra income at the end of the month when you don't think you have 2 or 3 dollars left over.

This is why you need, and I'll say it again, an experienced, local tax attorney. There is a certain way you want to present all this information. You don't want someone to represent you who doesn't understand the process. It is a difficult program, but that shouldn't discourage people who owe the IRS money because it can be done if you meet the requirements. If you do meet the requirements, the Offer in Compromise is the way you should resolve the debt because it's the best solution out there and it will give you the finality to this problem you are seeking.

BASIC REQUIREMENTS FOR AN OFFER IN COMPROMISE

There are some basic requirements in order to even apply for an Offer in Compromise with the IRS. This is one major place where many of the national tax resolution companies are very weak and really don't have a clue as to what they are doing. Here are a few of the basic requirements:

1. All your tax returns must be filed. You cannot have any non-filed returns from previous years.

2. If you are a business owner, the Federal Payroll Tax Deposits must be current.

3. If you are self-employed, you have to pay your taxes quarterly and you must be current on those quarterly payments.

If, for example, someone is not current on their estimated quarterly payments, the offer is going to be denied. This is what I encounter periodically. Someone comes to me and says, "I hired a national tax resolution company and everything seemed good. But I just received a denial of my Offer in Compromise. I've tried to call the tax resolution service and they won't answer the phone or return my calls. I don't know why this was denied and I can't get any answers from the tax resolution service I've already paid to help me." After I review their situation I find that no one ever told them that they can't miss their estimated payments because it's grounds for denial.

When an experienced local law firm, such as ours, is dealing with local revenue officers or dealing with a specific Offer in Compromise Unit, we have very likely dealt with them before and they know our firm is reputable and when we say we are going to do something they know we will do it. That doesn't mean we will get a better result as compared to someone that doesn't know them because it's not a matter of favoritism. But again, we're experienced with this process and our experience is the catalyst that drives better outcomes.

Keep in mind that the job of those in the Offer in Compromise Unit, in my opinion, is to find a way to deny an offer and they usually will. That means, in a lot of cases, we have to appeal that decision. Even before we appeal the denial, we will go back and forth with the Offer in Compromise Unit as many times as we can to get it resolved without appeal. But, ultimately, there may be a denial and then you have to go through the formal appeal process.

Who do you think is going to be better suited to deal with the Office of Appeals? Is it going to be someone that is an experienced tax resolution attorney or is it someone that took a test and is now able to represent taxpayers? Common sense dictates here. You want to be as well equipped as possible with a strong team working on your behalf.

THE GOVERNMENT ALWAYS HAS AN OUT

Another problem is that the government basically has an "out." Even if you meet most of the criteria, the government can still say, "No, we're not going to accept it because we don't think it's in the best interest of the Federal Government." Or "We're not going to accept this because we think you will be able to pay this in full before the statute of limitations expires 9 or 10 years from now." When the rules are stacked in favor of the government you always want to make sure you present the application, financial statements and every other piece of documentation in a way that is going to benefit you and not the Government. That's the issue I encounter when I have a client coming to me who previously used a tax resolution company. The problem is that we don't know what was presented before and we basically have to start from scratch.

Even if an Offer in Compromise is accepted, you need an attorney on your side to make sure the acceptance process actually comes to fruition. There are a number of rules that can breach the offer after it has been accepted by the IRS. For example, if you're paying off this offer over time, it has to be done a certain way. If you file your tax return one day late three years after the offer was accepted, the whole offer can be reversed. If you miss making your estimated quarterly tax payment sometime in the next five years, the whole offer could be reversed. So, if you have an Offer in Compromise accepted by the IRS, you will want to make sure someone is overseeing the process from beginning to end so that you decrease the possibility of getting it reversed by not meeting the IRS established requirements.

IT BOILS DOWN TO THIS

If you are facing any type of IRS problem …

1. You want someone who is a highly-experienced tax resolution attorney to represent you.

2. You want someone with a flat fee because hourly billing can accumulate very, very quickly when dealing with IRS issues.

3. You want someone who is local, so you can sit face-to-face with them to discuss your options.

I encourage you to do your due diligence when selecting an attorney to help you with your tax resolution problems. When trying to find the right attorney, call the Better Business Bureau. Call the State Bar to make sure they are in good standing. Google their name for "complaints" or "law suits." You need to know who you are paying to fix your problem. This is too serious of a problem to take lightly. When you have organizations like the U.S. Treasury and the IRS that can ruin you financially, it is crucial that you do your homework thoroughly with respect to whom you chose to represent you.

And please remember, if your Offer in Compromise is eventually denied, there are several other possible solutions that can give you a manageable way out of your IRS nightmare. So select your representative carefully... your financial future may depend upon it.

About Nick

Nick Nemeth is a Texas attorney and best-selling author who has been in practice for over 15 years. His law practice, The Law Offices of Nick Nemeth, PLLC, focuses solely on helping individuals and businesses resolve a wide range of IRS issues. Nick has been featured in *USA Today, The Wall Street Journal, Forbes Magazine, Yahoo Finance* and *Morningstar*, as well as having appeared on ABC, NBC, CBS and Fox affiliates around the country.

As a long-time resident of Dallas, Nick possesses a unique quality only present in those who truly love their home—a complete and personal investment in the lives of the people of his community. By creating a truly local presence in the Dallas-Fort Worth Metroplex, Nick brings his 15 years of legal experience to those who truly need it … individuals and businesses who are being threatened by the IRS.

Nick's ultimate goal in his practice, for any of his clients, is to provide efficient, cost-effective legal representation. He firmly believes that when any taxpayer is facing an "opponent" who happens to be a branch of the federal government, one who's able to seize your property and assets without going to court, that taxpayer should arm him/herself with an aggressive, experienced law firm. Nick's staff includes attorneys, CPAs, enrolled agents and tax professionals who are dedicated to keeping ahead of an ever-changing industry: solving IRS problems. Nick is known for constantly saying, "My only job is to keep the IRS as far away as possible from my clients' assets until I negotiate an acceptable solution to their problem."

Nick was driven to become an attorney by his desire to help serve others and make a positive impact on the world. He's pleased with having found a niche in which he has been able to accomplish both these goals. He loves the satisfaction of working for a diverse clientele who are unequivocally pleased with his representation. His dedication to his practice is a benefit to all in the area of law he's focused on—helping his clients solve their IRS problems.

Having traveled to places like Sweden, Austria, Denmark, Canada, Hungary and the Caribbean, Nick appreciates the ties that continue to bring him back to Dallas-Fort Worth: his law practice, his wife and five children, and the abundance of sports and community activities that keeps the family man busy.

To learn more about Nick Nemeth and his law practice, as well as his special report, *How to End Your IRS Problems Forever*, visit: www.myIRSteam.com or call (972) 484-0TAX (0829).

CHAPTER 45

EXERCISE PATIENCE
IN ALL THINGS

BY MYLES MILLER

In a frequently volatile marketplace that seems to shift direction like an untethered wind-whipped balloon, we continue to face challenges in making choices that have well thought out direction and rational, factual context to draw upon.

Finding SUCCESS in this new economy, requires the ever increasing need to be patient with oneself and others and the marketplace, rather than rushing pell mell into each and every scenario and situation that presents itself. There are better approaches that offer much better outcomes for all those involved.

There are many who may read these words and feel the need to always be first, rush to the front of the line, and get ahead of the crowd to win the proverbial prize. There may be many opportunities to do this and some may make perfect sense in a variety of situations. Your favorite band of all time happens to be coming to town and it causes you to sleep overnight in a tent to be the first at the ticket window to get the best seats, which might make sense to do in the midst of the circumstances. The person who gets up early in the morning to get a jump on traffic to avoid the inevitable backlog and traffic jams that will follow only 15 minutes later than the time they left their home. Makes sense to me, and I have definitely done this. Or how about that hot stock that everyone is talking about and its forthcoming IPO. Seems like a great idea and it might be worth throwing some money its way to see what happens. And here is one of my favorite examples of an impulsive rush to decisions that happens over and over again. The multi-million dollar lottery drawing that has a nine digit payout, causing those from all walks of life, fixed income seniors, upper and lower middle class, working and unemployed, retired and students, to spend time standing in line to put their money down on a longshot with amazingly unlikely odds. Yes, someone or some combination of people will win and it is just that possibility that garners such drive and ambition to tempt many to give it a try. Even I have felt drawn to participate on occasion, prompted by the sum offered and the siren song of unfathomable wealth.

All these situations and many more are ongoing examples of patience lacking in our lives that require us to take a moment to **reflect**, **reassess** and **refocus** to understand why we feel the need to make these impulsive and sometimes rushed choices.

> *Without reflection, we go blindly on our way,*
> *creating more unintended consequences,*
> *and failing to achieve anything useful.*
> ~ Margaret J. Wheatley

We should approach each situation with as an opportunity for awareness and knowledge, but before we move forward, make a decision, determine a course of action, there should be a time to **reflect**, based on the importance of the decision both on a short or long term basis. Let's look back at one of the previously mentioned examples and see how **reflection** may prompt a different response and potential outcome. How about that concert goer, willing to brave the elements and less than ideal sleeping conditions, to get the first tickets offered. Do they realize that there might be another way or two or three to achieve the same goal without putting themselves in such potentially uncomfortable situations? i.e., storms, high winds, temperature extremes and on and on. Options exist for those wanting early access to get it through a variety of methods that do not require a "sleepover." Of course, if the intent is to have stories to tell ones children or to share in the camaraderie of like-minded people and to hang out with others who share the passion for their group or artist, it may seem like a worthwhile pursuit.

Reflection is truly unique. It can be done at any point in time. Think of it this way, many people reflect back on the past, but what about reflecting on the current circumstances to weigh one's options. Or what about **reflecting** on a near or future term event that may or may not occur or **reflecting** on all the possibilities or "what-ifs" that may occur before the situation arises. Some would call this proactive and it is, but it is also being reflective of a potential future state.

So you can see that in any and all circumstances, some **reflection** into the past, in the present or about the future has tremendous potential and opportunity to make you more patient as you have contemplated on how things can and will unfold. This boasts your inner confidence and helps you to address situations with a greater degree of knowledge, due to time spent in patient **reflection.**

We live immersed in narrative, recounting and reassessing the meaning of our past actions, anticipating the outcome of our future projects, situating ourselves at the intersection of several stories not yet completed.
~ Peter Brooks

To exercise patience in all things we need to look to a by-product, or partner, in many cases of **reflect,** that is…**reassess**. While **reflecting** makes you think about the steps you have taken, are taking or will take, **reassessing** takes the next steps in improving our patience through options that are explored to achieve a desired outcome or a proposed path forward. I like to refer to these as my "Plan B" ideas. These "Plan B" ideas give me a great sense of control and understanding so that in many situations I could or will face, I have other directions and avenues available to me, thus making me more patient and more willing to be flexible as I know options do exist and can be explored. One caveat I have learned to acknowledge in my "Plan B" approach that comes from the very diverse and dynamic world we live in, is that a "Plan B" may not give you enough of an option. So, plan beyond one option to several others to diminish fear, concern, frustration, anger, and of course impatience. Make sure to have not only a "Plan B" but consider 'C', 'D', or 'E'.

By being able to **reassess** before we make decisions or choices, we open up our imagination and creative ideas allowing for the intermingling with our rational thoughts and experiences that will craft outcomes that have a great degree of SUCCESS because of the time taken to **reassess**.

Let's consider another one of our previous examples: the person like myself, who is willing to leave a little earlier each day to miss the potential traffic jams that may occur just a few minutes later. Through experimentation, experience, general knowledge and other factors used in the **reassessment**, one realizes, as I have on several scenarios, what will work best to get them to their destination in the timeliest fashion with the least amount of backlog and challenges. Could there be an unexpected traffic jam caused by an accident or construction? Absolutely, but by having taken time to **reassess**, the patient driver can have the additional plans in place to deal with the circumstances they face. Thus, they are calmer and deal with the situation in a patient manner.

Next time you are in traffic jam, look around at the drivers and try to determine from their expressions what attitude that they are exhibiting. The "patient" ones will be dealing with the situation calmly, might be singing a song on the radio, or talking with someone rationally about their circumstances and their plans, which they made in advance, to handle the current scenario.

Now it's your turn to do a little **reassessing** right now. Think of an upcoming event, meeting, trip or something that will require numerous logistics and thought to plan and execute. Oh, but before you get too far into your thoughts, let's set the proper atmosphere to do this right. OK, now this first one or two steps will be tough for some of you. Turn off your phone, PC screen, tablet, and any other electronic device that might interrupt you. Even better, walk away from them and go somewhere else, another room, outside, down the hall, etc. Now that we have the proper atmosphere we can begin to **reassess** the particular condition that may present itself. Think slowly through each scenario and potential outcome based on likely options or "plans" you may have available to you. It is important to note that you should only work on one scenario at a time. My recommendation is once you have **reassessed** your situation, stop there for now. Try to avoid tackling too many circumstances at one time if you can. In trying to increase your patience, you certainly want to minimize your stress levels by accomplishing one resolution plan at a time.

Now that you have been able to **reflect** and **reassess**, one additional step remains in exercising patience in all things…**refocus**.

Things do not change; we change.
~ Henry David Thoreau

This third step is often the most challenging. It continues to challenge me as I try to exercise patience in all things. True confession time: I am still learning and applying much of what I have shared with you here. So, let's get back to it and **refocus**.

So, after reflecting and reassessing now it is time to move forward in thought and/or deed. This is a crucial action step that builds on the foundation of the previous steps.

I have heard it said many times that change is hard, but "change we must". In the case of exercising patience in all things, it is this transformational idea that gives us the opportunity to use our patience to its fullest extent.

Remember back to our examples, that upcoming IPO opportunity looks like a pretty good idea, but after **reflecting**, **reassessing** and now **refocusing**, we realize that it may not be exactly what we thought it could be. In fact, through these efforts, clarity and decision-making become easier, preparing us through all these patient efforts, to be ready to chart a course to move forward, and to follow it.

We can now explore what path makes sense and pursue it. With patient reflection along with patient reassessment, we can confidently decide whether to take action and in what form; or in many cases to not take any action, because it would not be prudent to do so at this time.

Imagine the short and long term implications for you and others, with all the crucial and complex decisions and choices we have to make, if exercising patience was done frequently. Could money be saved, relationships be maintained and improved, possible mistakes be avoided and potential snap decisions be tempered by this effort. Put simply, the answer is a resounding and absolute…YES!!!

Some final thoughts for you to ponder. All throughout my life I have met many people who claim to be patient people and I have seen them prove this out over and over again. The ones who do this extremely well follow the approach that I have shared. They understand and know the value in taking time to **reflect**, many times a day. They constantly **reassess** their position and decisions to make sure they are choosing the right options. Finally, gathering what is learned from the previous steps shared here, these same people **refocus** their efforts to choose the path that leads forward. Sometimes this happens quickly, but often it takes time.

My hope is that you have been or are becoming people who each day in every way you can, exercise patience in all things.

About Myles

Myles Miller is the CEO and Founder of LeadUP (www.leadup.biz), LearningBreaks (www.learningbreaks.com) and SUCCESSHQ (www.successhq.net).

In January 2009, Myles started his first company, LeadUP, focused on providing customized training solutions to companies and individuals that will take them to new levels of success.

Other companies followed, and his efforts, along with those he has partnered with, continued to expand their market impact beyond local and regional companies to becoming national and internationally competitive training and professional development companies.

Each of his training companies was created with the foundational ideal to offer a variety of customized training, educational and speaking opportunities to professionals and their companies, that need to gain new and greater expertise in Project and Program Management, Business Analysis, Leadership Development and Team Building, Decision-Making, Critical Thinking, Problem-solving and much more.

During his career, Myles has influenced and impacted tens of thousands of people through his speaking and training efforts. His leadership and guidance has led corporations and non-profit organizations to new heights and enhanced abilities.

One life philosophy that Myles has tried to live out each day is to impact one life in a way that will last a lifetime. He puts this at the top of his To-Do list for each day and through a variety of methods takes steps to cross this item off this same list daily.

Myles has 30 years of experience in the project management field, across multiple industries including retail, defense, hospitality and state and federal governments. During his varied career, he has led projects ranging in budgetary size from $100K to $500B. His team leadership has impacted national and international companies, governments and non-profit organizations of all sizes from 100 to over 10,000 team members.

CHAPTER 46

RUNNING WITH THE BIG DOGS: TRUE WEALTH BUILDING STRATEGIES FOR REAL PEOPLE

BY VINCENT CORSI AND JOHN MARINO

Turn on the news any day of the week and out pours a deluge of stories about the wealthy becoming, well, …wealthier. Hard-working people and business owners become incensed that their dedication, work ethic and investments never seem to catch them up to the earnings of the super-wealthy. Like so many other business owners, we became interested in building wealth, both personally and as a company. While the politicos argue over flat taxes and massive debt, we quietly set out to revolutionize the way people earn money and reduce debt. We considered it curious that men like Warren Buffett would openly admit that making money was easy when for most people it remains a daunting task. What is the secret and how can we utilize it to help people reach their financial goals and perhaps retire earlier? The secret, we discovered, is arbitrage.

Arbitrage, taking advantage of the price differences between two markets to profit from the differences between the markets to gain wealth, was once a practice of only banks and brokerages, or those wealthy enough already to gain access to the secrets of those domains. Warren Buffett, an admitted arbitrageur, is rumored to have said that if you stripped away his wealth and allowed him to keep only $10,000, he could regain his fortune in only months. In fact, Buffett's annualized rate of return from 1980-2003 was a whopping 81.28%, according to *Warren Buffett and the Art of Stock Arbitrage* by Mary Buffett and David Clark. Few can imagine such a return, let alone the relatively small risks to netting that return.

The arbitrage system allows banks to make as much as $30,000 to $40,000 a day in profit on about $1million. They make their money by leveraging the time gaps between trades at different brokerages. In short, they use that money to profit during the seconds between the ask price on a stock at one brokerage and the sell price at another. These transactions happen at lightning speed. In fact, 65% of all trading happens via automation and most people do not even know it. In the time that it took you to read this paragraph, another "big dog" millionaire just got richer, why shouldn't you?

Until the late 1970's, when home computers were developed, only banks and major businesses had the computers and resources to track the time gaps between trades. Coincidentally, the gap between the rich and the super rich widened substantially between the late 1970's and today, as well. It is safe to say that the super rich know something that even the wealthiest around us must not know.

As we watched our own software business grow, we became increasingly dedicated to not allowing only the banks to profit from our hard-earned money. We wanted to profit more from our hard work, and we believe that most business people and those investing for retirement would agree. We work hard; we want our money to work hard for us too. With this at heart, we developed two software platforms to make options available to our customers to which only the super-wealthy have traditionally had access.

Our software, Automatic Day Trader, will revolutionize your personal or business financial future and afford you the opportunity to grow wealth just like the powerfully wealthy do.Unless you have a golden goose, the only way to make that much money rapidly is arbitrage. With the stock market trading just under $1 trillion per day, there is plenty of money to make.

After many years of research and development, we assembled a team of developers, mathematicians, specialized code writers and traders to build Automatic Day Trader.Our stock trading software, *Automatic Day Trader*, is a highly advanced algo trading system trading on arbitrage. Remember, arbitrage trading takes advantage of the price differences between two or more markets, then profiting from the difference between the markets.

Because of the leveraging laws in the United States, you do need to have approximately $25,000 in available capital to begin, but you do not need to close out your existing investments such as 401(k)s or IRAs. We have made it easy for people to use the software to access the money in their 401(k) to trade via Interactive Brokers without removing the money from their retirement accounts and paying penalties. Essentially, instead of trading within the confines of the currently available investments in one's 401(k), the person uses that invested money for stock arbitrage, or making money on the gaps between the prices on a certain stock at various brokerages. You will pay no penalty fees for using the money in your 401(k). Instead of the fund manager managing your money, you will have placed it within Interactive Brokers to orchestrate trades on your behalf.

Let's say, for example, that you had $25,000 invested in your 401(k). Instead of leaving it placed in Fidelity investments, you gain access to your money to take advantage of the price gap—sometimes only pennies—between the sell and the ask price for Disney stock. You could make 1 to 3% per day, but even a ½% *per day* return far exceeds the 6% annual return you might get in your mutual funds and achieves it with less risk. Those investors who lost signficant money in 2008 have the opportunity to recoup those losses, and even earn more than they lost, in a very short time.

With our software and your 401(K), you can utilize Interactive Brokers. We have no affiliation with Interactive Brokers in any way. They provide a great service for our software to execute trades, which is why our software trades through them. A banker once told us that, "banks have big buildings and people like you and I live in little houses because of arbitrage." Until recently, one had to have millions of dollars to enjoy arbitrage profits. What could your savings be today if you had been paid 10% or more, monthly, since you opened your savings account? What would you have if that amount compounded month after month? With a $50,000 investment account earning 10% per month and compounding monthly, you would earn over $105,000 in interest in only 1 year. Leave that money invested for a period of three years, and you would earn just about $1.5 million in interest alone. Imagine how quickly you could retire at that rate.

Businesses benefit from Automatic Day Trader as well. What do most successful business people do when they become highly profitable? They build bigger businesses or acquire other businesses. The growth potential of being able to work smarter—even create your own growth capital—increases exponentially when your business can run with the big dogs. Even a municipality could change their bottom line using this software.

The software looks at the differences, or gaps, in the prices between stocks. It makes instantaneous calculations on what the differences will be and buys, then sells, those stocks within seconds to profit the difference. You are pitting one brokerage house against the other at a very high rate of speed, faster than the rate at which you could buy or sell otherwise. It would be possible with Automatic Day Trader, for example, to purchase 100 shares of Apple and profit $200 within seconds.

Automatic Day Trader ensures you never have to worry about:
- Identifying the arbitrage opportunity
- Monitoring the price differences between brokers
- Tracking all of your trades simultaneously
- Calculating the potential gain in real time

Automatic Day Trader recommends stocks based on the performance of 2000 companies, selected from around 13,000 publicly-traded stocks, which includes all S&P 500, Dow 30 and additional highly rated companies. This fully automated trading software scans through stocks based on the user's choices to find ratings and provide a list of suggestions. These choices are determined, fundamentally and mathematically, the best picks for the immediate trading time. The software will also calculate ratings for your favorite companies that you add to the list. You are free from compiling manual research and analysis and the

Automatic Day Trader software identifies the arbitrage opportunities for you, tracks all your trades simultaneously and calculates your potential gain in real time. There is no guesswork because the system instantly captures profits of up to 3% per trade so that you **know** your potential profit when you place your trade. The software even safeguards you from losses.

If you are courageous enough to want to run with the big dogs, we want to teach you how to use our software to change your business and your life. If you are interested in quitting your job, earning extra income or saving for retirement, you can do all of those things with Automatic Day Trader. Automatic Day Trader offers the opportunities once granted to only the uber-wealthy to those with only modest monies to invest. Our webinars and customer support guide you to the choicest fruits, so you can begin harvesting bigger personal and business financial successes.

About Vincent and John

Steve Jobs said: *Innovation distinguishes between a leader and a follower.*

<u>Vincent Corsi and John Marino are leaders.</u> Their innovative arbitrage software, as unique as fulgurites, the sculptures created when lightening strikes sand, is the natural culmination of years of experience developing software about which others only dream.

 **Vincent Corsi** is a software developer and a partner of IQ Software Systems. Vincent specializes in the development of fully automated investment softwares for stock investing and Forex investing that are algorithmic traders. His most recent accomplishment has been the development of Automatic Day Trader, stock-trading software that trades based on arbitrage. The software: www.winningstocktrades.com revolutionized the industry as the one and only stock arbitrage software available to the public.

Vincent's extensive career has included Internet marketing, search engine optimization (SEO), data analytics and project management. He is also a partner with www.optimizeustoday.com, a website development and SEO company.

Vincent will be doing live weekly webinars where curious investors can learn more about stock arbitrage and how it empowers investors.

When he is not developing software, Vincent relaxes with his family. For more information about IQ Software products or Vincent Corsi, visit his website www.automaticdaytrader.com or email him iqsoftwaresystems@gmail.com .

 **John Marino** is a software developer and a partner of IQ Software Systems. IQ Softwares is a fee-based developer of investment and wealth building softwares including: stock investing, debt reduction and auto dialers. John's recent major development is: www.winningstocktrades.com. This collaboration with Vincent Corsi created a fully automated stock-trading platform that trades stocks based on arbitrage and is the first of its kind available to the public.

Throughout his career, John received numerous sales, achievement and other awards. He has held sales, marketing and software positions, and still owns and operates his first website design and SEO marketing company www.optimizeustoday.com.

John has done live interviews with some creditable big players such as Nick Nanton and George Ross, and was recently a keynote speaker with Steve Forbes.

You can find more information about John on Facebook or by viewing his websites: www.optimizeus.com and www.winningstocktrades.com .

CHAPTER 47

PAY YOUR TAXES –
BUT NOT A PENNY MORE!

BY LYUBIM KOGAN

The hardest thing in the world to understand is the income tax.
~ Albert Einstein

The year 2012 marked the first time since World War II when the US national debt exceeded our gross domestic product. In the near future, the IRS will be under enormous pressure from the federal government to increase tax revenue collections. This chapter will attempt to expose the fastest growing extra tax that is not getting enough attention- the Alternative Minimum Tax (AMT). This is one of the most convoluted areas of the tax code, but simply put the AMT is an extra flat tax added on top of your regular tax. If you are hit with it, you cannot legally avoid it. However, armed with proper knowledge, there are proactive ways to greatly reduce your extra AMT tax. To illustrate, we'll look at the publicly released tax returns of President Obama and Governor Romney. Two opposing parties, both affected by the same problem of having to pay the extra Alternative Minimum Tax.

	AGI	Regular Tax	Extra AMT	%Tax Increase
President Obama[1]	$608,611	$87,465	$21,221	+24%
Governor Romney[2]	$13,696,951	$1,340, 834	$674,512	+50%

Yes, Governor Romney did pay an extra 50% on his taxes because of the AMT. In the next few pages, I will take you step by step through a process that may help you greatly reduce both taxes, regular and the AMT. Before we proceed, there is another developing issue of great significance that affects practically everyone in the US. The roll out of the Patient Protection and Affordable Care Act (PPACA, ACA, or Obamacare). We are weeks away from October 1st, 2013, a major milestone date on which the national health exchanges are set to go live. Finally, after waiting for a period of three years, we'll be able to see the real cost of the new health policies. The level of anxiety associated with Obamacare is so high, that I'm compelled at this last moment to include this topic in this chapter. We will review important dates and which businesses will be affected. Most importantly, we will look at tax savings that your business may be eligible for through the **Small Business Health Care Tax Credit**.

AMT History. In the winter of 1969, Treasury Secretary Joseph W. Barr testified before congress that there were 155 individual taxpayers in the US with incomes above $200,000 who paid no Federal income tax. All used provisions in the tax code to legally avoid paying Federal taxes. This testimony created an overheated political debate, and to prevent the wealthy from avoiding Federal tax, Congress passed the original minimum tax. Later, it was modified and became its successor today know as the Alternative Minimum Tax (AMT). Generally speaking, to calculate the AMT income, certain items are considered preferential, and must be added to your income. Some deductions you take in normal tax years are disallowed in the AMT years. If the AMT is more than your regular tax, the difference is added to your taxes.[4] In 2012, a tax created to punish a few affected 4 million American households and imposed an additional $32 billion *tax*. The Congressional Budget Office projects that over 25 million taxpayers will become subject to the AMT in 2013, and pay a whopping $131 billion in *extra taxes*.[3] If not reformed, in the next 10 years practically every upper-middle class family with two or more children will have to pay the extra Alternative Minimum Tax. So let's take a look at three practical steps you may be able to take right now to combat this stealth tax. We begin with taking a look at a strategy on a personal level, and will integrate it with two tax smart ideas for your business.

STRATEGY #1
MAKE EVERY ITEMIZED DEDUCTION COUNT

	AGI	Itemized Deductions	AGI Reduction%
President Obama	$608,611	$258,385	42%
Governor Romney	$13,696,951	$4,681,842	34%

To be able to reduce AGI by a large percentage, this section must be carefully designed and crafted over a period of time. Most people, whose interactions with accountants are limited to the tax season, realize less than a 20% reduction to their AGI.[5] Here are some ideas that will get you started and on your way to making all your itemized deductions count. Remember, if you have any number on 1040 Line 45, you are subject to extra AMT taxes, making every deductible dollar more valuable. We begin with Schedule "A".

Medical and Dental expenses: This section provides a great opportunity for identifying tax savings. Most people lose tens of thousands of dollars in deductions because of income limitations imposed by the tax code. To make matters worse, an even greater percentage of your medical and dental expenses became non-deductible in 2013.[6] If you want to be able to avoid this limitation and be able to deduct 100% of your medical and dental expenses, consider setting up a Medical Reimbursement Plan through your corporation. All medical expenses paid or reimbursed by the corporation will become fully tax deductible.[7]

Taxes you paid: If you paid state and local income taxes, real estate and personal property tax in the years when you are subject to the AMT, you are not allowed to deduct these taxes. Even though a deduction actually appears on line 9, it is added back on a different form when figuring out your AMT income.[8] If you are losing this deduction in the current year, making these tax payments in the following year may enable you to realize this deduction. Be careful to not generate penalties greater than the tax savings you get in the following year. For this section it's best to use a CPA to run projections and help you figure out potential savings. I do not recommend doing this on your own, because you may generate a tax penalty higher than potential savings.

Charitable contributions:

President Obama gifted $172,000 to charities, and Governor Romney gave away $2.25 million. Both took a full deduction for their donations, and greatly reduced their regular and AMT taxes. If you regularly make charitable contributions consider making larger donations in the AMT years. By shifting more contributions into years when you are paying extra taxes, you will have more to deduct and increase your tax savings. How much you'll pay in extra AMT depends on many factors, and it's impossible to know what future increases will be. As we saw earlier with Governor Romney, it is possible for the AMT to add an extra 50% to your tax bill.

Starting in 2013, Pease limitation is imposed on your itemized deductions such as charitable contributions, mortgage interest, and property and state income taxes.[9] If we applied this limitation to earlier years, President Obama would have lost $9,258[10] in itemized deductions, and the Governor would have to forgo $410,000[11] of his deductions. In order to avoid Pease limitation, consider making donations out of your corporation. Additionally, the money you donate out of the corporation is not paid to you, and therefore extra regular and AMT tax is avoided.

STRATEGY #2
THE BEST TAX PLANNING TOOL - BUSINESS ENTITIES

Today, business ownership in America provides a plethora of great tax planning opportunities . However, choosing a wrong business structure can cost you millions in unnecessary taxes. As your business grows, it is necessary to change, leverage, and create new business structures in order to minimize your taxes. The lobbying force that represents corporate interests in Washington is very powerful. Consequently, whatever benefits large companies like Apple, Wal-Mart, Intel, and Exxon receive are available to every American business owner. When we look at "C" corporations, they offer many tax loopholes, but are faced with the issue of double taxation. What worked successfully for many business owners was to separate an activity like marketing, and to create a new "C" corp. to perform those activities. Then, set up and administer all benefits for the owners in this new company, thus reducing taxable income and avoiding double taxation.

Let's take a closer look at two areas that changed in 2013:

1) In strategy #1 we identified that many Americans are losing their medical and dental deductions because of rules applicable to the personal expense deductibility. One way to claim back those lost deductions is by setting up a Medical Reimbursement Plan (MERP). This plan is designed to pay or reimburse medical costs incurred, and gives you the ability to deduct all medical and dental expenses on a corporate level. Additionally, retirement plans, health insurance, and increasingly more important, long term care insurance, can absorb more earnings, again avoiding double taxation. If planned and maintained correctly, it is possible to soak up most or even all the earnings within the corporation, and zero out the effect of double taxation. If in some years not all earnings are absorbed by your fringe benefits, you can use retirement plans to minimize your income, or retain the earnings within the corporation for future marketing and fringe benefit expenses. Be careful with how much earnings you retain, because there is an annual penalty for accumulated earnings over $250,000.

2) There now is a 3% reduction on charitable contributions made for taxpaycrs earning over $300,000. If we apply this to Governor Romney's previous tax return, it would have reduced his deduction by over $400,000.[11] In order to avoid losing your charitable deductions, consider making gifts directly out of your corporation. Once again, not only may you be able to claim back your lost deductions, you will also reduce taxable income that is subject to double taxation on the corporate level, and on the personal return you will reduce your regular and the AMT tax.

STRATEGY #3
THE USE OF RETIREMENT PLANS AS TAX SHELTERS

Retirement plans allow business owners to generate hundreds of thousands of dollars in annual tax deductions. There is widespread disagreement and confusion amongst small business owners about company-sponsored retirement plans. Some feel that limited investment choices, combined with the cost and the time needed to stay compliant, does not outweigh the benefits received from having a company-sponsored plan. However, the deductibility of the retirement plan contributions is not restricted under the Alternative Minimum Tax rules. There are two main types of retirement plans, Defined Benefit (DB) and Defined Contribution (DC). These plans differ greatly. A Defined Benefit plan can provide much larger tax deductions than Defined Contribution plans. For example, a DB plan may require an annual funding of $200,000 for the husband, and $125,000 for the wife, who are both involved in the business. Incomes above $450,000 may easily get taxed as high as 48%[12] and a $325,000 retirement contribution would produce $157,300 in tax savings.[12] *A word of caution*- if you implement a Defined Benefit plan for your business, and its value drops below a legal requirement, you as the employer will be obligated to make additional contributions. In down market years, additional capital requirements may be substantial. In order to avoid being in a position of having to contribute more, look into funding your DB plan with fixed contracts.[13] If, after evaluating your situation, you decide that a DB plan is not appropriate for your current situation, then you may find something more fitting amongst Defined Contribution plans. DC plans are much more flexible and less costly, but they provide less tax savings than DB plans.

TURNING UNCERTAINTY INTO OPPORTUNITY

Most Americans agree that our health care system is in need of major reform. According to the Congressional Budget Office, ACA will combine savings of Medicare with additional revenues, and will reduce our deficit. For now, all we can do is monitor the progression of ACA's implementation and make necessary steps to stay compliant. As of September 1st, 2013, here are some important dates to note:

a). October 1st, 2013 the national health exchanges are set to begin open enrollment on the Small Business Health Options Program (SHOP) marketplace.

b). January 1st, 2014 is the earliest day that coverage begins.

c). The Employer Play-or-Pay Mandate- in July 2013 this mandate was postponed until 2015. Employers who employ more than 50 full time employees are mandated to pay for the employees qualified health insurance coverage, or face a tax penalty.

Currently, the highest tax penalty you may face is $250 per month for each employee.

The Small Business Health Care Tax Credit is a temporary loophole that allows a small business owner to receive a tax credit for providing health care coverage to its employees.[15] This credit is available to any business owner who employs less than 25 full-time equivalent employees, with an average salary of less than $50,000 a year (excluding owners' earnings). For tax years 2010 through 2013 the maximum credit is 35% of premiums paid for small business employers, and 25% of premiums paid for small tax-exempt employers such as charities.

For 2014 and later, there are several changes:

i). The maximum credit will increase to 50% of premiums paid for small business employers, and 35% of premiums paid for small tax-exempt employers.

ii). To be eligible for the credit, a small employer must pay premiums on behalf of employees enrolled in a qualified health plan offered through a Small Business Health Options Program (SHOP) Marketplace.

iii). The credit will be available to eligible employers for two consecutive taxable years.

How much can be saved on taxes if this loophole is used? Assume a company pays 50% of its 20 employees' $400 monthly insurance premium. If qualified for a full tax credit, the savings are as follows:

2010-2013 – $ 48,000 x 4 years x 35% = $ 67,200

2014-2015 – $ 48,000 x 2 years x 50% = $ 48,000

Total tax credit: **$ 115,200**

While many individuals experience anxiety over the potential negative effects of ACA, it is possible to benefit from it! Over $115,000 in tax savings was available in this example by knowing that this loophole exists, and filing the right paperwork with the IRS. As time passes, our lives change and situations become more complex. It happens quite often that we outgrow people who advise us. However, many of us refuse to see this fact of life. If you have not been informed of this small business tax loophole, or if you paid the extra AMT tax because *"there is nothing you can do about it,"* this may be the time to take responsibility for your situation and make changes. In essence, the aforementioned scenarios in this chapter offer examples of how tax planning is a lifelong **proactive** process of following the steps required by the Internal Revenue Code to pay 100% of the taxes you owe. But not a penny more!

REFERENCES

1. Information from the latest return available 2012 is used through chapter http://www.taxhistory.org/thp/presreturns.nsf/Returns/69751C3E8B0DE0CD85257B4B00687AB0/$file/complete_return_president_obama_2012.pdf

2. Information from the latest return available 2011 is used through chapter http://www.taxhistory.org/thp/presreturns.nsf/Returns/9F81699BC7D6DE238525798F0051C35F/$file/M_Romney_2011.pdf

3. http://www.taxpolicycenter.org/briefing-book/key-elements/amt/revenue.cfm
http://www.cbo.gov/sites/default/files/cbofiles/ftpdocs/108xx/doc10800/01-15-amt_brief.pdf

4. AMT is reported on line 45 of your Form 1040. If you have any number on line 45, the AMT limitations apply to you for that tax year.

5. To find your percentage reduction of AGI, divide line 40 by line 38 on your form 1040.

7. To find out how much you lost in medical and dental deductions, subtract line 4 from line 1 on Schedule "A".

8. Form 6251

9. Pease limitation named after former Congressman Donald Pease incorporated into the Omnibus Budget Reconciliation act of 1990. It is brought back for 2013 and later years. For every dollar you make over $300,000 you must reduce your itemized deductions by 3%, not to exceed 80% of the total for these deductions

10. (608,611-300,000) x 3% =$ 9,258

11. (13,969,951-300,000) x 3% =$410,000

12. Top federal 39.6% + 3.8% Medicare tax + assumed 5% extra AMT = 48.4% x 325,000 = $ 157,300

13. Most DB plans are funded through a mix of life insurance and annuity contracts. There are 2 major types of contracts available - Variable and fixed. Variable contracts have sub-accounts that work like mutual funds, and will fluctuate with the market. Fixed contracts provide protection to the funds they hold, and are not affected by market volatility. Historically, variable contracts were used because they have greater upside potential. However, recently fixed contracts have gained popularity due to their ability to capture a portion of market index upside, and at the same time enjoying contractual principal guaranty.

14. Form 1040 - subtract 300,000 from the number on line 38. Then multiply the result by 0.03. This is the amount you will not be able to deduct starting tax year 2013 and going forward.

15. Tax credits give us a dollar-for-dollar reduction on our tax bill.

About Lyubim

Lyubim Kogan is the founder and president of Kogan Financial Group, LLC a firm that specializes in proactive tax-based financial planning and risk management. For over 14 years, Mr. Kogan has helped hundreds of business owners and professional athletes, in the U.S. and internationally, to implement tax-reduction strategies, set up and protect investment and businesses interests, create powerful income strategies and efficiently transfer wealth to next generations.

Mr. Kogan is a graduate of NYU Stern School of Business with dual degrees in Finance and CPA Accounting. With hard work, dedication, and careful planning, all clients of Kogan Financial avoided losses in the 2008-2009 financial crisis. Mr. Kogan is well known for producing and hosting the *Secure Wealth®* radio show heard in Colorado, California, Oklahoma, and Wyoming.

Lyubim is an Olympic Athlete and participated in the 1998 Winter Olympic Games in Nagano, Japan.

One a personal note, Lyubim would like to express his gratitude to Steve Forbes for this opportunity to contribute a chapter to *Successonomics*. Lyubim went to NYU a few blocks down from Forbes Publications, and always knew that one day he would become a contributing writer for *Forbes*. Sometimes it can take 15 years to travel a few blocks, but it's never the distance we travel but the experiences we encounter on our journey.

Lyubim adds:

I thank my family, friends, and clients for their support and encouragement on my journey as a business owner. I would especially like to thank my wife Patricia for her unending love and support, and to my father Leonid, who had the courage to move his family to the United States in search of a better life.

With deep gratitude and appreciation,

-Lyubim Kogan
www.koganfinancial.com
lyubim@koganfinancial.com
Denver, CO
September 11, 2013.

CHAPTER 48

THE KEYS TO BUSINESS SUCCESS IN THE NEW ECONOMY

BY ELMER DAVIS, JR. MBA, ALM

What makes a strong business? A few Key elements for Business Success will get you on the right track in the New Economy. I'd love to share my thoughts on this with you.

In small to medium-sized businesses, the limitations of the owners translate into the problems of the business. More often than not, I begin working with clients to save them money, as well as implement cost control and budgeting to lower transaction costs. There are a number of ways to control costs that many business owners do not understand, which I'll explain.

Let's get started with Harry and his wife and partner, Ashu! When I started working with Harry and Ashu, I couldn't believe how little they knew about their business. They owned the Olympia IV Restaurant in Baltimore, Maryland which they had been operating for nine years. Since a lot of small businesses fail during the first 5 years, it's not everyday that I get to consult and share ideas with such well-experienced owners.

Here's an actual agenda and some work product from our Company Plan meeting for Olympia IV (with Ashu, Harry, and I), to illustrate:

BUSINESS DEVELOPMENT/GROWTH

A. <u>SHORT TERM GOAL: INCREASE SALES & PROFITS</u>

- Introduction to Break-Even—Break-Even is the point in the volume of Activity for the organization, where Sales and expenses are equal. (Knowing the break-even point is a key tool for decision making.)

- Cost volume and profit relationships—Look at Contribution Margin approach:
Sales less Variable Expenses = Contribution Margin
Contribution Margin less Fixed Expenses = Net Income

Objective: Break-Even Utilization for advertising decisions –Windfall of Sales and Profits (Groupon campaign—Kids eat Free). Later, expressing Break Even with a Graph will allow us to focus on Profits and Volume.

Principals of Finance: Overarching business goal -
Improve Asset Management

B. <u>LONG TERM GOAL:</u> Direct Market access as opposed to financial intermediation.

Banks have been at the heart of economic activity for centuries. How they function, what they do, and the challenges they face, are Keys to developing an understanding of Finance.

Here are a couple of Questions that illustrate a few introductory ideas:

Q.1. What are the two forms in which banks can hold reserves?

A.1 Banks can hold reserves in the form of vault cash or as deposits with the Fed.

Q.2. Suppose Tom takes a $100 bill out of his wallet and deposits it in his checking account at the Bank. Which one of the following statements most accurately describes what has happened?

(i). Tom's net worth has increased by $100.

(ii). Bank's assets and its net worth have gone up by $100.

(iii). The total value of Tom's net worth has not changed. Bank's assets and liabilities have both increased.

(iv). Tom's assets have decreased and Bank's assets have increased.

A.2. (iii) is the correct description of what happened. Let's analyze each statement in turn:

> (i). Tom's net worth has increased by $100. This is not the case. All Tom has done is to switch one asset (cash) for another (checking deposit). Hence, all the action is on the left-hand side of his balance sheet. Tom's net worth is not affected.

> (ii). Bank's assets and its net worth have gone up by $100. Bank's assets—in particular, its cash reserves—have indeed increased; but this is offset by an increase in Bank's *liabilities*. While the $100 checking deposit is an asset to Tom, it is a liability to the bank. The bank's net worth is not affected.

> (iii). The total value of Tom's net worth has not changed. Bank's assets and liabilities have both increased. This is the accurate description of what happened on the respective balance sheets.

> (iv). Tom's assets have decreased and the Bank's assets have increased. This is discussed under (i) and (ii), above.

C. <u>HUMAN RESOURCES PRODUCTIVITY</u>
(People engaged and effective)

- We start by addressing the impact of miscommunication.

Consider the communication environment:

Sender>encode>transmit>FILTERS>Receiver>Decode>Accept> Action

<<<<<<<<<<<<<<<<CONTINOUS FEEDBACK>>>>>>>>>>>>>>>

Sender has billions of nerve-ending brain cells encoding (defining thoughts) with a few thousand English words. Choosing the best language to express these thoughts. Overarching barriers like distractions and background noise, etc. Receiver hears the words and applies interpretation to create a cognitive thought or impression—(misunderstandings occur here). English is often ambiguous and paradigms and experience shape perception. Message often not accepted or inaccurate action results.

For communication to be effective, it must be free of needless miscommunication. When individual or team communication is fragmented, ambiguous, contradictory or short-circuited in other ways, businesses lose money. The cost can be in the form of:

- Time lost due to inefficiency and needless repetitions of a task (re-work)
- Missed opportunity
- Time and energy to repair ineffective communication
- Missed deadlines that slip by
- Lost or damaged customer relationships due to unclear or unmet expectations
- Loss of productivity and employee retention due to emotional distress and ineffective
- Reactions, such as gossip, complaining and backbiting
- Loss of repeat business and loss of long and short term strategic alliances due to
- Impaired relationships
- Waste of resources due to treating a technical problem as though it were a communication misunderstanding and vice versa

Here's an Example:
Imagine just one misunderstanding that is minor, but significant. Assume for example, that a team deliverable was vague and led to a misunderstanding about the standard required for successful completion. Assume further that the average Manager's pay is $80,000 for 50 weeks/year and 40 hours/week. This values a manager's time at about $40/hour.

If the misunderstanding is small and is caught and resolved quickly, we might assume the following:

- 8 people meet for an hour to discuss and resolve the issue. 8 x $40/hour = $320
- Follow-up with other key staff takes 30 mins. each for 4 people. 2 hours x $40 = $80
- Re-work to correct the mistake takes 2 hours for 2 people. 4 hours x $40 = $160

The hidden bill is $560 if all goes well. But imagine if the issue isn't resolved, and another round of meetings, follow up discussions and re-work is needed. The bill may double, going from $560 to $1120.

If the issue is still not resolved, let's assume that it impacts a larger team of 20, creating further technical and interpersonal challenges and leading to further loss of productivity. If the productivity of the team of 20 drops by 10% for just one week, costs are:

$80,000/50 weeks = $1600/week.

10% of $1600 = $160/person.

20 x $160/person = $3200.

The hidden bill for lost productivity has now jumped from $1120 to $4320.

So for one minor misunderstanding that is mishandled for only one week for a team of 8 and a larger group of 20, the cost for extra meetings and lost productivity alone is easily over $4,000.

Now multiply this by number of small groups in your organization and the number of miscommunications that take place. Remember this doesn't factor in all the other costs that may be associated with the mistake, such as customer dissatisfaction, lower team morale, lack of discretionary effort and inhibition of innovation.

IT CAN COST TOO MUCH

The previous example assumed simple costs, a clear resolution and a low price tag. But often the miscommunication is not simply resolved and can be astronomically expensive.

Some forms of miscommunication are by nature more expensive than others. For instance, miscommunication from and between executives costs much more than for someone in a more junior position. Their time is more valuable and the impact of what they say carries more weight and moves with greater velocity. The time to repair issues can also be much slower.

Keep in mind also, the time frame for completing a task. The greater the time frame, the greater the cost of a communication short-circuit.

If the task takes years to complete, you will pay for a communication mistake for years. This is especially relevant with project planning and execution. Complex work situations such as cross-functional, cross-site and cross-culture teams and business ventures simply cannot afford needless miscommunication.

Ways to improve communication:

Day one—Increase the understanding and effectiveness of spoken communication by 25-75% immediately by asking a question about the key content areas after a point is made. e.g., "That was just water you wanted with your meal Sir/mam." or "You needed the expense reports this afternoon, correct?"

D. <u>EXPENSE CONTROLS</u> (Budget & Profit Engineering)

If we were to build a very simple income statement, it would look like the following:

Revenues		$100
Less:		
Cost of Goods Sold	$ 35	
Selling, General and Administrative Expenses	$ 15	
Depreciation	$ 10	
Other Operating Expenses	<u>$ 5</u>	
Total Operating Expenses		<u>$ 65</u>
Operating Income		$ 35
Less: Interest Expense		<u>$ 5</u>
Income before Taxes		$ 30
Less: Income Tax Expense		<u>$ 9</u>
Net Income		<u>$ 21</u>

This is the traditional approach and treats profits as a residual or the remainders after all expenses are met. Our approach is to "Pay Yourself First."

Gross Revenues	As opposed to	Gross Revenues
- 25% Profits		- Expenses
= Expenses		= Net Profit

This is the very nature of budgeting.

Assignment for Harry and Ashu: Build in all costs in order to develop a monthly budget and breakeven in dollars and time for each monthly period.

Once true costs are defined, Effective Pricing is then possible.

E. <u>PERSONAL GROWTH:</u>

English language skills:

INTRODUCTION OF KEY TERMINOLGY: Acronyms, e.g., (TIP) To Insure Promptness, (RAS) Reticular Activating System (FEAR) Focus Emotional Commitment Action Responsibility, Cognition, Cognitive dissonance, Familial, Bi-dialectal, Paradigm.

Build a reference library in books and on Kindle: Read "The Power of Consistency" by Weldon Long---(loaner copy or purchase on Amazon), sign and deliver in the next meeting.

Reading and Study Skills:

1. Preview materials—discover the main points of the entire assignment first
2. Read—Use area hand motions, touch the page, left to right and right to left
3. Don't sub-vocalize
4. Post view materials

GOAL: Develop the Prosperity plan: Outcomes and action items.

Develop the habit of the **15 minute daily** quiet time ritual to review prosperity plan: outcomes and action items.

Email PowerPoint of Finance materials and Problem Set 1 Review in the next meeting at Olympia IV location.

In our first meeting, Harry and Ashu told me that they wanted to start by enhancing communication skills. I agreed that's a fine place to begin. We also discussed and worked through the correlation between personal limitations and business problems. We worked on increasing sales and profits, budgeting, cost control, break-even utilization, asset management, pricing and human resource productivity. Not bad for a couple hours on a Tuesday in Baltimore and the results are really stunning over time.

Simply focus on the key areas, create a plan and get moving. It's working out great for Harry and Ashu—No matter your business model, you can "follow suit" and find unprecedented business and personal success in the New Economy.

CHEERS!

About Elmer

Elmer Davis, Jr., MBA, ALM has over 25 years of experience in marketing and finance, including working with private and non-profit organizations, as well as Fortune 500 corporations. He began his business career in marketing with Bristol-Myers in Washington, DC in the early 80's, then moved on to work for industry giants like Mobil Oil.

He was a partner with Anderson, Philips, Davis, and Hoffmann in Washington, DC, NYC and Los Angeles, and served as Executive Vice-President and Chief Diversity Officer for Financial Dimensions, Inc.

A graduate of the Florida A&M University School of Business and Industry, Mr. Davis holds a Bachelor of Science in Marketing, as well as a Master's of Business Administration from Howard University. He also recently earned a Master's of Liberal Arts from none other than Harvard University in Operational Management.

He has conducted leadership-training forums for clients in numerous industry segments, including the public and private sectors and major Universities. Elmer has also written several articles, including *Understanding the Communication Environment, The true costs of miscommunication, Effective strategies for business growth, Financial management for cash flow and profits, Embracing Workplace Diversity* and *Eliminating Employment Discrimination.*

He was chosen as a Mortgage Bankers Association National Diversity Champion in 2005 and a Heritage Who's Who in 2004.

Elmer is well regarded as a facilitator of crucial information and trainer having worked with organizations in various industries providing specialized training to maximize profits through human resource productivity, asset management, pricing, and expense control. Elmer is a natural communicator and was a recent guest on MIT University radio WMBR.

His current company, TBK Ventures, Inc., has helped to control the costs and increase profits for businesses in the Pittsburgh, PA area and around the country. If you would like more information about how Elmer can help you or your business reach that pivotal next level, visit his site at: www.elmerdavisjr.net or call 855-293-0877.

CHAPTER 49

BULLET PROOF YOUR RETIREMENT IN TODAY'S ECONOMY

BY PETER BOMBARA

For years you have worked long hours to build what you have accomplished today, now what do you do with it? For some it's as simple as a pension plan and you don't have to worry about outliving your income and for the rest it could be a simple 401k or an array of investments. But how can you create an income stream that will last 20 to 30 years while adjusting for inflation and create spousal continuation without playing a guessing game?

You can follow the 4% rule and adjust your income over time due to inflation. Now if you decide to follow that rule, then how will your portfolio look if you continue to take income in a down market? Sad to say this rule no longer works in today's volatile market. Rules that are 10-15 years old will not work in today's economy as well. The way the markets change is the same way your mindset would have to change for planning purposes.

A lot of folks have a vision of a successful retirement. For some, it will include relaxation and travel – maybe even taking up a new hobby. Others may choose to continue to work.

With individuals living longer than ever before, one thing is clear: your portfolio should be able to provide income each and every year in retirement. Whether you're retired or about to approach retirement, your savings and investment plans should be properly adjusted to satisfy a guaranteed income stream to last your entire life as well as your spouse.

I would like to share a story with you. A story that inspired a lot of people all around me. I would like you to meet a couple named Marie and Joe. Why? Simply because they both represent the thought process of today's average retiree. A mindset that many financial advisors still fail to understand in today's economy.

More importantly Marie and Joe (last names are protected for compliance reasons) are real people; this is a real life story. This is not made up, and we do have permission to share this with you. So we would like to thank Marie and Joe for allowing us to share this with others.

Marie and Joe were both in their early 70's and have been investing in the market all their lives. They had NO interest in changing anything in their portfolio. With all the market gains they made in the 90's to the tech crash in 2000-2001 then going through a five year recovery. Their closest friend's insisted they should look at other ideas and not deal with market loss. She agreed to see what else would be available in today's world of investing.

I remember this day like it was yesterday. In 2006 Marie and Joe decided to come into the office and just talk business. Marie knew exactly what she wanted and didn't want to change anything she believed in. She kept her introduction short, sweet and to the point without wasting any of their time.

Marie and Joe explained they are knowledgeable about the markets and understand their returns over time. Like riding a rollercoaster the markets go up and down and they feel over time they have done just fine. So they didn't want to change their mindset.

After asking some important questions based on their lifestyle and situation we soon found out they were truly tired of watching the markets fluctuate. Marie and Joe felt they had a job and couldn't enjoy what is supposed to be a retirement. Joe said it can become tiring and stressful at times.

By understanding how Marie and Joe were thinking, we explained we didn't want them to draw back from the market but instead help them understand the new rules in participating in today's market. A way where you can be invested in the market and never experience a loss. This will help them free up time from negative market stress and enjoy the lifestyle they deserve, the real retirement life.

The planning process began and Marie decided to start small, $400,000 from her 401k. Based on their goals and what was suitable for them. They were put into a product that offered zero market risk, no volatility and potential returns.

This is where it gets really interesting. Marie and Joe were scheduled to come into the office about a year later. As time went by and the scheduled date came closer and closer, we couldn't wait anymore and was just so excited for them to come in to see how their product performed. So we asked to see them earlier than expected. And we did.

When Marie and Joe came into the office we were so excited to see what they had to say. We sat down in the conference room and said:

"Marie, did you see your recent statement?"

"Yes," she said in a low toned voice.

We really couldn't understand why she wasn't as happy as we were. So we asked her, "Well, did you see where it said 16% return?"

Marie said, "Yes, I saw that and I also see that the market did 21%."

"Yes Marie, the stock market did 21% and your fixed product did 16%."

Marie said, "Well, it's pretty close I guess."

We were amazed and our excitement and energy just disappeared.

So now let's fast forward a little. We did see each other a few times throughout the year at our client events and they both had a chance to interact with other clients who used to be veterans in the market as well as professional retired traders. What they have found out was most of them have become more and more conservative as time went on. So they started to understand when they spoke to others who used to be heavy market investors. They understood, it's not what you make but what you keep is important.

About a year goes by and it's just time for an annual review, we were not excited to see Marie and Joe. Due to the fact it was 2008 when companies were failing and in the middle of the credit crisis the markets were crushed and her account had a zero percent return. Marie and Joe didn't lose anything but they also didn't make anything. We were not looking forward to this meeting.

Marie and Joe have arrived said the assistant. We walk to the front and BOOM a smile from ear to ear. We were very confused to what have happened after understanding the last time we sat down. Marie walked up to us and gave me an apple pie and thank you card. She looked at my staff with tears and thanked us for a wonderful job.

My excitement finally came back to where it should have been since day one. I said to Marie; wait so I was able to help you with a 16% return last year and this year I showed you a zero percent return and you're happy? Marie raised her voice so everyone can hear: YES! She said, YES!

Marie said most of her friends and Joes big time executive friends all lost money. She added, "I didn't lose a penny! I look around to neighbors and relatives; they are all in the same boat. Not me! I gave you a shot and it worked. It was simple, I understand why it makes sense and I am so happy I was recommended to you. It's so true when people say it's not what you make, it's what you keep that counts! Thank you again."

To Marie and Joe, We thank you for trusting us. We can't wait for the years to come where we can spend more exciting times together.

Today's economy is different than what it used to be. The stages in life are different as time goes on. While growth is important, protecting against loss is extremely important.

We share Marie and Joe's story because we hope it will inspire not just you but the world. It's possible to enjoy market growth without market loss. In the years where you can make 5-10% returns and the years where you have a zero percent return, just remember others around you are experiencing huge losses. I personally rather make nothing than lose 40% of my portfolio. I wish you nothing but future success, happiness and love.

About Peter

Retirement expert, Peter C. Bombara, is the President of PCB Financial Advisory Group. He specializes in the area of retirement income, wealth preservation, and estate planning. He has helped thousands of individuals throughout the tri-state area retire successfully by using simple strategies that anyone can understand.

Peter has been involved in many publications, locally and on a national level. He often contributes to FoxBusiness.com and FoxNews.com. He is a proud Author and Co-Author on many financial topics. Peter continues to teach over 200 planners, bankers and insurance agents the basics and advanced strategies on a monthly basis. He has been featured on CNBC and a national radio show *A Roadmap to Retirement*.

Peter and his team of professionals would like to guide you through the financial road blocks that lie ahead in retirement. In today's economy, the strategies of the past will no longer assure you will have the retirement you hoped for.

Their planning process would help determine the proper investment risk that would be appropriate based on your current situation. Most people today have way too much risk in their portfolio and that can be devastating in their financial future. The proper risk often depends on multiple factors that the common investor does not take into consideration. A popular risk factor would be paying too much in fees. Fees can destroy your nest egg and even worse in down markets. Peter and his team are able to help you determine what the real rate of return is, after fees in your portfolio.

They have a team that specializes in custom plans that would help you hedge against future inflation. By positioning a portion of your assets into an inflation protection plan, they are able to create an income stream that considers future inflation, and will help you eliminate the fear of running out of money.

Having a written plan is more than owning mutual funds, stocks, bonds, or any other financial vehicle. Your investments should be able to work together to decrease your fees, participate in market growth, stabilize your retirement income, and protect what you have worked for. Guarantees in a portfolio will help you maximize what you are currently doing along with peace of mind.

CHAPTER 50

YOUR SILENT PARTNER IN RETIREMENT PLANNING

BY RONALD GELOK

We are taxing ourselves into economic exhaustion and stagnation, crushing our ability and incentive to save, invest and produce. This must stop.

~ President Ronald Reagan

President Reagan's words address an issue that many acknowledge is once again casting a dark pall over our economic lives. Fewer people realize, however, that the government, in the form of taxation, has become a silent partner in our retirement accounts, thus potentially limiting the individual's ability to provide adequately for his own future and that of his progeny. The goal of a financial advisor should be to not only advise and assist the client to accumulate wealth but also to lessen the influence of the silent partner on a client's retirement income.

I became interested in financial planning at an early age. When my grandfather and I were watching television, the news anchor was speaking about conservatives and liberals. I asked my grandfather, "Are we conservative or are we liberal? What's the difference?" My grandfather, trying to explain to an eight-year-old child said to me, "Well, in general, conservatives want you to be able to keep more of your money and for you to have the freedom to do what you think is best for you and your family with your money. Liberals want to take more of your money, and they feel that the government knows what is best for you, your family and society."

His over-simplification got the point across to me. I understood wanting to keep what is mine. Later, in law school and working as an estate and tax attorney, I became passionate about keeping people from parting with their hard-earned money. I was a partner in a law firm specializing in taxation, tax planning and wealth planning strategies. I promptly discovered the need for integration between tax planning and retirement planning. Knowledge today has become highly specialized, making it commonplace to work separately with a financial advisor, a stockbroker, an accountant and an attorney. Each player has limited knowledge of what the others are advising. Our office takes a holistic approach, harnessing all those specialties under one roof, to administer our tax diversification plan that uses the tax code advantageously for our clients.

We act as the quarterback bringing the correct professionals and ensuring the right information for our clients. We identify their needs and plan accordingly. For instance, if someone meets with us who needs life insurance, we ensure that they purchase such insurance in the most tax advantageous way. The prevailing thought in society is, "if I am going to have financial freedom in retirement, I need to accumulate, accumulate, and accumulate." It is not all about accumulation. The reality is that one must know the tax implications of the decisions one is making while investing for retirement. A person may be accumulating money in employee-sponsored plans such as 401(k)s or 403(b)s and think he is fortifying his financial future. Distributions from those plans are taxable, regardless whether the investor, the surviving spouse or the surviving children receive the money. Few people consider the "silent partner" in their retirement plan accounts, the federal government. That silent partner can change the percentage of the account that belongs to them by changing the rate of taxation on the money when the money comes out of the account or by changing how rapidly the money comes out of the account.

Last year, the Chairman of the Senate Finance Committee proposed legislation that would eliminate the ability of non-spousal beneficiaries, i.e., adult children, to stretch payments of an inherited IRA over their lifetime, which had been a planning advantage. If the government can eliminate that ability, they would, therefore, be able to compel accelerated taxation on the retirement plan assets. A big area that we hone in on is distribution planning which rescues these retirement accounts from confistcatory and predatory taxation. We try, then, to be proactive, not reactive in our planning. In the last 15 years, the federal government has changed the estate tax threshold 12 times. It makes it difficult to plan where the federal estate threshhold will be for a surviving spouse 30 years in the future. We study not just what the current laws are, but also what proposed changes to the current laws might be in the future.

"Permanent" change is a relative term when one is dealing with the government because permanent only means until the politicians deem it necessary to change it again. Therefore, the "permanent" threshhold for retirement of $5 million dollars indexed for inflation is not so permanent. In fact, in April 2013 the Obama administration proposed a decrease of the threshhold from $5 million to $3.5 million in 2018. What was supposed to be permanent is more like shifting sand. We must be concerned with the most tax efficient way to remove funds out of the qualified plan and reposition investments for more favorable tax treatments. It is not always the Roth IRA conversion that is the answer. Keep in mind that Roth IRA's are still part of the person's growth estate and are still subject to the state estate taxes and federal estate taxes depending upon where the threshhold is at the time the person dies.

Our strategy is to grow money tax-free, draw tax-free income and pass money tax-free to family members. Trust planning is one strategy that has been effective for generations. If the government is going to look at the upper middle class people as being wealthy, then the upper middle class need to employ the techniques or tools that the wealthy have traditionally used to plan for their retirement. Without proper planning, the wealth you have accumulated for yourself, your spouse and your family, will go to the government through taxation. Who needs the money more, your family and descendants or the government? Do not let the government decide who is more deserving; the family for whom you have worked hard to build a future, or whomever the government sees fit? In the end, it is not about how well you do, but about how you position your wealth and how you title it.

Beyond the federal estate tax laws, there are many states with estate taxes. A client can have provisions in his will that create a trust for the benefit of the surviving spouse. The net effect is doubling the amount of money that is not subject to estate taxes. A proper marital trust gets its own estate tax exemption. People wrongly assume that if they are not worth $5 million they do not need to do this type of estate planning. Trusts are not the only financial tools the wealthy utilize to protect their retirement funds.

Most people in or approching retirement, think they need more life insurance like they need a hole in their head. Their mortgage is often paid off or paid down, their kids' education has been funded, they have built up some assets, why then, would they need life insurance except to pay for a funeral? Why do they need to go to the expense of paying premiums for life insurance? There are provisions in the tax code that are favorable for insurance. Most people know that if a person passes away, life insurance proceeds are income tax free. You fill out the death claim, get the check from the insurance company, and there are no income taxes taken out. Depending upon who has the ownership of that policy, the policy could be brought back into the estate, or not, for estate tax purposes. Beyond that though, life insurance policies can be designed to build up cash value that can be accessed through what is called tax-free policy loans. When the person passes away, the death benefit is reduced by the amount in loan that was taken out of the policy.

We show clients how to reverse engineer what some would call an investment grade life insurance policy to perform in a superior fashion for purposes of accumulation of cash value without fear of losing earnings. Sometimes people buy a policy for the greatest death benefit, but sometimes it is more beneficial to work backwards and compute how little the client must receive at death in benefits in order to still be eligible for the tax-free benefits, while continuing to accumulate substantial cash value on the policy. It is important to have an advisor who knows how to use these tax laws to your advantage in accumulating wealth and who can recommend options that the investor might not have considered.

The closer you are to retirement, the more critical it is that your advisors have the correct skill sets for what you are trying to accomplish. Complacency can cost you. Do not stay with an advisor who knows only accumulation and does not know wealth transfer planning or is unfamiliar with strategies to grow money in the most tax-advantaged way.

Everyone wants to save to meet their income needs in retirement, but the government has the ability to raise tax rates while a person is in their retirement. Up until 1996, there was a 15% excise tax on IRA's over $1 million. What is to stop the government from bringing that back? It was repealed because the government surplus under President Clinton, the government did not feel it needed that money. Currently, the government is borrowing more than 40 cents for every dollar it is spending and needs additional avenues of income to cover the increased costs of social programs. Increased taxation on retirement accounts looms on the horizon.

Our office specializes in retirement income planning; solving for the gap between income coming in from fixed sources, such as social security and traditional defined pensions, and what a person's expenses will be to live the lifestyle they desire in retirement. We recognize that people have become frustrated with the limited guidance available to keep them from running out of income before they run out of breath. Life expectancy is improving. All elements of retirement planning converge in our office: we address guaranteed retirement income planning, which often involves insurances as a planning tool, tax planning, wealth planning and estate planning.

When it comes to investment planning, we want to look for strategies for clients that reduce risk and reduce expenses on retirement accounts, when possible. The expenses and fees, both disclosed and undisclosed, on retirement accounts can create a real drag on retirement income. Our goal is to provide clarity to our clients so that they can make informed decisions as to the direction they wish to take with their retirement investments.

We like to utilize tax diversification. People can become so focused on not having all their eggs in one basket that they overlook the fact that some of their chosen baskets put them in a position for unfavorable tax treatment. We look at not just investment diversification, but also tax diversification. We call attention to financial blind spots. You can do all the correct estate planning and investment planning to reduce risk and optimize income. You can also optimize your tax planning to transfer funds out of tax hostile accounts, but if you did not address the possibility of a catastrophic illness later in life, you might end up spending all your savings on long-term or nursing home care to cover the expenses of Alzheimer's disease or stroke.

Many people assume that if they are working with an advisor, and they are making money and amassing a significant retirement portfolio, that they are doing well. We take a holistic approach because we know that unless you have addressed all of the above issues, you leave the door open to disaster. You must plan for what will be the next shoe to drop. If interest rates are at a 50-year low, then the only place they are likely to go is up. What impact will that have on their portfolio? If the stock market is at a six-year high, then what impact would there be if we had another 2008-type catastrophic event such as the European nation was to default on their sovereign debt causing the market to go backwards. What we want to do is get people thinking properly, asking the right questions and being proactive, rather than reactive, and exploring the area beyond their rate of return.

People hear that they should sock away as much money as possible into their 401(k)s because by the time they take the money out, they will be in a much lower tax bracket. However, those same people, at the time they are heavily investing in their 401(k)s, are taking available deductions for dependent children and for their interest on their mortgages. When they enter retirement, those same people will have either paid off or substantially paid down their mortgage, so there is no more mortgage interest deduction. On top of that, they no longer have children to claim as dependents because they have grown up and left the nest, so they no longer have dependent deductions. Therefore, the idea that people are in a lower tax bracket when they retire is a fallacy; they are often in the same or bracket or one bracket lower in retirement than they were when they were working. As their retirement distributions increase, so does their tax rate.

To counter this tax change in retirement, we help our clients to look at tax advantage planning or tax-free alternative planning. We quarterback a CFR, complete financial review, for each of our clients to help them avoid financial blind spots and maintain their financial health so that they can enjoy the fruits of their labor.

There was a recent article in Reuters reporting that last year in France 8,000 people were taxed at 100%. You might ask, "What does that have to do with us?" Our government's spending addiction running out of control creates a scenario where tax increases are not only likely, they are unavoidable. The only decision as an investor is to choose to be proactive or reactive. Most successful people have built their businesses by paying attention to the world around then and proactively seeking opportunities for growth. They have invested for retirement with the same approach, so it makes sense to plan for the retirement road and not reactively wait for whatever lurks around the blind curves.

We want you to be able to keep more of your money and for you to have the freedom to do what you think is best for you and your family with your money. To do so, investors need strong retirement planning advice from professionals who not only understand accumulation, but also know and use all available tools to lessen the impact the "silent partner" can have on their retirement ahead. Quarterbacking for your retirement, we may not have a crystal ball to see the future, but we possess an extensive playbook and look for every appropriate opening to maximize your financial goals.

About Ronald

Ronald A. Gelok, Jr., JD is the president of Ronald Gelok & Associates, A Registered Investment Advisory firm with offices in New Jersey and Florida.

Mr. Gelok is an active member of the Financial Planning Association with over 20 years of financial services experience. He is a licensed New Jersey attorney and a member of the Elder Law and Real Property, Probate & Trust sections of the New Jersey State Bar Association.

Much sought after as a speaker, Ronald has appeared on WADB-AM and WOBM-AM discussing financial planning issues. He has addressed thousands of people locally, including Lucent retirees, union organizations, AARP members and government and religious organizations. He is known for making complex retirement planning issues clear and easy to understand. His clients often find that, after working with him, they have moved significantly forward in their planning, simplifying their finances and obtaining more understanding about their financial future.

Mr. Gelok holds insurance licenses in several states, including New Jersey, Pennsylvania and Florida, as well as Series 6, 7, 24 and 66 securities licenses. He is a Registered Representative of GF Investment Services, LLC, Member FINRA/SIPC, and an Investment Advisor Representative of Global Financial Private Capital, LLC, an SEC Registered Investment Advisor, 2080 Ringing Boulevard, Sarasota, Florida 34237.

Education:

    University of California, Juris Doctor, 1984

    Montclair State College, Bachelor of Arts, *magna cum laude*, 1980

Licensed Attorney:

    Admitted, New Jersey, State and Federal District Court

    Member, New Jersey State Bar Association

        Elder Law Section

        Real Property, Probate & Trust Section

Insurance Licenses:

    New Jersey Department of Banking & Insurance

Life, Health, Property/Casualty, Variable Authority

Pennsylvania Department of Insurance

Life, Health, Variable Authority

Florida Department of Financial Services

Life, Health, Variable Authority

Financial Industry Regulatory Authority (FINRA) Licenses:

Series 24 – Registered Principal

Series 7 – General Securities Registered Representative

Series 6 – Mutual Funds & Variable Annuities

Series 66 – Uniform Combined State Law Examination (Agent and Investment Advisor Representative)

Ronald has been seen on CBS, NBC, ABC and FOX television. He is known for making complex retirement planning issues clear and easy to understand. Ronald has a Sunday morning radio show WABC in Manhattan and is also featured weekly on The Financial Safari television show. Ronald has been featured in *USA Today* and has been recognized in *The Wall Street Journal*. He is active in several nonprofit organizations.

Ronald enjoys spending his free time outdoors with his wife and four children.

CHAPTER 51

THE #1 INGREDIENT FOR A SUCCESSFUL SMALL BUSINESS

BY SASHA BERSON

On a gloomy Tuesday morning, Jeff walked into the office consumed by his usual thoughts. TS WebPros, his 8-year-old company, was doing okay, but he was deeply dissatisfied because overhead ate up most of the revenue, leaving Jeff with a very modest income. There were never enough projects and hunting for new clients was dreadful. Without repeat business and referrals, TS would have folded years ago.

Jeff did all he could to build his business. He promoted on Google and advertised in trade journals, attended networking events, ran promotions, did cold calls, but nothing resulted in more than a few new clients. Often, the new business didn't even justify the cost of advertising. To change his luck, Jeff hired salespeople, but none of them lasted for more than three months, or in a single client.

Jeff was convinced that marketing did not work for his business and no salesperson could help. So, in addition to working on clients' projects, managing employees, and doing the books, Jeff was also the sole salesperson.

This is not what he had in mind when launching TS. At the last agency he worked, he was one of the best developers. Confident in his skills,

Jeff went on his own. It was a no-brainer. He was talented and deserved a bigger piece of the pie than he got working for someone else.

Ready for real success, Jeff worked hard. But running the business took more than just talent. And despite the limited success, he felt tired and frustrated.

To add insult to injury, some of Jeff's competitors, who started around the same time as TS, were rocking it with more, bigger, and better projects. The owners were living the lives Jeff wanted. They didn't work 60-hour weeks. They earned more money and had the time to sail to distant islands. They had it made, while Jeff worked hard to keep things afloat. He'd give anything to figure out what was missing.

Jeff is a fictional character. I made him up. However, I heard this story from hundreds of business owners from every industry. It seems that for every success story, there are thousands of struggling Jeffs.

Years ago, I, too, was a Jeff. Working hard but getting mediocre results while watching others enjoy all of the fruits that a highly-profitable small business could give. I was stressed out. I was tired. And I really hated working so hard for such limited results while my competitors seemed to be coasting.

Yet, I knew their success was not the product of luck. They had a formula that led to a better business, less stress, and a better life. I had to figure out what it was.

Fast-forward to the present. Through dozens of case studies and hundreds of hours of research on successful and not-so-successful business practices, I created that formula, profitably sold my business, and turned this journey into a new passion – helping small business owners get the results they deserve for all of the hard work they put in, and enjoy less stressful lives.

My contribution to this book is to reveal the #1 ingredient I used to create a better business and, in turn, a better life.

You see, just like Jeff, most business owners try to grow their business by using one-off tactics – a Facebook post here, a networking event there. Often, the tactics are random acts of desperation done when business is suffocating and needs new clients. And, usually, these do not work, leaving the owners with little to no positive results, stressed out and with less money.

To create a profitable business that is stable or steadily growing, you need to implement the #1 ingredient for successful small business – a Client Attraction System (CAS). Why? Because…

Better Business = Business with a Steady Flow of All the New and Repeat Clients the Owner Wants and the Company Can Handle

Basically, a CAS is a magnet that consistently drives clients to your business. And, in the following pages I will reveal the components of this #1 ingredient for your successful small business.

Imagine what your business and life would be like if you had a steady flow of all the new and repeat clients you wanted and your company could handle!*

Getting clients is not hard when you know what to do and how to do it.

The reason that Jeff and countless other small business owners think that marketing (client attraction) doesn't work is because they don't know HOW it works.

Think about it this way: I have no idea how to build a house, but if I wanted to build it myself, I'd have to learn about the hundreds of materials – concrete foundation, walls, roof, etc. that go into the house and the processes of putting those materials together.

A CAS is no different. But, unlike a house, it only has 5 components. Once you know what these components are and how they work together, you can build your very own CAS – the engine that drives new highly-qualified prospects to your business. Ready? Let's open the hood and see what's in a CAS.

PART I: MARKET

Remember when you were a little kid and went trick-or-treating? After a year or two, you knew which houses had the best candy, so you didn't

---

* Unfortunately, there is no room here to reveal how to maximize profits with your existing clients. For that, look for my upcoming book: *Better Business, Better Life.*

waste time on the others. These houses became your ideal clients and you made it your business to visit them on Halloween.

Now that you are all grown up, it is even more important for you to know who your ideal clients are. Insert the appropriate name to identify them: "If only I had 100 clients like _____, business would be great.

Once you have this client in mind, get to know everything you can about them: from their demographics (age, location, income, etc.) to the way they choose service providers and make buying decisions (their buying behavior).

Better Business Tip #1: The best way for you to learn everything about your ideal clients (the market) is to pick up the phone and call your existing clients.

Ask them:

Why did you choose me instead of my competitors? And why do you continue to be my client? (The answers will reveal what sets you apart.)

What do you like about me, my staff, and the way we do things, and how is it different and better than what you had before?

If tomorrow we closed the doors for good and you had to find a replacement, how would you go about it? What are the top three things you'd look for in a replacement or the top three concerns you'd have about doing business with them? (The answers will reveal what media your potential ideal clients use to find businesses like yours, and what concerns them when buying from a vendor for the first time.)

Once you have a good idea about who your clients are, finding more like them is easy. Take the information you learned and simply get a contact list of people who share the characteristics of your clients from a list provider. Will it cost you a few bucks? You bet. Will marketing to the wrong people cost you much more? Certainly!

PART II: UNIQUE SELLING PROPOSITION (USP)

A USP is a message that differentiates you from all of your competitors. You need to tell your prospects why they should choose you over everyone else. There is always someone with lower prices or claims of better service. And most of the time, these claims are ignored.

Better Business Tip #2: Tell your prospective ideal clients why they should choose you by using answers from Part I. There is something existing clients love about you, beyond price or quality. Use that to craft your USP.

Here is a good example: "We are number 2. We try harder." ~ Avis. In the mid 60's, this USP took Avis from 29% market share to 36% - a huge victory considering the size of the market.

PART III: IRRESISTIBLE OFFER

Use your USP to get attention. Then, provide an Irresistible Offer to stimulate action.

An Irresistible Offer prompts clients to jump at the opportunity to respond to your ad. What makes an offer irresistible? Give the client something of high value in exchange for something of a significantly-lower perceived value.

Better Business Tip #3: Create a no-brainer, high ROI offer to get your clients to purchase the actual, or introductory product, or get their contact information to continue marketing to them.

Examples:

A white paper that explains how to solve a relevant problem in exchange for your client's contact info.

A product that regularly costs $29 for free, if the client signs up for a monthly delivery of the product.

A super guarantee: "Done right or it's free."

PART IV: 12 STEP PROMO COMMUNICATION SERIES

Now that you gave your prospects a reason to choose you over your competitors – your USP, and a reason to contact you – your Irresistible Offer, create a series of communications to get them to act.

Expecting a customer to buy something the first time they see an ad is like asking someone to marry you after a first date: it's awkward, and anyone who accepts is probably not someone you want to commit to long-term. Most people and companies do not buy (or request for a meeting, sample, etc.) until the 7th, 8th, or even the 12th communication.

Whether the prospects come searching for you or you reach out to them, you need to deliver a number of communications, and make sure that all of those communications are seen by selecting the right media. You can find out which media are appropriate when you are doing research on your market (refer to Better Business Tip #1).

If you have ever advertised and the results were awful, you can, in part, attribute it to the fact that most prospects never saw your ad more than once or twice, or that you were using the wrong type of media.

Better Business Tip #4: Plan your promo communication

List the issues your business can solve for clients.

List how your services or products solve those issues.

Explain how your Irresistible Offer helps prospective clients address the issues.

Connect issues, solutions, and the Irresistible Offer to create 12 communications (letters, emails, postcards, whitepapers, etc.) that will "speak" to prospective clients and make them contact you to take you up on your Irresistible Offer.

Here is how I completed this exercise for my company:

The Issue: Not getting enough clients.

The Solution: We develop Client Attraction Systems that create steady flows of new clients by delivering a series of communications to the people highly-interested in buying the service and following up with them until they buy.

The Irresistible Offer: We offer a free 3-Step Roadmap to Doubling Your Clients' Calls that will help you clearly identify the group of people or companies that make up your ideal prospects. Then, we give you 2-3 strategies how to get more of them.

We use letters, postcards, newsletters and workshop presentations to deliver our message and deliver our Irresistible Offer, the 3-Step Roadmap, and get prospects to identify themselves and request more information, and ultimately ask us to help them with their business.

There is not enough room to explain it all here in detail, but I am confident that you can come up with 12 concerns and desires your clients have and create 12 communication pieces that reflect those ideas.

PART V: 7-STEP FOLLOW-UP SERIES

Don't leave money on the table by abandoning prospects that show initial interest but do not buy right away.

Better Business Tip #5: Similar to the promo communication series, create a 7-Step Follow-Up series.. This should use a variety of media (newsletters, emails, phone calls) to reach your prospects until they "raise their hands" again to buy your product or service.

THE COST OF INACTION

I'll be honest, this process takes time and a few bucks to do right. But if you want a steady stream of new clients, you have to put some fuel in your engine. Ultimately, the most expensive thing you can do is to do nothing at all. If you don't build your CAS, you will pay for it with fewer clients and a mediocre, stressful business.

I know that you don't want to end up like Jeff, our hero from the start of the chapter. Now that you know what all of the CAS components are, you just need the recipe to put them together. A step-by-step guide for developing your Client Attraction System is available. Remember that marketing works when you know how it works and make it work for you.

About Sasha

Sasha Berson is a natural problem solver. He helps small businesses tackle the most common headache – how to consistently get more new and repeat clients.

In 2009, after selling his first company, Interbank, a nationwide lender, Sasha was at a crossroads. Too ambitious to retire, he began searching for the next challenge.

As a successful entrepreneur, Sasha was often asked how to create a more profitable business. He freely shared many profitability strategies that helped business owners get more clients and grow their businesses.

One day, a friend pointed out that Sasha has such a natural ability to help entrepreneurs that he should seriously consider turning this passion into a business. Having mentored dozens of business owners and experiencing firsthand the difficulties and stress of growing and managing a business, Sasha fell in love with the idea of helping others who deal with these challenges every day.

He spent the next year researching and developing a system for helping business owners consistently get more new and repeat clients.

In 2010, Sasha launched his second business. Berson Business Development has one mission – helping business owners live better lives by making their companies or practices more profitable, stable, and less stressful to manage. Since then, Sasha's business development system has generated proven results for countless small business owners.

Sasha is also a sought-after speaker on the subject of developing a consistent flow of new and repeat clients as well as finding and retaining great employees.

If you would like to find out more about how Sasha's team can help your business or practice, or inquire regarding speaking engagements, call 877-355-1144 or visit: www.bersonbusiness.com.

CHAPTER 52

REAL ESTATE GAME CHANGER

BY SHANE PERKINS

WHY IS THIS A "NEW ECONOMY"?
WHAT'S NEW ABOUT IT? WHAT CAUSED IT?

I believe there are multiple answers that could be debated for days, or pages in this case. But I am here to focus on what I believe is the absolute primary reason for this long recession and longer recovery… *The Real Estate Bubble.*

Throughout my life I have seen many booms and busts in multiple industries. But my expertise and what I really want to talk about is the housing industry, the different cycles and where we're headed. I was in the manufactured housing industry in the 90's and saw that industry implode itself in much the same way the housing boom of the 2000's did. Back then, I saw lenders literally hop scotching each other for more deals. They introduced new programs almost weekly to "beat the competition." The underwriting was so loose that anyone that wanted to buy could buy with lower credit score requirements and lower down payments. A lot of the borrowers were literally living paycheck to paycheck and were one illness, one car repair or one significant home repair from losing their home. The lenders set these families up for failure. At the end of the 90's, I saw massive repossessions and lenders going out of business, which also led to manufactured home dealers and manufacturers going out of business. The entire industry went stagnant because there was no more money to lend to these bad investments due to their loose lending practices. The lenders literally killed the industry.

Well, fast-forward to the 2000's and what happened in the mortgage industry? The exact same thing but on a much larger scale. Credit became more and more available which drove up demand and home prices skyrocketed. As the lenders introduced "new programs" with little to no down payment required, low introductory payments, no proof of income, the writing was on the wall, it was an unsustainable model. The big difference here was these lenders were allowed to package these mortgages up and literally sell them to the world as mortgage-backed securities. The entire globe placed their bets on American Real Estate. These lenders set these families up to fail and it was literally one of the primary causes of the global meltdown. Global corporations, governments and the largest institutions around the world bought America's mortgage-backed securities. When the real estate bubble burst in 2008, real estate prices plunged across the nation and the foreclosure toll destroyed the credit of millions of families. But the bigger picture is the collateral that the world bet on was now devalued and was not producing profits but instead producing massive losses. Now you have all these global government pension funds, retirement funds, hedge funds and 401(k)'s absorbing these massive losses and unable to pay benefits, etc. Governments around the world are going broke and one of the primary reasons is because of these bad investments.

Why do I tell you all this? Mainly to have you understand why the recovery is so slow and how I believe real estate was one of the main causes and can also be one of the main cures. Currently, credit-based loans deny the American dream to over 90% of today's would-be homebuyers. The credit based funding system in America is broken and global investors are *gun shy* to *double down* on American real estate until we return to healthy interest rates again (6% to 8%). In order for interest rates to rise to healthy levels, home prices will have to come down or incomes will have to rise in order to comply with debt-to-income ratio guidelines. Banks have very stringent underwriting guidelines. Currently 8 out of 10 home loan applications are being denied.

However, there is an answer. Just like in previous cycles where banks tightened up, people had to look at other options to buy and sell their homes so they could move on with life. Job transfers, job losses, upsizing, downsizing and becoming empty nesters are only a few of the many reasons people need to sell or buy homes, but they are restricted because of a lack of knowledge of any other way to buy or sell a home besides conventional methods through realtors and banks. People should have an open mind when they consider buying or selling a house. Many of our parents and grandparents bought homes for our families without banks and conventional methods because that's all that was available. There are many investors that are very leery about putting their money into the stock market, and definitely don't want the ¼ of a percent that banks are offering. However, they are very comfortable buying real estate and selling these homes to families with owner financing. They don't base their decision the way banks do on credit alone. They understand that bad things happen to good people every day. They look at the home buyer and their ability to pay. The program is called **Income Based Funding** and it is one of the fastest growing trends in real estate.

Shortly after 2008, over 25 million jobs were lost which resulted in foreclosures, short sales and multimillions of credit files being ruined. Other reasons include divorce, identity theft, lawsuits, IRS liens, vehicle repos, medical bills, student loan defaults, credit card bills, cell phone companies, cable and satellite companies…the list goes on and on. Once you get behind, they start adding more fees and interest and it's almost impossible to recover, which many times can cause bankruptcy. All of these things destroy credit and make you unable to qualify for a home loan. The net result of all this in the new economy is that as many as 90% of would-be homebuyers cannot qualify for a home loan. People go through suffering and humiliation! Eventually they get a new job or a new business and get back on their feet. With a good income, they can now save money and start a new life, and what do they want to do? They try to get a home. And what does the lender say? They say NO! You haven't suffered enough! You need another 7-10 years of punishment.

When people have been through all this, they consider owner financing and they typically find limited choices. Everything is overpriced and the sellers usually want a big down payment and/or a high interest rate. You may investigate lease purchase, lease options, contract for deed or some variation. You will typically discover the same thing… limited choices and everything is overpriced! And even worse, if you have no deed you can lose your home even though you've paid as agreed. If the seller dies, gets a divorce, gets sued, files bankruptcy, doesn't pay the mortgage or taxes or gets an IRS tax lien, the buyer can lose the home. It's very risky to try to buy a home without getting a deed to the property. A lot of people resort to renting, which is like throwing money out the window.

In a nutshell…. homebuyers need financing and investors want to make money with low risk. This is a natural fit for these two parties to help one another.

Today, more than ever, investors are becoming concerned with how their investment dollars are making money. They want to know they're investing in a company that is reducing the number of foreclosures, creating jobs, and helping put their neighbors into the American dream of home ownership. The demand for socially responsible investing is growing in the new economy.

There are many families that have strong income and they cannot qualify for a credit-based loan. Case studies have shown that more and more people with good credit are walking away from upside down or underwater mortgages, which creates an abundance of good deals with equity, but you have to have cash to buy these good deals. However, without cash and the knowledge to get these good deals you're left with limited choices as described earlier. We've also discovered that people with strong income are very likely to pay if they have financing and strong equity.

Through all of this a powerful concept has emerged which is called **Income Based Funding**. If a family with strong income is allowed to find a great deal such as a foreclosure, a short sale, an estate sale or another home of their choice with equity, the chances of the family paying is very great. When a family is emotionally committed to a home it makes all the difference. It may be school district, nearby family, proximity to the job, floor plan, whatever the reason, when you combine equity, emotional commitment and financial commitment you create a low risk picture for the investor.

Enter the Transaction Engineer, individuals with the knowhow and resources to combine the homebuyer with the investor to get families in homes and investors great returns secured with real estate. Income Based Funding is the fastest growing trend in single family real estate and this trend is sweeping the country. It IS "Success in the New Economy" which provides a valuable service for families and individual investors, moving the economy toward a recovery in the industry that was one of the primary causes of the meltdown. Investors want to engage in socially responsible secure investing while helping their neighbors gain home ownership and moving the economy towards recovery – a true "WIN-WIN" in this new economy.

There are also additional benefits to both the investor and homeowner through this Income Based Funding program.

For the investor this is a much better scenario than buying real estate and renting it out.

1. The home is already sold before the investor buys it, therefore the cash flow starts the first month and this greatly reduces risk.

2. The investor is secured by a piece of real estate that has good equity.

3. Cash flow is typically higher than rent or lease payments.

4. Taxes and insurance are paid by the homeowner, there are no vacancies or advertising for new tenants, there are no management fees and a servicing company collects all payments and disburses all funds to the proper entities which includes taxes, insurance, underlying loan payments (if investor uses credit instead of cash) and best of all the positive cash flow to the investor.

5. There are no repair bills to the investor because all the repairs are the responsibility of the homeowner.

This is truly the best passive real estate investment available!

Benefits for the homebuyer; they are truly homeowners, they are on the deed of the house and not on a contract for deed or lease purchase or any variation thereof. It is also very important that this process provides positive mortgage credit for the homeowners. The Income Based Funding program reports all payment activity to all the credit reporting agencies so they can get a refinance at the best rates available usually within a year to two years. As most people know, it is much easier to get a refinance loan than it is to get a purchase money loan especially when there is equity. Most of the homebuyers that use the Income Based Funding program have good equity because of the home deals they are able to take advantage of because investors are making cash offers.

The Income Based Funding program is actually a hybrid combination of three proven real estate strategies that I have used for the last 17 years. It takes the strengths of each strategy, mitigates their weaknesses, and results in one SUPER STRATEGY. It is truly a "Real Estate Game Changer" that allows entrepreneurs to make money while simultaneously helping families gain home ownership, helping investors make money through socially responsible secure investments and helps sellers get inventory off their books. This "SUPER STRATEGY" creates jobs, helps society in general, and helps the mortgage industry, real estate companies and brokers. And best of all it helps fulfill the American dream of home ownership in a complete "WIN-WIN" scenario for all parties involved.

Success in the New Economy is business that serves many people and helps enrich people's lives through education and thinking outside the box. I am a proponent of the system and it works in all 50 states.

About Shane

Shane Perkins is a Best Selling Author and has been a leading expert in the Residential Housing Market for the past 17 years. Shane was also recently chosen as a featured speaker alongside Mr. Steve Forbes in the "Success In The New Economy" Conference in New York City. Shane is a Masters graduate from two of the most prestigious Real Estate Investment Educational Institutions in the world and has used his skills in helping families attain their dream of home ownership in over 400 transactions. He also teaches and mentors investors all around the country on how to overcome the challenges of the market and succeed in any real estate landscape. His passion for real estate is surpassed only by his passion for people and helping them attain their dreams. His niche is taking the so called "unconventional deal," the one no one can get done, and helping strategize and bring it to fruition. He knows that for most families their home is the biggest decision and investment they will make in their lifetime and he takes honor and pride in guiding them every step of the way.

CHAPTER 53

WHO WAS ROBERTO CLEMENTE? THE POWER OF A SUPERIOR TEAM

BY TOM PUENTES AND J. ERIK KIMBROUGH

Throughout sports history, there have been great players who have come and gone, who exist now, and whose names will carry on long after we are dust. They break records, they change the games they play and they even change the way we view the sport in which they operate. Unfortunately, they also end up as some of the greatest players never to win a championship. They may be fantastic athletes in their day, but, for some reason, other less talented athletes steal the sports headlines. Often, the public is led to dismiss the achievements of the superior athletes, in favor of less talented individuals. Why is that? How did the outstanding athletes become the lesser known? Well, the answer is simple. They were stuck on bad, unsupportive, or even misguided teams during their careers.

You can go down the list from Ted Williams, Dwayne Wade, Barry Sanders, Ralph Kiner, and some would even argue Dan Marino. Now, of course, as we read through sports history, we can note that there were definitely excellent players who were on crummy teams and who were not held back from success or popularity. Yet, there are many more who never achieved the glory that it would seem should have been their destiny.

Pittsburgh Pirate superstar Roberto Clemente died doing the two things he loved best: playing ball and helping people. His death in 1972 is as large a legend as his life. He was active in providing food, medicine and baseball equipment to underprivileged Latin American countries, but tragically his plane went down while on a mission to deliver aid to Nicaraguan earthquake victims.

His body was never found, but his memory lives on, and so do his Major League records. He played in twelve All Star Games and won twelve Gold Gloves. He led the National League in batting average four times and was its Most Valuable Player in 1966. During the course of his career, Clemente was selected to participate in the league's All Star Game on twelve occasions, and was recognized as the first Latin American player to be honored by the Baseball Hall of Fame.

Yet, with all the accolades he still never rose to the level of a Willie Mays or Joe DiMaggio. Could it be that he never understood or "embraced" the importance of the team? Was he not aware of the importance of the environment in which he was performing? Would he have achieved more success, more fame, before his death, if he had played for a better team?

The idea of embracing the concept of team is not just one that we can examine on the sports field. How would Roberto have performed in a corporate environment? Would he have continued to earn the equivalent of Golden Gloves in the business world, or would he have required a stronger team? Is the idea of team only present in our social and sports mentality, or can we implement it into our corporate strategy? Can this concept be used to expand our business? Can it help us to react faster and provide higher level of services than we would be able, if we acted, as Roberto did, alone?

To first understand why teams make such a powerful tool in the growth and development of an organization, it is critical to first understand the limitations of operating as a sole practitioner. As a matter of economic principle, the Law of Diminishing Returns tells us that the tendency for a continuing application of effort or skill toward a particular task or goal declines in effectiveness after a certain level of result has been achieved. An example of this would be a farmer's use of fertilizer to increase his yield of crops. The more fertilizer is applied, the greater the yield, until he reaches an optimal point of fertilizer to farmed land. After this optimal point of application is exceeded, if the farmer continues to apply fertilizer, we can expect the yield to begin to decrease.

The case is similar in a corporate setting. A financial advisor takes on clients for the purpose of asset management. As the advisor's business grows, there becomes a point where the effectiveness of the advisor's ability to properly service the clientele begins to decrease. When the advisor forms a team he not only solves the problem of diminishing returns, but also allows for greater growth, as now there are more resources to employ.

Teams allow us to achieve better success because we develop more efficient service models. We can isolate the need for teaming into seven simple reasons. These reasons allow us to measure and track success. These reasons can be listed as follows:

Increased utilization of resources – When we talk about the utilization of resources, we are trying to find that optimal point of growth vs. the employment of manpower. As we learned above in describing the Law of Diminishing Returns, this optimal point is lower as a sole practitioner than it would be in a team setting. For example, the optimal point for a financial advisor who is working alone might be 100 clients, whereas if he were operating within a team environment, the point, or client base, would be substantially higher.

1. **Overall quality improvement** – Continuous system improvement and improved customer service means that the functional barriers are eliminated and people are forced to co-operate with other positions in the team, not just within a function of the organization.

2. **Better able to respond to changes** – There is now a greater need to respond more rapidly to market forces and changes both within the organization and within the industry of operation. Organizations and structures are more complex and more flexible. This increases the need for collaborative decision making.

3. **Levels the playing field for members** – People have to be more interdependent in order to achieve more with less. The role of manager changes from director to that of facilitator, allowing a greater emphasis on the group/team.

4. **Greater availability of resources from senior management** – When it comes to the allocation of a firms resources, bigger (team vs. single) is better.

5. **Challenging expectations for growth** – Operating within a team raises expectations about contributing to decisions that affect growth. The group, as a team, can challenge the limits of "what is possible."

6. **Truly a case for stronger marketing** – More people bring more ideas which incorporate different centers of marketing. A Learning Organization is created. Members will tend to combine their experiences in order to learn how to do things better/differently in future.

In the financial service industry, our work is becoming so complex and intricate, it is becoming more like product development.

This insight is one that I think most organizations have been avoiding. They are happy to talk about speed and measurement, but not so much about the intricacy and complexity that is becoming commonplace in a more dynamic financial environment. There is no denying it; the teaming of individuals is becoming vastly more important and necessary.

Companies are trying to reach more customers through more channels, and reach them in a personalized, conversational manner. They are trying to do this simultaneously across global markets. This is extremely complicated and intricate work. Any denial in reaching a customer, or any weakness in the quality of that touch point, means lost revenue, so our worldview of process management must be adjusted. The solution is to do things faster, or do things in parallel.

Product development went through the concurrent engineering movement where companies realized that the massive advantages of being first, or taking control of a market, required reinventing service model development to allow more processes to run concurrently.

The financial service industry now has to do the same. We have to think in terms of concurrent management and find ways to remove inefficiencies from asset gathering, client retention, and asset management. We need to put time-to-market high on the priority list, and find ways to make our marketing processes run in parallel.

It is imperative to gain control of digital assets, while understanding the "defined relationship" with a targeted business area. This is time intensive and difficult when the professional is working alone. Building a team that can gain competitive advantage through concurrent global marketing is far more profitable than attempting this as a sole practitioner.

Maximum brand impact means communicating in a thousand different places at once with the most relevant, targeted message being delivered, conversationally, to highly segmented audiences. Print, social media, online, TV, YouTube, news groups, mobile phones, tablets, and traditional mail – all these channels now demand segmented messages to multiple unique market demographics.

The result? Advisors with a team act like a well-engineered machine that can move in multiple directions, as opposed to the outdated model of a single advisor with a desk and phone. There are hundreds of business parts that can be orchestrated in the ideal team– parts that are created by, and need to be managed across, a complex, creative partner network.

In today's financial world, an advisor must be able to react to changing market needs rapidly, effectively, and responsively. We must be able to reduce their time to market and adapt to changing environments. Decisions must be made quickly and correctly, the first time out. Advisors can no longer waste time repeating tasks, thereby prolonging the time it takes to acquire new clients, develop financial plans, manage assets, and provide adequate service. Therefore, teaming has emerged as the way of bringing rapid solutions to all needs faced by the advisor.

History tells us time and time again that greatness in leadership is achieved when the leader is backed by a supportive team. A game will never be won by the performance of one. An inflated sense of entitlement or a misdirected ego can actually lead to under performance by the individual. It can also weave its way throughout the corporate environment like an untreated virus. As a child, I often heard these wise words from my mother: "The greater man understands the importance of humility and disarms himself from unearned ego." I seek to lead my peers by my individual performance, but I do not neglect the importance of a successful team. As a team, we work together, supporting each other's talents, in order to represent ourselves as the best in the business.

Would Roberto Clemente have been a better player if he had been a part of the Yankees instead of the Pirates…who knows? What can be assumed is that as a Yankee, Clemente would have played in seven World Series, which is more than the two he participated in with the Pirates. Perhaps Clemente's popularity would have received more favorable press coverage in Manhattan during those seven championship seasons. For most of his career, Clemente and the Pittsburgh print media had a contentious relationship. The press considered Clemente a constant complainer and malcontent.

For his part, Clemente regarded the writers as racists who did not appreciate his many skills and never missed an opportunity to make note of his accented English. Clemente said his image suffered in predominantly white Pittsburgh because he was, in his words, "a double minority" — black and Latino. Additionally, Pittsburgh's slanted media treatment of Clemente hurt him with the national press. With such great success on the field, the Most Valuable Player voting reflected the writers' indifference shown in how few of these awards he actually won.

Consider, on the other hand, how a player of Clemente's caliber would have been received in New York, during the 1950s. When Clemente broke into baseball, the great wave of Puerto Rican migration was underway. Affordable air travel enabled tens of thousands of islanders to uproot and move to New York. His status as an All-Star player on the perennial champion Yankees would have made him a hero, not only in the Puerto Rican community, but also among African Americans. In 1955, Clemente would have joined Elston Howard as one of the Yankees' first two black players. Additionally, in the '50s, New York had six daily newspapers. Yes, Manhattan media coverage of Clemente would have been glowing and his national reputation enhanced accordingly.

Building a winning team takes time, but it beats working as a sole practitioner, and it definitely beats being a superstar on a lousy team. Wouldn't you rather be the greatest player on the greatest team, than the greatest player on the losing team? Right. Put your team together. Go win the Series!

About Tom

Tom A. Puentes has been in the financial services industry since 1985. His clients include family foundations, labor unions, health professionals, executives, Internet entrepreneurs, and business owners across the entire U.S.

From 1989-2000, Tom hosted a weekly financial show called *Your Money Matters*, on the Business Channel, Station KWHY, Los Angeles. He was also the financial correspondent for KADY-TV in Ventura, California.

For more information about Tom A. Puentes, visit: www.morganstanleyfa.com/tomapuentes/

About Eric

J. Erik Kimbrough was raised with the belief that giving is just as important as succeeding. In all his professional positions, he has illustrated quality and integrity because of the early philosophy instilled in him. Erik has brought this exceptional work ethic to the Investment Management industry. With 11 years of branch management experience, first at UBS and now with MSSB, He approaches every assignment with intelligence and patience. In a business that is always changing, his understanding and personal approach provides his office with the comfort needed to gain the trust and confidence that is necessary to obtain growth and development. His staff is important to him and he is not satisfied until he knows they have achieved a successful outcome for all their goals.

Erik's penchant for discipline was developed in his Olympic training days on the US Tae Kwon Do training team and through his studies at Boston University, where he graduated with honors in Economics. He continued with his economic studies at the University of Madrid, his MBA at Duquesne University and now is sitting for an MS in Financial Management and Banking at Boston University.

In addition to his extensive academic and professional life, he shares his time and knowledge with the Black Achievers, the youth at the YMCA and Inroads. He received the KDKA UpLift Award for his desire to pass on his knowledge of finance to the young people of Pittsburgh, and has taught a weekly economic class at Gannon University.

Living and traveling in Europe enriched Erik's aptitude for different languages and cultures, and has allowed him to communicate easily with all types of people. Erik is a person who loves to explore different landscapes and get to know the people living there. He speaks Spanish and Italian and has exchanged ideas with people from around the world.

A native of Pittsburgh, Erik is proud of his accomplishments and is looking forward to the opportunity to continue fostering cultural understanding and an appreciation of finance with the people and staff of La Jolla, CA.

CHAPTER 54

THE ART OF MOTIVATION

BY MARC ALFRED, (P.Th.)

*Start by doing what's necessary; then do what's possible;
and suddenly you are doing the impossible.*

~ St. Francis of Assisi

A lot of people, like I did, spend most of their life struggling to work out their purpose or passions.

The reason we do anything is due to internal and external drivers. Your internal drivers are how you speak to yourself; whereas external drivers are how others impact your thinking and your actions.

After over two decades of research, I've discovered one of the most important, but little talked about secrets to success, how you start determines both your level of success and how sustainable it is.

Drivers can be positive or negative, as with these examples:

Negative Drivers Include	Some Positive Drivers
Unrealistic parental expectations	Accountability
Loss or poverty	Skill development
Relationship breakdown	Planning and goal-setting
Guilt from religion or education	Inspiring philanthropy
Media projections of false realities	Reviewing what works
Bullying from peers or the workplace	Emotion and mindset development

In 1972, a young family fled from Uganda to the UK as refugees of Idi Amin's regime, with just a suitcase and the clothes they wore. Young son, Dillon Dhanecha, watched as his parents make a lifetime of sacrifices to ensure he had the freedom to create his own destiny. Dillon's parents became his first positive external driver. Aged six, Dillon watched the Ethiopian famine appeal on television with his mother, and tells how he wanted his Christmas presents sent to starving children. Dillon's mother made it happen and gave him the first taste of philanthropy. Positive internal drivers had developed at an early age. Early on, Dillon's father introduced him to compounding and money management. Dillon's first business was selling magazine posters on the playground to double his money weekly. Today, Dillon trains philanthropists around the world to trade the currency markets and invests millions of dollars in profitable businesses with a global social impact.

External drivers on people's lives are powerful. For Dillon, an episode of the Money Program showing how Sun Microsystems brought the Internet to the world led him into direct battle with his University Vice Chancellor who conceded to postponing Dillon's course so that he could join Sun's innovation lab.

Dillon now uses both technology and creative entrepreneurial strategy as the founder of The Change Studio, delivering a mission to leave the legacy of transforming how 'developmental aid' is used to 'help' communities. His world famous "Making Millionaires who Make a Difference" slogan and formula of: Passion, Purpose and Profit, places him on stages with the likes of Mark Victor Hansen co-author of the best seller, Chicken Soup for the Soul. Remember how it all started, his family arriving with just a suitcase – but I left out the words of Dillon's mother: "Darling, being financially and spiritually wealthy will make you a positive force for change in the world," and of his father, "Son, you will never help the poor, by becoming poor yourself."

Let me now show you how simply the Success Driver Matrix™ works.

THE SUCCESS DRIVER MATRIX

	- External	+ External
- Internal	Depression	Burn Out
+ Internal	Procrastination	Success

Internal and external drivers are obviously not necessarily separate. Here you can see both the links and their impact. If for example your parents or religion were highly critical growing up, this could then lead your self-talk to becoming damaged, leading to depression. However, this could also lead you to a common sub-conscious, "I'm-going-to-show-them" lifestyle. This leads to burnout, as unless you release the negative driver, you will never feel a genuine sense of peace or sustained happiness.

The opposite can also be true, an amazing upbringing and brilliant education can lead to positive self-talk. However, if your peer group, the media you consume or your workplaces are negative, this by default will create a stop, start, and stop to your success.

In 2006, Simon Alexander Ong had just finished his second year at the London School of Economics studying towards a BSc degree. He waited in anticipation for the exam results, though part of him already knew what would be displayed. And as he clicked the link he was informed he had failed his second year of university and would be required to repeat this year. He shares now that it was not exactly the best news you would choose to deliver to a Chinese family who have invested in you and expect you to pass exams with flying colours. What Simon did next was extremely powerful; Simon created this into a positive driver.

Within four months, Simon had landed multiple offers from investment banks for a summer internship. He accepted the offer from Lehman Brothers, which was converted into a full-time offer. In addition, Simon took this experience and began working as a coach, helping students land the jobs they wanted. As Simon discovered his purpose he signed himself up to 30 careers events and, importantly, met some amazing mentors.

Simon now believes in the 'awesomeness in everyone' and tells of the moment he helped an Oxbridge student who considered himself 'shy and not the most confident individual' land multiple job offers in weeks. Simon's transformation was the springboard for his global consultancy simonalexanderong.com that works with people in multitudes of other areas from all around the world. Remember how it started, failing at university and him embracing this negative driver and being open to it as a positive opportunity.

As one of my mentors once taught me, "We understand life backwards, but we can only live it forwards." So what about you, what have been your external drivers? Is what you say to yourself truly positive?

A study by the University of Chicago used MRI scans to compare brain activity of unusually aggressive 16 to 18-year-old males with conduct disorder, to those of 'normal' adolescent males, while they watched videos of people getting hurt, found the brains of aggressive males showed activity in the brain's pleasure centers. Normal males showed no such activity.

"It just dumbfounded us," said Benjamin Lahey, a professor of psychiatry. Co-activation suggested that activity in the amygdala and the prefrontal cortex is linked when shown something painful. In other words, when normal people see someone getting hurt, they respond with negative emotions.

"But in kids with conduct disorder, that connection isn't there," said Lahey, also professor of Behavioral Neuroscience, "They're not only indifferent to the pain, they love it, maybe." Lahey said.

I wonder if most people have 'conduct disorder' of a sort, with different types of negative drivers actually bringing 'pleasure'. We only really engage in any activity because it has a *perceived* 'benefit'.

Luke Bradford has brought his creativity to global organisations worldwide from the BBC's Top Gear to PlayStation but how did it start? His agency, *Frogspawn Creative* has a strap line, '*ideas that grow*' and uses the illustration of how frogspawn starts with that little black dot to exponential growth really fast. The black dot for Luke Bradford has been based on giving skills away for free. Whilst Luke was a senior producer at BBC Worldwide, he made films for charities in his spare time, either for free or at cost. When *Frogspawn Creative* was founded, 90% of the commissioned work then came as a result of the films he'd given away in the past.

When I asked the prolific British fashion designer Sir Paul Smith what was the one piece of advice he would give to entrepreneurs, he said, "think laterally." Working for free for most of us would be a negative driver, however, this lateral thinking has led Luke to being the film director everyone wants to work with. Celebrated author Sir Christopher Ondaatje describes him as "*the most creative and understanding film maker I have ever worked with.*" Successful entrepreneurs have an ability to take something others see as negative and mix it with a positive drive to see what others only dream of.

With Luke, it's been the likes of seeing the British Prime Minister's wife, Samantha Cameron, moved to tears at his film screened at 10 Downing Street about the school her late son attended, to hearing the reaction of 4,200 international leaders watching one of his films at The Royal Albert Hall. Luke once entered a competition to make a silent commercial for a client that had a High Street presence. Luke had no such client. He still made the advert for an international entertainment company and persistently wrote and emailed them until they saw it and loved it. It won and they got £100,000 of advertising space and he got an all expenses weekend in NYC – the film's budget was just £30.00. Luke had learnt from giving away his skills, how to act creatively with all opportunities.

Imagine standing at the edge of the dance floor of the club you own, to see it packed with people every night and Prince William and Prince Harry dancing on it! That has been a reality for Marc Burton of the internationally acclaimed Mexican themed club, Tonteria. What's amazing is how Marc managed to start this club with nothing.

Marc Burton explains how he "fell into nightlife by chance after arriving at Bath University." He had frequented London nightclubs and been fascinated how worlds merged and blended into one. In the real world, social groups were separated. If you went to a restaurant, people would stick to their tables and did not mix. You would see celebrities on TV and socialites in the magazines. Suddenly, in nightclubs, the barriers dropped. These people danced together and socialised at the bar with each other. He recalls the excitement and intrigue when he was at China White Wednesday (the hottest club in the late 90s), and there being the most incredible mix of celebrities, models, actors, business tycoons and socialites. Here, everybody interacted and seemed to know one another; it was like a dreamland to Marc Burton.

There's little doubt this external positive driver created a positive internal one in Marc Burton to want to create this dreamland community for others. While at Bath University, he learnt the model of creating 'success' without financial investment through inspiring shared success with others. The manager of the Blue Rooms Club, where he wanted this to happen, at first gave him a flat "no," but after months of persistence, it eventually led to a one off night there that became a popular student night. This led to Marc arranging entrance for friends into London clubs and meeting Nick House. Nick House, famous for 20-30 club nights in London, agreed to Marc bringing students to his clubs that started a great relationship between them. When Marc left Bath, Nick was about to open Mahiki. Marc thought this was going to be short-lived like nearly every other club, especially as they were going to play 60s to 90s music. However, Marc learnt the importance of reviewing his thinking in the light of others' expertise. Nick House did something unique and rather than being rude to it's guests, like others, it had a clear goal to be a friendly club. On the opening night everyone from Paris Hilton to Sting, Jennifer Lopez to Matt Damon, were there.

Marc Burton has gone on to create a world famous club due to his own set of unique talking points, like a train that delivers your drinks and the friendly family feel remains. The way Marc Burton has lived out his mantra of 'live your dreams' is a great example of allowing those internal drivers to connect with external action.

How does this mindset shift actually happen? To slightly adapt the famous Einstein quote, "The definition of madness is *thinking* the same thing in the same way and expecting a different result." Most success starts with creative entrepreneurial thinking. The current map in your mind has got you to where you are, if you want to get somewhere else, you need to punch a different destination into your mind's navigation system. In fact when we positively align our internal and external drivers, it also actually *creates* the thinking needed for organisations, as well as individuals, to enjoy true lasting success.

The world's media from FOX to The Times, have reported on the Dominic Knight Clinic creating change in incredible time frames. In the best selling book *Pushing to the Front*, that Dominic co-authored with Brian Tracy – selling over 42,000 books within an hour of release – Dominic talks about the 14 Second system, one example is when Dominic Knight himself cured 74 flight phobics in moments. Dominic also once worked with an average sales professional in London's famous street of tailors, Savile Row, who went on to break all sales records in his companies history selling $107,000 of suits within just one afternoon. What's important is how this demonstrates how quickly it's possible to change negative internal drivers into positive ones, there's even a 14 Seconds app that guarantees success.

Dominic Knight himself had to cope with the literal excruciating negative driver of three prolapsed disks that meant he couldn't walk or even sit normally, the doctors said he would be lucky to even be able to pick up a kettle. Interestingly, inspired by remembering reading about Bruce Lee's spinal injury, Dominic extracted this powerful driver to begin working on the only thing he could, his mind. This took him from being addicted to painkillers to healing his physical condition, to becoming a top ten finalist at Pride, one of the most extreme mixed martial arts competitions in the world.

Dominic talks of realising that when the 'why' he wanted to succeed became an all-consuming obsession, it happened. Overcoming these insurmountable odds, he initially started off his practice with no business card, advertising or permanent place to practice to generating incomes in the upper brackets of the top 20% in the UK through referrals alone. His clinical practice is now on Harley Street, a number one medical address in the world and Dominic is now in constant demand by companies from IBM to Virgin, but remember how it started; in Dominic's mind.

From these examples of just a few business I've worked with recently, they clearly demonstrate that when you or your organisation start by ensuring you have turned your internal and external drivers into a positive alignment, anything is possible. To understand your current purpose, start by ensuring negative drivers are not leading you. Then focus on your passions by regularly asking these now five famous questions we use at The School of Thoughts, as a starting point, to enable leaders and organisations to discover new levels of success:

- When have you felt most alive?
- What would you do for the rest of your life even if you never got paid to do it?
- If you only had 12 months to live but you would be well, what would you do?
- If you could only make one difference in the world, what would it be?
- If you knew you couldn't fail, what would you do?

About Marc

Marc Alfred, (P.Th.) as Founding Director of The School of Thoughts, is on a mission to bring entrepreneurialism not only to business but also to all areas of society, from education and charity to personal development. Over many years, Marc has shared his strategies from writing for international publications to being interviewed by the world's media.

His passion for understanding the mind began while studying counseling for his honors degree in Pastoral Studies and completing his postgraduate in education. Marc went on to be part of a research team at the prestigious Institute of Education and is dedicated to the lifelong research of human behavior.

As now a best-selling author and self-confessed "expert on failure," Marc's book *Failing To Succeed* enables its readers to overcome the fear of failure and answer one of life's most important questions: "If you knew you couldn't fail, what would you do?"

The School of Thoughts also enables businesses in a broad range of industries from entertainment to health to fuse together marketing with social responsibility. This mix of ethical advertising and philanthropy, which Marc has coined 'Adanthropy' have mobilized multitudes of volunteers and even gained the support of significant influencers such as Sir Richard Branson. Marc is also one of the very first mentors for start ups to be appointed by Virgin.

As a philanthropist, Marc has pioneered a number of projects—from working with young people in Kosovo after the war to producing media and web-based tools to tackle a range of social challenges, which has twice won him the Barclays New Futures Award.

Marc and his team of Consultant Coaches also enable organizations to apply a range of psychological tools to develop the mindset of its leaders and teams to see new levels of success. One way this has been achieved is by developing global training programs for large multi-national organizations.

As an in-demand keynote speaker and educator, Marc Alfred brings his interactive approach to a range of audiences and has communicated with thousands over the last two decades — from hosting national conferences on human behavior to giving annual lectures at some of the best universities in the world.

You can connect with Marc here:
marc@theschoolofthoughts.com
twitter.com/hellomarcalfred
facebook.com/TheSchoolOfThoughts
TheSchoolofThoughts.com

CHAPTER 55

MAILBOX MONEY — ACHIEVING ADEQUATE MONTHLY INCOME IN RETIREMENT

BY DON B. BERGIS AND JARED M. ELSON

Mailbox money. Growing up, I listened to my grandfathers, who were both very successful investors, talk about their "mailbox money." One grandfather had a pension from the telephone company, which he called his "mailbox money." The other grandfather had made some good investments and had some rental properties, so he, too, had mailbox money. Mailbox money is the money that comes to you as a check every month--residual income. Today, with direct deposits, we don't have the opportunity to venture to the mailbox each month for income, but the goal is to achieve residual income just the same.

Sophie Tucker, Vaudeville actress, and inspiration to Bette Midler's career, once said, "From birth to age 18, a girl needs good parents. From age 18 to 35, she needs good looks. From 35 to 55, she needs a good personality and from 55 on, she just needs cash." As you get older, growth can still be important, but your real need becomes reliable income. The biggest complaint that most people have about their financial planner is the planner's lack of proactive planning for retirement.

History indicates that people purchase life insurance from one advisor, purchase stocks and bonds from another advisor, and then visit a tax preparer once a year. They are then dissatisfied with their income at retirement because the components they purchased do not fit together, nor were their tax liabilities taken into account with regard to those components. Much of the confusion arises, not because investors are unintelligent; to the contrary, most investors are highly intelligent, technical and business-minded, but because they lack an education about managing their finances. The three hardest things in life on which to make decisions are marriage, children and money. Unless you have a finance degree, you likely have not had much formal training in managing your finances. You might not understand the Rule of 72 or that tax-deferred and tax-free are very different.

If you take a dollar and double it every year for 20 years, at the end of the 20 years, you will have $1 million. However, if you have to pay tax on that money every year, you would have a greatly reduced amount in the 20th year, as low as $51,000. Likely, your stockbroker never informed you of the tax burden or tax loss you will have from your investments. The right financial planner will winnow out the unsatisfactory portions of your retirement plan, so that you enjoy the best retirement possible.

Neither rain, nor sleet, nor snow…

The Discovery Process
If an important fact or piece of information affects your retirement, when would you want to know about it? You want to know about it now, especially if that piece of information will put your money at risk. It is imperative to work with a financial advisor who specializes in retirement income planning, or the "preservation cycle" of life. You want the advisor to ferret out and identify those pitfalls, and to protect you from financial distress in your retirement. Retirement pitfalls are the rain, sleet and snow that keep your mailbox money from reaching your mailbox each month of your retirement.

Our discovery process starts with a 1040 tax review. Yes, some financial planners do want to review your tax return. We know if we can find any taxable dollars that can be re-directed; we can save you money on social security taxation. We then have a much more efficient income plan that can make a significant difference in your retirement income. Next, we do some income planning, because as Sophie Tucker said, cash will become very important at retirement. Finally, we do some risk analysis so that we can minimize the risk, according to your desires.

A Little Advanced Warning on...

Phantom Gains and Taxes

There are times when investing, especially with products like mutual funds, is a lot like gambling. Before you invest, you need critical pieces of information about Wall Street and mutual funds, such as phantom income and phantom taxes that cause you to pay taxes on a losing mutual fund. If you invest $500,000 into a mutual fund or a series of mutual funds, the fund company may charge you as much as 5%. Therefore, you have actually invested $485,000 and the fund company gets their $15,000 share off the top. Imagine that the market had a bad year that year, and the value has dropped to $400,000. You lost $85,000 in the mutual funds and $15,000 in fees so far. Come the next January as you are preparing your taxes, you go to the mailbox and find a 1099 from your broker that shows a gain in your mutual fund. A gain? How can you have a gain when you lost $85,000? On paper, because of the way the mutual fund manager traded, your 1040 will list a financial gain. You now have a $2,000-$5,000 tax event that you did not anticipate. Statistically, if you hold on to a mutual fund for a 10-year period, you will likely have gone through this 2-3 times. Your tax advisor will not find this. A financial planner needs to look at your statement while looking at your taxes and comparing the two to find phantom taxes.

Fiduciary Responsibility

The second thing to learn before investing in mutual funds is how Wall Street is paid and how they are licensed. The court case of Bill Metzger makes an excellent example. Mr. Metzger was a successful software specialist. He had managed to save $2 million and at the age of 46, he invested it in the stock market. Unfortunately, for Mr. Metzger, Wall Street took his $2 million and brought it down to $1.1 million. Mr. Metzger sued the firm he was with. The judge told Mr. Metgzer that although his loss incensed him, he could only legally award him $10,000 because Mr. Metzger had signed a suitability agreement with the stockbroker. The suitability agreement essentially said, "We have the capacity to lose all your money, but you have the capability, outside of this investment, to live if we do lose your money." Suitability means that if the broker loses all your money, you would still be okay. A stockbroker does not have a fiduciary, or trust, or obligation to do what is best for the clients, frequently, their fiduciary duty is to their firm and it's shareholders. They have a fiduciary responsibility to the shareholders of the firms they represent. The alternative to this one-sided lean against the investor, is to work with a Registered Investment Advisor as a portfolio manager who has a responsibility to the client and the client's best interest as a fiduciary.

Hidden Fees
Nestled amongst the little known facts about Wall Street lurk the hidden fees built into many investments and those charged by broker dealers. A Registered Investment Advisor's fees are fully disclosed and may offer clients a savings of 30-50% in total fees paid over working with a broker-dealer investing in mutual funds. Making sure that you are working with a fiduciary that is beholden to you, dramatically changes how much of your money you will keep. It's important to ask that your advisor show you the hidden fees in your current portfolio, advise you if those fees are out of line, and discuss the risk to your current portfolio as well.

Truth in Advertising
The stock market has performed okay over the last 20 years, with an annualized return of 8.2% on the S&P 500, however the timing of market ups and downs needs to be considered, and if you look at the volatility over the last decade you'll see most of that return came during the first 10 years of the last 20. You'll see that the stock market can be a risky environment if what you want is steady mailbox money. There are more variables on Wall Street than there are in a Las Vegas casino. We would never suggest that you invest your money at a Las Vegas casino; it follows suit that we would not recommend you invest your money 100% in a market with unpredictable returns and volatile ups and downs if what you are seeking is a steady income and preservation of principal. Wall Street does a wonderful job, with their billions per year in advertising, convincing us that it is exactly where we should invest the majority of our money.

Inflation
The next critical fact is inflation; inflation is the silent killer. We like to talk to our clients about inflation because in planning, we believe it's necessary to account for a 2-3% raise each year in withdrawals to deal with inflation.

Long-Term Care

Statistically, 630 out of every 900 retirees are going to need long-term care in their lifetime. You do not have to pay the insurance industry for something you may, or may not use. There are investment products that allow you to get your money back if you don't require long-term care. The benefits are accessible whether you need help at home, at an assisted living facility or at a critical care/nursing home. The money is always there, and if you do not use it, you get your money back plus interest.

Taxes–Tax Deferred or Tax-Free

We established that hidden fees can squelch retirement plans but taxes can too. Eighty million baby-boomers are leaving the workforce and this natural exodus of workers is putting an unbelieveable pressure on Social Security. Seventy percent of all 70 year olds live at or below the poverty level. Many retirees are frustrated because they pay taxes on the social security that they paid into while working, so they feel this is a form of double taxation. Your advisor should examine tax returns to discover ways to keep their clients from paying avoidable taxes on social security income.

If you plan correctly, a person can collect over $1 million in social security benefits during a 30-year retirement. This is not a small chunk of change. One way to reduce your taxable income is through tax-deferred products like pensions, IRAs and 401(k)s and an under-utilized product called an annuity. Certain annuities are excellent, some can produce as much as 30-50% more income than a stock and bond portfolio utilizing guaranteed income riders from the annuity companies. For deferral of funds for future income it's important to keep in mind that a dollar that doubles every year for 20 years will grow to $1 million. The key is to eliminate or reduce the taxes on the money during the accumulation period. Even better than tax-deferred income is tax-free income. Some insurance products offer not only the tax-free advantage, but also offer living-care benefits as well.

Proactive Management and your Portfolio

Two men participated for over 30 years in their retirement plans; they both invested a good amount of money and both got the same average rate of return, but one ended up with $562,000 at retirement and the other retired with $1 million. What was the difference? The one with

$562,000 had some very bad down years between the ages of 55-65. What we learn from their example is that average returns mean nothing, annualized returns mean a great deal, and that having negative years in sequence during the 5-10 years before retirement can deflate your retirement balloon dramatically. You are better off having flat years or very little return during that period. You will not have the time needed to recover from significant losses, potentially cutting your nest egg in half.

In 2002, investment guru James Stack, President of InvesTech, created a demonstration of the S&P 500 to illustrate the impact of market volatility on a portfolio. He "invested" $10 in the market and tracked its cycle from 1928 until 2002. Over that 75-year period, the $10 grew to almost $11,000. Next Stack illustrated the effect of bullish increases of the best 30 growth months of the 75 years by removing them from the chart. The portfolio value was now $154. Then his financial team suggested he look at the portfolio after removing the 30 worst months, just to see what happens. What they found was shocking. When they removed the 30 worst months, the value of that $10 investment was now $1.3 million! Stack's study shows it's far more important to stay away from the down than it is to achieve momentous gains on the up.

Proactive management provides the key to saving a portfolio from disaster. Sometimes you have to cease all operations when disaster seems imminent. A surgeon understands the importance of aborting a surgery that will do more harm than good. The foreperson at an industrial facility will shut down production when the line is not producing the desired results. In contrast, many mutual fund managers lack a panic button and cannot go to cash to preserve the portfolio. Going to cash is the primary means of minimizing losses; active fund managers cannot do this because of the restrictions of the fund documents. When was the last time that your stockbroker called you and said, "We need to go to cash." Never?

In 1980, when Wall Street lobbied Congress to create the 401(k), 403(b) and all these new retirement accounts to allow more people to invest in the stock market, only 5% of families were in the market. For the next 20 years, while the baby-boomers were at the height of their careers, they invested heavily in the stock market. By the year 2000, 90% of households were invested in the stock market. Of course, the market grew as a result. The volatility of the market in recent years correlates to those same baby boomers exiting the market as they retire.

Traditionally, stockbrokers advise that you can pull 3-4% of your money out annually and not lose your principal or run out of money in retirement. Why is it then, that those same stockbrokers are now advocating only a 1.5% or 2% payout per year? They have changed their tune because the top mathematicians in the country worked the numbers and computed that an investor would have only about a 50% chance of being able to make their money last in retirement when extracted at the 3-4% rate. Would you get on an airplane if the chances of it crashing were 50%? Not likely. Working with an advisor that offers products that guarantee income (income guarantees based on the strength and claims paying ability of the issuing insurance company) with as little risk and tax implication as possible for a portion of your portfolio, and offers active fund management for your other funds, is exactly what you need in retirement.

Your mailbox money, the money that you can count on every month, might be the difference between enjoying your retirement or living at the poverty level. Proactive management of your retirement assets to fill holes in your bucket and to keep the tax collector at bay will ensure your mailbox money continues to arrive in a steady stream.

Jared M. Elson is a Registered Investment Advisor. Investment Advisory Services are offered through Global Financial Private Capital, LLC, an SEC Registered Investment Adviser. Don B. Bergis is not registered with Global Financial Private Capital, LLC. Insurance products are offered through Regent Financial & Insurance Services, LLC.

About Don & Jared

Don B. Bergis and Jared M. Elson have been helping clients with their financial goals for the last ten years. They take a practical and personal approach with their clients, assisting them with numerous strategies. These various strategies focus on the fundamentals of implementing tax efficient programs, income building, income distribution, and legacy concepts. As trusted professionals, Don and Jared specialize in retirement and estate planning. They believe in thoroughly educating their clients about the advantages and disadvantages of every financial decision they make, and then help them to accomplish and execute their personal financial plan to retire with confidence.

Don and Jared have enjoyed being the trusted authority for hundreds of clients, friends and associates throughout California. Don and Jared are both members of the National Ethics Bureau.

Don is a graduate of Cal Poly University with a successful background in the high tech industry. He was raised in Los Alto Hills, California, and resides in the foothills of Gilroy with his wife, daughter, son and their three dogs. Don enjoys living in the country, horseback riding, fishing, music and reading a good book. He is involved in his church and several community groups.

Jared is a graduate of San Jose University with a degree in Communication and Business. He also has a background working in the high tech industry having spent nearly a decade taking on multiple roles with Yahoo! Prior to working as an investment advisor. Jared offers investment advisory services through Global Financial Private Capital, an SEC Registered Advisor. He has lived in the south county area all his life. He was raised in Morgan Hill, California and calls Gilroy his home. Jared enjoys playing amateur ice hockey, outdoor activities, reading, and spending time with his family and friends.

CHAPTER 56

REAL ESTATE'S BEST KEPT SECRET

BY CHRISTOPHER MEZA

There is no dispute that more millionaires have been created in real estate than in any other industry. That's why so many people inherently see the value in investing in real estate. The only point to consider is that the majority of people that do invest in real estate ONLY invest in one type of real estate, DEVELOPED REAL ESTATE: condos, homes, shopping centers, apartment buildings, hotels, so on and so forth. To be clear, *whenever the majority of people are investing in the same or similar investment strategy that particular type of investment will tend to yield lower returns usually with greater risk.* You may be asking yourself, what's the alternative? Before I explain the alternative to you, I would like to share with you a little bit about myself and how I discovered the biggest secret in real estate.

I have a degree in electrical engineering and computer science – which makes me a computer engineer. I have worked for Fortune 100 companies such as IBM and The Boeing Company. Although engineering is my profession, my passion, real estate and investing, has allowed me to retire at a very young age. I'm going to share with you the greatest way to financially succeed in any economy. First let's start with how an engineer by profession became an investor.

Back when I was in high school I was doing well for myself and what I mean by that is, I had good grades. One day my family had a gathering and one of our family friends that attended happened to be a real estate developer and multi-millionaire. When I was walking around the room I came across this gentlemen and he said, "Hey Chris, aren't you excited you are going to be graduating high school pretty soon and you are going off to college to become an engineer?" And I replied, "Yes, I am very excited." However, there was something that I had been feeling for quite some time that I had never shared with anyone and for some reason I decided to tell this gentlemen, "Sir, although I'm excited, I feel like all I have is good grades and that I'm not living to my potential. I feel like I could be doing so much more but I don't know what to do. I think maybe I need a mentor." To my disbelief, almost without hesitation, this gentleman said, "WOW...well...I'll mentor you." I was shocked for several reasons; I wasn't sure why a multi-millionaire would want to spend time with me. I also thought, he's a real estate developer and investor how could he possibly mentor me when I'm getting ready to become an engineer. However, without reluctance, I jumped at the chance and said, "GREAT. Okay. Thank you!"

Our relationship started off very much on the surface. It was always, "Hey, how's school?" or "Hey, how's business?" Until one day he said something that changed my life. I know he didn't do it intentionally, nevertheless, let me share with you how the conversation went. I gave him a call and I said, "Hey how's it going today?" and he responded in very high spirits, "Chris I'm doing FANTASTIC, things are going so great, I'm getting ready to get into this DEAL, you know and blah, blah, blah..." I *psychologically* couldn't hear anything past the word "deal". The word deal for me started a very strong emotional response. As I mentioned, I'm an engineer and consequently very analytical and the first thing I thought to myself was how could he possibly know he has a deal, can he *prove* it? However, instead of appearing pessimistic I carefully asked, "So how do you know you have a deal?" He said, "Chris that's EASY, all you do is crunch the numbers, if it pencils out, you do the deal!" I got excited and I said, "Oh wow, can you teach me how to do that?" He said, "Sure, if you want to learn." That's where my mentorship really began.

So for over 15 years as his sole project manager, one of my duties was to evaluate potential deals by doing some pretty intense calculations and reverse engineering. First, I would have to determine what we were going to build and how much we were going to sell it for. Second, what are our hard costs such as construction and materials? Third, what are our soft costs such as planning and pulling permits? Lastly, what can we pay for the land to make a profit? In brief, I became very proficient in how developers think, analyze and determine opportunities, and ultimately earn huge profits. After working on several projects, I found my mentor's genius. His genius is the ability to see something that nobody wants and turn it into something everyone loves.

Let me explain just one of our many creative deals. Imagine a run down, dilapidated, 11-unit apartment complex where the maintenance has been deferred so much that the rents in Los Angeles are literally only $400 to $500 per month per unit. Because the rents are so low and the cash-flow so poor, this building was worth a maximum of $600,000 but the person that owned the building needed $1 million dollars just to clear the debt on the building. The building sat on the market for two years and was not able to sell. My mentor saw this <u>deal</u> and almost instantly bought it ALL CASH for $1 million. My mentor knocked it down immediately and built twelve luxury townhomes in its place. When I say luxury, I mean Berber carpet, travertine tile, granite counter tops, stainless steel appliances, etc. He built twelve luxury townhomes and sold them each for $500,000 that's a total of $6 million! Now remember he bought the apartment building for only $1 million when nobody would dare offer more than $600,000 for it...and still made a profit in the millions of dollars. Once more, he turned something that most people avoided into something people really desired.

Now after working on project after project, there was something that I personally discovered. It didn't matter what we built: homes, apartment buildings, etc. It was always profitable. This made me realize that the value is not in the end item. It's not in the house, townhome, or apartment building. The value is not in the developed real estate, <u>the value is in the land and it has been all along</u>. All my mentor is doing is simply going to that piece of land and unlocking that land's MAXIMUM value even IF there was already a structure on it. So that made me want to understand how does this asset known as land perform? More importantly, is it possible for me to buy land that's affordable in a growing area and later sell it to a developer for substantially more than what I paid? Remember, my mentor paid $1 million for a property that no one else would dare buy for more than $600,000 just to acquire the land. The answer is absolutely yes, it is possible and even probable that you can buy land affordably in a growing area and later sell it to a developer for significant profits, and that is exactly what I've learned to do best. Investing in development-ready land is exactly how I was able to retire young.

One of the things that my mentor always told me was to buy at least one piece of real estate every year to truly build wealth over time. Because of his advice, I've invested in just about every type of real estate strategy such as buying properties to rent them to build cash-flow or buying properties that I would rehab and sell quickly for profit. Let me tell you something, all of those different types of real estate investment strategies work. If you know what you're doing they're all profitable. The only point to consider is that all of those traditional real estate investment strategies fall into one category: Developed Real Estate. I mentioned before, there is no dispute that more millionaires have been created in real estate than in any other industry. But the masses, the majority of people that do invest in real estate ONLY invest in developed real estate: condos, homes, apartment buildings, shopping centers, hotels, so on and so forth. Please understand that: *whenever a majority of people are investing in the same or similar investment strategy, that particular type of investment will tend to yield lower returns usually with greater risk.*

Good judgment reveals that to make greater than average profits with less risk, you have to be doing something that the masses are not doing. That is why I teach people how to properly invest in PRE-DEVELOPED Real Estate. Most believe there are only two types of real estate categories; undeveloped and developed real estate. However, there is a third type of real estate that only exists for a very short period of time as it transitions from undeveloped to developed called pre-developed real estate. Pre-developed real estate is so misunderstood by the masses that most confuse it with undeveloped real estate, which is to buy land in the middle of nowhere, and based on pure speculation that someday somehow something *might* happen. **Pre-developed real estate is buying land that already has some infrastructure and is in the PREDICTABLE path of development where for very specific reasons something *will* happen and very soon.** Pre-developed real estate is like buying land directly next to Disneyland *before* Disneyland is built. Can you imagine the explosion in capital returns of real estate near such a massive development like Disneyland?

Let's compare two different real estate categories: developed real estate versus pre-developed real estate. Let's say you happen to have great reliable information showing that Disneyland is going to come into an area and you decide to invest in that area by buying an apartment complex. Let's say you pay $1 million for the apartment complex and five or six years later Disneyland is complete and there has been a surge of new restaurants, hotels, retail shopping, businesses, and population growth. As a result of the growth, the demand for places to live and the rents in the area have considerably increased. Now the apartment building you bought for $1 million is worth $2 MILLION. That's a great investment! Furthermore, that is the type of investment most real estate investors look for which means there would be quite a bit of competition in purchasing the apartment building to begin with.

Now let's consider instead of purchasing the apartment building for $1 million, less than one mile away on the same street, same side of the street, with the same zoning, and with utilities, you purchased a piece of land large enough for you to build THREE apartment buildings. Now because it's "ONLY land" to the mass public, you could have bought it with very little competition and for only $90,000. Within the same five to six years Disneyland is complete and developers are rushing into the area looking to cash in on the surge in prices and growth by buying land, developing it, and unlocking very large returns. In fact, developers want to buy your land and build three apartment buildings to sell for $2 million each; that's $6 million to the developer. Can you sell your land for only $1 million to the developer? ABSOLUTELY! That leaves plenty of net profit, in the millions, on the table for a developer. Selling the land you purchased at $90,000 for $1 million results in OVER a ONE THOUSAND PERCENT (1,000%) RETURN. Keep in mind, had you purchased the apartment building you would have invested $1 million and sold it for $2 million, which is only a one hundred percent (100%) return by comparison. The pre-developed real estate takes less capital to get in (because there is virtually no competition), so your risk is lower and your profit margins are SIGNIFICANTLY higher.

Here is a quick summary of the above-mentioned example, which compares the performance of developed and pre-developed real estate in a high growth area in terms of return on investment (ROI):

$$ROI = \frac{(Sale\ Price - Purchase\ Price)}{Purchase\ Price}$$

Developed Real Estate ROI:
e.g. Apartment Building

VS

Pre-Developed Real Estate ROI:
e.g. Apartment "Development-Ready" Land

Purchase Price = $1 million
Sale Price = $2 million

Purchase Price = $90,000
Sale Price = $1,000,000

$$ROI = \frac{\$2,000,000 - \$1,000,000}{\$1,000,000} = 100\%$$

$$ROI = \frac{\$1,000,000 - \$90,000}{\$90,000} = 1,011\%$$

Many people have questioned if 1,000%+ gains were true and/or even possible and the answer is YES. What's equally impressive is that if you know what you're doing and exactly how to do it, these gains can be achieved in a relatively short period of time. A high-growth area that has a growing population, growing infrastructure, growing developments and several other sources of economic stimulus places overwhelming market pressure on the shortage of developable land in that area. The growth is demand and the land is the supply. It's basic supply and demand economics, the shrinking supply of land and growing demand causes the remaining development-ready parcels of land to become *exponentially* more valuable.

Again, it is clear that the returns in developed real estate are not even close to the returns in pre-developed real estate. Nonetheless, you must know what you are doing no matter what type of investment you are getting into. You can use the following ten key growth indicators to help determine pre-developed real estate that is in the growth path of development. If even one indicator is missing, I wouldn't invest in the land and neither should you. The ten key growth indicators are:

1. The land must be flat, useable, and developable.

2. Authoritative population projections and studies must show the area is growing.

3. The area must have an abundant water supply.

4. There must be master-planned government infrastructures.

5. There must be accessibility by freeway, air, and rail.

6. There must be adequate utilities in the immediate area.

7. There must be <u>existing</u> *and* planned commercial, residential, and industrial developments within three miles.

8. The area should be within close proximity to a metropolitan city.

9. There must be existing government and private educational, medical, and public related services.

10. There must be affordable housing to accommodate a diversified job base.

I am proud to say that I no longer regard myself as an engineer. I regard myself as an investment land banker. Just in case you missed it, land banking is the practice of buying pre-developed land in the path of growth. My company's core competency is the ability to stay in front of the PREDICTABLE development process. As those developments complete, my investors and I are left in the unique position to profit SUBSTANTIALLY. John D. Rockefeller, the first American billionaire and arguably the wealthiest man in history said, "The major fortunes in America have been made in land." We've helped people from all over the world to discover the hidden wealth in land banking and we can help you too. Land banking is truly real estate's best kept secret.

About Christopher

Christopher Meza, also known as the leading authority on pre-developed real estate, is a nationally recognized speaker and best-selling author. He was the keynote speaker with Steve Forbes, Chairman and Editor-in-Chief of Forbes Magazine, at the "Success in the New Economy" conference. Christopher has also been a guest on the Brian Tracy Show interviewed by the legendary Brian Tracy on Christopher's expertise in land banking and pre-developed real estate. Christopher's feature interview can been seen on ABC, NBC, CBS, and FOX affiliates across the country or you can visit: www.ChristopherMeza.com.

Christopher is the keynote speaker for Real Titan Acquisitions, Inc., a world-leading investment company focusing primarily on pre-developed real estate and land banking. With a Bachelors of Science in Computer Science and Electrical Engineering, he has worked for Fortune 100 companies like IBM and The Boeing Company. Due to his remarkable investment savvy, he retired at a young age and now spends his time investing and successfully teaching people worldwide how to achieve financial security using his real estate investment strategies.

There is no dispute that more millionaires have been created in real estate than in any other industry. That's why so many people inherently see the value in investing in real estate. The only point to consider is that the majority of people that invest in real estate ONLY invest in developed real estate: condos, homes, apartment buildings, hotels, shopping centers, etc. Good judgment reveals that to make greater than average profits with less risk, you have to be doing something that the masses are not doing, and pre-developed real estate is just that.

To learn more about Christopher Meza visit: www.RTALand.com
or call (424) 209-RTA1.

CHAPTER 57

BEING SUCCESSFUL IN LATIN AMERICA TODAY

BY LUIS VICENTE GARCIA

Small opportunities are often the beginning of great enterprises.
~ Demosthenes, Prominent Greek statesman, 384–322 BC

We have heard for many years the importance of the opportunities that arise in new markets or new economies. And we have also heard that in some cases, some of those opportunities pass us by when we are not ready to grab them or to take advantages of them. This is true whether we are talking about introducing new products or services or when entering into new markets.

Several economies have been growing slowly during the past few years and some have not been growing at all. And if we look at companies, the same might also be happening. However, even under these economic conditions, some countries are doing much better than others as some have developed new competitive advantages, and many companies have been performing better by introducing new products, services, and technologies or entering new markets which have allowed them to grow at rates very difficult to imagine in today's world.

In simple terms, you and your company would probably prefer to be in a different position than the one you are in today; that is, to be in a bigger and faster-growing market, with more possibilities, and maybe, be present in countries that you have not thought of being in before.

Emerging markets or the now-called "frontier" markets have always interested many companies, but some are still undecided to invest in those areas. In today's economic environment we have to be open to the new market conditions and economic realities, particularly since we live in a globalized world in which the possibilities of international trade, commerce and investments are bigger than before. Even in a downward market, or when economic growth is slow, there are still many possibilities if you position yourself in the correct place. This is why part of my job is to help business owners and entrepreneurs understand about the opportunities and possibilities they have in expanding to Latin America and entering some of those key markets in the region.

There is a lot of potential in a continent as big as Latin America. Just to give you a brief overview of what I mean:

- There are 21 countries in Latin America and over 25 state islands in The Caribbean.
- It is a market of almost 600 million people.*
- Latin America's GDP was USD 5.6 Trillion in 2012, which is over one third that of the U.S. GDP.**
- Several countries in the region are some of the fastest growing economic areas in the world, which means increasing income and higher standards of living.

And this means that Latin America is growing very fast.

Its population is becoming increasingly educated, and is traveling much more; technology, the Internet and social media are enabling people to get exposure to products and services from all over the world, thus creating a demand for those products back in their home markets. Now, it is important to understand, as it has happened previously, that the company which gets to the new markets first and takes on the opportunities will have a bigger advantage over its competitors.

Several news reports which appeared in Brazilian Journals during 2010-2011, indicated that more than 40 million people in Brazil had already moved up from the poor sectors of society into the middle class of the

---

*. US Census Bureau. US & World Population: http://www.census.gov/popclock/
**. International Monetary Fund. World Economic Outlook. IMF, Washington, DC

economy; and that happened in the eight years prior to 2010.*** The interesting fact is that this is continuing to happen, not only in Brazil, but also in other countries throughout the continent. Another interesting fact is that this continent is still a very young market, where the average age of the population in Latin America is estimated at 28.9 years, according to recent information presented by the United Nations.**** Therefore, I am sure you'll agree with me when I say that if today you are not present in Latin America, there might be opportunities and potential for growth which you and your company are missing at this very moment.

Sometimes we reach a destination and do not know exactly how we got there. Have you ever driven from your office to your home and then did not realize how you got there? You probably do not remember the road you took, which houses or buildings you passed by or at which corner you turned. When you arrived, you probably felt strange not knowing how you got there, realizing that you probably passed by buildings, cars, or shops that you were not aware of. And let me ask you a question, where those buildings, parks or cars there, even though you did not notice them? The obvious answer is yes!

There are people who are searching for new ideas, products, services, strategies or possibilities that are not present in their home markets; and sometimes we, as business owners or top management, are not able to see that they might be looking for our products and services. The truth is that there are always new opportunities that are present in new markets, but sometimes we do not notice them; like we did not know how we got to our destination. We could get to a point at which, without noticing, we might let opportunities go by, as we do not look for them or act upon them when they are in front of us; and by this time, some other company will have gotten to the new markets first, and they will be the one providing a similar product or service that you could have been selling in that new market or that new economy. And again, those opportunities were there and you probably did not see them. So, how could you be the one to take up those opportunities?

I was born in Venezuela and have lived there most of my life. I have also been able to travel extensively throughout Latin America while

***. Marco Press. South Atlantic News Agency: http://en.mercopress.com/2011/06/28/almost-40-million-brazilians-climbed-to-middle-class-in-the-last-eight-years

****. United Nations Data. Average age of Population. Latin America and the Caribbean http://data.un.org/Data.aspx?d=PopDiv&f=variableID%3A41

on vacation, while working for other companies, and more recently as a business performance coach. It is very interesting to see what has happened during the past 10 to 15 years in some of these countries. As the population is growing and as the standard of living is increasing, foreign companies are coming in very fast into certain markets in the region – with new and better products and services, with new and more efficient ways of doing things. And many are still wondering if they should invest there or not. When you visit Chile, Mexico or Peru, you see that they are very different to what they were 10 or 15 years ago: they have changed and their population has changed.

I have been helping businesses and business owners grow their companies, increase profits and improve performance. As a business coach, I can see the possibilities that exist in some of these markets, the challenges that some countries present, and the growth opportunities that companies could have by entering some of the Latin American market. And my job here is to help these companies grow.

There are three main factors that you would need to understand as you prepare your company for investing in Latin America.

First: How do you engage with the local people you want to do business with? How do you connect with them? This is something that many business owners - who are looking to do business in other countries - forget about and so they immediately put themselves at a disadvantage. And it means that you need to understand that each economy is different.

- There are large and small countries, with different standards of living;
- Some have very large natural resources or vast expanses of land;
- Others are net importers of natural resources and foodstuff;
- Some countries even have a much larger manufacturing capability within the region;

And there is a very large intra-regional economic trade and you would probably want to be part of it. One bright spot in global economic news is the growth in intraregional trade among emerging markets[*****]. In total, intraregional trade makes up one-fifth of the world's total trade and is expected to surpass North-South trade flows by the year 2030.

[*****]. World Trade Organization, WTO: https://www.wto.org/index.htm

And Latin America is an important part of this growing market.

As all the economies are different in size, capabilities, educational level, development and in the way businesses perform, you need to understand the possibilities you could have in each of the markets you would like to enter, because there would be different needs for different products and services in each country.

Second: Our cultures are different and the history of each country is unique, although they may have similar roots; the fact is that our history and our cultures are different. All the countries in the region have a different geography, which presents challenges as well as diverse resources, and this differentiation would also include a mixture of people from countries of the world.****** It means that you need to know the culture and history of each of the countries where you would like to do business in, and invest in the future.

In each country you have a large cultural diversity, with different customs, different tastes, and it would explain why Pepsi will sell more in a certain areas because it tastes sweeter, or why McDonald's adjusted the flavor of its sauces to the particular tastes of each country. Some companies even do manufacturing outsourcing already in some of the Latin countries, as they are already taking advantages of the different possibilities in natural resources and educational levels.

Third: Once you understand the people and the economies, when it is time for your company to go to Latin America to invest or manufacture, you will find sometimes certain restrictions and limitations you need to be prepared for. You will be required to get permits, approvals, go through official offices and you will be confronted with the need for local help, such as advisors, counselors, coaches or consultants.

And while you understand the different cultures, realize that you would need to get the right contacts that not only speak Spanish or Portuguese, but who can also help you find the right people and put you in the right direction. It is very important to be ready and to go prepared, as you will need to make your investments and your efforts worthwhile.

Now, start to think of the opportunities you have probably missed out,

---

****** There are many sources with information on cultural issues in Latin America. Please visit UNESCO (http://en.unesco.org/), the World Bank (http://www.worldbank.org/) or one of the many organizations available.

and understand the huge potential that many of the Latin American economies are presenting to your companies at this very moment. In fact, what I have tried to explain is that there is a very large market of almost 600 million people, in a region that has been growing at an average rate of 3% per year, with a forecast GDP growth just revised by the IMF to 3.4% for 2014[*******]. It is a continent with vast natural resources, with very young, talented and qualified people, and with untapped potential.

And Latin America today has a much different reality that 10 or 20 years ago. It has developed an entrepreneurial quality and spirit that is required to bring the region to its new standards. According to the World Economic Forum, there are three Latin American countries in the top 50 of the Global Competitiveness Index for 2013-2014[********], which itself poses a bigger challenge to the whole region as it needs to grow and develop further, while becoming more competitive, if it wants to win in a globalized world.

As you know, it is entrepreneurs who invest in new businesses, promote new ideas, and who create new jobs; and they are the ones who take on the opportunities to create prosperity and growth. So seize the opportunities, act when they are presented to you or go out there and look for them, and begin to consider Latin America as an ever-expanding possibility for your company's future growth and your future development.

[*******]. International Monetary Fund, World Economic Outlook Update, July 9, 2013. http://www.imf.org/external/pubs/ft/weo/2013/update/02/ @IMF; Washington, DC.
[********]. World Economic Forum (http://www.weforum.org/), World Competitive Report 2013-2014. http://www3.weforum.org/docs/GCR2013-14/GCR_Rankings_2013-14.pdf

About Luis

Luis Vicente García is a business performance coach who has helped business owners and organizations achieve higher levels of performance in their home markets and internationally. A motivational international speaker and best-selling author, Luis has studied how personal motivation and positive attitude influence the performance and success of Businesses and Business Owners. He has lived and worked for companies with medium and large operations in Latin American countries, which has allowed him to get to know and understand many of the different cultures, economies and business climates in many of these countries.

An Economist with an MBA, with Master's Degrees in Service Enterprise Engineering, and Leadership and Management; and having just finished a Master's Degree in Strategic Organizational Leadership and Management from Michigan State University, among other studies, he is a firm believer in continuing education. Luis worked mostly in the Corporate Financial field, in both the manufacturing and service industries, and in a variety of companies: including multinational corporations and publicly-traded companies, start-ups and family-owned businesses.

Luis has published two franchising books in Spanish, *Motivando al Futuro Franquiciado* in 2010 and *101 Preguntas y Respuestas sobre las Franquicias* in 2013, and in 2013 he co-authored the best-selling book *The Ultimate Success Guide,* featuring Brian Tracy, as well as the #1 International best-selling books *Dare to Succeed* with Jack Canfield and *Ready, Aim, Influence* with Carlos Slim. He also writes his own Blog called *Motivando El Futuro* (www.motivandoelfuturo.com), a Blog on Motivation and Personal Growth. He has been married for 21 years, and has two sons.

The year 2013 marks the beginning of his new business coaching practice, as he became a Certified Business Performance Coach with FocalPoint Coaching, a company founded by Brian Tracy. Luis also has been speaking on motivation, personal development, Success and Leadership since the late 90's. In 2013, he was invited to join the Public Speakers Academy in London, and the National Academy of Best-Selling Authors in Hollywood. He was recognized with two Quilly® Awards and an EIPPY Award in September 2013, as an International Best-Selling Author.

He believes in providing people with the right tools and opportunities to learn, in motivating and coaching them to perform better, while at the same time being a promoter of continuous training, personal growth and professional improvement. A team builder, a motivator and a confidence generator, always with a positive attitude towards life, Luis Vicente believes in being a leader for the people and organization he works with.

Contact information:
www.luisvicentegarcia.com
lgarcia@focalpointcoaching.com

CHAPTER 58

THE INDUSTRY WHOSE TIME HAS COME

BY LYNN LEACH

Did you know that there is a recession proof, virtually untapped, global industry that has steadily grown for the last 20 years and actually had an 80% sales increase over the last 10 years, according to a recent Forbes Magazine report? With over $105 billion worldwide and $30+ billion in US sales, only 70 million people worldwide and 15 million US citizens are currently involved in this industry – and that is less than 1% of the world's population. The prospects for long-term global expansion are excellent. This is an industry that has steady annual growth, healthy cash flows and a high return on capital. It is an investors dream and one of the best-kept secrets in the business world. It is also, in my opinion, an answer to many financial stresses for the American economy. What is this intriguing industry? It is network marketing: the new franchising opportunity of the 21st century and a revolutionary shift in marketing.

Let's talk for a moment about why I feel network marketing can be an answer to so many of the stresses on the American economy. A recent personal development in my husband's employment has brought a new issue to light for me. My husband Norman has worked at a power plant for more than 30 years. Some devastating news was delivered to the employees of the power plant several weeks ago. Norman's plant is joining the growing list of coal-fired power stations that are closing. Because we had not been affected by any of the downsizing patterns that so many in the US have had to face, I was not particularly aware of the impact on lives this really made. I knew some people struggled with downsizing, but I had not dwelled on it, or given it much thought. But with the touching the personal lives of so many friends and co-workers, a glaring fact has reared its ugly head, and now I am aware of the impact this actually makes for certain segments of the population.

In particular, I want to address seniors. Many of the employees being let go fall into a group that is not able to retire comfortably. And when you reach a certain age, it becomes difficult to acquire a new position with a different company. And yes, I know there is not supposed to be age discrimination for hiring…but the reality of finding a job after the age of 50 is definitely difficult. Jo Ann Jenkins, the President of AARP Foundation, sent me an email yesterday and stated, "Right now, more than *2 million* Americans age 55 or older are officially unemployed. Many of these people are former – and would-be – workers who are suffering in the wake of the latest economic downturn as they compete for a limited number of jobs. Even as the economy shows signs of improving, recovery for older Americans remains painfully slow. Older workers sometimes lack the technology skills for today's jobs. Others face discrimination from employers who want younger, "more energetic" employees. As a result, older adults remain unemployed for twice as long as younger workers, approximately 54 weeks!! NETWORK MARKETING can be an answer to this issue for many who have fallen into this category.

In addition to the senior segment of the population, non-profit charities and faith-based organizations are also feeling the stress of the economy, and many are recognizing the wisdom in adopting a network marketing company to help in producing monthly residual income for sustaining programs and ministries. As non-profits build success with network marketing, more and more non-profits and churches are jumping on board with open arms of acceptance for this funding opportunity. As these groups become educated about network marketing, they begin to see how it is a powerful, legal, viable distribution method that benefits everyone on many different levels. Network marketing can help the non-profits overcome the downward dip in charitable donations and funding opportunities.

If you want to make money in today's world, you have to recognize that you need to own your own business. BUT, 90% of new brick and mortar businesses fail within the first 5 years. Business owners work long hard hours without pay for years, sometimes for 5 to 10 years. And the cost for these new start-up brick and mortar businesses is astronomical. An attractive alternative to building from scratch was buying a franchise, because all of the groundwork was already done. They are attractive, because the normal person can buy in, regardless of their business experience, education, marketing expertise, management skills, people skills, or accounting skills. It doesn't matter what your skill sets are, what your strengths or weaknesses are. You get a complete business model that is duplicable and will work for anyone. And the franchise you select has the national advertising in place for you, so the brand is recognizable and will work for anyone.

According to the International Franchise Association, 30% of all retail dollars spent in the United States are spent in franchise establishments. However the start-up costs to begin a franchise business can be extremely high, and the statistics show that 1/3 of all franchises fail. The reality is that the risk factors and the dollar investments are very high, and these put this option out of the range of most people. Network Marketing offers the same type of duplicable business model that a traditional franchise offers, but without the high costs and high risk factors.

Robert Kiyosaki, Donald Trump and Warren Buffet all recognize the wave of the future and the tremendous wealth-generating opportunity of the network marketing model and have taken advantage of adding it as one of their own personal investment strategies. An interesting fact to take note of is that 10% of new millionaires made their money in network marketing. It is not only the wave of the future, but in fact the new franchise opportunity of the 21st century.

Here are a few interesting quotes on network marketing:

Steven Covey: Bestselling author of *Seven Habits of Highly Effective People*, "Network marketing affirms people's worth and potential and can open up a whole new alternative income stream that can make a huge difference in their life. It's an entrepreneurial opportunity where people can use their talent and passion towards a greater good."

Bill Clinton: "…gives people a chance to make the most of their lives."

Tom Peters: Bestselling author *In Search of Excellence* and *Circle of Innovation* called Network Marketing "…the first truly revolutionary shift in marketing…in over 50 years."

Warren Buffet, Berkshire Hathaway, Billionaire, 2nd richest person in the world, has been out trying to buy up network marketing companies and now owns three including *Pampered Chef* – which he said was: "the best investment I ever made."

Robert Kiyosaki: author of #1 NY Times bestseller *Rich Dad, Poor Dad* has said, "Network Marketing gives people the opportunity, with very low risk and very low financial commitment, to build their own income-generating asset and acquire great wealth."

Donald Trump: "…it has proven itself to be a viable and reliable source of income."

Paul Zane Pilzer: Bestselling author of 5 books including *Unlimited Wealth*, *The Next Trillion* and *The Wellness Revolution*. He is a Wharton economist and economic advisor to two US presidents. "Yesterday's fortunes were in physical distribution: Target, Wal-Mart, Home Depot, FEDEX, etc. …For those looking to create long term wealth today, educating people one-on-one about products and services is now the #1 business opportunity – called 'intellectual distribution.' Direct selling is the perfect intellectual distribution business for today's economy."

Sir Richard Branson is one of the world's most innovative entrepreneurs. He founded Virgin Airways and Virgin Records and now owns a network marketing company called Virgin Cosmetics.

1. So why is network marketing a smart choice for so many?
2. You can start with a very low initial investment and you have little capital risk.
3. You own your own business, you are your own boss and you make your own schedule.
4. You can work from home or you can travel and work from virtually anywhere. We jokingly say, "Have cell phone, have computer – will travel!"
5. You control your income and your future. You are not dependent on what others think of you, as in the case of a boss responsible for your reviews and raises.

6. The IRS allows us amazing, legitimate tax benefits for in-home offices and owning our own small business. It is my personal belief that EVERY household should have a home-based business to take advantage of these tax benefits.

7. It allows you to have a Plan B in place in case of emergencies. A second stream of income to remove the stress and pressure of financial surprises is priceless.

8. You can build a very nice residual income stream that you can depend on – month after month after month. This is bread and butter money that can pay bills, supplement retirement and build savings.

9. You build as big or as little as you like. There is no glass ceiling.

10. You can fit this into your lifestyle and build according to your own work preferences and schedule. There are thousands of ways to market a product or a service, and you can select the ways you are comfortable with.

11. You are in business for yourself, but you are not by yourself. You have a company and mentors behind you that are vested in your success. Training is always available to you.

12. Your success is dependent on you alone and no one else. Your personal discipline and consistency will build your business as big as you desire. No one can hold you back.

13. You can become as independent as you desire.

14. Instead of trading an hour's worth of work for an hour's worth of pay, you can do the work once and get paid over and over and over again. Building with a consumable product or monthly service has a built-in reorder business for you that grows each month you continually work it.

15. You get a road map, charted course or blueprint to work from. Network Marketing businesses provide a simple, proven business plan or model just like a franchise provides, but without the extremely high costs.

16. You do not need a college education or a pedigree to join a network marketing company. Personally, I do not care how much someone has to work with – I am more concerned about the desire in their heart to change their financial situation.

- Did you know that there are over 175,000 people joining a network marketing company each week?

- Did you know that there is a new home-based business started every 12 seconds?

- Did you know that the US alone has over 38 million home-based businesses?

- Did you know that more than 2/3 of Americans would prefer to be self-employed?

- Did you know that 44% of home-based businesses are started for less than $5,000?

- Did you know that 70% of home-based businesses succeed within 3 years as opposed to 30% of the traditional brick and mortar businesses?

Many people dream of owning their own business, being their own boss and having the freedom to make their own schedules. Network Marketing gives you that time and freedom and can reduce the stress and pressure of financial problems for many people. It is not just those seniors who are at risk because of a failing economy and downsizing. Think about the average household in the United States in this era. Most people are living paycheck- to-paycheck. For many, it is not a question of becoming a millionaire. Some people just need an extra $300 to $500 a month, and that could make all the difference in the world to them. Did you know that an extra few hundred dollars a month for some people could mean that they can keep their car from being repossessed? Did you know that a few extra hundred dollars a month could save some families from having their homes foreclosed on? Unfortunately, that is the reality for many people in our country now. A few hundred dollars a month can mean some seniors can buy food in addition to needed medications, instead of trying to choose between medications and food.

How easy is it for us to share this with others? If we go out and have dinner and enjoy it, we tell our friends, family, neighbors and co-workers. But we do not get paid for it. If we see a great movie, what do we do? We share it and tell others about it so they can go see it. But again, we don't get paid for advertising that movie. Word-of-mouth advertising is so powerful. It is recognized as the best form of advertising. That is all that Network Marketing is – sharing a product or service that we love with others. And because Network Marketing relies on word-of-mouth advertising, the companies that use this form of distribution HAVE to have the best products. They have to have products that work. Because no one wants to attach their name to a product or service that is substandard. It has been proven over and over again that Network Marketing companies have some of the highest quality products and services in the market place today.

The reality is, that you can not only build a nice future for yourself with a Network Marketing business, but you can share with others and make a world of difference in their lives. How fun is it to build a solid future for yourself, create wealth for yourself, establish time and freedom for yourself while you share products you absolutely love and help other people discover financial aid in the process? Is there any reason why you would not want to get started with a Network Marketing opportunity today?

About Lynn

Lynn Leach (1952) was born in Washington, Pennsylvania, and grew up in southwestern Pennsylvania. Her birth name is Elizabeth Lynne Yankovitch, but her nickname until the age of 27 was Nikki. Her parents were the late Maryjo Handel-Mueller and Joseph Yankovitch. She lives with her husband Norman and they have 3 sons and 6 granddaughters.

Lynn has been involved in ministry since 1969, and is a retired pastor. She served on 8 different boards of directors and has been a volunteer with many non-profits and faith-based organizations since 1969.

She was in restaurant management for 13 years and enjoys cooking. She has also been involved in direct sales and network marketing since 1968. She was the first to reach PREMIER, the top position, in her primary company: Q International, and she is also the Director of Corporate Training for Emmutec. She owns COMMON SCENTS HEALTH RESEARCH & WELLNESS CENTERS, COMMON CENTS VACATIONS and LEACH PUBLISHING.

She is a #1 Best-Selling-Author who has not only co-authored several books, but has also developed her own *MENTOR WITH LYNN* Marketing Series, *WILDERNESS VOYAGE* 40 Day Devotionals Series, *IT IS WHAT IT IS* Health Series and *COMMON SCENTS COOKING* Series. She is working towards getting them all published, and is also currently working on a children's series entitled, *ADVENTURES WITH RAINBOW AND COCO.*

Lynn conducts monthly BOOT CAMP INTENSIVES, Seminars and Workshops and is available for speaking engagements.

Her main website is:www.lynnleachconsulting.com

CHAPTER 59

ONE STEP AT A TIME

BY DOUG TRAYLOR

My six-year old little girl is one of the best sales people I know. I think all of us start out trying to find out how we can get what we want in life and "learn" to put up barriers to our success along the way. That's a big part of our job as parents, managing the "no fear" attitude. If you have kids, you know exactly what I'm talking about. By the time my girl was three, she had established multiple closing techniques. She usually started with the "assumed close" and would just state what she wanted, she learned to add a "please" later. That would turn to the "pretty please" close, and of course you are all aware of the "temper tantrum" close. By the time she was just shy of five, she had honed the best one yet. We call it the "pookie eyes" that comes with a sweet voice and "butter-up" disposition. Usually works on me. What happened to that gift at birth? Loosely quoting Plato, I recall he said "as children most of us are afraid of the dark, as adults most of us are afraid of the light."

Sometimes it takes a desperation moment to get what you want to light that fire to figure out how. I started writing this based on a golden ticket moment that changed the direction of my career and realized that what I gained from the experience was not about a resume builder or the financial gain, but a change in philosophy that would alter my life. I had worked with many wealthly people in my life and this would turn out to be a very unique and perspective- changing experience. I'm now face-to-facc with a legendary Texas Billionaire.

The gentleman in question is a life-long achiever, and I have learned that people of this caliber and time on earth genuinely want to impart wisdom to everyone they work with. I was fortunate to be on the receiving end of some of his life lessons. He enjoyed competition and was very good in getting your full attention to earn his business. In one of our first few meetings, he had asked "do you want to win this?" and of course I jumped in emphatically and said, "Yes Sir." Soon after, I was feeling the education; he let us know that nobody that works with him doesn't want to win. Winning is nothing special at this level, and that only people that prepare to win and can execute to win, will actually do so. Lesson number one, bring your "A+" game because your "A" game might not get the deal done.

Fast forward to the end, yes, after almost a year of working, me and my fellow teammates did earn the largest financial client in our company's history. I can't give you all the details on how we prevailed, but I can most confidently tell you that it was far more about what was LEARNED vs. what was EARNED. I can tell you that the months it took to win this man's business was nothing short of a typical great story. It was your usual 3-act play. Imagine any of your favorite classics like the *Wizard of Oz* and you might find that many of them follow this basic story line.

Act I: As you might imagine we were simply ecstatic to have the opportunity to earn even a sliver of this man's business, and thrilled we were going to get to work with his team. The phone rings, we're not the only ones working on it. We get thrown a "winner takes all" curveball!

Act II: We were using all of the skills we usually use to get the deal done and encountering massive roadblocks. It was time to find out if we could think outside the box, and in this case, ditch the box altogether. Were we capable of beating the competition? It was time to stretch our minds and perspective.

Act III: We present the final proposal and ask ourselves if we had prepared enough to win, did we execute to win? In Quentin Tarantino fashion, you know the answer. A typical Tarantino film starts with almost the end. So what is left of this story? The story of my greatest reward, a new philosophy.

What did I learn from this experience and the many significant clients and mentors I have enjoyed since then? I said it was about a change in philosophy. I can never learn enough, grow enough, or stretch what that means far enough. I hope to have a hundred things on my bucket list when I actually do kick it. For the sake of delivering quick takeaways that hopefully some of you may recognize in yourself, I will start with five things I was convinced I knew were right and follow those up with my post philosophy change.

How I thought before:

1. Always Be Closing! This is the very root of the sales training I had growing up – The ABC's.

2. Double your efforts to double your results.

3. If it is to be – it is up to me. YOU have to make the deal happen.

4. I need to cast a broader net to catch more fish.

5. I'm so good now I only need to focus on my selling.

Tips from a better philosophy:

1. NEVER BE CLOSING. The best clients or relationships don't want to be closed or sold, they want to be served. Focus on how you and your product or service can serve their wants and needs. Alphas have a tendency to extend beyond authenticity to get a deal done without the forecasting of what this may cost them in the relationship. We do business with and buy into people we trust, you can never give up authenticity to a sales technique. It does not mean that you should not be Convincing, Confident, and I emphatically recommend Caring. What it does mean is that you should avoid popular sales techniques like answering a question with a question to "control" the conversation. If you have the ability to answer the client's questions you should try and do so, and then continue to gather more necessary information. If you have ever bought a car you have probably asked the salesman what the bottom line was and found the avoidance of the true answer and a concentration on how much you can afford a month. Your clients appreciate this about as much as you do. I realize many of you will be sending me the Alec Baldwin movie clip from Glengarry Glen Ross.

2. Double down on efforts and you may just blow a gasket in the whole engine. Our natural tendency says if we want to double our income we have to double everything you're doing today. This is usually just not plausible and it really doesn't force you to stretch your talents. My coach has taught me that the answer to too much is not more, but to imagine what my environment has to look like for my goals to be met and its usually easier to double your income or sales by imagining an x-factor. I have proven this in my own life.

3. I found the "I" in team and it's hidden in the A-hole.' A photo of this t-shirt was e-mailed to me and I think it was a message. You can be the star; the franchise player, the rainmaker, whatever, but YOU CAN'T DO IT ALONE! Respect, inspire, and empower those with different talents than yours. If you are the rainmaker and those around you are the implementors, be careful you are not the "I" in TEAM.

4. For most of us in sales and marketing, a strategic approach will move the needle more than a tactical one. Don't count on casting a wide net to yield your dream clients. Focus on identifying who they are and go after them with focus, drive and determination. This goes for your entire sales community. If everyone is on the same page of identifying a perfect client for your product or service, you increase the odds dramatically. It's actually easier than most people think because it's part of our human nature. Technically it's called your Reticular Activating System. But in terms of an analogy, have you ever bought something you thought was new and unique only to see several other people with the same purchase shortly after? It's that easy to get people to find the best prospects you want. When you find them, treat them special.

5. You can never stop sharpening the saw. I will save you the story because if you are reading SuccessOnomics, you probably have already heard that one before, but many of us get complacent with our talents and forget to keep studying, working to better ourselves, and overcoming our internal objections to more success, higher achievement and greater personal fulfillment.

This adventure in a new and revised philosophy of achievement is barely a few years old for me; you may ask what has happened since? I will tell you that I have sought the best information from the best advisors, coaches, and mentors I could find. I have gained more and given more than at any other time in my life.

The rest of this chapter is dedicated to why you will read this and possibly understand and agree with most everything I say and do nothing in your life to make any change at all.

I always loved the quotes in the back of Forbes magazine on the "thoughts of business of life" and kept a folder of my favorites. One of the first I loved to use when I was a young restaurant manger was a Zen quote I read in the 80's in the back of Forbes. "To know and not do is not yet to know" I wrote this on the wall of the kitchen before staff entered the dining room as a reminder of my management message.

Many years later this would come to my mind and I would realize the message was for me. I would get motivated, listen to the greats like Tony Robbins and Stephen Covey and the motivation would wear off shortly. I would always fall back. In other words, to know and not do.

Why do we wash ourselves with great information and never take action on the takeaways or golden nuggets that we get from our endeavor to sharpen the saw? Is it our fear or flight response? According to the great Wikipedia it is in response to the negative. I will tell you that this is most abundant in me at the point of great opportunity. It's the fear of failure at the point of great opportunity that sends my flight response. Fear-freeze and runaway is our most primal fallback position. Stress and nervousness is often greater at the point of anticipation than it is in the middle of the very act that got you going to begin with.

The day I'm not nervous stepping onto the first tee,
that's the day I quit!
~ Tiger Woods

I will admit that a golden ticket moment sent me running to expand my mind. But I hope that it does not take that for you. It could just start with a simple question, "Do you still have a sense of amazement?"

My golden ticket moment was only a trigger to start seeking the best of the best in advisors and friends. I was now more receptive to other signs and signals that my real work started with working on myself. That moment came and went just like the seasons do and I needed to work towards a new spring. Just like the three act play, I was thrown a few more curveballs in my life. What I can tell you is that I recently met a man through my awesome business coach that has put my prescription for change better than anyone before.

Step into the pain. If you hear, see or read a concept you believe in, don't just agree with it, surrender to it and make it happen.

The conversation you have been putting off the most is probably the one you need to have next. *Step into the pain.*

Don't feel like going to the gym, *step into the pain.*

Figure out who the engines and anchors are in your life and you know what to do next. *Step into the pain.*

I am grateful for all of the people who have told me that success is a series of corrected failures. Otherwise I may have given up a long time ago. My father always told me if it was easy, everyone would do it.

So here is to your own SuccessOnomics, one step at a time!

About Doug

Doug Traylor is the President and Co-Founder of VIP Insurance Group as well as the founder of ROE1.com, a consulting company. Doug is a financial product designer, distributor, marketer, collaborator and consultant. In addition to entrepreneurship, Doug is dedicated to education, writing and speaking on the topic of personal growth.

Over the past twenty years Doug has worked with millionaires, billionaires, celebs, pro athletes, politicians, and professors. He has been endorsed by professional associations and contracted by top Banks to provide training and product to their financial advisors.

"The greatest title I've ever had is Daddy. I have found that people don't follow titles; they follow people willing to risk the lead. My daily battles are: procrastination, focus, fears of failure, fear of great success, not being a morning person, how well did I 'show up'? and how full is the glass?"

CHAPTER 60

CHOICES AND NOT CIRCUMSTANCES WILL MAKE YOUR DESTINY

BY SHANDON PHAN

My story starts out in Saigon, Vietnam where I was born. After the communists had taken over South Vietnam, my father was sent to re-education camp and my mother forced to work far away. I spent the first few years of my life living with my aunt in meager conditions.

Even when my father returned home, he couldn't get a job and was forced to live as an outsider in our neighborhood. I was taught throughout my childhood that the key to survival is to stay low profile, take the safe path, work hard, and do what I'm being told. I thought that was the formula and I should stick to it.

That formula wasn't a bad one. Following it led me to hold first or second place in all my classes from first grade to tenth grade when I and my family immigrated to America. Following it led me from being a social outcast in my early childhood to being admitted into the top high school in Vietnam for gifted students.

It wasn't until I came to America that I could really develop my own personality and build my confidence. I arrived in Lake Charles, Louisiana. As I grew to be more adventurous, more confident, and more optimistic in my outlook, I realized that there is no fixed formula for success in life.

The past eighteen years living in America did magic on me as I grew, adapted, and transformed into who I am today. Living my freedom to the maximum – I took on every opportunity along the way, determined to chart my own path.

After one week of settling in, my aunt took me and my sister to the local public high school and enrolled us. I didn't speak much English, was very shy, and felt out of place. There were only a few Asian kids at my high school and most were born here, from other Asian countries. I didn't have many friends and spent most of my time studying. I worked after school in a Chinese restaurant, washing dishes, waiting tables, and doing whatever kitchen chores required. It was hard work and I experienced loneliness and embarrassment sometimes, but I decided to focus on all the positive things and strived to make the best of it.

In America, my siblings and I had free lunches and free tuition. Our teachers were nice and caring, campus was much cleaner, and classes were much more interesting. I only had a very old bicycle in Vietnam, and as a kid, could never make any money. Here, I was able to work in different part-time jobs, saved my money and bought my first car. I enjoyed the fact that I could choose which classes I wanted to take. I loved my freedoms and all the opportunities here in America.

There was no ESL (English as a Second Language) curriculum at my school district and all classes were conducted in English. Even though I had finished my tenth grade in Vietnam, I was required to retake my ninth and tenth grades. That didn't seem to make any sense to me and there must be a way. After a few days of thinking, I approached my counselor and requested her help to get me to where I need to be – in eleventh grade. It turned out that if the school district does offer basic course tests for those two grades and if I can pass all of them, I can obtain sufficient school credits to move me into eleventh grade. I studied hard, took all required tests, and two months later, gained fourteen credits to skip two grades and join the school's junior class.

One day, Ms. Hannum, my Chemistry teacher, asked me if I thought of going to college, and when I said yes, she asked me what school I planned to attend. I had no idea. She told me she would help me pick a few schools to request application materials. I eventually got a scholarship to attend Tulane University, one of the best colleges in the

South. I graduated from my high school seventh in my class, and was the first one in my family to go to college. My family, especially my father, who had moved to Houston, Texas to find a job, was proud of me.

I never forgot the kind guidance and encouragement Ms. Hannum provided me. Like other great friends and inspiring mentors who appeared later on in my life, Ms. Hannum saw potential in me and helped guide me in the right direction and gave me the extra push to go further.

Fast forward ten years later, I had moved to Washington, DC and obtained my law degree, fell in love with a beautiful lady and started a family with her. By this time, I had charted an interesting path for myself: holding a high-level non-profit executive position, running a consulting business, receiving a gubernatorial appointment, being elected as a delegate to the Republican National Convention and serving in a leadership role for my Senator John McCain's presidential bid in 2012, participating in various leadership programs and honor societies in Washington DC, running marathons, and traveling the world in my free time.

Then the urge of entrepreneurship hit me. Against the advice of most of my friends and family, I left my steady salary job to launch my own law practice. It was a risky move as my savings wouldn't last more than three months and I knew nothing about starting and running a firm.

After several years of hard work, I have built a good client-base, won over a million dollars in aggregate settlement for my clients, and am currently working with a selected group of other entrepreneurial-minded lawyers around the country to pioneer a new law practice model that can better serve my clients with fixed fee, personalized legal services and create positive changes in the legal profession.

I take pride in having the trust of my clients – among whom are many multi-millionaire business owners, including one who built a billion-dollar international business. As I counsel and represent them on legal matters, I have learned from them valuable lessons on life and business.

Many of my attorney friends who have practiced law much longer than I, have frequently complained about their law practice or chose to return to work for big law firms. What is the reason for my happiness and entrepreneurial success?

I believe in the power of faith and courage in business. Every time I stick to my guns and make a decision to take on a big risk, I let go of any backup plan or escape ship, so that I only have one way to go – to keep moving forward and doing whatever it takes to succeed. Oftentimes, people, despite having all the resources and advantages, never truly move forward in business and be successful. We have to decide to go all-in to make it work.

I burned my bridges when I decided to leave everything behind in Washington, DC to move across the country to pursue the BP Oil Spill case. I turned down an attractive partnership offer to lead a top real estate and business brokerage firm, a highly coveted civic leadership program, and other opportunities to devote myself to learning a new area of law and providing the best representation for my clients.

I swallowed my pride and borrowed money from families and friends to rent a new office, buy equipment, and hire staff even though I knew I wouldn't be able to make it back in legal fees for at least another year! When the money didn't come as expected, I even sold my Lexus, my only means of transportation, and my wife's ring, to continue representing my clients.

A recent study points out that immigrants are four times more likely to become millionaires than those who are native-born, despite the fact that they encounter numerous challenges, including linguistic barriers, cultural differences, lack of social connections, and other obstacles. Is it because they are smarter or work harder? I think not.

What separates the successful ones from others is that these individuals maximize their freedoms and have developed the mindset of constantly learning, adapting, and doing what is necessary to achieve success. My growing up time in Lake Charles, Louisiana remains my fondest time as I woke up every morning with the belief that America is full of opportunities and I set out to find them and seize such opportunities. I washed dishes, cooked and waited tables, painted houses and mowed lawns, but never saw myself as a dish-washer, a waiter, a house painter, etc. I had a dream of where I wanted to go, who I wanted to be, and those hard jobs were necessary sacrifices; they were the price I must pay in order to achieve higher stations in life. So, I embraced these times as they helped build my perseverance and character for the bigger games later.

The choices you make will shape your destiny. It is choices, not circumstances, that define your success in life. So I focused on making good choices and not letting circumstances control my future.

Being American has special meaning to me. Freedom has empowered me in so many ways and allowed me to grow into the entrepreneur I am today. My experiences in community service, political activism, and entrepreneurship have taught me a lot about life and even more about myself.

A year after graduation, I was asked to give a speech to Army personnel about my American experience. I sat down and wrote a list of lessons I learned from my own experiences and the wisdom of many other mentors who guided me along the way. The lessons below are an extended version of that list.

LESSONS I LEARNED

1. *Develop your vision.* You decide what kind of person you want to be, the lifestyle you want to live, and the legacy you want to leave behind. You only have one life to live, live well and realize your own life vision.

2. *Develop a success mindset.* The human mind is the most powerful thing on Earth. Yet, it works just like a computer program. You get out of it what you put into it. If you feed it with positive thoughts and train it for maximal performance, it can lead you to accomplish extraordinary results. If ill-equipped through lack of knowledge and weak mental power, it will lead you towards the path of failure and misery.

3. *Never Say No to an opportunity.* A year into launching my own law practice, a friend called and asked me to consider moving to the Gulf Coast to represent fishermen and local businesses affected by the BP Oil Spill. The law was complex, the chance of recovery uncertain, and the cost of representation is high — as few firms can afford the up-front expenses required. Yet, I knew the demographics and could connect with most clients better than many attorneys. I appreciated the strategic impact of working on such a significant case. So, in less than 48 hours, I talked to my wife, packed up, and

moved my young family in a U-Haul to Biloxi. It was a long, hard, and at times, lonely fight, but more than a year later, my efforts bear fruit and I successfully won recoveries for many of my clients. I saw an opportunity, a risky one with strategic impact that can leapfrog my firm above others if I succeed, and I decided to run with it.

4. *Take action and keep moving forward.* Many people have good ideas but few achieve success because they never set out to develop a plan and act on it decisively and consistently. The most common reasons are that they become intimidated by risks and challenges, and their minds naturally start to lead them away from their dream in favor of staying the same course, doing the same safe and familiar things. You must master the ability to shift your mind from focusing too much on risks to what is possible… and chart a path forward.

5. *Be willing to do what others are not.* Channel your faith into making that courageous decision and make necessary sacrifices to reach your goals. Nothing in this life is free. If you want to make a positive change in your life, you have to be willing to pay the price for what you want. What you are doing now is paying for what you will be getting. Pay it forward.

6. *Build Your Brand and Guard your Reputation.* Your words are your brand. Commit and stay true to your core values and principles. Reflect on your own experience and write down your core values on paper. This helps gain clarity and focus to make the right decisions against temptations or challenges.

7. *Stand your ground in the face of adversity.* Any road to success will be filled with obstacles that you must persevere with and overcome. As a young solo practitioner with no money, I struggled to keep my practice afloat and fought against much more powerful competitor firms. There were days of despair and self-doubt when I did not have money to buy printing paper or lunch. But I kept pushing on – one thing at a time – with the belief that I could finish by taking one step forward at a time. I told myself that these hardships are only temporary and if I gave up, I would have to face a loser every morning in the mirror. I just had to overcome these setbacks, one at a time. I believed things would get better. And they did.

8. *The How matters.* Your actions, no matter how just your motive is, are only effective when they are carried out in the right way. How you do something is just as important as why you do something.

Your tone, voice volume, facial expression and body language are just as important as your words. I learned this costly lesson when my words to a trusted business partner were taken the wrong way and led to the deterioration of our partnership. It cost both of us our investment as the partnership fell apart, and looking back, I know I did not really exercise good form in communicating with him.

9. *Any decision is better than no decision.* We live in an abundant society with so many choices, so much data, but with the same 24 hours a day. An essential trait you must develop, whether in managing your own life, family, or organization, is the ability to make decisions quickly. Do not wait for the perfect scenario to happen before you act.

10. *Always be learning. Embrace change.* It is insanity to expect to get a different result by doing the same thing over and over. Many people want to change their lives, but at the same time, they don't want to step out of their comfort zones to make any real changes.

11. *Prepare. Prepare. Prepare.* There is no such thing as overnight success. It is the months and years of intentional struggle and preparation leading to that moment when everything comes together. <u>Discipline is the key to your achieving success</u>.

12. *Donate your time. Give generously.* It will come back threefold. We live in an ever inter-connected world and it is important that you add value to your community. If you develop a purpose greater than yourself, you will enrich your life with more love, trust, respect, and long-lasting relationships. Not only that, giving with compassion will make you feel very good inside, it will transform you into a better human being with a ripple effect on others around you.

About Shandon

Shandon Phan is the Founder and Managing Partner of the Shandon Phan Law Firm located in Houston, Texas. Shandon is dedicated to serving as trusted advisor to families and businesses and guiding his clients in making the very best legal, financial and business decisions throughout their lifetime and ensuring the long-term wellbeing of their families.

Though he focused on litigation in his law study and early career and successfully won approximately one million dollars in aggregate settlements for his clients in several high profile cases, he has discovered his true passion is helping his clients build a strong foundation for their success and preserve their family legacy. He has developed a highly personalized practice in estate planning and business planning to help individuals, families, and business owners.

Shandon Phan has been designated by the Family Wealth Planning Institute as a Creative Business Lawyer™ and a Personal Family Lawyer®.

As a Personal Family Lawyer™, Shandon helps families with young children, special needs families, business owners, unmarried couples and individuals with protecting their family wealth and legacy. With a unique ability to listen to client concerns, he has translated his client's vision into a plan that meets their desires and exceeds their expectations.

Shandon is also a Creative Business Lawyer™, helping entrepreneurs and business owners with the myriad of legal, financial and tax issues that arise, and designs a plan to ensure that the business not only has the best chance of success, but continues to "live on" long after the founder is gone.

He is also a member of the Wealth Counsel, a nationwide organization comprised of estate planning professionals, including attorneys, tax and financial planners who utilize cutting edge techniques for sophisticated planning.

He is the author of *Legal Guide for Families* (currently being published) and frequently speaks to both public and private groups as well as Attorneys, Accountants, and other financial professionals.

Shandon is proud to be among a new breed of entrepreneur-minded, dynamic and pioneering attorneys who embrace the newest technologies and constantly seek new ways to provide the best values to their clients. In addition to serving clients at his offices in Houston, Texas and the Gulf Coast, he also serves clients around the country and internationally with online estate and business planning legal services — via phone, email and a secure online platform.

Coming to America as a young immigrant, Shandon appreciates his American freedom and strives to give back to his community and country. He has volunteered his service to local and international charities, held many civic leadership positions, founded a chamber of commerce, served in voluntary bar associations, and been recognized by U.S. Congress and U.S. Coast Guard for his legal contributions and service to his country.

In his spare time, he practices martial arts, enjoys the outdoors and running, and has completed three Marine Corps marathons. He aspires to compete in an Ironman full triathlon one day.

CHAPTER 61

RETIREMENT PEACE OF MIND THROUGH SAVING AND INVESTING

BY MARC KORSCH, MBA, ChFEBC

As a culture, we focus a lot on performance. We want our athletes to be all-stars, our cars to be hotrods and our singers to blow the roof off the concert hall. That's understandable, but as a financial advisor it took me awhile to separate this cultural love affair with performance from my primary obligation to my clients. Once I did, I soon discovered not only the entire context for my conservative business model, but a compelling way of demonstrating its value based on three principles: stock market history, the dangers of "reverse" dollar cost averaging, and the ability of income-generating investment options to deliver something even more important than performance.

There's a natural tendency in my business to automatically assume that what a person wants first and foremost when he seeks the guidance of a financial advisor is to see his money "perform" well. Translation: portfolio growth and capital gains. While that may be true in some cases, I have found that most people who come to me for advice are at a point in their lives where they have priorities that trump performance, whether they realize it or not.

We all know that the risk-tolerance level of most people decreases with age, and since most of those I deal with are either at or near retirement age, they already instinctively recognize the potential risk and shortsightedness of an overemphasis on performance when it comes to their money. Naturally, they want to see their savings and investments "do well" and for their portfolio to grow, but ultimately that's less important than being able to enjoy their retirement years comfortably and with a genuine sense of security.

Now, earlier I used the term "whether they realize it or not" because I've discovered that many of these people don't even know, themselves, where their priorities lie until I help them figure it out. I do that by posing a simple and direct question: "Would you say that your financial goals are primarily performance-based or purpose-based?"

I elaborate by explaining that "performance-based" means they are mainly interested in getting competitively better returns than the next guy on their investments regardless of their personal financial needs, while "purpose-based" means they are mainly interested in earning enough, with reasonable risk, to achieve their goals – which usually include never running out of income and possibly leaving something behind for their loved ones. The vast majority of people I deal with – 99% in fact – say their goals are "purpose-based." That's not really surprising, but what is surprising is how many of them have never really asked *themselves* that same question, or thought about their financial goals in those terms.

Once a person has come to that important realization, his mind invariably leaps to the next logical question, which is: "What are my best options for achieving my purpose-based financial goals?" For me, that's a question that can only be satisfactorily answered "in context," and some of the information most relevant to providing that context has to do with stock market history.

Most people have read or heard somewhere that the stock market generally delivers about a 10% average return over time, roughly 7-to-8% of that in growth, the smaller percentage in dividends. What they don't understand, however, is that the growth average is determined by factoring together long, long periods of time when the market delivers 12-to-15% growth, and equally long periods when it delivers zero. That is the reality of long-term secular market cycles, which can be graphed with incredible precision over the course of two centuries of market history:

- 0% growth secular bear cycles: 1899-1921, 1929-1954, 1966-1982, 2000-?

- 12-15% growth secular bull cycles: 1921-1929, 1954-1966, 1982-2000

Dig a little deeper into market history and you realize that not only has the duration of these secular cycles been remarkably consistent (16-to-20 years or more), but that they share other important characteristics as well. Most significant among these is that every secular bear market cycle has included at least three *major* market drops. In addition, certain economic indicators, such as price-to-earnings ratios, have always foretold the switching points between secular bull and bear cycles.

So how is this condensed history lesson relevant to the purpose-based retiree or near-retiree? Well, obviously getting 0% return on any investment over a 20-year stretch (actually less than 0 if you factor in inflation), is not conducive to *either* purpose-based or performance-based objectives if we happen to be in the middle of a long-term secular bear cycle – which, as of this writing, we are.

The problem (and the reason investing can be so challenging) is that many people aren't even aware of the concept of long-term secular market cycles; they think only in terms of *cyclical* market cycles, which play out in months or just a few years, as opposed to decades. Of course, this lack of common knowledge about secular cycles is hardly surprising when you consider that brokers, most advisors and the financial media *only* focus on cyclical cycles because that's an easier way of selling optimism. Wall Street knows people are more apt to stay invested in the market when they're optimistic and believe it's on an upward trend. What sounds more optimistic: that a cyclical "bull rally" is in full swing or that our current zero-growth secular bear market cycle is likely to drag on for at least another five years?

What's more, many people become accustomed to paying close attention to cyclical cycles because they have 401(k)s and are saving for retirement using a dollar cost averaging strategy: investing equal amounts regularly in a mutual fund, thus purchasing more shares when prices are down and fewer shares when prices are up, reducing their average cost-per-share over time.

I bring this up because one of the most common financial mistakes people make is to maintain a mutual fund post-retirement and start drawing regular income from it. Essentially they are "reverse" dollar cost averaging because by removing level income they end up taking out a greater percentage of assets when values are reduced and less when they are improved, ultimately "cannibalizing" the fund. Nothing could be more counter-productive to a "purpose-based" retirement strategy than reverse dollar cost averaging, especially if your objective is to make sure you never run out of income.

So now that we've established this important context, let's go back to that question: "What are my best options for achieving financial goals that are more purpose-based?" In short, the answer is instruments designed to deliver consistent income through interest and dividends, specifically: CDs, government bonds, fixed annuities, municipal bonds, corporate bonds, preferred stock and some real estate investment trusts (R.E.I.T.s).

Surprisingly, just as most people are unaware of the very concept of long-term secular market cycles, many are also extremely limited in their knowledge about the universe of income-generating investment options. That's probably due in large part to the issue I talked about earlier: our cultural obsession with performance. The plain truth is, these instruments *aren't* hotrods or all-stars and they won't ever blow the roof off the concert hall. They're not as sexy as investment tools geared toward reaping huge capital gains or massive portfolio growth. In fact, you might even call them dull, boring and old-fashioned. They are not "performers" in that flashy sense of the word, but they *will* deliver if your goals are purpose-based – and, again, that covers about 99% of the people I work with!

As a matter of fact, income-generating investments aren't merely the "best" option for achieving purpose-based financial goals, they're really the *only* option for three reasons:

1. They pose little risk (many are insured).

2. They work *regardless* of secular cycles, cyclical cycles, major drops or anything else going on in the stock market.

3. They generate income through interest and dividends, which means your portfolio has much less volatility and can, in fact, enjoy strategic "organic" growth.

Most people immediately understand the common sense in a strategy that allows them to live off income generated through interest and dividends without ever having to draw down on principal. It's actually as far from reverse dollar cost averaging as you can get because not only are you not "cannibalizing" your nest-egg, but you can take the income you don't need immediately and reinvest it in *other* instruments designed to generate even *more* interest and dividends. I like to describe that as growing your portfolio "organically" – in other words, naturally and safely. It's my alternative to the "Miracle-Gro" strategies touted by many performance-based advisors promising fast, phenomenal growth. While those kinds of strategies can, indeed, sometimes work as advertised, they can also destroy or greatly damage an otherwise healthy garden! I have seen this happen far too many times, but let me share just one example:

A nice couple I know, Jack and Mary, went to see an advisor when Jack turned 60 to help them plan for his retirement at age 65. This was in 1999, just before the major stock market drop of 2000 that kicked off our current secular bear market cycle (remember, every secular bear cycle has at least three such drops). Unfortunately for Jack and Mary, this advisor simply presumed their goals were performance-based and came up with a plan based on "miracle growth" and capital gains. Well, not surprisingly, their garden shriveled and they lost money for four straight years. By the fifth year, of course, it was time for Jack to retire and he and Mary finally recognized the need to plan for income. Only then did they realize the extent of the damage. Instead of a portfolio capable of generating their desired $54,000 a year in income, they had to adjust that down to $30,000 a year. It was either that or face the likelihood of depleting their entire savings by 2012 – just eight years after Jack's retirement! Not only did they lose principal in the downturn, even worse they lost nearly half their retirement income.

Now, what might have been the difference if Jack and Mary had realized in 1999 that their financial goals were primarily purpose-based? Well, potentially they would have enjoyed a lifetime's worth of income at the level they wanted...with money to spare!

Unfortunately, this story is not unusual for many of the very reasons I've talked about: People tend not to realize, themselves, that their financial goals are more purpose-based than performance-based until you pose the question in those very terms. They're generally unaware of secular market cycles and the lessons of stock market history. They don't know about the dangers of reverse dollar cost averaging, and they have a limited knowledge about the universe of income-generating investment options.

On top of all that, there is simple human nature. Even when people do recognize the sense and logic in purpose-based financial planning, if there is one thing I've learned over the years it's that most people don't make decisions based on pure logic. In fact, most financial decisions are driven by two very basic human emotions: fear and greed. That's not a bad thing, necessarily, just a fact. We're all simply hard-wired to a certain extent to want as much as we can get as quickly as we can get it. That's why the stock market looms so large on our cultural landscape, why it's the first thing most people probably think of when they hear the word "invest." It is tied to performance, after all, and intrinsically linked to those very basic human emotions.

Years ago, that connection used to throw me off, and lead me to make quick and false assumptions about what people really wanted in a savings and investment plan. But once I began asking them one simple question, I discovered – and helped them discover – that performance wasn't really their highest priority for their hard earned savings. They had a higher *purpose* in mind and, thankfully, I soon had a way of showing them exactly how to achieve it.

About Marc

Marc F. Korsch, MBA, ChFEBC is a native of the Sarasota area and has been in the financial services industry for over ten years. Marc previously spent time as a CPA, and auditor, for the big five accounting firm KPMG. Among other accomplishments, Marc strives to educate his clients on how to invest profitably and avoid loss by providing conservative options. He is dedicated to helping his clients reap the rewards of a well-planned retirement.

In addition, Marc Korsch is a well-established speaker in the Gulf Coast area and is committed to educating the community with his workshops on topics relating to conservative alternatives, educational workshops on savvy Social Security planning, and his courses at State College of Florida. Furthering his dedication to education, Marc is an approved educator of the nonprofit group S.A.F.E. He is also a member of the Better Business Bureau, National Ethics Association, and Chamber of Commerce.

CHAPTER 62

DISPELLING THE MYTHS OF WALL STREET

BY MARK H. WITT

INTRODUCTION

The crowd eagerly awaits the emergence of the star from backstage. The moment has arrived. The roar is deafening as he walks on stage. No, I'm not at a Kenny Chesney concert. I'm at a Broker Dealer conference with hundreds of my colleagues, fellow investment advisors. We await a *rock star* money manager to espouse his philosophy on how to "beat the market." And beat the market he has done. For the previous decade he was ranked as one of the World's Best Money Mangers. With the retail mutual fund industry in decline, the ability to partner with the world's best institutional money managers is intriguing.

The well-dressed gentleman confidently walks onto the stage. He has the presence of Paul Harvey. There is an air of sophistication as he speaks. He travels the world in search of the best stocks. He manages money for some very powerful and influential people. We learn firsthand about his money management philosophy; a system based on extensive quantitative research and technical analysis. His tactical portfolio practically guarantees *participation in bull markets while avoiding participation during inevitable market downturns*. It's as though he has discovered the magical formula that ensures investing success: exceptional profits in rising markets and a knack for avoiding losses in down-market cycles.

Trouble is this *rock star* manager fell from the top echelon of his profession to mediocrity in the span of two years. He was unable to duplicate his past heroics. The magic was gone. He did not have a crystal ball nor had I found the holy grail of investing. So one day I called his office to talk about his firm's dismal performance. He gave me a number of excuses from monetary policy to extreme weather patterns (yes, he even blamed the weather). My response was "you are willing to take credit when returns are outstanding but are unwilling to accept responsibility when returns are negative." And I will never forget his answer: "Listen, we can't get it right every time. Deal with it."

Intellectually I already knew the truth: no one can *consistently* predict the movement of the stock market. And, at that moment I began a relentless journey to discover the truth in investing. Stay with me for a few minutes and I will reveal the fundamental principles to becoming a confident successful investor.

RETURNS COME FROM THE MARKET NOT THE MANAGER

Admit it. You want to find the next "genius" to manage your money. Who wouldn't? Peter Lynch's record as Fidelity Magellan's manager still stands as the most remarkable in mutual fund history. While other fund managers have gone on notable streaks, nobody can touch Peter Lynch's run – not before, during, or since. Lynch was one in a million.

According to John Bogle in *Common Sense on Mutual Funds:* "roughly 80% of all mutual fund managers fail to even meet the return of the S&P 500 every year, let alone exceed it." The other 20% can't sustain their above average performance for more than a few years. If mutual fund managers with graduate degrees in finance from Wharton or Stanford can't beat the market, do you really think you can?

Investors must realize that true stock market returns are realized by owning a highly diversified mix of assets across multiple asset classes on a global scale and **not** by constantly trying to find a mutual fund manager who is all too willing to prove his investing prowess with *your* money.

My investing philosophy is simple, yet powerful. We design portfolios using structured engineered asset class funds. We purchase institutional class funds only. These funds are typically available only to the most sophisticated investors. These funds buy a cross-section of stocks in any given asset category, and often employ highly effective trading strategies to minimize trading costs to the portfolio.

Check out how generous market returns can be:

- U.S. Micro Cap stocks, 12.26%; 1927-2012
- S&P 500 (Large U.S.), 9.82%; 1927-2012
- Small Cap Value, 14.77%; 1927-2012
- Large Value, 11.64%; 1927-2012
- International Small Companies, 14.40%; 1970-2012
- International Large Companies, 9.06%; 1970-2012

Quit looking for the next Peter Lynch. Returns come from the Market not the Manager!

WHY MARKET TIMING IS A BAD IDEA

So you want to be *in the market* when equities are soaring and *out of the market* when equities are falling? Etch this in your memory: For a market timing approach to succeed, you must be correct *twice…* when you leave the market **and** when you get back in. Time and time again studies show that investors who try to second-guess the market's direction will get burned. Market timing is any attempt to guess the direction of the market. Remember the *rock star* manager? His sales pitch was: *our tactical portfolio will participate in bull markets and avoid participation during inevitable market downturns.* Reread that last sentence. Does that sound too good to be true?

"After nearly 50 years in the business, I do not know of anybody who has done it (market timing) successfully and consistently. I do not even know anybody who knows anybody who has done it successfully and consistently" – John Bogle, Founder of Vanguard Funds.

From 1991-2010 a Dalbar Research study found if you stayed fully invested in large U.S. growth stocks, a $100,000 investment would have grown to $565,610, a 9.05% average annual gain. **If you just missed the best 30 days, over the entire twenty-year period, your rate of return now drops to 0.85%.**

Another market timing ploy is the product sale. Instead of just guessing when equities are good or bad, financial firms push the hot product. You've heard the pitch…you need to own precious metals, commodities, hedge funds, managed futures, REITS, or variable annuities. Never buy financial products on impulse or just because they are the hot product. This is merely market timing in disguise.

So this idea of timing the market – trying to guess when stocks are hot, when they're not, is one of Wall Street's worst ideas, EVER! If you want all the profits you must be invested all the time!

RETAIL VS. INSTITUTIONAL

You may not be aware that there are actually *two* mutual fund industries. You're well aware of *retail* mutual funds, but you may never have heard of *institutional* funds.

According to David Swenson, chief investment officer of Yale University's $20 billion endowment fund, there is "overwhelming evidence that proves the failure of the retail mutual fund industry."

When my company decided to leave the retail mutual fund world, it was a relatively easy decision. Today the industry is more concerned with making profits for itself than serving its shareholders. Retail mutual funds have two glaring problems: high fees and poor performance.

Institutional funds have numerous advantages over retail mutual funds:

- Institutional funds rely extensively on an academic approach to money management
- Institutional funds are engineered and structured for true asset class performance
- Institutional funds are designed to capture market rates of return over multiple asset classes using extensive global diversification
- Institutional funds generally have lower fees
- Institutional funds generally produce higher rates of return

Because my company is a Registered Investment Advisory firm, we have access to institutional funds. We consider Dimensional Fund Advisors (DFA), to be the best institutional fund family. With $315 billion currently under management, DFA's list of clients includes high net worth individuals, public funds, major corporations, Taft-Hartley funds, and non-profit organizations. Individual investors can only access funds managed by DFA through authorized financial advisors. In the United States, there are a small number of advisors who have completed the training necessary to be approved by DFA. I am happy to say that my firm is an approved provider of DFA funds.

THE WALL STREET MARKETING MACHINE

The year is 1979. John Houseman, the actor with a distinctive mid-Atlantic English accent is sitting in an elegant restaurant. Lights! Camera! Action! It's a commercial for Smith Barney, the Wall Street investment firm. John Houseman proclaims "Smith Barney makes money the old fashion way…They earn it!" I remember that commercial like it was yesterday. In that brief 30-second commercial, America knew Smith Barney meant business. Invest your money with Smith Barney. We will make you wealthy at Smith Barney.

Ladies and gentlemen, therein lies the danger. America was duped by an actor with an English accent. America would invest their hard earned money with a Wall Street firm because Madison Avenue advertising executives had created an award-winning commercial that caught our attention. Let me introduce you to a very dangerous adversary: the Wall Street Marketing Machine.

Wall Street is everywhere. Its marketing reach is limitless. According to Joshua M. Brown, author of *Backstage Wall Street,* the securities industry spends $15 billion a year in advertising. To put that number in perspective, the alcohol and beer industry spends only $2 billion per year. There isn't a televised sporting event in the country that doesn't count a financial firm as a sponsor. There isn't a newspaper in the nation that doesn't count on at least some ad revenue from a fund company, brokerage firm or bank. There is a common theme that runs through all investment marketing: "We know what we're doing in the market." It's outrageous to think we can be manipulated by their advertising campaigns. But turn on the TV and there's Sam Waterston, straight from the set of Law and Order, pitching investments for T.D. Waterhouse and there's E-Trade Baby….isn't he cute? And just for fun let's throw in the 24/7 media, talking heads on TV, radio, the Internet, books, magazines, newsletters, smart phones, oh my gosh, make it go away! You can't even go to the gym or your favorite restaurant without ten 60" flat screens blaring out market reports. The Wall Street Marketing Machine is here to stay and it's only going to get worse.

Studies of neuroeconomics show that emotions drive investment decisions more than objective data. I can tell you exactly how to invest your hard-earned money to maximize your returns and minimize risk. My recommendations will coincide with the finest minds in finance today, backed by reams of academic studies. You will agree that this long-term disciplined approach is right for you. But the Wall Street Marketing Machine will try to convince you otherwise through slick advertising campaigns.

It's a fact that most people don't respond to reason when it comes to investing decisions; they allow their emotions to get in the way. The Wall Street Marketing Machine knows this so they feed us what drives us to act—the feelings of fear and greed. **Do Not Let The Wall Street Marketing Machine Control Your Mind and Emotions.** Turn off the noise. Prudent investors win. Emotional investors lose. Period.

THREE SIMPLE RULES TO INVESTING

The diet industry is a multi-billion dollar industry. They trot out the latest and greatest ways to lose weight but really there are two simple rules for weight loss: Eat Less and Exercise More. Simple rules – but not necessarily easy to follow.

The financial services industry is a multi-trillion dollar industry. They would have you believe that investing is complicated but in reality it is simple. There are three rules to investing. Let's break down each rule, see what it means, and why it is so critical for your success.

Rule #1: Own Equities
Equities are the greatest wealth creation tool known to man. Since 1927, an investment in the S&P 500 has produced an annual rate of return of close to 10%, while stocks of small and value companies have produced returns of 11% to 14% during this same timeframe.

Our institutional portfolios consist of 12,000 stocks spread over multiple asset categories and adhere to the landmark research of two distinguished professors of finance: Eugene Fama and Kenneth French.

Fama is widely recognized as the "father of modern finance" and is the distinguished professor of Finance at the University of Chicago Booth School of Business. French is the distinguished professor of Finance at the Tuck School of Business at Dartmouth College. The Fama-French Three Factor Model is considered the gold standard among Nobel Prize laureates in economics. The three factors involve owning domestic and international equities across multiple asset categories, global exposure to small company stocks and global exposure to value stocks. We strictly adhere to the Fama-French Three Factor Model. (Fama was awarded the 2013 Nobel Prize in Economic Science, a validation of his rigorous work in finance and investment management.)

Warren Buffet once said, "In the 20th century, the United States endured two world wars and other traumatic and expensive military conflicts; the Depression; a dozen or so recessions and financial panics; oil shocks; a flu epidemic; and the resignation of a disgraced president. Yet the Dow rose from 66 to 11,497." (And the Dow has risen above 16,000 since Buffet's quote.) Intelligent investors who believe in capitalism and focus on equity ownership, have been richly rewarded over the past century.

Rule #2: Diversify

While reviewing a portfolio from a Wall Street firm a few years ago I noticed a major flaw. The account held twenty-three mutual funds but was largely allocated in only three market sectors. The flaw...lack of diversification. What is diversification? Too often investors believe that owning a bunch of "stuff" means true diversification. However, true diversification is owning distinct asset classes across multiple lines of investment sectors, with an emphasis on correlation, a statistical measure of how two securities move in relation to each other.

My company partners with Matson Money and Dimensional Fund Advisors to provide institutional portfolios for our clients. Mark Matson, CEO of Matson Money a $5 billion dollar investment firm was once in a meeting with Nobel Prize winner Myron Scholes. Mark commented that our institutional portfolios are "as diversified as a Fortune 500 pension plan with billions in assets." Myron Scholes interrupted with, "That's not accurate. They are better diversified." A ringing endorsement from a Nobel Prize winner for our diversification model!

Our portfolios include stocks in 45 countries. Here's a list of free market economies that are included in our institutional portfolios:

Argentina, Australia, Austria, Belgium, Brazil, Canada, Chile, China, Columbia, Czech Republic, Denmark, Egypt, Finland, France, Germany, Greece, Hong Kong, Hungary, India, Indonesia, Ireland, Israel, Italy, Japan, Malaysia, Mexico, Netherlands, New Zealand, Norway, Peru, Philippines, Poland, Portugal, Russia, Singapore, South Africa, South Korea, Spain, Sweden, Switzerland, Taiwan, Thailand, Turkey, United Kingdom, and the United States of America.

Pretty cool, huh? Your money is invested in all of these free market economies! Now that's Diversification!

Rule #3: Rebalance
Rebalancing is a way to ensure your portfolio is no more or less risky than you intend. To give an example, if the equity portion of your portfolio increases in value more than the bond portion, you have a riskier portfolio than the one you created because the allocations to stocks is now higher. The simple solution is: sell some stocks and buy more bonds to bring your asset allocation back to target.

Rebalancing forces you to do the opposite of what you think you should do. Emotionally you want to buy more of the asset that rose in value and sell the asset that under performed. Here's a great example: in 2008 long term government bonds rose 26%. Small U.S. stocks fell 37%. Human nature would say buy the bonds that are up 26% and sell the stocks that are down 37%. That would have been a huge mistake because in 2009 the bonds fell 15% and small U.S. stocks rose 47%.

Ever heard the expression *buy low and sell high*? That's exactly what rebalancing is and if you're not rebalancing your portfolios on a regular basis, you certainly are at risk of losing potential market gains.

SUMMARY

Wall Street and the 24/7 media want you to believe they have all the answers. So, why have the majority of investors lost faith in Wall Street? <u>Investor Alert:</u> It's okay to lose faith in the Wall Street institutions. They deserve it. But never lose faith in the *stock market*. Your investment in the *stock market* provides capital to businesses around the world to provide the products, services and technologies to make the world a better place. Just remember three simple rules... Own Equities, Diversify and Rebalance. Follow these rules and you will be in an elite group of investors who have confidence, clarity and peace of mind.

About Mark

Mark H. Witt is the President of Witt Financial Group, LLC, a Registered Investment Advisory firm. With over fifteen years of experience in the financial industry, Mark dedicates himself to working with investors who are interested in learning how financial markets work and are seeking a disciplined approach to investing.

Mark's approach to investment management is the culmination of years of study grounded in academic research from the University of Chicago. Mark teaches his clients the truth about how Wall Street really works and educates them on how they can achieve true peace of mind and win at the investment game. Mark wants each client to achieve clarity and confidence on their financial journey.

As a dynamic public speaker, Mark has shared his message of free markets and global investing with thousands of people around the country. His direct approach and enthusiasm make him a compelling speaker and fierce proponent of free market capitalism. Mark currently teaches public and private seminars on Investing, Asset Allocation and Modern Portfolio Theory.

Mark co-hosted "Main Street Money" which aired on Public Broadcast System (PBS) in 2012. Mark was featured in the documentary *Navigating the Fog of Investing* and has appeared on *Matson Money Live!* – a popular Internet financial show.

Mark and his wife, Glenda, have been married since 1983. They have two sons, Jordan and Grayson. Jordan graduated from East Tennessee State University and is Vice President of Witt Financial Group, LLC. Grayson, a beautiful child with special needs, is an active participant in Special Olympics.

CHAPTER 63

PASTORAL COUNSELOR TO MATCHMAKER

BY MARSHON THOMAS

There have been some bumps in the road in my life and there were times when I wanted to give up. I learned at an early age that anything worth having has to be earned. In order to succeed in and make a difference, one must go beyond the norm. I'm the owner of Matchmakers Plus, a Christian-based matchmaking and life coaching service located in Brentwood, CA. My quest to become a matchmaker and life coach was a little different than most because of my unique business model.

I wasn't always a man of God and my journey from non-believer to believer was a difficult one. I had a pretty rough upbringing as a child, but l never stopped believing that one day, my world would turn around.

Then in May 8, 2001, a very tragic event happened in my life. My mother died of cancer and it changed my life forever. When she died, I was forced to face my own mortality. I was so afraid of dying because of my fear of the unknown. I saw my mom take her last breath but she seemed at peace. Just weeks before, she talked about her conversation with Jesus and speaking to angels in her sleep. I thought to myself, 'Was she imagining things? Or was she really telling the truth?' I was so confused.

In 2002, while watching a religious service on TV, I decided to give my life to God. I felt the results immediately. I felt a change in my heart and a new zeal for life. But I still had an uncaring Spirit. I also held grudges and became judgmental. I scared a few people off and was labeled a "judgmental Christian." Hmm? Was I really a "judgmental Christian?" The answer was a resounding "Yes!" It took me years to basically get over myself and actually help others. But when I finally help others, I felt an unspeakable joy from above. When you help others with a pure heart, you›ll be blessed in return.

In 2005, I enrolled in Bible College and was ordained in 2008. In the latter part of 2008, I received a certificate in pastoral counseling, and an Honorary Doctorate of Divinity. I was already spreading the word of God since 2002, but I felt that I still needed to earn a biblical degree to validate my credentials. I learned later on, that God doesn't go by your credentials; He goes by your heart. Silly me.

In 2008, I founded Shiloh Christian Ministries - a non-profit dedicated to pastoral counseling and raising money for charities. I was able to help charities raise money but was unable get the non-profit going. I still continued to help counsel others biblically and would help raise money as well. I was content with helping other organizations grow and flourish.

In 2012, I saw a reality show that dealt with matchmaking. I really didn't know much about matchmaking or how one could make a living doing it. I was very entertained by the show but didn't take it seriously. Then one day I googled different matchmakers and learned that some of them made $125,000 a client. Lets just say that sparked my interest. :)

I later stumbled upon Paul Carrick Brunson (also known as: The Modern Day Hitch) who has a series of dating and relationship videos on YouTube. Paul Carrick Brunson is a internationally-recognized matchmaker and relationship coach who's received an NAACP Image Award nomination for his first book entitled: *It's Complicated: But It Doesn't Have to Be*. I read his book and loved it!

I attended a seminar in San Francisco on February 23, 2013, where Paul was promoting his new book. The seminar was on my birthday (this must be destiny!) and I loved every minute of it. He signed my book after the seminar and told me, he would help me become a matchmaker. He also informed me of a matchmakers conference in New York and suggested I attend.

Over the coming weeks, Paul took me on as a mentee and gave me valuable advice about the industry. I decided to take matchmaking and life-coaching courses simultaneously and started my business after I completed the courses. I discovered yourtango.com, a well-known dating and relationship site and had the opportunity to write several blogs for them. The blogs were well received and I eventually developed quite a following. I attended the matchmakers conference, which my mentor suggested in New York, and made valuable contacts in the matchmaking industry. I revamped my business model to fit the Christian community and immediately started to receive clients. I have reached thousands of people with my business in a short amount of time, and I am still learning the business. I have found my true calling and am blessed to have so much support from my colleagues. I really enjoy having my own business and I get to help people as well. How cool is that?!!

According to statistics published by the Small Business Administration (SBA), about two-thirds, or 66 percent last past the first two years, leaving only a third of businesses that fail within these two years. The number of surviving businesses decreases to only 44 percent, at four years and about 56 percent of businesses fail at the five-year mark.

To help you become a successful entrepreneur, I've gathered priceless information that will help you succeed. Feel free to use some or all of them and I hope this information will prove be invaluable to you in your in business endeavors:

1. Find a mentor

I can tell you first hand that finding a mentor is one of most important steps in being successful in any field. Ask for referrals from your friends or colleagues and be clear about what you're looking for. The mentor has valuable experience to share with you and can help you hone your skills. I suggest if you find a mentor that fits the business model you are interested in, it will be easier for you to incorporate what you have learned. Make sure the mentor is a match for you and *vice versa*. Set aside enough time in your schedule for your mentor and know what you want to achieve out of the relationship.

2. Get a Website

Having a website gives your business credibility and strengthens your brand. Let's be honest, customers don't buy from businesses.

They buy from people they know and trust. Your potential customers will not spend a dime on your product or services until they know more about you first. That's why your website is a great way to introduce yourself to your customers. Having a website is a great way to showcase your services and expertise. If your customers like your website, they'll more than likely refer others to it.

You can also include a newsletter to communicate more with your customers and build a valuable client list. It is much easier to retain satisfied past clients than it is to acquire new ones. This is the only medium that customers can gain access to your services from anywhere in the world. The best part is that the website is open 24/7 and customers can access it at their convenience.

3. Social Media marketing

What is Social Media marketing? Social Media marketing involves sharing content of any kind on social media sites like Facebook, Twitter and the like, for marketing purposes. I'm telling you now, if you're just using social media to stay in contact with friends, you're losing money! There are so many potential clients you can reach by simple chatting on these sites. But first you have to decide what messages you want your audiences to receive. Have a plan of action in place and use relevant content as a way to connect with your audience. Mix up the content by using pictures, text-based content and videos to get your message across.

4. Become a guest blogger

Writing on someone else's already established blog is a great way to introduce yourself to potential clients. Building these connections can result in high yields for your business. Be selective of what sites you submit your content to. Some websites will take any content, but only the picky ones are worth your time. The goal is to add to your credibility and give more exposure to your brand. It's also helps if you're interacting with your audience as well. For example, if someone has a comment or question in the comment section of the page, it is beneficial for you to engage in conversation with them. But I suggest to always keep professional! Adding backlinks in your blog is a great way to drive traffic to your site. Another added benefit is that Google will crawl your blog and the link you posted in the content.

5. Give away free stuff

This may sound kind of strange but giving free stuff can actually help you generate more income. I can't tell you how many referrals I've gotten from giving free services to my clients. Believe it. There is a method to this madness. If you give away high quality free services to your potential clients, they will automatically assume that your paid services are even better. Your free services are for promotional purposes and a way to draw in your potential clients. It's also a way to show your expertise in your field, without looking-like a typical salesperson. You can also provide high quality content via a newsletter and have them sign up to receive the free information.

6. Use YouTube to grow your business

YouTube can make you an Internet celebrity expert if you market yourself correctly. Only the highest quality content will separate you from the crowd. You can also add your commercials, special training, promote upcoming events, client testimonials, etc. The sky's the limit! One of most important aspects of YouTube is the viewer feedback. No need to hire a market research team. Viewer feedback will give you all the information you need. I can't stress enough the importance of using keywords and tags in the title descriptions to help you target the right audience.

You can also link your YouTube video to your website, Facebook page, blog, etc. If potential clients RSS your video channel, every time you upload a new video, a notification will be sent to them. The best part is its automatic; you don't have to do a thing. In time you will grow your brand and gain much needed brand recognition. This is an opportunity for people to see and hear first-hand what you have to offer. YouTube can be a great marketing tool for your business only if you plan ahead and present creative video.

7. Networking to success

Networking is a great way to meet other businesses and possibly partner up on future projects. You can also help each other grow through business referrals. The main purpose of networking is to build a productive relationship with each other. Understand that networking requires some effort but it will all pay off in the long run. A couple of websites I use to network with other businesses are Meetup and LinkedIn. You can also check your local Chamber of

Commerce to search for business groups. Make sure to check each group's rules and regulations to determine if they're a good fit for you. Be sure to mix and mingle with everyone when attending social gatherings pertaining to business. "A closed mouth doesn't get fed!" So go out there and build some relationships. Once you meet new business contacts make sure you stay in contact with them. Have your business cards ready and available, and don't forget to ask for theirs. Be attentive when meeting new contacts and make sure you don't come across as overbearing. Stay positive and give them that million-dollar smile!

8. Write a book

Writing a book can help your business grow. Think of your book as an expensive business card. Writing a book is a great opportunity to show your industry expertise and build your credibility. This can be an added advantage to any business and not just a niche one. Whatever business you own, you'll be a sought-after consultant or motivational speaker. Think of the book as a different source of additional income to your business. The actual book sales won't make a huge difference in generated income, but the added promotion and distribution efforts can aid in surges of cash flow due to exposure to your business. For example, you can be an exhibitor at a business conference and promote services, but you're also offering a free copy of your new book to anyone who subscribes to your newsletter. This is a great way to draw potential customers in and ultimately gain business sales. Instead of spending all your time and money on paid ads alone, write your book and gain exposure for your business through media interviews and coverage. This will make you a Celebrity Expert and increase your status in the community.

9. Conduct your own business seminar

Conduct your own seminar for the exposure of your new-found celebrity status. The seminar should hit on the top topics that are essential points you want to convey. Make sure you know your target audience before you conduct your seminar ahead of time. The way you conduct your seminar will depend on whether you're addressing businesses owners, students, executives, etc. The event must be tailor-made for your audience in order for you to connect with them effectively. Make sure you secure a good location that is aesthetically pleasing to your attendees. I attended a seminar once in a mall. It was a little different but it didn't feel boring or stuffy, that's for sure.

10. Give back to your community

I'm big on giving back to my community. If you don't give back with a pure heart you're better off not giving back at all and I'll tell you why. You'll end up looking like a big phony and this will soil your reputation. For those who do give for the right reasons, it's a great opportunity to volunteer and meet some dynamic individuals who are making a difference in others lives. There are so many worthy causes that need your support and you can be the main ingredient in helping a cause get the support it needs. This will help build your reputation in the community and in turn other businesses will follow suit. This makes you more of a well-rounded individual and business owner, who values the importance of helping others and changing lives.

These are just a few ways you can acquire new clients and establish yourself as a successful and well-respected entrepreneur. Remember that honesty and integrity are important in our personal and business relationships. Have patience and believe that you are destined for greatness. With hard work and dedication you can make it. I look forward to hearing your remarkable stories some day. Walk on faith!

About Marshon

Marshon Thomas has founded a Christian-based matchmaking and life coaching business named Matchmakers Plus. Matchmakers Plus is located in Brentwood, CA. Marshon was the previous founder/pastoral counselor of Shiloh Christian Ministries, a non-profit dedicated to pastoral counseling and raising money for charities. He has a certificate in pastoral counseling and an Honorary Doctorate in Divinity from World Christianship Ministries.

Marshon is a Certified Life Coach who received his certification from Fowler Wainwright International. He received his matchmaking training from the Matchmaking Institute. Marshon has written articles for yourtango.com and for more.com.

Marshon Thomas has over 10 years experience as a pastoral counselor and continues to encourage others through Christ. Marshon became a help professional because he truly believes that God put him on this earth to help others.

I feel that when you bless others with a pure heart, you will be blessed in return,

~ Marshon Thomas.

CHAPTER 64

CAN YOU AFFORD STATUS QUO? BEWARE OF THE HIDDEN COST OF COMPLACENCY

BY ROBERT DAY

I attended a conference with Terry Jones (founder and former CEO **of Travelocity.com) who is currently the chairman of Kayak.com. Terry** was talking about how fast things change today in comparison to how fast things used to change. Some people say that technology doubles every 24 months, while others say it doubles every 18 months. I think it's safe to say, regardless of who is correct, that it feels as if the pace we are living is at the speed-of-light. Every day, new technological advancements make it possible to create new items that will replace some of the items we, as consumers, bought just a week ago.

I have been active in the financial world for almost 30 years. I ran several companies, while spending almost half that time as a commercial banker working closely with hundreds of companies. The number one thing I see as detrimental to companies is the belief that "if it's not broken, don't fix it," with the "I KNOW what to do" syndrome coming in a close second.

I get it; it's hard getting your job done every day, as well as remaining aware of the new technological advances that emerge as you sort through new products to improve your business—not to mention fighting any skepticism that may arise as a result. After all, you have been deceived more times than you care to remember. And so you assume the fix is in keeping your head down and plowing ahead, right? Wrong! In order to survive, you must keep your head up, watch the trends in your industry, and do at least a fairly good job of predicting the future—not just in your industry, but also in all areas.

Today, I run an auditing firm that specializes in finding the overbilling that takes place in merchant processing fees generated by banks and processing networks. We are on the "bleeding" edge of technology. The techniques we use today weren't even available 10 years ago—and some of what we use wasn't even around 12 months ago. Our firm is four years old and we have rebuilt it four times, almost from the ground up. I realize now, as we have grown, that change is becoming more and more difficult to initiate. But as I remind the members of my team, the only thing more difficult than change is being snuffed out by the competition.

Our Firm's newest team members push back and say, "We don't have any competition." In some ways that is true, but what would you say about a company that dominated the 8-track business in the 1970s? Their competition was not the other small companies that made 8-track tapes, it was the company that was working on developing the cassette. And the guy working on the cassette had no idea that his product would almost become obsolete by the time he sold his first cassette because the CD was right at his back door. The CD has had a good run, but it too is at risk of extinction, due to cloud technology. One thing I know for sure is if we don't perfect what we do, and constantly work to improve our services while finding ways to cut costs, the death of our firm is certain.

You may remember the Eastman Kodak Company, which filed for bankruptcy in January 2009. The company was obviously not on the front side of the digital world. Eastman Kodak was not alone. Many reports cite failing companies, showing anywhere from one a week to as high as 50 per day. Those companies are subject to what you consider failed, including being acquired by the competition, laying off massive numbers of employees while trying to regroup, or putting out the "Closed for business" sign in the window for the last time. While the numbers vary, in my opinion, more businesses are in trouble now than in the past.

Most blame the economy for the failure of so many companies, and while there's some truth to that, the fact remains that some companies have become stronger in spite of the poor economy. While many companies had new ways of doing business available to them, they chose to disregard them, thinking "they have always done it this way," or "this storm will pass." Others were on the lookout for change, and they embraced it by cutting costs and changing the way they did things, sometimes to the point of pain, while others completely reinvented themselves.

Bookstores took a major hit when Amazon came on the scene. They found it hard to compete. The local bookstore could not sell enough books to get the buying power they needed to get keep their profit margins healthy while competing, and so they had two choices: either go out of business or reinvent themselves. Some opted for the first choice, while others made the decision to sell used books along with new ones. I'm not saying the latter was a cure-all, but it kept many bookstores in the game until they could figure out how to get to the next step and gain back a little more ground.

My best friend of 30 years has an online store (Rimz To Go) from which he sells tires and custom rims. He started out with a local brick-and-mortar store, but after the boom of online shopping, he realized that people will go for lower prices more often than they will go to the local guy they know down the street, and so he sold his inventory. He now conducts all of his business online. Some might say how sad it is that he is gone. He will tell you how blessed he is to work from home. Now he can spend more time with his children, while not having to worry about inventory. The poor economy pushed the consumer to do more online buying, and because my friend was able to embrace change, he now makes more money while working less. If he had fought change, he would have been forced out of business and would have looked for someone, beside himself, to blame. **Those who don't adjust always look for someone else to blame.**

If you are going to survive, or better yet, thrive in today's economy, you can't just embrace what's new, you need to lean into it! Most people did not buy the first in-home microwave oven when it came out 1967. They thought of it as a strange way to cook food; but today some think that cooking food on a stove is strange.

Change is inevitable, and everyone is part of it. We must act so that we reap the full benefits of embracing change first, or we'll pay the price of being late. We now see that most consumers eventually caught on to the idea of cooking with a microwave oven, which costs about 91 cents a month to run versus the average cost of $5.21 per month to run a range—not to mention the countless hours that cooking with a microwave saves. But before consumers purchased microwaves, how much money and time did they waste while watching and waiting to see if the new technology would take off?

The change I'm most familiar with is in the merchant processing fees that businesses incur, and the impact it has on those businesses.

The top three processing networks (Visa, MasterCard and Discover) have recreated themselves. For about the first 50 years, these networks operated in the same old status quo. They have made some amazing changes and have transformed themselves into super giant companies with a business concept that is so basic—and simple—that it's crazy. Think about this: They issue a card to a person, the person uses the card to buy something at a store, the person pays the network a small fee to use the card, and the store pays the network a small fee to accept the card. That's the entire business model, and they made a little money while doing it. Then someone said, hey, let's see if we can take this to the next level—and did they!

The change - You will see below the massive change the banks and processors have made. These changes have resulted in huge profits for each one of them. In 2012, Visa reported a net income of $4.2 billion, MasterCard $2.8 billion, and Discover $2.3 billion.

The Processing Networks (Visa, MasterCard and Discover) get a very small cut of your processing fees. On average their cut is only about 0.11 percent of the sale. That's not a bad profit on such a small cut.

To implement the changes, the processing networks and banks used the "frog in boiling water" trick. For those who are unfamiliar with this concept, I will explain: If you put a frog in boiling water he will jump out; however, if you fill a pot with cool water, the frog will swim around in it thinking life is good—he has a cool new swimming pool. As you turn the heat up, the frog never notices and he soon becomes someone else's delicacy.

The cool water - In 1946, the first traditional bank credit card was introduced by John Biggins, a banker in Brooklyn. It was great; it offered convenience to both the user as well as the business for a very small and simple fee. The user knew the fee, the business knew the fee, and all was well. While the fees continued to grow, the simplicity of the operation remained the same for almost 50 years.

The warm water - In 1991, four interchange categories emerged: Visa Card Present, Visa Card Not Present, MasterCard Present, and MasterCard Not Present. Any bookkeeper that could run a basic calculator could validate the fees. It was a time of transparency and fairness.

The hot water - Today, in 2013, it's no longer Card Present or Card Not Present. It's Data I, Data II, Data III, Electronic, Level II, Level III, Standard, Merit III, Rewards, World Card, Signature, Enhanced, Corporate, Business, Commercial, Purchasing, Fleet, Breakeven, Large Ticket, World Elite, Premium, Super Premium, High Value, and Emerging Market. This is not even close to being a complete list, since there are *hundreds* of interchange categories—and new categories come out every spring and fall. My favorite is EIRF; you can ask your processor what that is and they will tell you EIRF means Electronic Interchange Rate Fee. Wow, that explains it, right? Wrong.

When speaking at conferences, I explain how Card-Not-Present merchants are paying 0.50 percent more for transactions that fall into the EIRF category. Next I ask, "So now that you know this, how many of you will stop letting your transactions fall into EIRF?" Without fail, half the people in the room raise their hand (these, obviously, are the people who raise their hand for anything). I then ask, "Can anyone tell me what EIRF means?" At that moment you can hear a pin drop (if it weren't for the nervous laughter). I go on to explain what it means in plain English: "It means you did not enter the zip code or the numeric street address." Oh, they say, well then why doesn't my processor just tell me that? And that raises a good question; why don't they? It may be because they don't want merchants to get it right.

This is the part you really need to understand because it explains why and how banks and processors overbill their cardholders in the first place. Let's go back to EIRF. If a card clears at EIRF, the bank that issued that card gets the extra 0.50 percent, so why would they want to tell you to enter the zip code or the numeric street address? After all, they benefit when you don't enter those items. Letting your bank or processor give you advice is a little like paying a tutor a premium for every "F" your child gets, and next to nothing for an "A." Would you do this? Of course you wouldn't. But if you did, would you honestly expect good results?

You also must factor in other games processors play, such as the "enhanced billing" game. This is what occurs when processors place an additional surcharge on top of a current surcharge. Often times, the extra surcharge is even higher than the processing network's base surcharge. I have seen processors add as much as 0.95 percent on top of a surcharge. How can this happen? Is this legal? Here is what Senator Dick Durbin said about it, *"Interchange is unregulated with hidden fees and is non-negotiable," "Businesses are being overcharged by credit card companies without restraint" and "Interchange is a Price Fixing Scheme. Period!"*

The lack of change – Business owners and key decision makers are not doing anything about this, because they are under the false assumption that everything is fine. In the meantime, they are losing tens of thousands of dollars, and in some cases millions, as they lay people off, close locations, or go out of business while banks and processors celebrate the highest earnings in decades!

Make a change - I will arm you with information to help level the playing field. This information will bring about change. It will help you increase your profits, and get them back where they belong—on your P&L statement, not on your bank's statement.

Below are the top six questions banks and processors hope you never ask.

Q. What's my discount rate?
A. 0.02%-0.10%

Keep in mind: Y*our discount should never be more than 0.10%*

Q. How many basis points are you charging over Base Interchange on downgraded transactions?
A. Zero. It's pure Interchange Pass-Through.

Keep in mind: *Banks should never surcharge you on top of the surcharge fee being assessed by processing networks.*

Q. Do you have an interchange management program?

A. Yes.

Keep in mind: *While they all claim to have it, ask the next question...*

Q. Please explain how it works, and give me an example of how it helped me with my previous downgrades.

A. Let me put you on hold.

Keep in mind: *This is where you will need to endure the elevator hold music.*

Q. Was my statement reviewed last month for any avoidable downgrades of which I should be made aware?

A. Yes.

Q. Great, who received the report?

Keep in mind: *Get ready for more elevator hold music.*

At this stage, the most important thing for you to do is to get all of your answers in writing; if not, the information you are verbally provided won't be binding.

Don't be the person who falls prey to overbilling. Be proactive; don't let it happen. Companies are being overbilled by more than a million dollars a year. That's about three thousand dollars a day. Don't be the one who loses all of his or her hard-earned profits, while sitting on the sidelines thinking about it.

It's been said, "The only thing constant is change." This is so true and applies to every area of your business and your life. Whether you are a CEO, the guy in the cubicle, or a domestic engineer, your success will be in direct correlation with your ability to embrace change. Never stop pursuing. Never stop seeking solutions to problems. Keep your head up and look around as well as looking forward. Say no to *status quo*!

About Robert

Robert Day is the Managing Partner of Merchant Relief Council, a one-of-a-kind auditing firm that is revolutionizing the world of merchant processing by protecting merchants' profits, often cutting their fees in half. Recognized as the "Industry Expert" of merchant processing by every major credit association (National Association of Credit Management, Credit Research Foundation, Credit Today, and Riemer Credit), he is a highly sought after speaker with his witty anecdotes and paradigm-shifting perspectives, giving him a rare ability to not just educate, but entertain.

For 13 years, Robert was a top executive for one of the largest credit card processors in the country before crossing the aisle and co-founding Merchant Relief Council (MRC). Now Robert has one simple goal: to educate merchants on how credit card processors use hidden fees to drive up fees by 30-50%.

As a former corporate executive and former business owner, Robert has a special blend of experience and an intimate understanding of the needs of small to mid-sized merchants as well as Fortune 500 companies. It is Robert's personal mission to lower merchants' processing costs in order to "right the wrong" in the credit card processing industry and protect every businesses' profits, ultimately defending and preserving the American dream.

Robert is a nationally-recognized speaker, blogger and bestselling author and has been quoted in *The Wall Street Journal, Washington Business Journal, CNN Money, Yahoo Finance, Business Week, Business Credit, Credit Today,* and the *Credit Research Business Journal.* Robert has appeared on Fox, NBC, ABC, and CBS television affiliates speaking on how merchants can lower their credit card processing fees.

CHAPTER 65

FOUR STEPS TO SKYROCKET CLIENT RETENTION

BY MILES BODZIN

I've always been an entrepreneur. I can recall hot humid days in Miami Beach, pulling my wagon around the neighborhood selling the avocados from the trees in our backyard when I was 10. I can still smell the scent of the fresh cut grass from all the lawns I used to mow.

Why it took me so long to go into sales I don't know. But it wasn't until I was 19, when I got my first job selling clothes at a surf shop in San Diego, CA. Boy, did I discover a talent for getting moms to spend money on their kids.

I have no idea how I ended up going to San Diego State University studying Electrical Engineering. Well, that isn't entirely true. When I was a freshman in high school, I took my first computer programming class with Mrs. Brenneman, and I excelled in software design from the start. We've all had those teachers that believed in us, and for me it was Mrs. Brenneman who fostered my artistic creativity using software programming as a medium.

With two of my brothers already engineers, it seemed natural for me to pursue that career. In college, I further honed my creative skills in software development, earning many accolades from my professors.

But I felt something wasn't right.

Have you ever woken up just knowing you were living someone else's dream? Someone else's purpose? For me, it was the beginning of my senior year of college. A brutal year of engineering studies lay before me, and my heart was screaming - "Get out, you won't be happy!"

What I did next changed my life forever. I went to the beach and spent a few hours surfing, clearing my mind and getting in touch with what made me happy and feel alive. When I was mentally clear, I sat on the warm sand, the sun on my back with a pad and pencil and started to write the story of who I would be when I grew up. I knew I wanted to help people, be in charge of my own business, make a good living and have fun while doing it.

When writing my story, it was as if I had put on a pair of rose-colored glasses, tinting everything I saw. There are times in everyone's lives when we experience things that forever change our destiny. The day you met your spouse. The day you had a great idea. The day you accomplished a goal. My day was upon me.

At this time in my young life, I was seeing a chiropractor every month to stay healthy. When I was twelve, I had injured my neck diving into a pool and his care kept me in 'tip top' shape. On one particular visit, with my rose colored glasses, nothing about the routine changed, yet somehow everything was different. What I heard him saying suddenly became very clear to me. What I saw him doing suddenly seemed like something I would love doing.

Like a light bulb flashing on, I said to myself, "I should be a chiropractor." This guy is having the time of his life, helping lots of people, running a successful business, and people respect him.

Leaving engineering to pursue another career was a scary idea. But I couldn't get it out of my mind. I found myself in the college library looking through medical books until I found one about chiropractic. In that book I read something that changed my life. It was so simple, yet so profound, I knew I would spend the rest of my life embodying the idea.

What I read went something like this: *"The nervous system is the master system of the body. It controls and coordinates everything. Interference to this master system causes dis-ease in the body, ultimately leading to illness if left unresolved. The role of a Doctor of Chiropractic is to analyze, detect and remove these nerve system interferences thus allowing normal function to return to the body."* This spoke to me not only because of its simplicity, but because I had been studying electrical engineering and software development. After all, the nervous system is the electrical system of the body.

So in a moment that is forever etched in my mind I remember asking my girlfriend, who I would later marry, "what do you think about me becoming a chiropractor?" Let's just say her initial reaction was less than favorable. Looking back I guess I could see her point. She was prepared for me to graduate the next year so we could get on with our lives. But to her credit, she said, "If you feel it's your calling, let's do it!"

And just like that, we made the decision and I went to the head of the engineering department to share my news that I was leaving the program. He looked at me like I was insane - and I loved it!

About a year or so later my new education in chiropractic college began. It was so exciting to study subjects like human anatomy, physiology, and biochemistry and no longer be buried in calculus, thermodynamics, and physics. The human body was absolutely amazing to me!

I've always been a problem solver. So when I came to realize that the class notes for my spinal anatomy class were poorly done, I decided I wanted to type a new set of notes. It was really just my way of studying. The "new" notes I had created were so well done my classmates asked to buy them from me!

By the time I had graduated from chiropractic college with honors, I had written over 25 sets of notes, sold hundreds of copies to fellow students, employed 2 of my classmates (they received free copies for helping me) and grossed over $40,000. Some of the teachers even started using *"Miles Notes"* to teach their class.

So it looked like the story I had written on the beach so many years earlier was really happening. There was no doubt I was going to succeed beyond my wildest dreams! I was going to serve thousands of people and create an amazing life!

By the time I graduated in 1993, I was married, had a daughter and was over $100k in debt. With a family to support, the pressure was on to get my career going …and fast! On the day my license to practice arrived in the mail, I opened the very first wellness practice in San Diego with high expectations. I thought, if I taught people what I knew, they would get as excited as I was and become my patient.

Now imagine if you owned a flood repair company. You know, a company that repairs your home after a pipe bursts. Do you think most of your revenue would come from the homeowners or from their insurance company? What about if you owned an auto body shop? Again, where would most of your revenue come from? Insurance claims of course!

Now picture this. You own one of these companies and your customers expect their insurance to pay for your service. But it turns out, the insurance industry is no longer willing to pay. What do you do?

What I'm going to share on the following pages can be applied to any service business. I just happen to have learned these lessons because I was in the right place at the right time. As a chiropractor in the mid 90's, it became painfully obvious that people were still expecting their insurance to cover their care. However, the HMO's were growing, and either not covering care or approving very limited care.

To succeed in that economic environment meant I was going to have to learn to do things very differently from what had worked in the past. I spent the next five years with trial and error research in my practice learning what worked and what didn't. I made it my mission to figure out how I could make my care affordable so people could pay without depending on their insurance.

Eventually I did figure it out and it was time for me to systematize the process. I once again put on my software design hat and went to work developing a web-based application giving me the tools I needed to run my practice. As of this writing, over 3,000 chiropractors have used my software to increase their patient retention and collections. And I am 100% confident that if you apply the business principles I based my software on, you will experience happier clients who continue to use your services, refer family and friends and are happy to pay you themselves.

What I discovered in practice was a four step process that led to incredible client retention. For me, that was the measure of success. Where the rubber met the road was how many of my patients consistently used my services for many years.

In a service business, it's all about building long-term relationships. By following this Four Step Process, you will increase your client retention tremendously. In my own practice, my patient visit average was over 200 visits over a 5-year period. The average chiropractor in America struggles to see a patient more than 12 visits on average. My retention was 1,600% higher than the national average! Clearly my clients were very satisfied too - or they wouldn't have stayed or referred so many people to me.

What I learned became my secret formula for incredibly high client retention. And once I discovered this formula, I quickly realized why some things I tried worked, while others did not. Like all great ideas, the secret is very simple.

THE SECRET FORMULA FOR INCREDIBLY HIGH CLIENT RETENTION

If you identify and remove the situations that cause a client to question whether they will start or continue your service, they're more likely to start and continue your service.

Once I realized that it's the "situations that cause the client to question," I spent the next few years identifying those situations. For example, situations such as when they make a payment, or when they have to decide to transition to another program of care, or when you present your findings or that their insurance was no longer paying. It became my mission to figure out how all these situations affected the patient's decisions.

I studied what I could do to neutralize them so the client was never triggered to think about whether they should start or continue care. And to my amazement, it worked. When people were no longer being triggered by situations to question starting or continuing, more started and more stayed longer. Simple as that.

This Four Step Process is simply a system for doing exactly that - removing the situations that cause your clients to question whether they should start or continue the relationship with you. I often refer to this as "expectation management."

STEP 1 - TRACK YOUR CLIENTS' RESULTS AND EFFECTIVELY COMMUNICATE THOSE RESULTS

Clients need to know where they stand with you. If progress is expected, they need to know they are making progress. As a chiropractor, part of my job was to re-evaluate my patients at regular intervals and let them know how they were progressing. If your clients are not aware of their status or if they are making progress, it will create a situation that causes them to question whether they should continue with your service or not.

Think about it. Let's say you hired a personal trainer. And after one month they showed you that you had reduced your weight by 15 pounds, reduced your blood pressure and increased your grip strength by 10%. As compared to just hearing them say, "You're doing a good job, let's keep it up." …wouldn't you be more likely to continue working with the trainer?

Without a doubt, people will stick with a service much longer if "how things are progressing" is communicated based on test results and not just your opinion. But the real power is in *how* you communicate those results.

Remember when you were in school? How did you know you were doing well in the class? You took tests, did assignments and received grades to let you know where you stood in the class. So simple! Give your clients a report card with a grade letting them know how they're progressing!

STEP 2 - OFFER AFFORDABLE PAYMENT OPTIONS

When you see a commercial on TV for a car, how do they advertise the price? Do they show the price of the car? No! They tell you the lowest, most affordable, monthly payment. I will keep this short and sweet. You have to do the same. Offer your clients affordable payment options that include monthly payments as a choice. This is a game changer when it comes to starting new clients with your service. Not doing this will definitely create situations that cause your client to question if they can start your service.

STEP 3 - STOP REMINDING PEOPLE OF THE MONEY

This step is will have a significant impact on your business. It is based on the following law I formulated.

> *The frequency of the conscious purchasing decision significantly influences your retention. The more often a client thinks about money, the less often they will utilize your services.*

The best way to stop reminding them of the money is to use auto-payments. In my practice, nearly 100% of the patients left a credit card or bank account on-file with an authorization for us to auto-debit their payments. We never had to send them bills or statements, never had to wait to be paid and we could always count on consistent cash flow.

Among all the different types of people I took care of, the only thing that the high retention people had in common was the fact that they paid for their care with monthly auto-debits. Even Disney World is now selling their annual passes with monthly auto-debits.

STEP 4 - AUTOMATE YOUR CLIENT EDUCATION

You must continuously educate your clients on the benefits of your services. The fact that the education needs to be done continuously, it makes perfect sense to automate most of it. I trademarked the term "Drip-Education®" years ago to describe the idea of repeatedly "dripping" your message on your clients via email. It is simple and effective. You never want to have a situation where your client didn't know something you thought they did.

So there you have it. My story of how I discovered the secret to creating lifetime clients. Track your client's results and effectively communicate them. Offer them affordable payment options. Use auto-debits to process those payments. And continuously educate your clients on the benefits of your service.

I am proud of my company's successes and products. I feel like this is just the beginning of the story. Everyday I continue to listen to my clients' needs and talk to thousands of doctors across the country to learn and see how I can continue to solve problems they face day in and day out.

Thinking back to that kid laying on the beach writing his story, it just amazes me how powerful it is to have a vision. As Stephen Covey so eloquently says in *The 7-Habits of Highly Successful People*, "Start with the end in mind."

About Miles

An unlikely combination of talents, education, and experience have led Dr. Miles Bodzin to the success he's achieved at an early age in his life. After leaving the study of electrical engineering, Dr. Bodzin pursued a career as a chiropractor where for nearly two decades he built a very successful wellness practice. A big part of his success was the result of developing systems that removed the obstacles to patient compliance, thus allowing patients the opportunity to get the best results possible. Ultimately, this led to his understanding of how to build a service business with extraordinarily high client retention.

He now brings that knowledge to others by helping them build practices and businesses where their clients become lifetime clients. A big part of this process is helping doctors of chiropractic free themselves from the shackles of insurance dependence. Dr. Bodzin teaches a business model that promotes patient compliance while making care affordable for uninsured and underinsured patients.

Raised in a family where lessons in independence, leadership and creativity were the daily norms, he was armed with the ingredients for success. His success in private practice eventually led to the launch of his company Cash Practice® Systems in 2003, where he now assists other chiropractors to succeed in creating non-insurance dependent practices.

Dr. Bodzin's technologies are built on his idea that "if you identify and remove the situations that cause a client to question whether they should start or continue your service, they are more likely to start and continue." His goal is to help his clients implement systems that neutralize those situations so the customers don't disappear.

Dr. Bodzin has a unique combination of talents. He's both analytical and artistic, giving him unique software development skills. He's been an entrepreneur his entire life, where he honed his skills in building teams and leading himself and others to success. Lastly, he's a people person, so he understands why people do what they do.

Dr. Bodzin's clients range from those who are fresh out of school to some of the most successful practicing chiropractors in the U.S. and from around the world. Dr. Bodzin studied electrical engineering at San Diego State University, however in his senior year he realized he wanted to pursue a career in chiropractic. He graduated *Cum Laude* from the Los Angeles College of Chiropractic in 1993. In 1995, Dr. Bodzin was honored by the California Chiropractic Association as Outstanding New Doctor of the Year.

Dr. Bodzin has written dozens of articles published in *The American Chiropractor,* *Chiropractic Economics, The Chiropractic Journal, Spizz Magazine* and countless other newsletters. He's an international speaker who has educated on the topic of running a cash-based practice at some of the biggest chiropractic seminars and state conventions. Dr. Bodzin is interviewed regularly by leaders in the chiropractic profession who routinely refer their clients to his company.

You can connect with Dr. Miles Bodzin at:

DrBodzin@CashPractice.com

www.facebook.com/DrBodzin

www.facebook.com/CashPractice

CHAPTER 66

SUCCESS ON YOUR OWN TERMS

BY NICOLE MARKSON

I wasn't supposed to be in the family business. But wound up there anyway. It was supposed to be "just for a little while." That turned into 15 years at the dealership and 5 years on my own for a total of 20 years experience. I had always wanted to be a singer. I went to college to study theater and communications at NYU (New York University). I wanted to be on the stage.

My stepfather, the owner of several car dealerships made me an offer I couldn't refuse... a job on the used car lot to sell cars earning money so I could have the freedom to come and go to auditions. That beat waitressing, so I ventured onto the lot. I was the only girl in a sea of men. It was a hard, and very competitive environment. You had to have a thick skin to survive. The competition was fierce. I quickly learned how to operate in a man's business, and took on an exterior of steel. I had to stake my claim for customers and deals.

I had a double issue. I was a woman, and I was the *"bosses kid."* Some might think I received special treatment because I was the boss's daughter. It was quite the opposite. No one cared at all. I had to work twice as hard to be respected.

My father was just as tough in public. He didn't want anyone thinking he was giving me special treatment either.

Fast forward three years, I was engrossed in learning the business and my singing career had gone by the wayside, and I became a top salesperson. My father took notice of my sales ability and suggested I go to dealer school.

I attended the National Automobile Dealer Candidate Academy, a program that trains Children of Dealers, and High Level Managers in all aspects of dealership operations. I spent that year learning about the different departments from Sales, Service, Parts, and Finance and Insurance (F&I)/Business office.

Over the next few years I worked my way up to high positions such as Sales Manager, General Manager and Finance Director. In the Finance office, I would unlock my true potential, make a difference, and discover my true passion… Helping women.

As a finance manager, I worked with women in dire situations, experiencing serious personal and financial hardships. Some were Divorced, getting Divorced, abused, abandoned by their husbands, widowed, and for some, it was their first time buying a car and dealing with money matters on their own. It was clear the financial commitment they were about to enter into was about more than just buying a car. It was about survival and addressing unique life circumstances. These women needed guidance, comfort, connection, and compassion, elements missing from the typical car buying experience. They were relieved to see me, a woman on the other side of the desk. I would listen to each one's life story and come up with a customized deal to fit their lives.

I could see the need to educate women about the car buying process, as no one is taught this in schools. My specialized knowledge made a real difference in their financial lives. I knew there had to be others who could benefit from my service. (Even men if they wanted the help.)

There was a serious disconnect in the way dealerships treated people, specifically women. The business lacked empathy and sensitivity to the difficult situations people faced. No one was catering to women and their specific needs. No one seemed to be listening. The purchasing process was unfair, antiquated, and few knew how making a poor financial decision could impact their lives for years to come. It had been proven that women statistically pay more for cars than men. The culture of the business still had not caught up to the reality of the power of the purse.

As a woman working in the auto business, I identified with the gender bias. It was still very much a man's world. As time went on, I wanted to contribute my ideas to the business to improve it. I liked making decisions and being in charge. My ideas were not always valued or met with the same enthusiasm I hoped for. It became disheartening to me. I had a different business philosophy and style from my Father.

One day we hit a turning point, which became the catalyst for me to leave. We were caught in Father/Daughter (Father/son) syndrome characterized by so many family business relationships. He was conflicted between his feelings of wanting to teach me all he knew, and his ambivalence to be in charge and release the reigns. Our working relationship was a dichotomy of 'let me teach you and open up your world'… to 'hold on just a minute, not so fast' micromanaging.

We had our share of differences, but I've always had great admiration and respect for his incredible business knowledge, and self-made accomplishments. He taught me one of the most valuable business lessons of all, the value of having a strong work ethic. My mother instilled it also. She always said, "What you put in, is what you'll get out, it's your choice." A strong work ethic, extreme focus and commitment to follow through, are three critical components required for creating and maintaining success. I am grateful for all he taught me and owe many things to him. He is still a great mentor and a great sounding board for me when I need advice or run into an obstacle.

In reflection, my leaving turned out to be a blessing. Our relationship is the best it has ever has been. I think he respected me for stepping out.

The truth was, I just didn't belong in business with him. This was hard to admit because working "in the family business" was part of my identity for so long. I knew in order to get to the next level of my career, I'd have to give up the comfort of a steady paycheck and start over. It would be uncomfortable. Not following my vision would be more uncomfortable. For a while, I was devastated, angry and sad it wasn't going to work out. I had already felt badly about selling out on my musical dreams, and I had dedicated my life to *his* business. I was determined to turn my feelings around, and not allow them to block me from progressing. This brings me to another core principle of success: the skill of overcoming obstacles quickly and not getting stuck in your tracks. By redirecting your emotions, having a positive attitude, and asking yourself questions like, "How can I turn this challenge into an advantage" or "What is the gift or lesson in this situation?" and "How can I use my experience for the betterment of others?" focuses your attention on coming up with solutions that propel you forward, rather than wallowing or having a pity party for yourself. How fast you overcome barriers gives you a greater advantage toward success.

I finally summoned the courage to leave, change course and create my own future. I didn't want a boss, I didn't want to be the "kid," and I didn't want to regret not trying. Staying in the business was the "safe," "secure," "comfortable" choice, but to do things my way I had to take responsibility for my own destiny — even though I feared the unknown. In my never-ending quest for self improvement, and in an effort to re-examine my life and gain new direction, I attended a Tony Robbins seminar. He spoke about designing your life by creating a compelling vision for what you want, defining your goals, seeking out mentors and communities that support you and hold you to a higher standard, and taking action in spite of fear. Getting a handle on fear can be the difference between succeeding or not. It is important not to allow fear to paralyze you just "because" you are afraid. But rather to make the distinction between doing something risky and taking a calculated risk. When evaluating new opportunities, I suggest looking at each situation independently using critical thinking, rationale, facts, numbers and careful analysis. Asking yourself what is the worst thing that can happen is another way of reigning in your fears. If you answer the question and you can survive the answer then you can keep fear in check. Make a decision and trust your instincts. Then, surround yourself with the best people you can find to support you. You want to find people that are better than you in areas you are not as well versed in, so you can concentrate on what you are best at making use of your time effectively.

So many people never give themselves a chance to succeed because they are afraid for "fears sake." They stop themselves before they start. Fear will present itself over and over again so if you are going to be in business or try new things personally, it is something one has to learn to handle. Each time you face your fears, you build the muscle to take the next step forward. By allowing yourself to step out of your comfort zone, you mature into your higher self, realize your own self worth, develop your true potential and grow your personal power.

Belief and faith in your self is paramount to success. It takes extreme determination and the will to believe in your own concept even when naysayers tell you it can't be done. You have to trust in your vision more than everyone else and create what you want to happen. It takes strength to do and say what others won't. Especially when tradition has dictated it be done a certain way.

Creating and sustaining a successful business is seeing what's missing in the marketplace, addressing it, and seizing the opportunity to fulfill the need. By filling the void, you can create new systems, processes and extraordinary new experiences. By doing business in a new way, you differentiate yourself in places where people least expect it.

I knew in my heart of hearts there was a better way to transact business and defy the common reputation that car dealers had earned to their own detriment. As I spoke with women about their car buying experiences, they all too often reported being ignored, not listened to, disrespected, or made to feel stupid despite their role as either a primary or key decision maker. They feared being ripped off and taken advantage of and just wanted to "*get it over with*" even if it meant accepting a less-than-stellar deal. Women were settling and not getting the deals they truly deserved because they were selling themselves short. They felt intimidated, worn out by the process, and feared dealing with numbers. How could dealerships ignore the fact that 85% of all brand purchases were made by women? 75% feel misunderstood by automotive marketers, and women control two thirds of consumer wealth in the United States and stand to be the beneficiaries of the largest transfer of wealth in history. The trend was clear and still women were being ignored.

To me this was unacceptable. So, I set out to create a new kind of company despite sexism or discrimination. I had fears about going out on my own but I decided I was going to do it anyway. I decided that the business as it stood didn't have to be this way. I saw the need to set a higher business standard. I saw an opportunity for more female leadership and to create something women were longing for, customized care. It is important to identify what you want your name and company to stand for and how you want to portray yourself in business. Having a clear vision points you toward being successful because you know who you are, and your values are clearly defined.

Autoempowerment operates on the premise that integrity comes first, relationships matter, all deals are not created equal, and the financial success of a deal is woven into a larger story including each person's unique set of life circumstances, responsibilities, Cash position, Credit Standing, Budget and lifestyle needs. By taking the time to understand the dimensions of people's lives, and collaborating with a client, we can create a deal focused on what they value most. Productive relationships begin with listening and weighing the potential benefits, risks and costs of a deal to create a strategy that fits a client's needs and benefits them not just for today, but tomorrow and in the future. In turn, newfound confidence is built through education, and information vital for financial preparedness, in other facets of life for the future.

The mission of autoempowerment is to:

1. Make a difference in the economic security of women.

2. Revolutionize the auto industry by demystifying the typical purchasing process making it easy to understand, while creating transparency, making it enjoyable, and stress free.

3. Give clients insider access to the "hottest" deals, rebates, incentives, and rates in the marketplace so clients save thousands of dollars, time and aggravation.

4. Cater to women's specific needs by "holding their hand" through the process, and creating customized purchasing/leasing/financing strategies that fit their personal circumstances.

5. Establish a supportive community where women feel safe to discuss money issues, not let embarrassment, or shame get in the way of getting answers to the questions they need to make informed decisions.

6. Banish money fear by empowering women to feel more comfortable dealing with money matters by providing educational programs and seminars to inspire women to take back control of their finances, control of their deals, economic security, and ultimately transform their financial destiny.

I identified with women I served because I was a child of divorce and watched my mother struggle financially. As a child, I felt hopeless and vowed when I grew up, I would never be at anyone's Money Mercy, …EVER. My mother encouraged me to "Always be able to support yourself and never depend on a man for money." She made it a priority to teach me to be financially independent. She enrolled me in a class called "WOMEN AND MONEY." I learned about different ways to save, invest, and how important it was for a woman to have a financial plan. The class had a great effect on me. Little did I know how much these early experiences would impact my professional life.

Being self-sufficient and having financial security was important to me. Early on, I made the decision to be disciplined about money. I always worked and saved most everything I earned. This brings me to another success tip. SAVE MONEY. Don't underestimate the power of saving money in your business and personal life. A key to remaining successful is being financially prepared for the unforeseen. It's important to make a habit of saving money and having a reserve fund. Even if you are just starting out, start with small amounts. Don't judge yourself on how little you are saving. You will be amazed how quickly your fund will grow. You never know what financial burden lies around the corner, so just start.

In 2009, I was diagnosed with Breast Cancer. Anybody who goes through a serious illness can relate to the astronomical medical costs. If you are not prepared, it can break you financially not to mention emotionally. I underwent a 13-hour surgery, double mastectomy, eight courses of chemotherapy and a hysterectomy. I could have allowed this actuality to derail me in my quest to succeed. Instead, I made the choice to use the experience to push me even harder. Living through an illness brings a sense of urgency to your life. My advice is to act now, not later. Time suddenly isn't what it used to be and accomplishing dreams and goals becomes even more important. Having success isn't just about being successful in business. It is about defining what success means to you, and finding personal fulfillment doing things that you want to do. They may be simple things or extreme challenges. It doesn't matter. What does matter is that you pay attention to what you do want and go for it. Don't go through life numb. Don't let life pass you by.

I know I don't want to live with any regrets, so I am fulfilling as many fantasies as possible.

The lesson here is simple. There is only so much time, so respect it and don't wait. Create your plan and take massive action. Remember, the road to someday leads to the road to nowhere. Facing death shines the light on the importance of figuring out your life's vision.

So live your legacy!

About Nicole

Nicole Markson is an Automotive Expert with 20 years experience in the automotive field. She is a graduate of New York University and The National Automobile Dealers Association Dealer Candidate Academy where she earned her certification to operate an automobile dealership. She started out studying Theater and Communications at NYU and studying voice to become a singer. She began working in the family business at the dealership as a means to earn a living while pursuing her musical career. As time went on, she decided to enter into the family business. Working her way through the ranks, she held the positions of Sales Manager, General Manager and Finance Director and specialized in working with credit challenged customers. It was at this juncture, she discovered her passion for helping women secure the right deal to meet their individual life circumstances. She realized women needed a compassionate, transparent, fair approach to the purchasing process and weren't being taken seriously.

With 15 years under her belt, she left the family business to launch Autoempowerment, a company dedicated to changing the purchasing experience women are subjected to at auto dealerships by recognizing women as a major consumer force. Her goal is to help clients create economic stability by taking back financial control of their car deals, their lives and their financial destiny so they are no longer afraid to deal with money matters. By serving as a personal guide through the purchasing/leasing process, women are able to make informed financial choices, and use the experience to build confidence in the rest of their lives. Nicole's philosophy is that "a deal is not a deal unless it works for you, and everybody's life circumstance is unique and deserves careful evaluation in order to execute the right purchasing strategy." Nicole has helped plenty of men along the way and welcomes them as well.

Nicole, dedicated to being a leader in her field, created a video educational series dedicated to teaching women and teens strategies for negotiating amazing deals. She is a radio host on "The Autolab" a live call-in automotive talk show in NYC that educates listeners on automotive matters. She has conducted interviews with Consumer Reports, The Insurance Institute for Highway Safety, National Institute for Automotive Service Excellence (ASE), and leading manufacturers. She has written articles for She Buys Cars, TravelingMom.com and has been quoted in *Forbes*. She has appeared as an Automotive Expert on ABC World News Tonight with Diane Sawyer, Nightline, and CNBC's Closing Bell. Nicole conducts her own educational seminars and is a public speaker. She covers a range of topics on financial education and personal development. She is also a Breast Cancer Survivor and shares her survival story to help newly diagnosed women make informed choices about their treatment …and how to survive, strive and thrive after experiencing an illness. An avid life learner, she loves reading business books, attending business and motivational seminars, working on real estate projects, taking spin classes, recording music, and can be found weighing in at Weight Watchers. She adores spending time with her wonderful husband Jed, amazing daughter Sydney, and their fluffy Shitzu-Poodle, Goldie.

You can connect with Nicole at:

AUTOEMPOWERMENT.COM

By calling (551)579-4227

Nicole@autoempowerment.com

www.facebook.com/Nicole Markson

CHAPTER 67

SMART IS THE NEW RICH —HOW TO RETIRE ON 6% TO 9% INCOME FOR LIFE—IN A 3% WORLD

BY STEVE JURICH,
Certified Income Specialist®

When Baby Boomers were growing up and growing their hair, people said: "these kids don't know what they want." Today, Baby Boomers are becoming very clear about what they want in their financial plans: No BS, sustainable income equivalent to their lifestyle, more simplicity, less risk, and upside growth potential. Did I mention *no BS?*

The generation that told their parents to quit worrying and "chill," now wants to chill and enjoy life themselves. Early statistics tell us they will be drawing on their savings for 30 to 40 years, without adding a penny. This is gonna cost some money—will low interest rates and volatile markets torpedo their plans?

The Bureau of Labor Statistics tells us that 50,000 baby boomers a day turn age 60 to 65. As they enter a *new* brave world, they are asking new questions about money. Not ready to accept their parents' solutions to problems (hey, they wouldn't be Boomers otherwise), they are demanding new answers. They saw and felt the crash of 2000-2003.

They saw it again in 2008. Now, apparently, *'My Generation Won't Be Fooled Again!'*

Their grandparents were lucky to make 15 years in retirement. People were considered "really old" at age 75. Today's 65 year olds are still kicking butt, and many 75 year olds are very active—hitting the gym, playing golf, still traveling. Health-wise, that's good news. Money-wise—they've got work to do. Withdrawing money for 30 or 40 years at a five percent or six percent clip, when some years may lose forty or fifty percent? Even if you got a C in math, you get the picture.

Meanwhile, Wall Street continues to ladle out the same old porridge: "If you want more income and more growth, simply take more risk." If it's that easy, one can only wonder why it's called risk? If indeed more risk equals more money, it's not risk.

Retirees are seeing through this foggy "logic." The market has risen to uncomfortable levels on the 'waiving magic wand' of Ben Bernanke. One day, he will 'wave' the other way. The message is clear: Wall Street should not be viewed as a trusted custodian of the only nest egg you'll ever have.

Look, this is serious business. Retirement for most Boomers and those born right before them, will last around 30 years on average—about the same length of time it took to accumulate their money piles. What is going to be the safest and most reliable way to now turn those piles into streams of income into their 90's? A man of 62 may have a spouse of 57. Statistics now say she has a 30% chance of making it to 97. That's forty years of withdrawals.

Bottom line: You will likely live longer than you think and need more income. Wall Street may not be able to provide the income you want, and it certainly can't guarantee it. Interest rates have fallen for 32 years since 1980, when bank CDs were doling out close to 18% interest. Today, the bank wants to pay you a little less than that. Try 0.25% for the privilege of keeping your money on their side of the marble counter. I almost said for keeping it in their vault, but the money is not kept there. They're taking it in at 0.25% and lending it out at 15% on credit cards. Good work if you can get it.

It's pretty easy to see that math and time are not on your side once you hit the chronological and financial age of 55. Biologically, you may still be in your 40s or 50s. *Biologically* speaking, that's a good thing. Financially speaking, you have work to do. A strategy change is in order.

Consider the math:

- A $500,000 account paying income at 1% a year pays only $5,000 annually.

- A $500,000 account paying income at 4% a year, pays $20,000 annually.

- A $500,000 account paying income at 6% a year pays $30,000 annually.

Which do you prefer? Obviously, the $20,000 to $30,000 range is more appealing, but where will it come from? How long will it last? How much risk will you need to take in order to secure it?

Imagine securing an income of $25,000 to $30,000 annually(or more) on the same $500,000, without risking a penny in the market, and with a contractual guarantee to last your lifetime, backed by the claims paying ability of a one hundred year old insurer, backed by regulated reserves, that has never lost a penny for any customer at any time. If financial security in any economy—up, down, or sideways is important to you, it's time to do a little more research.

DON'T LET THE MARKETS EAT YOUR MONEY —YOU'RE GOING TO NEED EVERY DIME OF IT

If you aren't careful, the markets can and will eat your money. Full disclosure: I am not a "perma-bear". I love the market, especially when it loves me. Who doesn't? But the lessons of 2000-2002 and then again in 2008, should be all you need to know—in your *withdrawal* phase. Stuff happens. Arm yourself with the facts. Experts like Ned Davis Research tell us Bear markets occur statistically about every 5.2 years and last nearly two years. Don't fight the facts. Stick around for 30 more years, and you could live to see at least five more bear markets (market declines of 20% or more). Try withdrawing five percent when your money is cascading downward for a few years. The phenomenon is known as "Reverse Dollar Cost Averaging, or RDCA."

In the same manner that Dollar Cost Averaging works to build money, Reverse Dollar Cost Averaging works to eat money, especially if losses come early in retirement. What happens when you reverse the process and start withdrawing instead of contributing? Bad things. A study by Ernst & Young in 2012 determined that many of today's affluent retirees are at risk of a fifty-six percent failure rate in their income plans. That means what you think it means: running out of income *and* money. Why? Today's low interest rates, plus market volatility, combined with steady withdrawals and inflation.

CONCLUSION? IF THE NEW GENERATION OF RETIREES STAYS WITH THE OLD GENERATION OF INVESTING IDEAS, THEY'RE TOAST

Instead, a New Revolution of income planning strategies has emerged. It involves innovations in the arena of annuities (eek, an annuity!). I know, I know—you would never consider an annuity as a younger investor, and I would not recommend an annuity to you as a younger investor. But shift happens, my friend. You are no longer a younger investor.

Instead of listening to a biased or under-informed broker tell you why you don't need an annuity, do your own research.

See what the Wharton School of Business, Texas Tech, and even Roger Ibbotson of Morningstar have to say about annuities. It may surprise you. In fact, Ibbotson is quoted as saying that annuities are the "new bonds."

Face it, this is the only nest egg you will ever have. Before you count your financial chickens, make sure they will hatch. First things first:

- Preserve your nest egg's income producing capability, no matter what kind of market we are in.

- Pay yourself an income in the range of 6% to 9% – regardless of market conditions--based on your age and when you start your income.

Let's check this observation by Professor David Babbel of the Wharton School of Business:

The consensus of the literature from professional economists is that lifetime income annuities should definitely play a substantial role in the retirement arrangements of most people. How great a role depends on a number of factors, but it is fair to say that for most people, lifetime income annuities should comprise from 40% to 80% of their retirement assets under current pricing. Generally speaking, if a person has no bequest motive, or is averse to high risk, the portion of wealth allocated to annuities should be at the higher end of this range.

~ Professor David Babbel,
Wharton School of Business, University of Pennsylvania

Smart Is The New Rich: Sustainable Cash Flow, Not Cash, Is The Essence of Real Planning.

Your income plan for retirement in the new normal should look like this:

- **Sustainable** - Your income must last as long as you do. Period.
- **Measurable** – In dollars. You can't manage what you can't measure.
- **Attainable** - Your income needs to be real, not based on hope.
- **Reliable** - Cash flow with no interruption, even in poor markets.
- **Timely** - The income is ready for you when you are ready for it.

GOOD PLANNING IN RETIREMENT BEGINS WITH INCOME PLANNING

Building the income floor is the first order of business, just as pouring a concrete foundation is the first step in building any structure. Therefore, smart assets in retirement must have the capacity to generate cash flow safely, for a long, long time. Safely means without putting your irreplaceable nest egg assets at risk.

In the Old Normal, you could just "live off the interest" in retirement. All you needed was a 'paid off' house, money in the bank, some muni bonds and a few Ginnie Maes. That was a 6% world, and that world no longer exists. The new normal is a 3% world. That old plan will pay you a poverty wage and, perhaps, leave your family with very little – if anything – when your time passes one day.

YOUR GOOD HEALTH AND LONGER LIFESPAN MAY TURN INTO YOUR BIGGEST EXPENSE

Jeffrey Opdyke writing in the *Wall Street Journal* pointed out that an annuity holder with $600,000 placed in annuities could live as well as a traditional investor with $1,000,000 in stocks and bonds. That's buying the future at a $400,000 discount. Annuities don't cost, they pay. After 2008, the annuity holder with $600,000 in annuities still had $600,000 in annuities with income guaranteed. The investor with a million in the markets likely was down to around $500,000, with confidence shaken.

As always in financial planning, there is no "one-size-fits-all" solution to every set of circumstances. Annuities aren't right for everybody nor are they ever right in unlimited amounts for *anybody*. However, when clear thinking about statistical fact and academic research get applied to the finite realities of managing money, annuities can't be ignored.

A VERY RISKY TIME REQUIRES A FULLY INTEGRATED PLAN—AND FOR YOU IN RETIREMENT, THIS IS A VERY RISKY TIME

A fully integrated retirement plan must include an income replacement plan, an investment plan, a tax plan, a healthcare plan, and an estate plan. However, most people don't have a complete plan in any one of those areas let alone all five.

Wealth is defined differently by each person. For some, it is the attainment of an actual numerical goal in terms of dollars and possessions. To others, it is the knowledge that you have provided for loved ones, paid all debts and made good on your promises. Still others measure their progress by their ability to help the less fortunate or their church. A simplified definition might be: "No more money worries, no matter what." Regardless, getting there and staying there requires a fully integrated financial plan.

The old fashioned pie chart model of financial planning—the 60/40 stock bond portfolio has seen better days. New risks have emerged, but here's the good news: Managed correctly, your retirement "Number" need not be as big as you once thought. When you start enjoying more sustainable income with fewer dollars, regardless of the markets, you'll understand why more people are discovering that retirement planning has more to do with math, than markets. Since hope is never a strategy, choose solutions that exchange risk for guarantees in the income portion of your plan. This is *your* retirement, and this is *your* turn to make it happen. Get smart, cut the worry—increase the income. As the late, great Stephen Covey might say, "Begin with the end in mind." *Yes, Smart IS the new rich.*

About Steven

Steve Jurich is a Certified Income Specialist®, President of IQ Wealth Management, and a popular business radio commentator. His comments have been seen on Bloomberg, TheStreet.com, MarketWatch, and CNBC.com.

As the manager of IQ Wealth Advisory, LLC, a Registered Investment Advisor, Steve is licensed in securities, as well as insurance and real estate. His new book on retirement, *Smart Is The New Rich* is available now on Amazon.com. Steve is the editor of one of the top google-ranked annuity websites in America, MyAnnuityGuy.com™ and works with affluent retirees and pre-retirees seeking to preserve and grow their retirements. His clients range in background from engineers, teachers, and medical professionals to business owners, government workers, and accountants. His firm has offices in Scottsdale and Los Angeles.

CHAPTER 68

THE SEVEN LAWS OF THE UNIVERSE AND YOUR MINDSET FOR SUCCESS

BY CHRISTIAN HIDALGO LIMONGI

Success is a state of mind. Like everything in life we can't obtain success without doing something; because of the law of cause and effect we know that it's impossible to obtain any result without an action. It doesn't matter if we use all the other laws, without the law of cause and effect we can't get results. We have to carefully choose the actions that we take so that we can increase our probabilities of success.

Success is the achievement of something desired, planned, or attempted. To be successful we must know what we want first, and that's the first thing that we have to be successful in – finding our passion. What do we really want to do in life? …Because what we have and who we are is related to what we do, and what we do is something that we choose to.

When we know what we want, we can plan how to get it.

The map is not the territory. It's our state of mind, attitude, emotions, imagination and our actions that determine everything. When we change the map we also change the territory because of the law of correspondence.

There are 7 laws in the Universe and these laws act, whether we know them or not.

The laws are:

1. Cause and Effect

2. Mentalism

3. Generation

4. Vibration

5. Correspondence

6. Rhythm

7. Polarity

These laws are called Universal because they exist and act for everyone. These laws don't make a difference due to beliefs, social classes, religion, political party or profession.

We are responsible for our lives because we are responsible for our minds and emotions. We decide what goes into our minds and emotions and this determines our lives. If we fill our minds and emotions with positive information our lives are positive, if we feed them with negative information our lives will be negative. The law of correspondence works in anyway. This is something that we choose, nobody can choose for us what goes into our minds. That's why it's important to train our minds in the best possible way. Even with problems and conflicts, if we work on the cause we can solve them in an easier way. The cause is inside and therefore that's what we have to work on every day. Through personal development we can change our lives in any way as long as we understand and use these laws.

1. THE LAW OF CAUSE AND EFFECT

"Every cause has an effect and every effect has a cause."

The Law of Cause and Effect is the most important because without this law we can't achieve anything. The imagination can't be transformed in reality without the Law of Cause and Effect. This Law also teaches that everything has an effect. Even after people die, their actions have an effect on future generations, positive or negative, depending on the causes. Positive actions bring rewards and negative actions consequences.

The purpose of life is always the good. As Saint Germain states: "Life, in all Its activities everywhere manifest, is God in Action; and it is only through lack of the understanding of applied thought and feeling that mankind is constantly interrupting the pure flow of that Perfect Essence of Life which would, without interference, naturally express Its Perfection everywhere.

The natural tendency of Life is Love, Peace, Beauty, Harmony, and Opulence, for Life cares not who uses It, but is constantly surging to pour more of Its Perfection into manifestation, always with that lifting process which is ever inherent within Itself."

This is why we have to be clear in what we want, we have to be clear in our goals everyday, we have to keep notes of them everyday, we must have something to live for, as Malcolm X said: "If you don't stand for something, you will fall for anything."

We can do this by writing our 10 or more most important goals in:

- Family and Relationships
- Health. Physical, Emotional and Mental
- Finance
- Business and Career

After we have clarity in regards to our goals, with deadlines we can start working on our achievements. We also need to know the importance of a coach or mentor because they can show us the way and we just have to follow it. Everyone that is successful obtained their goals because they used the laws in the right way.

Using this law we can change reality, which is the territory, because everything that we see is the result of something that's inside. And to change everything outside we have to first change the inside, starting to work on the place where everything begins, the mind.

2. THE PRINCIPLE OF MENTALISM

"The all is mind; the universe is mental."

The most important Law is the Law of Cause and Effect because the Law of Mentalism can't act without the Law of Cause and Effect, even if someone thinks, talks and imagines positive things it's not possible to obtain results without action. Physical action produces physical results.

That's why we have to work on all the areas of our life.

To have great financial results in our lives, we have to work on ourselves, especially in our way of thinking.

We have a conscious, subconscious and super-conscious mind. We have to discipline our conscious mind so that the right information goes to our subconscious mind and when we receive ideas from the super-conscious mind we are ready to take action.

The mind is influenced by the emotions according of the quality of the emotions and feelings in our lives, this happens because all the laws are related. With the mind and emotions we generate a vibration, these are two other laws that work all the time.

Financial success is a state of mind. Everyone with a fortune first created a fortune internally. First the mind has to be able to imagine. Where there is no vision people perish because everything is first created inside and through action everything is created outside.

To change the action we have to change our internal state. All rich people think in the same way in many things, all poor people also think in the same way. There are beliefs and ideas that make us think in a rich way: Spend less than what you earn, save and invest the difference, pay yourself first and many other ones.

But when we get around the right people, our lives can change because their philosophy, their positive thought and feelings will also go to our subconscious mind and we will produce positive results in our lives. Everything that we read and see goes to our subconscious mind and that's something that only we can decide.

3. THE PRINCIPLE OF GENDER

"Gender is in everything; everything has its masculine and feminine principles; gender manifests on all planes."

It's really important to understand this law. We can see the results of everything that mankind does, but to solve everything we have to understand how reality works because reality and circumstances are created by humans. Circumstances reveal everything that's inside of everyone.

Our world in every area is the result of what we have inside. The way of solving difficulties is to work on inside ourselves, because there is always correspondence between what is inside and what is outside. Reality is the result or the effect of something that is inside us first – in our emotions, minds, imagination and most importantly, in our actions. Our choices are also happening inside ourselves and that's why we have to train our minds in the best way possible so that we can make the best decisions.

To have the best results we have to have the best minds. To master all the areas that we have to master in life we need to study them as much as possible. Here are four areas of Focus:

(a). Relationships

This is one of the most important things that we have to have because this determines our future and the future of the world also. When we stop being around negative people we can be positive. To do this we also have to be around positive people, and when we are positive we can help other people into being positive.

We are not the only ones in the world, to achieve anything we will always need the help of others.

(b). Health

This is also something that we have to work on inside ourselves. Health is emotional, physical and mental, all of them are related. Looking at the world we can see how healthy everyone is, not only physically but also mentally and emotionally. This is related to our relationships in finance and business and career. There is no point thinking that we can have one area in order and not the others. We have to work on all of them to be successful.

(c). Finance

There are hundreds of books that teach people how to be successful financially. There are also many seminars and coaches that help people in this aspect. It's very important to be successful financially because this also elevates our self-esteem, improves our relationships and even our conversations are more interesting and positive when we have goals…when we know where we are going and what we have to do to achieve what we want. With this the first law is the one that we have to use in order to be really successful, because there is no real success in doing something that later will come back to us. That's why it's good to be financially free, but this has to be done thinking in terms of serving other people, changing the world for good and in that way making a lot of money. Our philosophy has to be of-service if we want to make money in the right way. That is to think in terms of what we can do for others instead of what others can do for us.

(d). <u>Business and Career</u>

To be successful financially we have to be successful in our business or career, and to be successful in this, we have to work really hard. First of all, we have to know what we want, and second of all, we have to find a way to get everything that we want doing something that we love—that's success. Obtaining everything that we want, doing something that we love with the people that we want to work and be with.

To obtain everything we have to work on our own Personal Development, this makes us stop making excuses for everything. When we understand that we are responsible, we stop making excuses.

4. THE PRINCIPLE OF VIBRATION

"Nothing rests; everything moves; everything vibrates."

Our emotional world has a vibration that attracts thoughts to our minds. These thoughts become actions and all those actions have reactions. Even the smallest action has a reaction, big actions are the group of small actions that can create massive results over time.

All humans have a vibration that is created by our feelings and minds. These vibrations create a state of mind in us and the same vibration will attract everything that's in harmony with the vibration. That's why in some holy places in the world, the vibration is so positive that it makes people feel good and positive. Our vibrations can be felt by plants and animals and they also react to our vibrations.

Disorder also creates a vibration of disorder and attracts more disorder. The key of this principle is to work on our own vibration rather than the vibration of others, because to change the vibration of others we have to change our vibration first. As Gandhi said: "Be the change that you want to see in the world." Just by changing ourselves we can change others.

5. CORRESPONDENCE

"As above so below; as below so above."

When we change our vibration, by the law of correspondence everything in our life starts to change. When our vibration is higher it will automatically attract better things, people, opportunities, situations, job opportunities, relationships and everything that is related to our vibration.

Because of this law, we attract people that are similar to us. Something that we will always notice when we change our vibration is that a lot of the people around us will change. We will always attract people that think in the same way so when our thinking changes, the people around us change.

This law also teaches us that we have to seek advice from the experts to do anything in life. When we want something in life, we can think about someone that already has what we want. We then can start tracing the actions of that person to the causes and so that we can learn from them and copy them.

6. RHYTHM

This is the law that will give us critical mass in all these aspects of our lives. To have great lives we must have great actions and that's why it's important to work on our psychology because our psychology and our emotions determine our actions.

These are the internal things that we have to develop all the time. As we said before, first we must know what we want, how do we see our lives in 1, 3, 5 and 10 years. We need to have realistic goals in all areas of life and then we have to work on our goals. When we do that we will achieve everything that we have to achieve. One of the reasons why people don't succeed in life and start to look for escapes is because they are not clear on what they want.

7. POLARITY

A loser can become a winner using these laws. Everything works according to these laws but the impatience of people makes them give up on their goals and their vision of happy lives. Nothing is achieved straight away because we have to escalate from fear to faith, from poor to rich, from doubts to certainty, ignorance to wisdom, hate to love and revenge to forgiveness. Everything in life is a process, and the accumulation of wealth is done cent-by-cent and dollar-by-dollar, until the point of critical mass where the positive mind controls the territory. Our job is to work on the cause of everything, those causes are inside ourselves. There is a price that we have to pay to be successful, this price we can only pay for ourselves, we can only change others by changing ourselves.

Even when someone wins the lottery but the money is not in correspondence with that state of mind that will keep it and grow it, that person will lose everything because it's all about developing positive ways of thinking. If we change our feelings and our thinking processes, we will also change our actions including the people that we surround ourselves with. Contrary to that example, if someone with a rich state of mind loses everything because that situation does not correspond with that state of mind – that mind won't settle for less than excellence and will accumulate wealth again usually more than ever before because it's not possible to go back in the law of polarity. The way is always forward because the human's evolution is also emotional and mental. The quality of the mind and emotions evolves everyday and we can accelerate this process by learning from the experts.

These 7 Laws connect the invisible with the visible.

As Frank Sinatra said: *"The best revenge is massive success."*

About Christian

Christian H. Limongi is a young entrepreneur that started with nothing as have many others.

He owns a firm that largely specialises in niche areas of the property market, and is now expanding to niche areas of the hospitality industry.

His goal is to solve the cause of the world's problems, and by so doing, how we will resolve the effects. All the causes of everything are internal and that's why we have to work on the inside to see results on the outside.

He studied Metaphysics since the age of 16, that's when he discovered self development, something that changed his life and now continues to do so. Christian had been working with a FocalPoint coach since he started his firm, therefore he knows the importance of mentorship. We all need others to help us succeed in the journey of life.

You can connect with Christian at:
christian@newage-intl.com
www.twitter.com/christianhlimo
www.facebook.com/christianhlimongi

CHAPTER 69

YOU CAN RETIRE IN 3-5 YEARS

BY CURTIS BROOKS, G.G., CLC

Can YOU really retire in 3-5 years?

The answer is unequivocally, **YES! *You can***. The question however, is, "Will you do the things necessary to retire in that timeframe?"

Face it. You have probably read many business books. You may already have a successful business, if so the question then becomes, "Will you look for *what you don't know* to find that one gem of information that will **transform your business and your life into true financial freedom?**

I have taught many people who attained that 'retirement' goal, some in less time some in more. It all came down to their application of the systems and processes we teach to multiply and manage their money and give themselves the real retirement they wanted. Not the, "Can I make it on $5,000 a month?" kind of retirement, but the real retirement of your dreams. Others have done it. The question is, *"Will you learn what you need to learn so that you can earn what you need to earn, in order to be able to retire in three to five years?"* People from every walk of life have succeeded with our plan. Why not you?

Steve Forbes and I agree wholeheartedly that America has a bright future. We are the innovators of the world. Innovation arises from our roots as free individuals who know that *all is possible if we seek specialized knowledge and the wisdom to use it.* We also know that the choices our elected officials have made have taken a terrible financial situation and amplified it.

America and the world financial markets have changed. Those changes will not reverse in our lifetime or the lifetime of any child born today. If you intend to thrive, not just survive, you need to acquire that special knowledge and the acumen to use that knowledge to surf the tsunamis of the Financial Earthquakes ahead. Do you want to learn to surf before or after the financial tidal wave has struck?

What is not obvious are the real ramifications of the 'Free Money' to the Banks and the non-stop debasing of world currencies with worldwide forms of "Quantitative Easing."

We expect to see the DOW cut in half over the next two years, a de-leveraging of debt which will crunch the credit markets, gold to dip to $800, and oil to fall below $50 a barrel. This also means the propped up housing market is going to take another hit and could see drops as much as 40% in some areas. Likewise, commercial real estate will suffer. **There is no substance to the "economic recovery"** so optimistically created by the administration, the media, and of course Wall Street – who wants you to buy more stocks. The hucksters on Wall Street will say, "Look how much the market has recovered," when, in fact, its historical highs come from 'out of thin air' money.

Ask yourself, "Is business overall at historically high profits, or near their lows? Are you seeing people going to the malls to take a walk to just hang out while looking around, and then going to the discount stores to purchase? Even top performer Wal-Mart had horrible "Back to School" sales in 2013 and had to lower stock estimates which means that people are not buying, because they just don't have the money. Going into more detail here would take the rest of the book, so I'd like to invite you to go to www.HighOctaneWealth.com for more insights, information, and discussions about this and other financial awareness tips that will protect your hard earned money.

I want you to retire in 3–5 years. I want you to build cash reserves to **protect yourself from the economic slide and stagnation of the next 10 years**. None of us who looks at the economy through non-political eyes sees any real recovery beginning until 2023. *The upturn supposedly* *happening now is simply manipulated statistics and hidden inflation creating the illusion of rising markets; it is "smoke and mirrors" to fool the masses.*

If you are reading this book, you are neither ignorant nor a fool. If you believe anyone owes you anything in life, this book is probably not for you. If, on the other hand, you are ready to explode several myths about how fast you can create money, and use the techniques that the rich and the financial institutions use so you can retire to a beach or a penthouse, then read carefully and take action. I promise, if you are dedicated and diligent, this can and will help you.

As "International Director of Development" for a division of Mason Best Merchant Bank, I traveled the world building companies and ensuring we stayed ahead of the world's economic climate. I have coached individuals who led their companies to the Forbes Fastest Growing 100 companies, and I know I have the best method to enable the average bright person to achieve the life of their dreams. I am writing this from my 25th and 26th floor penthouse that overlooks the entire central valley, mountains, extinct volcanoes and San Jose, the capital of Costa Rica. I spend time in a penthouse just a short drive away that overlooks the beaches and tropical forest of one of the top 10 National Parks in the world.

Life is great, yet just a few short years ago, this was not the case. I had lost my wealth to unscrupulous business partners. I had cancer with a diagnosis of a 20% chance at living five years. My wife left; my dad died; my dog died. The list, was long and growing longer, until I realized it did not matter what cards life dealt me. I had a choice: Fight on because my daughter deserved her real Dad back or should I just quit life altogether? Mental and physical pain at times obscured the obvious answer. I am sure many of you know this pain first hand, I have been where you are, and I have come back stronger than ever and *you have the ability to do it too, with the right education.*

I invested six years locating and refining the best team of practical, real-life real-time "Financial Education" trainers in the world. Their Real World executable knowledge about the currency markets can not only *insulate you from the financial meltdown,* but also make you wealthy in the process.

I believe my team (because we have done it before) can train the average person how to trade currencies on the world market and make ¼% to ½% per day of trading. On average, there are 22 days of trading per month giving you a potential of 11% increase Per Month. Below is a chart (a) that shows you the potential of what a $10,000 account would look like after just 4 years.

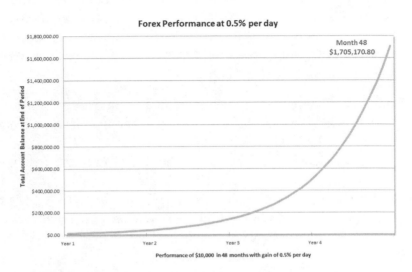

As you can see at the Beginning Of Year 2 at 11% per month your account could compound up to $40,219.54; and B.O.Y. 3 = $145,337.98; and B.O.Y. 4 = $525,195.60 and by the End Of Year 4 a potential of $1,705,170.00. At this point, you can retire to trading for a few hours a week and still spin off $500,000 plus per year. We have many students who have reached this level of making that 0.25 - 0.5% and a few stars who really dedicated themselves to being top traders and are doing better than 18% per month. The main variable is you.

I can't promise you success. You might lack the dedication and diligence to succeed even with this proven method. However, we have trained some of the best private traders, as well as training International Fund Managers and Multinational Corporate Money Managers to trade currencies with the exact same systems. These systems were set up to take the financial novice to success. That is why they work so well.

I am well retired and only do what I want to now, so a fair question is, "Why am I still educating people, when it is really not a lucrative job?" There comes a point in a person's life when they have it figured out; they have it made and their future is secure. This level of success affords them the opportunity to explore the ways they can impact the world around them.

During my quest for a way to change the world, a friend, who passed away early in life, challenged me to find a method to give away to meaningful charities $1,000,000,000.00 – yep, 1billion USD. Now that is a huge number and individually that hill seems insurmountable. However, what if I could teach you and 10,000 folks in the next 10 years how to become wealthy and great stewards of money, and YOU then support the goal of 1billion to charities. *We can succeed if we do the following, together:*

I teach you how you can double your money, and double it again, and again, *by learning the professional way to trade currencies for a living.* Then one day a month, you join the cause with us, and we all trade for 15 minutes to 4 hours *and* give those earnings away the next day. **Imagine what it would be like to be so wealthy that you could just give away money and not feel the pinch.**

Folks that is my personal goal! To get you to the point of wealth where you are able to dedicate a few hours each month, and average $834.00 to a worthy charity each time. We could each give away $100,000 in 10 years. I have a heck of a job set for myself without your help! With your help, it becomes an achievable and worthy goal: Personal Wealth and Philanthropy! A question, Can you commit to a higher calling than just achieving personal financial success? If so, this method of learning is for you.

I have built several fortunes, and I have witnessed many friends and worthy strangers struggle to make a difference in their lives and the lives of their families. They spent years flailing around trying to find the way and somehow thinking that their idea was going to set the world on fire. You can still achieve the "American Dream" a thousand different ways, but frankly, most people, including many family members and friends, don't have a clue how to "Make It Happen." With the help of my dedicated associates, you will have a proven *modus operandi* to turn lives around. By teaching people in every walk of life how to become wealthy and how to become good stewards of that wealth, we will change the world. *This becomes a pathway to generational wealth that will change entire families' lives*.

Here is the 'catch', there are two keys to becoming a successful world-class trader: first, the tenacity to learn and stay current with the systems that produce 70-90% winning trades, and second, to learn the emotional controls that allow successful implementation of proper money management techniques. This is not a get-rich-quick scheme. This type of training must last a year for it to be effective.

Bear in mind, every trader – even the best in the world – has losses and wins. Currency trading is not an all win game, therefore, we excel at teaching you to manage your mind and emotions. Some say you need nerves of steel; others say you have to be cold and unemotional. Frankly, those are both recipes for disaster. You need to be just as happy with your losses as you are with your wins! You must have the systems and the money management to give you the strength to **trade happily, and therefore confidently, in any outcome**.

My team and I teach a select few each year to do this professional training and we charge the "Mercantile Boys" from Chicago $30K for a year's training, but for you, we have a different view. For the non-industry person we provide a special program to those who are committed to learn, with a huge discount to those who also agree to join our charity challenge. What does that mean? When you have learned how to trade profitably, you voluntarily raise your hand and attend a special webinar that we hold once a month (except Aug.) to trade for charity. The charities will vary from drilling fresh water wells to orphanages and self-sustaining villages, and the incredible Micro lender to the poor, Bank Grameen. [Visit us at: www.HighOctaneWealth.com for more information on the charities and our mission.]

If you possess the desire, we provide the knowledge. We can, with your diligence, teach you how to make that +/- 0.5% per day and the money management skills needed to build your wealth and retire in 3 to 5 years. We do this with two separate educational paths: a quick start program for a full freshman (raw beginner) to Graduate 5 Level training that many Professional International Fund traders are required by their companies to attend. *The multiple weekly live trading sessions and training sessions are integral to your learning curve, as is the ability* *to reach out and talk to one of our top traders when you are stuck.* We guide you from the beginning basics to a full working knowledge of how to enter and exit like a pro, and how to control the 6" between your ears that represent the difference between you being just another 'Wanna-Be Trader' and being a "Money-Making Professional Trader."

If you know nothing about trading, then you are like many of our successful traders who came in green. Our 60-lesson self-paced fast start modules can have you up and going within a couple of weeks (no, we don't use robots). Next, you learn to win better than 50% of your trades using our proven trading systems. Your year-long training includes 5-8 live sessions training and trading each week, everything archived, over 100 video lessons, multiple levels of training and our annual *"Success"* boot camp – you have every opportunity to win big. We have made it comprehensive yet simple to understand! We also made it all-inclusive. We make it a 'no brainer' to jump on this express lane to fulfilling your personal best life.

This is the Real World of Financial Freedom and a Real World Training, therefore I cannot promise you anything because I can't read your mind or dedication. Do you quantify your success not by meeting your goals but by exceeding them? Do you dream of changing the world one water well, one house, one small farm and one family at a time while learning how to be wealthy to boot? If you are willing to dedicate yourself part-time for one year to education that will change your life, then we stand ready to help you in a unique training program that is ready to help you reach your 'retirement freedom.' The only thing we are missing is YOU!

About Curtis

From humble beginnings growing up with dirt floors and a grass roof to living in his 26th floor two-story penthouse overlooking a tropical paradise, Curtis Brooks, G.G., CLC, has been helping his clients achieve their financial dreams for decades. Curtis knows how people can come from humble beginnings and reach the pinnacle of success. He has done it himself and has seen it done over and over again with the two keys he says you must have: 1) a learned specialized knowledge, and 2) the "bull-headed" persistence to make it happen.

With these keys, he himself has started from zero. Starting from humble beginnings, he educated himself and had a wildly successful career helping corporations achieve their financial goals and helping families create an individual financial fortune that many of us only dream about. Unfortunately, his life was turned to ruins after a series of personal catastrophes starting with the complete and total theft of his sizable fortune, deceit of a business partner just as he was rebuilding his business, an emotionally devastating divorce, and life-threatening 3rd stage Malignant Cancer. He is a true comeback story, which he is willing to share with you, so you too can learn and create your financial security.

Curtis holds a Graduate Gemologist degree in Geology from the Gemological Institute of America and did his undergraduate work in Business and Finance at New Mexico Military Institute, as well as University of Johannesburg, and U.Wit., S.A. He worked extensively with the Smithsonian, the Museum of Natural History, NYC, with the geology departments of the Museum of London, Museum National d'Histoire Naturelle, Paris, as well as working with the University of Texas, UCLA, Yale, Harvard, and The Royal Museum of Canada. He then went on to build several manufacturing facilities and was hired by Mason Best Merchant Bankers to develop a fine jewelry division. One of the well-known directors at MB became his mentor. That man was the ex-Treasurer of the United States and past Governor of Texas, "Big John" Connolly (historically known as the man who was shot in the car with Pres. Kennedy). Curtis was taught by "Big John" how to profit from Currency Exchange and the arbitrage of Gold and Silver. This knowledge was and is highly specialized information, and it held the secrets to making vast amounts of money – which is still unknown to most of the general public. It was closely guarded by corporations and the banking industry and very few outside of the international financial world knew of its existence. It was not until the early 2000's when computers, Internet, and broad market culture changes within the trading industry made it possible for the layperson to participate. That is when Curtis started assembling the team that has, and can, change lives.

Having lived, taught, and run businesses in eight different countries as Director of International Development for M.B., Merchant Bank gives Curtis a unique perspective on how and what it takes to succeed. He has trained countless thousands of people in the real world application of generating significant cash flows for income and long-term generational wealth over the past 40 years.

Curtis has a set of true gifts – the ability to make the complicated simple, and to take the average, but dedicated person and make them a superstar. Curtis and his team show you how to take a modest amount of money and with diligence, study, and simple rules-based systems, learn how to double or better that money each and every year.

He says learning how to make money is only part of the equation to wealth, many people make it and then lose it all. When you want self-sustaining long-term wealth, that means getting a good financial stewardship education at the same time. Get both by finding more information on creating your true wealth and how to keep it growing at: www.HighOctaneWealth.com.

CHAPTER 70

SOME GOLDEN RULES OF SUCCESS

BY JIM WHITENER, AAMS®

After a successful career as a business entrepreneur, I decided to enter the Financial Services industry to help business owners and retirees build and maintain their financial wealth. I started my new career from scratch in August of 1998. Today I manage over $100 million in assets for my clients. That is a milestone in my industry.

I built my practice one client at a time and entirely by referrals. I never had to use cold call lists or mass mailing techniques. I never put on any sales seminars or invited people to free prime rib sales luncheons. I built my practice with these core traditional values – Integrity, Trust, Commitment and Service.

The core values I implemented from the very beginning of my Financial Services career have served me well. I have also had the good fortune to have been chosen to mentor and train many new advisors. In addition to my core values, I have instilled in them numerous business principles that have enabled me to be highly successful. In this chapter I would like to also share with you some of those success principles that may help propel you to success in your own business.

ALWAYS DO THE RIGHT THING

After passing the licensing requirements enabling me to begin my career in Financial Services, I showed up for my first day of training.

To say I was immediately disappointed would be an understatement. The instructor wrote on the board in big letters: "THIS IS A SALES POSITION." My great disappointment was based on the fact that I didn't want to be a salesman. Instead, I wanted to teach, help others, and share information so my clients could make informed decisions.

I have always considered myself an employee of my clients, not the company I represented. I always teach those I mentor that it's not the trades you make that keep you successful; it's the trades that you don't make which will make you successful. You see, some investment products pay good commissions, but they are not always good for all clients in all situations. Sometimes the "easy" trade is the wrong trade. It is of utmost importance to always do the right thing. That is, do what is in the client's best interest. The commission should simply be a bi-product of doing what is right for the client. Just as a dog can sense fear, clients will eventually sense truth, honesty and sincerity or the lack thereof.

The most difficult part of my job is to manage behavioral finance. That is, the psychology that drives people's investment decisions. People often make emotional decisions that end up going against their interests. A rational investor buys when prices are low and sells when the price is high. The emotional investor does the exact opposite.

As a responsible advisor, I must always direct my clients to do what is best for them and help them understand why the decision is in their best interest. Whatever business you may be in, the same principle applies. You must always do the right thing for your client or customer, even if it means you will not benefit as much from the transaction. I taught my children that the formula for success was measured by the value of your character, not by the value of your estate.

BECOME A MASTER AT YOUR PROFESSION

I am registered and licensed to do business in 17 states. I am licensed to offer Life Insurance and Long Term Care Insurance. I hold a series 24 license. I also hold series 66, 7 and 63 licenses.

As you can see, my credentials enable me to do a variety of things. However, instead of being a *jack-of-all-trades and master of none*, I have chosen to tighten my focus. It is analogous to an athlete that is good in multiple sports but chooses to play basketball like Michael Jordan or someday represent the U.S. in the Olympics. Although I am licensed and qualified, I often refer specialized work to those that I know and trust will serve my clients' best interest so I can focus on what I do best for my clients.

It is important to know what you are, but even more important to know what you are not. For example, I am a moderately conservative Financial Advisor. I don't like to speculate with other people's money. I prefer an "Income with Principal Preservation" type of financial portfolio. In very simplistic terms, I look at an investment strategy as a ride in a car. Income is in the front seat. Principal Preservation is in the back seat. Growth is in the trunk. Growth is along for the ride and if I get it, great. But if I don't get it, that's fine.

Income with Principal Preservation is what I do best. Those who favor this investment philosophy are the people that come to me for my expertise. That is my laser-like focus. I have become a Master at that component of my profession even though I could be doing many other things. What is your laser-like focus? If you are a "Jack-of-all-trades," it is likely you are not as successful as you could be if you became a "Master" at a specific component within your profession.

KNOW YOUR REAL BOSS

In my profession, I always teach those I mentor to never lose sight of that fact that it is the client's money, not the firm's money, and that the reason you have work is because of your clients, not because of the firm. You might be a business owner and believe that you are your own boss, but you really work for your clients or customers. They, in essence, are your boss. They are the ones who have given you the work to accomplish. They are the individuals you need to please.

This is precisely what led my career to what it is today. I am an Independent Advisor with one of the largest independent advisory firms in the country. No conflicts of interest, no pressure quotas, no proprietary products, no business practices with investment banks. I don't work for anyone except my clients. While your particular circumstances may be somewhat different in that you may be tied to a particular "boss" in the traditional sense, you can always treat your clients or customers with the same respect as if they were your employer. Whether you are an employee or a business owner, never lose sight of the fact that your customers drive your income and they need to be treated with the utmost respect and dignity.

DON'T WALK, TALK OR ACT LIKE THE OTHER GUY

Your clients or customers already have access to "the other guy." If you are going to enjoy the spoils of success, you need to out-work, out-perform, out-study, out-practice, out-research the other guy and try your best every day to be the best that you can possibly be in every way. You need to bring your "A-Game" every single day. People will be attracted to you when you set yourself apart from others in your industry.

My business is like a meteorologist predicting weather patterns (economic conditions) and storms (market crashes). Even the best of the weather reporters mistake weather patterns from time to time, but they have to strive to do their best because lives depend on predicting a hurricane's path of destruction. None of us have a crystal ball. Since we can't predict the future, we must be prepared for it.

As you can understand, the Financial Services industry can sometimes change unpredictably much like weather patterns. But, by doing what many others are not willing to do in preparing for the unforeseen in the best possible way, I set myself apart. You can do the same with your business by taking the extra steps that others in your profession or industry are not willing to take.

ALWAYS FIND A SOLUTION EVEN WHEN OTHERS SAY IT CAN'T BE DONE

In the mid-90's I owned a successful photography business. While on a trip to Colorado I saw a very impressive digital imaging display. Since the 1996 Republican National Convention (RNC) was going to be held that year in my hometown of San Diego, someone suggested to me that I should capitalize on the digital imaging opportunity at the upcoming convention. Unfortunately, I only had about three months until the convention.

Accepting the challenge, I flew back to San Diego and went to the convention center where the RNC was to be held. I went from one resource to another and finally found out where I needed to go to inquire about doing the digital imaging for those attending the convention. When I arrived at the appropriate location, I was questioned about the reason I was there. They were quite surprised that I was even able to gain access to their offices through security. But before they ejected me from their facility, they allowed me to tell them the purpose of my visit. I explained to them my interest and they quickly informed me they already had that outsourced and I was too late for the bidding process.

However, I didn't allow that to stop me. I called the person in charge and was able to get him on the phone. To my surprise, I found out he was the former marketing director for the San Diego Chargers. He told me about the three major companies with which he was dealing. I was just a small business owner wanting to "get in the game" and was just a fraction of the size of my competitors. I learned that he was frustrated with the major companies because they wouldn't give him what he wanted. I pressed him for clarification. He told me he wanted a life-like image of Bob Dole, the Republican candidate for President at that time, so convention attendees could get their picture taken with the image. The major companies told him it was green screen technology and wasn't feasible to deliver what he wanted at the convention. I quickly responded, "I've got an idea. Let me check on a couple of things and I'll get back to you on Monday."

I immediately went to the local Walmart where they had these life-size standing cutouts of Michael Jordan. On the packaging I found the manufacturer located in Northern California and a contact number. I called them and they told me they could make a life-size cutout of Bob Dole for me, but they would need a full-length picture with the appropriate permission to use the photo.

My next challenge was to find a full-length picture of Mr. Dole. After a couple more phone calls to the East Coast, I found someone that might be able to help me with the picture, but it would require research to find a full-length picture. There were no guarantees, but the person on the other end of the phone sensed my passion and drive to accomplish this task and told me they would do their very best to find something for me. A few days later I had a full-length picture of Bob Dole from their archives and I paid them $500 for the rights to use the picture for two weeks.

I received confirmation from the company that made the cut-outs that they could have the image made by the time the convention started. I called the marketing director for the convention and told him I could make it happen. He quickly told me to come to his office to sign a contract.

Because I was willing to find a solution when others said there was no feasible solution, I was able to do something three other multi-million dollar companies with six-figure sales representatives thought could not be done. The San Diego Business Journal picked up the story and there was a significant financial benefit to me for my effort. You see, successful people will always find a way.

BE TENACIOUS

In 1997 the Green Bay Packers and the Denver Broncos came to San Diego to play in the Super Bowl and I decided to go after official Digital Imaging Rights for Super Bowl XXXII. Those around me thought I had lost my mind. There was a national company that had secured the contract I wanted for the past three Super Bowls. But, I didn't let that deter me. I kept trying to get to the right people to discuss the contract and I was constantly turned away by security. Someone asked me why I didn't give up after several attempts. I responded, "Because there are 446 days until the event and they're going to have to tell me 'no' 446 more times and then I'll go away."

Eventually, because of my persistence, I was able to talk with a decision maker at the NFL and I convinced him that they would benefit by making it an open bid process to at least give the local community the impression that they gave local people an opportunity to bid instead of just giving the contract to a national company as had been done in the past. I argued that it would also make the other guys sharpen their game if they want the contract. He agreed, but I had the distinct impression that he agreed only to get me out of the way. So, he opened up the bid and sent a bid letter to me and to the national company who had acquired the contract for the previous three years.

The major company initially ignored the letter and did not respond before the established bid deadline. Needless to say, that didn't set too well with those in charge. To make a long story short, they gave me the exclusive digital imaging rights to the 1997 NFL Super Bowl! I even received field level tickets as a sponsor. It was one of the greatest experiences of my life!

All NFL teams have rights to their team's logo and the NFL logo, but not the Super Bowl logo. So, a letter went out to every corporate sponsor in America and every NFL team saying, "If you want a digital imaging experience with the Super Bowl logo, you have to contact James Whitener." That my friend is success! It happened because I was tenacious. I didn't give up! When I set my mind to accomplish something, I will do whatever is necessary to make it happen. I have always acted with tenacity. That is a key component to accomplishing goals in life.

What about you? Do you act with tenacity? Will you keep going back 446 times if necessary? Do you have a drive and a spirit that will never give up until you accomplish your goal? Tenacity is a major driver of success. Without it you will be crushed. *Even if you've been knocked down, you can always get back up and keep going until you achieve your goal.*

About Jim

Jim Whitener, Registered Principal at LPL Financial and President of Whitener Wealth Management of La Mesa, California, possesses a depth of investment knowledge that can only come from years of experience in the Financial Services industry. Serving his clients since 1998, he has earned the prestigious designation of Accredited Asset Management Specialist (AAMS®) with training in asset management; risk, return and investment performance; asset allocation and investment selection; investment strategies; and deferred compensation and other benefit plans.

Jim's unrelenting dedication to provide his clients with quality, ethical services led him to become an independent financial advisor. He is devoted to helping his clients create financial stability and confidence in their investment decisions. He is under no pressure to promote certain financial products or to meet any kind of sales quotas. He is able to offer his clients truly unbiased advice and is free to search the marketplace for whatever insurance and investment products best serve his clients' needs.

Jim's dedication to his clients' best interests has not gone unnoticed. He is a four-time winner of the prestigious "Five Star Wealth Manager" designation by San Diego Magazine. To earn this award, wealth managers are rated by their customers in regard to service, integrity, knowledge, value for fees charged, quality of recommendations and overall satisfaction. For more information about the award visit www.fivestarprofessional.com/wmresearch.

Because of his expertise in the financial services industry, numerous professionals have sought out his counsel to help them become established in their business or to take their business to the next level. He has been chosen as a mentor by many individuals who have benefited from his extensive knowledge and accomplishments. Jim has also appeared on San Diego's local television channel 6 during the "San Diego Living" segments where he addressed financial issues of interest to the viewing audience.

Originating from Florida, Jim has been a California resident since 1982 and lives in San Diego with his wife, two lovely daughters and a son. Additional information about Jim Whitener and LPL Financial can be found at: www.jimwhitener.com or by calling his office at: 877-574-8295.

CHAPTER 71

FIVE KEYS TO MANAGING YOUR WEALTH

BY ERIC KEARNEY

Have you ever come home at 5 o'clock on a Friday night and thought to yourself, "Wow, what just happened?" When you look back on your week it seems as though it was just Monday morning and before you know it, it's Friday. It sometimes feels like a blur. Maybe you can't even remember what you had for lunch on Wednesday or where you had the meeting with your client. Time goes by very quickly and the older we get, the worse it seems. The same may go with your money. Many times people will come into our office and tell us that they should have come in years ago, or that they haven't looked at a statement in a long time. Although our money is important to us, the day-to-day tasks that demand our attention have disallowed us to make that a priority in our lives while time moves forward rapidly. A man showed up one day in my office. He sat down and passed his portfolio. As I flipped through the pages I would look at him and ask him questions about his thoughts on about his investments. He seemed withdrawn from the process as if he wanted to detach himself from the situation.

I asked him a few questions on the service of his account and he couldn't seem to answer. I told him we would provide him with a Portfolio Blueprint and would see him soon. There are many clients who will say something to me in the first meeting that I never forget and he was not any different. As I held the door for him and said goodbye, he slowly turned to me and said, "Please help me." He is not alone, there are many

people that feel that their portfolio has some kind of a broken steering mechanism and is unable to ever move forward without some serious changes. Many people feel that they are in a financial no man's land and end up staying there. One year leads to another leading to another and they end up doing nothing. They wonder why their portfolio just isn't working while friends, coworkers and family members seem to do better. I believe that many people's portfolios typically don't have just one thing wrong but usually there are 3-4 major things wrong that make it difficult to have any positive forward direction. Let's take a look at five keys that could help in the success of your portfolio.

Do you really know what you own in your investments? everyone that comes in our office receives a Portfolio Blueprint. We complete these for people across the country. This blueprint shows your strengths and weaknesses and provides a deeper analysis into your portfolio. It also proves how many people still are not properly diversified. It still amazes me after 12 years in the business how many people still lack a truly diversified portfolio. I consider up to 24 asset classes when constructing a portfolio. We also pay attention to relevancy of what's happening in the world. Most people go into an advisors office and they want to measure what their risk tolerance is. That's important but nothing has changed in that process in the past twenty years. I want to add something new to that process. I want to pay attention to what is relevant in the world. In other words, after an event like 9/11, I moved my clients out of large capital companies such as IBM, Wal-Mart, GE, etc., because the overall economy was about to take a large hit and probably for quite some time. It takes a lot of money to feed these large companies to keep going with payroll, benefits, research and development, real estate and so forth. If the economy slows down, they are usually the first ones to take a hit. Now, if you read in the news that gold is going up and you know you have it in your investments, you know that portion of the portfolio is relevant. I love technology, but yet I still see tech companies from the 90's that are not relevant as much as they were. If you're filling up your SUV and gas is at $4.00 and you know that you have energy in your portfolio, you know your portfolio is relevant.

Currently there are 10,000 baby boomers a day turning 65 so I love healthcare. US Healthcare is the fourth largest economy by itself in the world. If you pay attention to what's going on in the world, look at your portfolio to see if it is relevant to the world's economy and events. Remember, once we feel that an asset class is irrelevant, we tend to move out of that or decrease our exposure to it so that we can provide our client with a new relevant asset class, therefore providing us with a nicely truly diversified portfolio. My father is 79 and his portfolio is relevant to what is happening in the world and I believe that is more important than being diversified in several non- performing irrelevant asset classes that don't seem to be providing any growth and end up stagnating the portfolios growth for many years. If your advisor tells you to hold on, they'll come back, it's probably time for a second opinion. Holding on and hoping that they will come back is not a strategy and could possibly mean the advisor is not capable of providing you a relevant, sophisticated, diversified portfolio. Have you and your portfolio graduated from your existing advisors capabilities?

Let me ask you this, "Does your portfolio tell you a story? I look at hundreds of portfolios every year. Many times I open my email and someone has sent me their portfolio to review. The first thing I do is look at and see if it is telling a story of what you're trying to accomplish. Are you seeking preservation of capital? How about monthly income? Maybe you need some growth and income in your portfolio. The bottom linc is that if you don't see what your portfolio is trying to accomplish, it could be working against you. Constructing a portfolio should have investments that work together so that you have a chance at surviving any kind of market. The market can move up or down, right? It can also move sideways and can move sideways for a long time. Is your portfolio set up to take advantage of these moves? I have seen portfolios where the client needs income and the investment objective is aggressive growth. The owners of the investments do not realize that the investments they are currently in will take a dive in a down market and will struggle through a flat market. Typically we will set up three sides of a portfolio. One will be fixed income, the second will pay dividends and distributions, and the third one will be growth oriented that is again relevant to the worlds events. If the market goes up, everyone makes money, but in a sideways market I can rely on dividends and distributions that are typically paid on a quarterly or monthly basis. On a down-ward market I can rely again on the second portfolio and on the fixed income. essentially what I have done is provide a nice toolbox and no matter what job I have to tackle in the market I have the proper tool to do so. If you can take a look at your portfolio and it tells you a story of what you're trying to accomplish, then you've done OK.

How much does your life cost in retirement? I think that many people find retirement planning overwhelming and possibly intimidating so they end up doing nothing for a long time. There are people who will plan months for a two week vacation and yet don't think about retirement planning that can last thirty years. I like my clients to get used to the idea of retiring typically five years before they do so. I usually start out with a budget worksheet. I always enjoy the look on their face when I say, "Let's take some time and fill it out now," then I tell them I'm just kidding and they always let out a huge sigh of relief! I do send them on their way and the next time they come in we will review it. Why is this so important? The average person does not realize how much they spend on a monthly basis to cover their bills. They want to retire, but how do they know that they are financially capable of it? When they return for the following meeting, they are usually surprised at how much they do spend on a monthly basis. I will usually add another 10% monthly and that's approximately how much they spend. At that point we will look at their income from social security, pensions, rental income, and royalties, etc. We then take a look at their investments and figure out how much they will need from those and make sure that we build a portfolio that they will be comfortable with and provide them the income that they need. Again, if you start this process five years before retirement, you will feel like you know what your life will cost you financially and the bud- get worksheet will help you to keep track of what you spend.

How much will retirement cost me? Forget about groceries, insurance and car payments. There are always several concerns that most retirees have. Most people have the worry "What if I run out of money? What if my investments do not keep up with my lifestyle?" Healthcare is becoming a number one competitor with money issues. There is another expense that most people do not consider and that is taxes. For many years, we have been growing our 401(k)'s, IRA's, pension plans and we forget that we have been deferring all of our taxes for so long. As soon as we take out any distribution, we are hit with taxes! Taxes are typically going to be one of your largest expenses in your retirement, if not the biggest. Ask yourself this, "Are my investments tax friendly?" There are many ways to make your money more tax friendly. Do you have a Roth IRA, tax-free bonds, or specially-designed cash value life insurance? It's not necessarily how much you have, it's actually how much you get to keep. By using tax friendly investments, it can significantly reduce how much of your taxable income you are using, allowing your money to last longer by paying less in taxes. you can also implement Limited Partnerships and Master Limited Partnerships into your portfo- lio. These can be tax-friendly investments that can possibly provide you with tax benefits while providing you a regular income. According to the National Association of Publicly Traded Partnerships, the first MLP was launched in 1981 by Apache oil. Its purpose was to raise capital from smaller investors by offering them a partnership investment in an affordable and liquid security. Today's MLP's are primarily focused in the energy-related industries and natural resources and their purpose are to provide both income and tax advantages. MLP's pay out their earnings not needed for current operations to their unit holders in the form of quarterly distributions. There is no double taxation and the income is sheltered by tax deferral on distributions. These may be valuable to you if you are seeking income or yield and want to reduce or defer your taxes. Those interested in estate planning, as with other securities, the amount of units are stepped up to fair market value at death. The heir or heirs receive a fresh start with no taxation of previous distributions. As with any other investment, there are pros and cons to each and must be considered before making any decisions.

Have you heard the buzzword "transparency" in the financial industry in the past few years? When I think of that word, I feel as though my clients can see and visualize what they're paying in fees and what they are getting for it. I am a fee-based advisor. I get paid a fee for what money that I manage for my clients. Many people actually think they are not paying a fee but no matter what you invest in, there will always be fees involved. Let's say that you are invested in mutual funds. Are they front-loaded with fees? An example is if you own an "A" share, you typically pay an upfront fee that can range anywhere from 1 to 5.75%. After that, each year you still may have an internal fee of up to 1.25% or higher. Every year you are paying that fee. If you have a "B" share or a "C" share, you are not paying that front-end charge but you are still paying a higher internal fee and usually higher than an "A" share. If you choose to go with a no load fund or an exchange traded fund, your fees are typically much less expensive. Think about if you have a $500,000 invested. In Portfolio A that has loaded shares, your annual internal fees could be $5,000 based on a 1% internal fee. If you take a look at Portfolio B that has no load funds, stocks and exchange-traded funds, your internal fees would be approximately $750 based on a 0.15% fee. That's a $4250 savings every year to you. Remember, you have to consider that if you're paying your advisor 1% to manage your portfolio, what are the other costs involved? you have to also consider what you are getting for service? Do you have an Investment Policy Statement with your advisor that lays out how often you will be meeting and what services you can expect from them? Most people do not have an IPS and so it is difficult to understand what service you will be receiving on a regular basis. I met a client once who had a large portfolio. Every time he put in more money, the portfolio's investments never diversified, the existing investments only got larger because of the added money. I asked him if he was the advisor's largest client and his answer was yes. The advisor didn't know what to do with a larger portfolio and ended up being detrimental to my new client's money.

I leave you with this; take charge of your investments and portfolio. If you feel you're not headed in the right direction, interview with three advisors and ask a lot of questions. Make sure that the portfolio makes sense and your fees are understood. Make sure that the people in charge of your retirement are capable of it and understand your lifestyle and always have your best interest in mind. Strive for excellence, your wealth deserves it.

About Eric

Eric Kearney has more than 12 years of experience providing comprehensive financial planning for affluent individuals and families. As a relationship manager, Eric oversees and manages all aspects of his client relationships. Eric is actively involved in creating customized plans, retirement planning, estate tax planning and investment portfolio development and analysis.

His diverse client base is represented by successful individuals, small business owners and those either nearing retirement or enjoying retirement. He recognizes that each client has their own unique financial needs and challenges. He takes the time to listen and gain a full understanding of your current financial picture as well as your overall goals.

After recommending appropriate investments, he regularly maintains and monitors performance to help ensure that stated objectives are being met. His practice is focused on innovative fee-based investments platforms through RWA. He works out of his SW Florida office as well as his upstate New York address.

Eric holds his Series 7, 66 and Life, Accident & Health, and Annuity registrations, held through RWA.

CHAPTER 72

RECLAIM YOUR RETIREMENT —THREE KEYS TO A RETIREMENT OF CONFIDENCE, CLARITY, AND PEACE OF MIND

BY BRADLEY M. OLSON, CPA/PFS

With the "lost" investment decade that we have recently gone through and seeing almost every retiree that comes through our doors with a retirement plan that does not work, I felt that I could no longer wait to write this. The idea for this came from the countless clients who I have met and worked with and who have made these mistakes with their retirement plan. The frustration grew out of seeing the same mistakes being made over and over again. These are mistakes which can be devastating to a successful retirement, but also mistakes that are totally preventable! I hope that you read this and take the necessary action to correct the mistakes and live a "worry free" retirement. That is the ultimate goal of this writing and of my professional practice.

Those who know me know that I am a straightforward advisor. This is written based on my experience and professional knowledge. My knowledge was gained by having over 20 years of experience dealing with retirement planning and countless hours of meetings and presentations with clients. This is not meant to be technical and was not written for the financial professional. It is written for the ordinary person – so that they can learn the strategies that can allow them to live the retirement that they worked their whole life for…and dreamed of having. It was written for the person who has their life savings in investments with a stock market advisor and cannot afford to lose that life savings and is looking for the kind of advice that is appropriate for them in order to live a worry-free retirement, a guaranteed retirement with guaranteed income.

My opinion is that every retiree should have, and deserves, a WORRY-FREE retirement! If you are working with a stock market advisor, a worry-free retirement CANNOT happen. Every type of stock market investment vehicle they propose to you carries some sort of risk in it. Here you will find great information to take action on, information that cannot only provide you with the retirement that you deserve, but the retirement that you saved your whole life for. A retirement that is one WITHOUT worry, one that has potential for reasonable asset growth, and one that has the capability for GUARANTEES and peace of mind.

The retiree's that have placed their trust in the stock market retirement system have learned the hard way that that system is set up for failure. With the historic declines in the stock market over the last 15 years, it's no wonder that many retirees' dreams of a worry-free retirement were crushed. No one can predict when the next market crashes will come, but you can avoid them (just not with the stock market advisor system).

You need to look at the only system out there that promotes and provides GUARANTEES and SAFETY. The insurance institutions and strategies used in my G.R.I.P. system have been around for over a century and have proven time and again when the market corrects itself, their products are unaffected. They provide certainty, guarantees, financial security, and most importantly, peace of mind.

Retirement represents a fundamental change in your life. Doesn't it make perfect sense that your retirement investment portfolio should fundamentally shift as well? Without question, this mistake tops my list. If you are like most people, during your working years you invested for your future retirement through some type of retirement plan, usually a 401(k), 403(b), IRA or something similar. In most of these plans, you had a "menu" of investment choices. This "menu" was probably comprised of a variety of mutual funds. You could select from stock funds, bond funds, and some type of money market or interest bearing fund. In some plans you could even invest in your company's stock, and sometimes even at a discount. This is called your **Accumulation Phase**. You are saving for when you retire. Your retirement plan was probably with a big financial firm and you probably interacted with this firm for 20 to 30 years. You know how their website works; you know what funds are available and how to switch between them. You are very comfortable with them. THEN YOU RETIRE.

What did you do? If you are like most people, you made few, if any changes to your portfolio. At most, you may have moved more money into the bond fund and less in the stock fund, but odds are pretty good that you didn't even do that. Then you retire and need regular income from what you have saved. You are now in the **Distribution Phase** of your life.

So, what does that mean? This means that you need to make a fundamental change in how you structure your investment portfolio when you are retired. Fundamental change means that now you have to be more involved and observant with what is going on with your portfolio. Guarantees now become extremely important. YOU have to decide to make the fundamental change and then have to act on it and actually make the change!

Simply changing from one set (or family) of mutual funds to another set of mutual funds does NOT represent a fundamental change in your portfolio. Fundamental change is changing (and by changing I mean SIGNIFICANTLY reducing) the amount of RISK you are taking in your portfolio. You MUST reduce the amount of RISK so that you can free yourself from the worry of running out of money. What is the reason for this? When you are retired, what do you have less of that can never be replaced? TIME!

You have to ask yourself this question, "Can my retirement assets afford to take the kind of dramatic reductions that happened in 2000 and 2008?" Most retirees cannot. Now, no one can predict when the downturns will occur, but if you make the fundamental change in your portfolio, you will be more prepared to handle them. Like I said before, changing to different mutual funds is like changing the color of the paint on your car. What was appropriate for building a portfolio is no longer appropriate when you are preserving and distributing income from your money in retirement.

Have you ever heard of the "Rule of 100"? It's the financial rule of thumb that says you should take your age and subtract it from 100. The result tells you how much of your portfolio should be "at risk". This rule recognizes that as you age, you should be taking less and less risk with your money. As you get older, you are losing time to make up for the losses. This is especially true if you use your assets for income. Then you should lower the risk number even more.

Let's look at an example. Say you are 65 years old. Then simple math gives us the following:

Start With:	100
Minus your Age:	65
Amount at Risk:	35%

What does the Rule of 100 tell us in this example? If you are 65 years of age, you should have approximately 65% of your money invested in "safe" investment tools and you can take risks with the other 35%. Like I stated above, if you use your assets for income then your amount at risk should be lowered another 10%, to 25%.

How does your result match up with how your portfolio is currently invested? If you are like most retired people, you are probably taking on far more risk than you should be. And you've probably seen a couple of big drops in your portfolio in the 2000's. How much did you lose in the nasty market years of 2000 - 2002? How about in the 1½ year stretch from October 2007 to March 2009? I don't know when the market drops are going to come, but I do know that they will happen again. And they have been happening more frequently during the last decade

What you have to be asking yourself now, is, why have I not heard of this type of advice before? The answer is pretty simple. You have been dealing with the stock market system. The stock market system does not want any competition from any other type of planning system, regardless of the benefits for the retiree. You HAVE to understand that when you retired, your income from work stopped, and you may need your assets to generate an income to you and you have less time to recover from downturns in the market. This message is not getting to the retiree because the stock market system does not want it to, and they will spend millions of dollars a year to promote their system as the best system. It is not the system that a retiree wants any part of. You, the retiree, should want to protect and preserve your assets so that they can create a guaranteed income stream for life.

The stock market system may work for younger people who have many years to go before retiring, but it has proven time and again that it doesn't work for the retiree. How do we know that? Because I see the retirees coming into my practice on a daily basis with all sorts of financial issues and they have received little to no useful advice from their stock market advisor. And in most cases, the advice they receive is like, "Don't worry the market always comes back," or "The longer you are in the market, you will earn 8-10% rate of return," or "You have to take risk to get a higher return." This type of advice given to retirees not only is dangerous, but it is completely FALSE! NONE of those statements are true! But they spend a lot of money making you believe that they are. My G.R.I.P. planning system uses products that have been around for over a century and have always been in the business of protection and guarantees. It is a system that has been protecting and providing the retirees who use it a safe and worry-free retirement plan. You just will not hear about it from the stock market advisor system and now you know why. When you retire, you simply cannot keep investing as though you are still working. There is a better way, the G.R.I.P. system.

And I will say this again, so as not to confuse you, this advice is for the retiree and not the regular investor. The retiree has special circumstances that they have to deal with that the regular investor does not, e.g., less time to make up losses, no income from wages to replace lost principal due to market losses and the need for income that has to be produced from the assets. NONE of these circumstances affect the regular investor BUT they have a tremendous impact on the retiree. When you retired, you went through a philosophical change in your life and it only makes sense that your investment philosophy goes through that same change as well. Then and only then will you be able to go down the correct retirement path. The path of protected assets, guaranteed income, and reduced taxes. That is what the G.R.I.P. system can do for you.

As of this writing the state of our economy remains on shaky ground. Unemployment is far worse than is being reported. Government spending is out of control. Our country's debt is over 14 TRILLION dollars. There are political issues around the world that affect us daily. The unfunded liabilities of Medicare, Social Security and Prescription Drugs are almost $113 TRILLION dollars. The threat of terrorism is just as bad as it was after 9/11. There are natural disasters happening more often. I state these facts not to scare you or create a panic, but to get you to realize that your retirement assets and your retirement future are at RISK. You must take the necessary steps to protect and guarantee your retirement!

About Bradley

Bradley Olson CPA/PFS is the founder of Olson Wealth, a premier retirement planning firm in Cincinnati, OH and is a frequent attendee and speaker at national retirement planning conferences. He is a licensed CPA and has earned the prestigious AICPA PFS (Personal Financial Specialist) designation.

Brad is a Best-Selling Author and has been helping people retire with confidence and clarity for over 20 years. He specializes in developing retirement strategies that protect and preserve retirement assets. Bradley has developed the renowned G.R.I.P. system, which he uses in his planning. Brad has been seen on ABC, NBC, CBS and FOX affiliates across the country as well as in *Newsweek Magazine, Forbes, Yahoo Finance, Marketwatch* and other major media outlets.

Brad is also a proud husband and father of three happy, healthy, active children.

CHAPTER 73

EVERYONE IS A WINNER — THERE ARE NO LOSERS

BY ROCK LA SPADA

Many wealth management experts will tell you they go the extra mile to make and save money for their clients – but when I claim that I do that for people, I'm not just talking metaphorically. Back in the late 90s, the moment I was made aware that a company and the organizer I had recommended was misappropriating funds, I immediately traveled to Central America to help investors get their money back from a so-called expert at setting up funds – who turned out to be less than reputable. I had been hired to lecture about investments by a global firm, which asked me to introduce them to a fund organizer who currently formed and managed a number of mutual funds in Central America. I managed to locate an individual who had come to me highly recommended. When I found out that he was misrepresenting his fund and the people who invested their money with him were losing their investment, I flew to where the organizer was based.

At my own expense, I engaged local attorneys, who then contacted the police. We went to his offices and confiscated all of his computers and files. I told the fund organizer that I would press charges with the local authorities and also divulge his activities to everyone I knew in the financial world if he failed to offer restitution. Fortunately, I was able to retrieve almost 100 percent of the funds for the benefit of the investors. His unlawful activities eventually caught up with him as he received his due and was incarcerated in the United States.

I believe that my success in this business is partially due to my ability to think outside the box and tell it like it is – even if the truth is hard to hear. I am always trying to determine the pulse of what is going on, and have a-long established history of protecting my clients – not only in the kind of extreme circumstance I mention above, but also in regular day-to-day investing. Sensing the disastrous changes that were looming, I pulled all of my clients out of the market before the crashes of 1987, 2000 and 2008. This was contrary to the views of many stock market experts in each case.

THE EMERGENCE OF A NEW PHILOSOPHY OF LIFE

There are some downsides to growing up in a small town for those of us whose destinies take us beyond that. When you are raised in a conservative environment, you only spend money on essential things. I had to deal with that ingrained philosophy and change my perception of money. Later, when I chose to go into finance and deal with people on a higher level, it was crucial that I start thinking differently. In that environment, it's all about spending money to make money – a concept completely at odds with my initial environment. It's a very different world for me now. This became a reality a few months ago, when I went back for a visit to my hometown of Vandergrift, PA. and went to our local coffee shop to talk to some friends I knew from long ago, as well as some new faces. I found that they had not changed. I was the one who had changed. We now had few areas of common ground that we could agree on. They have always been great people and still are today, although their philosophy about politics, money and life is still maintained within a very conventional mindset.

From being out there in the world for so long, I realized that I had developed a philosophy for business and life that is very different. I think I can sum it all up in a nutshell by saying, **"Everyone's a Winner, There are no Losers!"** We are all exactly where we have chosen to be and want to be at any point in time. Only our subconscious knows our true reality. We can be successful, whomever we are, wherever we are, and in whatever we're doing. It is my belief that God didn't put us here to make mistakes. If people look back on say, a failed marriage, what they did may have turned out badly – but it was right at that point in time. When we start realizing that sub-consciously both parties made that choice, and it was the right one whatever the ultimate result, that's when we can start moving forward and changing. We need to change, or rather re-evaluate our past and look at it from a new perspective, before we can change our present and future.

Many years ago, I found a competent attorney to work with in California, he started sharing some of his past issues, and I learned that he was living in his car because he felt as if he didn't deserve to live in an apartment or house. I told him he had to work through those issues that were holding him back. He had to change his past in order to change his future and move forward. We are all a product of our initial socio-economic environment, which heavily influences the mindset we bring to our present lives.

But if we're going down the wrong path and making harmful decisions for our lives today because of input we had when we were growing up...well, the only way to change what we are doing today is to change our perception of the past, and use that as a building block towards choosing the path towards success. When we realize that we are all winners, not losers, we look back on our past mistakes as the building blocks we learn from. Much of the population in America either are not aware of or do not recognize that the United States has gone through a paradigm shift. This is analogous to the proverbial frog, which, when placed in a container of water at room temperature, remains content. As the temperature slowly increases to boiling, the frog is unaware that he is slowly transcending to frog heaven and is totally oblivious to what is occurring. Why be a frog?

When this paradigm started is a matter for debate - although strong contributing factors are the steady decline of the dollar, and US companies moving to Asia and Mexico, taking their jobs with them. Remaining companies started cutting back and laying off personnel. The bottom line is that Americans wanting to maintain their style of living, would now seek a second job and spouses would have to go back to work. Families could then feel that not much had changed, as they were able to maintain their previous lifestyle.

The most obvious result of this paradigm shift is that **nothing is as it was before and will never be the same again.** We may look back 20, 30, or 50 years and attempt to use the mindset of that era or our fathers to achieve a secure and successful future. Utilizing those parameters of the past will almost assuredly lead to our ruin and ultimately our financial demise.

GAMBLING VS. GROWTH: CHANGING THE WAY WE THINK ABOUT MONEY

How does this philosophy apply to investments and wealth management? It's about advising people to think unconventionally, convincing them to open up to new possibilities beyond the concepts of investments (and about the financial industry as a whole) that they have embraced and accepted, based on all the factors from their past experience. Investors must forego that intense desire (translated as avarice) for high returns - which normally carries with it high risk. A while back before the real estate crash of 2008, an elderly couple of modest means (the man was 83 and the woman 79) came to me not to seek my advice but to proudly inform me that they had just refinanced their home and were able to obtain $200,000 cash. They wished to purchase stock on a "hot tip" they had received from a cab driver. I told them I would not, and in good conscience I could not, allow them to purchase any investment. I was able to convince them to deposit the money in their bank. After the real estate crash, they thanked me profusely and were able to keep their home.

HARD TRUTHS/INSIDE PHILOSOPHIES

People must be in tune with the core philosophy of retraining their mindset of the past to embrace creative new ways of thinking. What we have been taught is not everything we need to know. Our schools and our government teach and follow "Keynesian Economics," after John Maynard Keynes. On August 15, 1971, President Richard Nixon, effectively removed all dollar connections to gold, thereby establishing the U.S. dollar as a fiat currency open to infinite levels of inflation. President Nixon then stated, "We are all Keynesians now."

This philosophy is a major contributing factor to our extremely high debt situation. A simple explanation is that the majority of our country lives way beyond their level of income. This is another reason why the United States has had such a high standard of living. We incur much more debt than we can ever possibly hope to accommodate, i.e., more expensive homes, automobiles, clothes, vacations, and much more. This practice was an extremely strong contributing factor to the bursting of the housing bubble, which we have just experienced.

The philosophy that I advocate, adhere to, and attempt to instill in my clients, is the "Austrian School of Economics," as professed by Ludwig Von Mises. This philosophy follows the concept of living within your income and following a balanced budget. When proper and strategic planning is formulated and utilized to accommodate a person's lifestyle, unexpected emergencies and 'the bursting of economic bubbles' will not affect them.

#1. Never take a "hot tip" from anyone

An excellent high profile example of this in recent years is Solyndra, a solar panel company that received a huge government-backed loan but then went bankrupt, leaving taxpayers stuck with the bill.

#2. Don't Trust Your Own Timing Of The Market

No matter how good you think you are in timing the market, chances are you are going to be wrong because the market is not static. *Ceteris paribus*, or "all things being equal or held constant," the market can be manipulated to appear like it's going up when it's not. Every time there's a downturn, the government puts in their "plunge protection team," comprised of large institutional buyers such as Goldman Sachs and others, strongly advising these big players to start buying in large quantities to prop up the market. So the layperson thinks, "Great, my investment is safe, or going up" and they stay in.

#3. Invest in Foreign Currencies

One of the largest markets in the world is the foreign exchange market, also known as Forex, FX or currency market. It is a global decentralized market for the trading of currencies whose main participants are the larger international banks and interbank FX trading platforms. Although FX trading can be very lucrative it should not be attempted by the inexperienced, as it comes with extremely high risk. The only effective way for an individual to invest in foreign currencies is through a currency fund managed by experts.

#4. Utilize IUL and IA

Two very popular vehicles that are currently being utilized by financial advisors for their clients are indexed annuities and indexed universal life insurance. An IA usually requires a lump sum investment while an IUL can be funded on a monthly basis. These vehicles participate only in the gains of the market, not the losses. When these investments are structured properly, it is possible to receive the benefits without taxation.

THIRD PARTY MONEY MANAGERS

Beyond these ideas, I highly recommend utilizing professional fund managers available to the large institutions who specialize in certain sectors. The key is finding money managers for clients to work with who invest in sectors that are not offensive to people. By that I mean that the investments don't go into industries that the client would disapprove of. When I lectured at a large conference, I recommended a couple of defense stocks. Two nice elderly ladies spoke up and said, 'How can you recommend these? They are stocks of war!' I told them that people were asking for advice on investments that could possibly achieve a very high increase in price. Although I do understand their ethical objections, those stocks indeed went up 90 percent shortly thereafter.

LIVING AND INVESTING FULLY IN THE PRESENT

To summarize, the key to averting mistakes and falling into traps is breaking free of those past philosophies that didn't work and living fully in the present. We tend to assimilate the social and economic environment we grew up in or live in at present with the world economic situation, expecting that certain positive things will happen. Although if we don't take note of the changing tides and plan for the future we could be in dire straits when the time arrives to access our funds.

My job is to engineer my clients' investments around a single overriding concept: if you're sleeping well at night, I can sleep well at night. To make that happen, we need to remove ourselves from the past and leave that behind in favor of forward, practical thinking. The world and its economies are changing dramatically and the past we know will not be the same as the future – so those of us of a certain age, set in our ways and stuck in conventional thought patterns need to think differently. If you want to invest in order to be solvent and whole in the future, you have to adjust your thinking by changing your past. If you do not change your past, it will become your present thus sabotaging your future.

As the economy becomes increasingly precarious you must analyze and evaluate every investment recommendation that is offered to you. Request—no, demand—that your financial advisor fully explain and document all recommendations that he proposes. Today allowing *Ceteris Paribus* to formulate and guide your actions could lead to financial ruin.

If you want to remain solvent, the most important critical thought I can leave you with is: *do not follow the sheep. **ALWAYS, ALWAYS, ALWAYS**, think outside of the BOX!*

About Rock

Rock La Spada has been in the financial services industry for over 25 years. He formed his own business management company, providing services for income taxes, securities, insurance, real estate, and budgeting. Upon leaving initial active duty, he immediately signed on for a new US Air Force flight program. He was then able to maintain his commission as an officer and fly specific missions worldwide while working and attending graduate school. The mission that his unit was responsible for was transporting troops and supplies into combat zones in overseas locations. He eventually retired from the Air Force as a Major after 23 years.

When he left his initial tour of active duty, he returned to school at USC to complete doctoral studies in economics and finance. After graduating from USC, he attended additional schools to further his education in order to obtain degrees in International Business and Real Estate. He taught investment and finance courses as a professor at the college in Nevada. His services as an investment advisor and lecturer have been requested by numerous corporations both in the US and in other countries.

Rock has worked with a number of well-known actors, entertainment celebrities, and physicians. He provides complete business management plans, retirement plans, and investment services. Before the crash of 2008, he was considered to be way too (ultra) conservative. After the crash, many new clients were referred to him by satisfied existing clients. Those that followed his advice did not lose a cent and thus showered him with accolades. Those that did not follow his advice expressed extreme regret and wished they had.

His motto is:
"I ensure that you can sleep at night like a rock, so that I can sleep like a rock."